CIMA

PRACTICE & REVISION KIT

Stage 4 Paper 14

Strategic Management Accountancy and Marketing

BPP Publishing
January 2000

First edition 1994
Seventh edition January 2000

ISBN 0 7517 3858 1 (previous edition 0 7517 3877 8)

British Library Cataloguing-in-Publication Data
A catalogue record for this book
is available from the British Library

Published by

BPP Publishing Limited
Aldine House, Aldine Place
London W12 8AW

www.bpp.com

We are grateful to the Chartered Institute of Management Accountants for permission to reproduce past examination questions. The answers to past examination questions have been prepared by BPP Publishing Limited.

Printed in Great Britain by Ashford Colour Press, Gosport, Hants.

CONTENTS

The headings indicate the main topics of questions, but questions often cover several different topics.

Long case studies (up to 60 marks) cover several areas of the syllabus. Their mark allocation means that they must be given the bulk of your time in the examination. It is vital that you spend time practising case studies and there are 11 examples from previous papers collected together at the beginning of the kit.

Tutorial questions, listed in italics, are followed by advice on how to **approach the question,** thus easing the transition from study to examination practice.

A date alone (11/97, say) or 'specimen paper' after the question title refers to a current syllabus paper.

Questions preceded by * are **key questions** which we think you must attempt in order to pass the exam. Tick them off on this list as you complete them.

REVISION

This is a very important time as you approach the exam. You must remember three things.

Use time sensibly
Set realistic goals
Believe in yourself

Use time sensibly

1. **How much study time do you have?** Remember that you must EAT, SLEEP, and of course, RELAX.
2. **How will you split that available time between each subject?** What are your weaker subjects? They need more time.
3. **What is your learning style?** AM/PM? Little and often/long sessions? Evenings/ weekends?
4. **Are you taking regular breaks?** Most people absorb more if they do not attempt to study for long uninterrupted periods of time. A five minute break every hour (to make coffee, watch the news headlines) can make all the difference.
5. **Do you have quality study time?** Unplug the phone. Let everybody know that you're studying and shouldn't be disturbed.

Set realistic goals

1. Have you set a **clearly defined objective** for each study period?
2. Is the objective **achievable**?
3. Will you **stick to your plan**? Will you make up for any **lost time**?
4. Are you **rewarding yourself** for your hard work?
5. Are you leading a **healthy lifestyle**?

Believe in yourself

Are you cultivating the right attitude of mind? There is absolutely no reason why you should not pass this exam if you adopt the correct approach.

- **Be confident** - you've passed exams before, you can pass them again
- **Be calm** - plenty of adrenaline but no panicking
- **Be focused** - commit yourself to passing the exam

QUESTION PRACTICE

There is little point in simply opening this Kit and, beginning with question 1, attempting all of the questions. You need to ask yourself three questions.

Am I ready to answer questions?

Do I know which questions to do first?

How should I use this Kit?

Am I ready to answer questions?

1 Try to fill in the blanks on the **Do you know? checklist** for a particular syllabus area. Compare your answers with the corresponding **Did you know? checklist**.

2 If you are happy with what you have written, you can go ahead and start answering questions. **Do not attempt questions if you could not fill in any of the blanks**. Go back to your BPP Study Text and revise first.

Do I know which questions to do first?

1 **Start with tutorial questions**. They warm you up for key and difficult areas of the syllabus. Try to produce at least a plan for these questions, using the guidance notes following the question to ensure your answer is structured so as to gain a good pass mark.

2 Don't worry about the time it takes to answer these questions. Concentrate on producing good answers. There are 13 tutorial questions in this Kit.

How should I use this Kit?

1 Once you are confident with the Do you know? checklists and the tutorial questions, you should try as many as possible of the exam-standard questions; at the very least you should attempt the **key questions,** which are highlighted in the **question and answer checklist/index** at the front of the Kit.

2 Try to **produce full answers under timed conditions**; you are practising exam technique as much as knowledge recall here. Don't look at the answer, your BPP Study Text or your notes for any help at all.

3 **Mark your answers to the non-tutorial questions as if you were the examiner**. Only give yourself marks for what you have written, not for what you meant to put down, or would have put down if you had had more time. If you did badly, try another question.

4 Read the **Pass marks** in the answers very carefully and take note of the advice given and any **comments by the examiner.**

5 When you have practised the whole syllabus, go back to the areas you had problems with and **practise further questions.**

6 Finally, when you think you really understand the entire subject, **attempt the mock exam** at the end of the Kit. Sit the paper under strict exam conditions, so that you gain experience of selecting and sequencing your questions, and managing your time, as well as of writing answers.

EXAM TECHNIQUE

Passing professional examinations is half about having the knowledge, and half about doing yourself full justice in the examination. You must have the right approach to two things.

The day of the exam
Your time in the exam hall

The day of the exam

1 Set at least one **alarm** (or get an alarm call) for a morning exam.

2 Have **something to eat** but beware of eating too much; you may feel sleepy if your system is digesting a large meal.

3 Allow plenty of **time to get to the exam hall;** have your route worked out in advance and listen to news bulletins to check for potential travel problems.

4 **Don't forget** pens, pencils, rulers, erasers.

5 Put **new batteries** into your calculator and take a spare set (or a spare calculator).

6 **Avoid discussion** about the exam with other candidates outside the exam hall.

Your time in the exam hall

1 ***Read the instructions (the 'rubric') on the front of the exam paper carefully***

Check that the exam format hasn't changed. It is surprising how often examiners' reports remark on the number of students who attempt too few - or too many - questions, or who attempt the wrong number of questions from different parts of the paper. Make sure that you are planning to answer the **right number of questions.**

2 ***Select questions carefully***

Read through the paper once, then quickly jot down key points against each question in a second read through. Select those questions where you could latch on to 'what the question is about' - but remember to check carefully that you have got the right end of the stick before putting pen to paper.

3 ***Plan your attack carefully***

Consider the **order** in which you are going to tackle questions. It is a good idea to start with your best question to boost your morale and get some easy marks 'in the bag'.

4 ***Check the time allocation for each question***

Each mark carries with it a **time allocation** of 1.8 minutes (including time for selecting and reading questions). A 20 mark question therefore should be completed in 36 minutes. When time is up, you *must* go on to the next question or part. Going even one minute over the time allowed brings you a lot closer to failure.

5 ***Read the question carefully and plan your answer***

Read through the question again very carefully when you come to answer it. Plan your answer to ensure that you **keep to the point.** Two minutes of planning plus eight minutes of writing is virtually certain to earn you more marks than ten minutes of writing.

6 ***Produce relevant answers***

Particularly with written answers, make sure you **answer the question set,** and not the question you would have preferred to have been set.

7 ***Gain the easy marks***

Include the obvious if it answers the question and don't try to produce the perfect answer.

Don't get bogged down in small parts of questions. If you find a part of a question difficult, get on with the rest of the question. If you are having problems with something, the chances are that everyone else is too.

8 ***Produce an answer in the correct format***

The examiner will **state in the requirements** the format in which the question should be answered, for example in a report or memorandum.

9 ***Follow the examiner's instructions***

You will annoy the examiner if you ignore him or her. The **examiner will state** whether he or she wishes you to 'discuss', 'comment', 'evaluate' or 'recommend' (see the section on examiners' instructions on page (xxvii).

10 ***Lay out your numerical computations and use workings correctly***

Make sure the layout fits the **type of question** and is in a style the examiner likes.

Show all your **workings** clearly and explain what they mean. Cross reference them to your solution. This will help the examiner to follow your method (this is of particular importance where there may be several possible answers).

11 ***Present a tidy paper***

You are a professional, and it should show in the **presentation of your work**. Students are penalised for poor presentation and so you should make sure that you write legibly, label diagrams clearly and lay out your work neatly. Markers of scripts each have hundreds of papers to mark; a badly written scrawl is unlikely to receive the same attention as a neat and well laid out paper.

12 ***Stay until the end of the exam***

Use any spare time **checking and rechecking** your script.

13 ***Don't worry if you feel you have performed badly in the exam***

It is more than likely that the other candidates will have found the exam difficult too. Don't forget that there is a competitive element in these exams. As soon as you get up to leave the exam hall, ***forget* that exam** and think about the next - or, if it is the last one, celebrate!

14 ***Don't discuss an exam with other candidates***

This is particularly the case if you **still have other exams to sit**. Even if you have finished, you should put it out of your mind until the day of the results. Forget about exams and relax!

THE EXAM PAPER

Format of the Year 2000 exams

		Number of marks
Section A	one compulsory case study question	60
Section B	two questions from four	40
		100

Time allowed : 3 hours

Recent pass rates

The UK pass rate for the May 1999 exam was 43.7%, which was the highest of the Stage 4 papers.

Analysis of past papers 1995-1999

The analysis below shows the topics which have been examined in the ten sittings of the syllabus and the CIMA Specimen Paper for *Strategic Management Accountancy and Marketing.*

November 1999

Section A (Compulsory case study, 60 marks)

1 International and diverse group, with distinctive and successful brand, charismatic chairman and distinctive management style. The brand is stretched across different products and services with particular success in airlines. Latest venture into the domestic railway market has not been so successful.

- (a) External forces on worldwide business development
- (b) Divisional performance evaluation for airline and railway companies
- (c) Brand extension strategy in new countries
- (d) Factors contributing to commercial success; responsibility to stakeholders

Section B (2 out of 4 questions, 20 marks each)

2 Market defence strategies

3 Benchmarking programmes

4 BCG matrix and strategic business units

5 Outsourcing

This paper forms the mock exam at the end of the Kit, so only an outline of its contents is shown here.

May 1999	*Question number in this Kit*
Section A (Compulsory case study, 60 marks)	
1 Public service radio and television broadcasting organisation, relying on licence fee income, considering possible separation of radio and television services.	11
(a) Rational planning model	
(b) Stakeholder views	
(c) ROCE calculations	
(d) Implications of the separation for the organisation's objectives	
(e) Financial and non-financial information needed	
(f) Marketing research programme for new radio service	
Section B (2 out of 4 questions, 20 marks each)	
2 Customer account profitability analysis	39
3 Customers, profitability and marketing strategy	59
4 Strategic issues associated with establishing an overseas subsidiary	46
5 Experience curve and the product life cycle	51

Examiner's comments

The overall improvement in candidates' performance noted in November 1998 was continued in this sitting. Successful candidates tackled the compulsory first question with confidence. In Section B of the paper, questions 3 and 4 were preferred. Most candidates did not rise to the challenge posed by question 5.

Candidates continue to appear unwilling or unable to separate the relevant from the irrelevant, both in analysing case study information and writing answers generally. There is still the temptation to 'write all I know about X'.

It is worth repeating that candidates may answer the questions for this paper in any order, although answering the parts of individual questions out of sequence is not recommended.

November 1998	
Section A (Compulsory case study, 60 marks)	
1 Global pharmaceuticals company: product development; marketing ; competitive forces; profitability analysis; marketing and strategic alliances	10
Section B (2 out of 4 questions, 20 marks each)	
2 Attack strategies for increased market share	60
3 Management accountant and product quality	52
4 Environmental influences on public service industry	14
5 BCG matrix and the public sector	37

Examiner's comments

Performance overall improved on this paper, largely due to confident handling of the compulsory Section A question, which often compensated for poor marks in Section B. Disappointingly, many candidates seemed to have difficulty with the issues and concepts in Section B. The SMM paper has two distinct sections and each examination will contain wide syllabus coverage.

Successful candidates tend to be those who recognise the theory and apply it. Questions often imply by their very wording the theoretical approach to be taken, so only those students who have the underpinning knowledge will be able to answer a question successfully. There is still a tendency for candidates to write all they know about a topic, and leave the marker to dig out the relevant bits. Candidates must practise giving incisive answers in the time available.

A handful of scripts were impossible to decipher. Language skills must be sufficient for the marker to be able to make sense of what the candidate has written.

May 1998

		Question number in this Kit
Section A (Compulsory case study, 60 marks)		
1	Ecologically friendly natural cosmetics company with niche market domination. Trying to decide between quality improvement or increased promotion to protect its position. Write a corporate appraisal, decision analysis; reaction of competitors; strategic environmental aims; recommend a strategy	9
Section B (2 out of 4 questions, 20 marks each)		
2	Porter's Generic Strategy model; Experience Curve	31
3	Brand strategy	57
4	Divisional performance measurement	47
5	Disclosure of forward-looking information	69

Examiner's comments

There was a slight general improvement in the quality of scripts. It seems that candidates have finally recognised that a compulsory 60 mark question requires the bulk of time available to be devoted to it. There was more evidence of answer planning and better time management.

Many candidates still resorted to general discussion techniques rather than relevant commentary, and yet again candidates failed to answer the precise question set on too many occasions. The "write all I know about X" style of answer was much in evidence for question 2. Candidates must be prepared to apply their knowledge to the particular circumstances of the scenario given in the question. Rote learning is not sufficient to pass this examination.

Some candidates encountered difficulty in manipulating the numbers contained in question 1. Numbers feature regularly in this paper; it does have "management accountancy " in its title and is not entirely discursive in nature.

November 1997

Section A (Compulsory case study, 60 marks) — *Question number in this Kit*

1 International phone company seeking to expand and diversify faces the establishment of a regulatory organisation

(a) PEST forces influencing the company

(b) Ansoff matrix — 8

(c) Evaluate investment in new technology and quality improvements for closing the gap and achieving strategic development aims

(d) Planning gap: recommend strategy

Section B (2 out of 4 questions, 20 marks each)

2	Strategic management accounting and environmental change	22
3	Management accountant to assist sales director in planning a research programme	65
4	Central determination of transfer prices – reasoning and ethics	50
5	Value chain analysis and strategies	38

Examiner's comments

There were far too many candidates who were confused by the simple calculation requirements in question 1. Candidates must be prepared for calculations to appear in the question requirements and use them to support an argument. The core strategic planning models required in question 1 also caused confusion. It is foolish to believe that this examination can be passed without first having acquired the appropriate knowledge. Answers relating to ethical issues surrounding transfer pricing in question 4 were often not convincing.

The last part of the case study had ten marks attached to it. Too many candidates either failed to answer this part at all, or paid very little attention to it. One of the first things a candidate should do is to determine how much time needs to be allocated to the individual parts of each question.

It is also worth mentioning that, although it is acceptable to answer whole questions out of order, answering parts of individual questions in the wrong sequence is a risky approach as it becomes easy to lose the logic of the sequence. Very often the answer to an earlier part informs what comes later.

Candidates are expected to be able to apply their knowledge. Proper and thorough preparation can be helped by wide reading of quality newspapers and published texts. Awareness of current business affairs is always useful.

May 1997

Section A (Compulsory case study, 60 marks)

1	A joint venture company, owned by two conglomerates, faces performance problems: Assess performance. Suggest indicators. Discuss objectives and opportunities. Acquisition problems.	6

Section B (2 out of 4 questions, 20 marks each)

2	Effects of share issue on an owner-managed business; planning processes	17
3	Performance in the public sector; measurement problems	21
4	Constituents of BCG matrix; its use in strategic planning	36
5	Environmental accounting and reporting	30

> **Examiner's comments**
>
> Candidates had problems with time management. The questions in Section A are designed in a sequence and should be answered accordingly. Candidates' answers are too short: bullet points without 'additional comment or elaboration .... [indicate] ... that the candidate is unable or unwilling to expand the answer and construct a rational argument ... Bullet points are quite acceptable provided they are supported with appropriate expansion'. Candidates also see the syllabus as compartmentalised. Few attempted question 5. Candidates failed to answer properly question 4.

November 1996

Question number in this Kit

Section A (Compulsory case study 50 marks)

1	A small haulage firm faces competition. Present a position appraisal. Establishing the need for strategic management accounting information. Recommend a marketing strategy	7

Section B (2 out of 4 questions, 25 marks each)

2	Benchmarking: objectives and introduction	54
3	Buying behaviour in consumer and industrial markets	56
4	Strategic and operational management: culture and segmentation issues	16
5	Social and ethical implications of acquisition	70

> **Examiner's comments**
>
> Again, many candidates relied on 'common sense' - this is insufficient to pass, as candidates must know what the models are and how to apply them. A mere list of points, not grouped together in support of an argument, is insufficient. The examiner also mentioned candidates' poor handwriting.

May 1996

Section A

1 A shipping services company aims to increase international activities, employee development and capital investment.

- (a) Assess corporate objectives
- (b) Flexibility and conflict — 1
- (c) Divisional performance
- (d) Five forces model. Market share
- (e) Environmental audits

Section B

2	Marketing services; life cycle implications; competitors	64
3	Customer account profitability and marketing/sales orientation	35
4	Barriers to entry and low technology industries	27
5	Transfer pricing at home and abroad	49

> **Examiner's comments**
>
> Overall, the standard of scripts was disappointing in comparison with November 1995. Evident problems of exam technique include poor time allocation, and an inability to read the question. Answer plans are helpful - but are not substitutes for a proper answer. Question 1 revealed a surprising lack of familiarity with Porter's five forces model. In Question 2, many candidates restricted their marketing suggestions to promotion activities. Question 3 was generally well answered, although some candidates had difficulties in relating two areas of the syllabus. Question 4 was popular and well answered. Question 5, on transfer pricing, was shunned by most.

November 1995	*Question number in this Kit*
Section A	
1 A national supermarket chain is proposing an out-of-town development	
(a) Reconstruct DCF calculation for appraisal	
(b) Market opportunities and threats	4
(c) Stakeholders	
(d) Joint venture or go-it-alone	
(e) Management accountant's contribution	
Section B	
2 Diversification strategies	43
3 Manufacturing overseas	26
4 Information and strategic decision-making	20
5 Performance indicators and behaviour	48

> **Examiner's comments**
>
> Question 1(a) required a very simple DCF calculation: 'many ... were unable to calculate a simple net present value'. Some candidates merged their answers to parts of the question, making it hard for markers to mark. Answers to Question 2 tended to ignore risk. In Question 3 (environmental factors) PEST was adopted, although Porter's competitive advantage of nations could have been applied. Question 5 was unpopular and poorly done.

May 1995	
Section A	
1 A bank is restructuring its organisation to enhance profitability. Investment centres have been set up, and the new mission statement is setting a new direction. Discuss these changes.	5
Section B	
2 Marketing organisation and marketing SWOT	-
3 Strategic analysis models: Porter and Ansoff	42
4 Putting social responsibility into practice	68
5 Product life cycle. Brand capitalisation	63

> **Examiner's comments**
>
> Performance indicators and investment centres caused problems in question 1. Question 2 was answered badly; candidates seemed confused about the role of a marketing department. Most avoided the question on social responsibility.

Specimen paper

		Question number in this Kit
Section A		
1	A diversified conglomerate is seeking to divest one of its businesses, under pressure from institutional shareholders. Assess strategies, conflicts of interest and communications with different stakeholder groups	2
Section B		
2	Relevance of management accounting	-
3	Product life cycle: risk and return characteristics	-
4	Mission, conflicting objectives, ethics	-
5	Marketing objectives and management accounting	19

How the syllabus has been examined - an overview

	11/99	5/99	11/98	5/98	11/97	5/97	11/96	5/96	11/95	5/95	Specimen
Establishing the corporate objectives											
Organisational mission, aims, goals and objectives	✓	✓	✓			✓		✓		✓	✓
Long term and short term objectives: quantitative and qualitative evaluation	✓	✓		✓			✓		✓		✓
Application of decision theory								✓	✓		
Role of strategic management accountancy											✓
Internal and external influences on decisions; implications of 'short termism'	✓		✓				✓	✓			
Appraising the environment											
Impact on the organisation of changing national and international influences	✓	✓	✓		✓			✓	✓		
Use of renewable and non-renewable resources: ethics; environment						✓					
External sources of information, including databases				✓	✓						
International market integration: impact on goods, services and labour					✓	✓					
Comparative performance: market share and production capacity	✓	✓	✓	✓			✓				
Position appraisal and analysis											
SWOT analysis				✓			✓		✓	✓	
Identifying and quantifying the planning gap					✓						
Closing the planning gap: efficiency, improved products, new markets etc			✓		✓		✓		✓	✓	
Use of alternative strategies	✓			✓	✓						
Quality implementation and management			✓		✓				✓		
Comparing performance with competitors; benchmarking	✓			✓		✓	✓	✓	✓		
Measuring divisional and subsidiary performance	✓	✓		✓					✓	✓	
International and multinational trading; transfer prices		✓			✓			✓			
Customer outlets and customer profitability analysis		✓						✓			
Strategy in the marketplace											
Developing marketing strategies to meet organisational objectives		✓	✓				✓				
Assessing the nature and size of the market	✓	✓	✓		✓						
The marketing mix; relevance of the product life cycle		✓		✓						✓	✓
The product portfolio; formulation, management, brands	✓		✓			✓				✓	
Consumer power within the marketing environment							✓	✓			
Managing markets through mergers, acquisitions and divestments			✓			✓	✓	✓	✓		✓
Assessing performance of foreign subsidiaries		✓				✓					
Corporate social responsibility and professional ethics											
Profit motive versus other corporate objectives			✓							✓	✓
Stakeholders in business and the obligations of the organisation	✓	✓					✓		✓	✓	✓

The full syllabus is on pages (xxviii) to (xxx).

CURRENT ISSUES

Summary of recent articles

The content of articles published before July 1999 is reflected in the BPP Study Text for *Strategic Management Accountancy and Marketing*. A list of other articles has been noted briefly below.

The customer continuum, Deiric McCann, Management Accounting, January 1999 p 38

Customer account profitability analysis was examined in May 1999. This article looks at what it calls 'the customer continuum', that is, the varying degrees of relationship that can be fostered with customers. This continuum ranges from low to high 'lock in'. 'Lock in' to quote from the article 'is the measure of the security you can win in any customer account for an investment in developing business relationships with that account'. Some customers want a relationship with their suppliers (and will be alienated if this does not materialise). Others operate on deal-by deal basis, and will desert as soon as competitors drop their prices. Customers in low lock-in relationships with suppliers are promiscuous. High lock-in offerings tend to include large value-added service, such as management consultancy. Companies must decide where on the continuum individual customers are, to be able to decide how much to invest in building relationships with them.

Green and social issues and the management accountant, JG Williams, Management Accounting, February 1999 p 64

This article offers a useful and realistic overview of developments in environmental and social issues from a strategic and management accounting perspective. As well as covering the variety of pressures on organisations to respond to environmental and social improvement, the article discusses possible further developments and the role of the management accountant.

Investment appraisal for marketing and strategy, Malcolm Hazell, Management Accounting, March 1999 p 68

This article gives practical applications of investment appraisal techniques, and demonstrates the importance of strategic analysis.

The interface between finance and new product development, Pauline Gleadle, Management Accounting, July/ August 1999 p 24

The strategic issues surrounding new product development have been examined in the past, particularly in the section A compulsory question, and this article examines the specific example of 3M (UK). According to the article, 3M (UK) is innovative in product development and yet manages to meet stakeholder objectives via appropriate financial controls. The ability to innovate is often a crucial differentiating factor for companies subject to increasingly global competition.

The writer gives a good general background to the diverse activities of 3M and a summary of its performance measures.

The foundations of strategic management, Richard Bull, Management Accounting, September 1999 p 24

This article (the first in a two part series) looks at the complexity of strategic management and the contribution to be made by the management accountant. Using the analogy of a business as a building, the foundations are what gives a business its 'strength, capability and potential for future development'. The article gives a strategic perspective on business by providing a model which can be used to chart the development of any business, from its foundations to its summit. The second article in the series (October 1999) looks at the various schools of thought on strategic management.

Focus on quality, David Lynch, Management Accounting, September 1999 p 30

Quality and the role of the management accountant was examined as recently as November 1998. This is the first in a series of three articles dealing with exactly that topic, with the emphasis on the role of the finance function as a support activity. The author's belief is that 'helping the organisation to achieve quality is central to the purpose of the finance function'.

> Two articles by the examiner are reproduced on the following pages. You are strongly advised to read through them in detail.

Richard Smith provides some insights as to his aims, as the Examiner, in setting the SMM examination paper, and offers some practical suggestions for approaching the examination. If you work hard at understanding the subject and practice answering the questions, there is no reason why you should not pass

What is he getting at?

Possibly the most frequently heard question on the lips of any student as he or she leaves the examination hall. Or maybe when students are trying to fathom out the questions in their preparation for the examination. What *is* the examiner aiming at? What is he/she actually trying to do? Is it an attempt to catch us out?

Well, my answer to the last question is very clearly 'no'. 'Oh, but he would say that, wouldn't he?' Of course I would, but if I genuinely was intent on being obtuse or difficult in the examination, I could ask questions in a far more obscure manner than I do.

What I do admit to is that I try to set papers which deliberately test the candidate's ability to apply his or her knowledge. The reason for this is clear. At Stage 4, I am not simply looking for regurgitation of knowledge. Employers expect qualified Chartered Management Accountants to be competent as well as knowledgeable. This means that they must have the ability to analyse information and present a coherent approach to a particular problem. Examiners understand the artificiality of the scenario which may be set in the contrived atmosphere of the examination hall. Nevertheless, that in itself creates some approximation of the pressure under which the management accountant is expected to work.

I aim to set a fair test and there are many 'examination audit' procedures instituted by CIMA to try to ensure that this occurs. Not all information is given in a case study or scenario—but then it couldn't be, given the time which is available to assimilate the data. That is consistent with the real-life situation. I constantly point out to my undergraduate students that real management accounting problems do not come in neat examination-style packages, with all information supplied, such as you might expect in a straightforward variance analysis question. At Stage 4, there needs to be recognition that the management accountant must be able to determine what information is required in order to analyse the situation and provide cogent and competent advice.

The candidate needs to be able to manipulate the information (including numbers and management accounting techniques—yes, even in SMM) and apply the theory and knowledge in the particular circumstances identified in the question. This is essentially what sets SMM apart from studies at earlier stages. I will not ask for a simple description of a model or theory unless that leads to a more thorough analysis.

To satisfy the demands of the employer, the management accountant must demonstrate competence, and that implies a good grasp of theory and the ability to apply it to given situations in order to provide advice and solve complex business issues. This includes the ability to research the topic, rationalise the issues, deal with uncertainty, synthesise and evaluate the data, and communicate a rational solution or recommend alternative approaches. These skills are not obtained by a mere description of a model or theory, and consequently the examination paper for SMM requires depth of thought and application. If it did less than this, it would be failing in its responsibility to satisfy the requirements of employers and thereby devalue the high standards set by the Institute.

Aims of the SMM syllabus

There are four syllabus aims. These are concerned with relating the organisation to its environment, formulating strategies and recognising the need for flexibility, understanding the principles of strategic management accounting and appreciating the role of the management accountant in providing a service to the marketing and other functions of the organisation. These aims are encapsulated within the syllabus overview which explains the requirement 'for the management accountant to evaluate alternative courses of action to promote a more adaptive stance for the organisation...'

The aims of the forward- and outward-looking syllabus clearly emphasise the role of the management accountant and this has played a prominent part in previous papers. The management accountant has a crucial role in developing and shaping business strategy by applying strategic management accounting concepts and techniques to real-life problems. The examination paper seeks to provide a fair and realistic test of competence, with the syllabus aims very clearly in focus.

Syllabus components

The SMM syllabus is wide in range and clearly overlaps with other Stage 4 subject areas. One of the clearest examples is the area of performance appraisal within section 14c (Position appraisal and analysis) which overlaps with 16c (Performance and management control) within the MCS syllabus. There are overlaps with other subjects which feature earlier in the CIMA syllabus, notably Organisation Management and Development (OMD) and to a lesser extent Management Accounting Applications (MAA), both at Stage 3. Candidates coming forward to Stage 4 who have been granted exemptions from these subjects should take care to note that it is assumed they have a very good grasp of the syllabus contents. The onus is on the candidate to be sure that he or she is fully familiar with the subject contents for which any exemption has been granted. This is particularly important for OMD at Stage 3, as this subject provides the underpinning for much of Stage 4.

The candidate must recognise that it is not sufficient to rely on common sense alone to pass. A solid base of knowledge is needed before commencing SMM. This needs to be enhanced through the study of the subject. It should also be noted that the SMM subject itself is not as compartmentalised as it may appear from the sections of the syllabus. That is to say the candidate should be prepared for individual questions which require breadth of knowledge across the whole syllabus. This means that a specific question may relate to more than one area of the syllabus. Of course this mirrors life, as management accounting problems do not fit neatly into individual watertight compartments. Naturally, issues and problems impact on each other, and resolution of one problem might well result in the creation of another.

For example, the depreciation of a foreign currency may reduce demand for the export of a particular product as it becomes more expensive to the foreign customer. What should the exporter's competitive response be to this situation? Should the exporter look for another market for their product or remain loyal to their current customers and hope that the exchange rate will improve in the near future to make their product more attractive? To look for another market would demonstrate that the exporter was not willing to keep faith with customers when they encounter difficulties beyond their control. To remain loyal could mean a prolonged period of reduced profitability. It may be that the exporter cannot afford to remain loyal, as this may mean pegging prices in the foreign currency which then lose value after being exchanged for the home currency. What is the impact on the rest of the exporter's market? How is the future market in this particular foreign country viewed? Is it tactically more important to keep faith rather than go for short-term profitability? The decision on the strategic action which should be taken impacts on a whole range of issues. These include: environmental appraisal (section a of the syllabus); long- and short-term objectives and balanced growth and development (section b); closing the planning gap, use of alternative strategies, impact of changing price levels and customer outlets (section c); development of marketing strategies, consumer power and the product portfolio (section d); and stakeholders and the obligations of the organisation (section e).

Tackling the SMM examination

It should be clear to the reader by now that it is necessary for a thorough knowledge of the syllabus to be obtained before an attempt is made at the examination. Wide reading beyond the manuals or texts will enhance the candidate's likelihood of success as he/she can bring contemporary examples into the arguments. At least, candidates should keep up to date by reading quality newspapers as well as journals such as *Management Accounting* and *CIMA Student*. Of course, I am dependent on tutors and other 'diligent' students bringing this article to the attention of those who do not read widely!

Practice at the examination questions is very important. It is necessary for the candidate to acquire the skill of analysing and synthesising the information contained in the questions and constructing a valid answer. There is no better way of doing this than practice at answering the past questions. If you can, it is a good idea to ask a tutor (or even a qualified colleague at work) to look over your answers. In addition, the Institute publishes its Suggested Answers at the conclusion of every examination diet. These are answers which represent a 'good' pass. That does not mean to say that these are the only possible answers to the questions. If the suggested answer refers to a particular model in answering a question, it is quite reasonable for the candidate to suggest an alternative, provided that it is relevant and the case for its application is well argued. Markers are willing (and encouraged) to accept answers which vary from those which I put forward, provided that they are relevant and properly argued.

Forgive me for lapsing into 'grandfatherly' advice for a moment, but this technique worked for me when I was studying for the Institute's examinations all those centuries ago. I established a work pattern and devised a plan for each day. I found I could not cram for examinations anyway and therefore had to apply the drip-feed approach. Having set the plan, which consisted of about two hours' study a day after work, I set time aside to ensure that it was done. If I missed a day, then I encountered feelings of guilt. Starting in February each year, I spent a full weekend per month working through a set of past papers. My idea was that, if I could do three sets of past papers, one each in February, March and April, then when the real thing in May came around it would be an extension of the same process and psychologically should not feel much different. Of course, May always did feel different, but at least I felt reasonably prepared. Yes, OK, to use current jargon I was 'sad'—but I passed, which was my main objective at the time.

The main point is that practice is needed at presenting the answer in a logical and coherent way which takes account of the knowledge acquired. One of the main skills needed is to be able to apply that knowledge to the circumstances presented in the question. Be prepared to link themes within the syllabus and whatever you do, DON'T PRESENT AN UNSUBSTANTIATED LIST OF BULLET POINTS. Bullet points are fine, provided that they are supported with narrative or explanation. Headings followed by a paragraph or two of explanation for each which develops a series of points to argue a case is encouraged. The bullet points on their own will not secure a pass.

Steph Edwards-Nutton and I wrote an article on how to use answer plans in the February 1997 issue of *CIMA Student*. This was intended to help candidates to structure their answers and we worked through a full exam paper as an example. Answer plans often help candidates, but remember, they should not replace the answer itself.

It is vital to think carefully about what the question actually asks. Often candidates see a topic and enthusiastically proceed to deliver all they know about it, without answering the specific question. This is just a waste of everybody's time. A good example was question 2 on the November 1997 SMM paper. This required an explanation of how strategic management accounting can provide information which meets the requirements of senior managers in seeking to realise corporate objectives. The question did not ask for a description of strategic management accounting techniques, but that is exactly what was supplied by many candidates. Such an approach could have been used for part of the answer. Many candidates missed the point, which was to explain how these techniques help in the achievement of corporate objectives. It required much deeper analysis than a recital of such techniques as customer account profitability analysis, interrogation of databases and provision of non-financial as well as financial information. Citing these was fine, provided that an explanation was given as to how they help in the achievement of corporate objectives. Why is customer account profitability analysis being carried out in the first place? What are the long-term and short-term issues which should be addressed? How might the techniques help to achieve long term owner value? Will this help to anticipate the response of competitors?

It is better that a candidate provides an in-depth answer and deals in detail with a few key issues rather than skimming briefly over a lot of topics. Markers accept in-depth answers more readily than those that are superficial. They also reward relevant contemporary examples or practical experience which is used in support of a point. They do reward ingenuity—indeed, they go into raptures of delight (well, they are quite pleased anyway) if they see an answer which is relevant, well constructed and demonstrates the candidate's deep understanding of the topic.

Of course it is most important that candidates are able to get to grips with the case study. This is worth 60% of the whole paper and it is self-evident that, to pass, the candidate must score well on it. Answering the questions in the case in sequential order will allow the natural flow to develop. I spend a lot of time trying to get the questions in the case in the right order. Often the answer to one part of the case informs another. To answer them out of sequence, e.g. part a, c, d then b, may destroy this flow and usually the candidate does him- or herself no favours by approaching it in this way.

Having said that, I believe it is perfectly reasonable for the candidate to answer the full questions in the order which suits him or her best. There is a lot to be said for building confidence and if questions in section B (optional part) of the paper are more appealing than the case, then go for these first. Of course it is essential that sufficient time is left for the case—which at 60 marks is about 110 minutes!

You would expect me to implore candidates not to 'waffle'. The markers see through this and wafflers achieve nothing more than filling the pages and tend not to pass. There is a difference between constructing an argument which builds a case from apparently unrelated topics, which are then brought together at the end, and simply mentioning numerous unrelated and incoherent ideas which 'fit the question where they touch', or using a 'scatter gun' approach. The scatter gun method is 'here, this is what I know about this, sort out the bits you want!'.

'Page filling' techniques do not impress anyone either. You know the sort of thing I mean. The page-fillers certainly do. Writing on every other line, starting each line in the centre of the page or managing to fit no more than three words to a line is the type of thing I have in mind. There are no prizes for weight of answer or for filling the most answer books. Most prize winners manage to present their answers in a concise and logical fashion. I don't mean that answers should be written in the least space possible, but that a sensible approach should be adopted. Spacing is very important in layout and is encouraged, providing it is not simply a page filler.

Markers recognise the pressure under which candidates take the examination. It is also recognised that sometimes the neatest of scripts deteriorates as the examination progresses. Thankfully, most handwriting is readable. However, at each diet there are some scripts which are illegible. I ask the markers to point these out to me. Candidates must realise that if their handwriting cannot be read by either the marker or me, they cannot possibly achieve a pass. Further, such poor handwriting is unacceptable in the business environment, even in these days of word processing. Some things still need to be hand written.

Conclusion

The intention of this article is to provide some insight as to my aims in setting the SMM examination paper. I also hope that I have been able to provide some practical suggestions for approaching the examination. If the candidate works hard at understanding the subject and practices answering the questions, there is no reason why he or she should not pass. You do not need to be a genius to pass CIMA Stage 4, it is not rocket science. I and many others are living proof of this! Your answers to SMM examination questions must be applied to the particular situation contained in the question in order to achieve the success for which you are aiming.

FOR STAGE 4 STUDENTS

Outsourcing—a strategy for increased profitability or catastrophe?

This article, by Richard Smith (the SMM Examiner) and Steph Edwards-Nutton is aimed principally at candidates studying for Stage 4 examinations. It concerns outsourcing and is intended to assist in examination preparation as well as providing some discussion within the context of the wider working environment. The key issues discussed in the article are:

- *rationale for outsourcing;*
- *processes in outsourcing;*
- *benefits and problems of outsourcing.*

Introduction

According to Elmuti, D., Kathawala, Y. *et al* (1998):[1] *'Outsourcing has become a useful tactic to lower costs and gain a competitive advantage.'*

They go on to explain that companies are achieving a 9% cost saving and an increase in capacity and quality of 15% on average as a result of outsourcing.

This is all very well but what actually does the term 'outsourcing' mean, what is the rationale for it, how is it done, how is the quality of the outsourced service assured and what are its benefits and pitfalls? This article considers these questions in turn.

What is outsourcing?

Martin Stacey (1998)[2] states that, *'Organisations have taken the opportunity to transfer services and internal resources to a third party and then control the supply (sourcing) through contract and partnership management'.*

So outsourcing is about an organisation obtaining the benefits from the provision of services without actually having to own the physical resources which generate those services. Outsourcing requires the organisation to enter a contractual commitment for the provision of the services, which may in itself be something of a culture shock for many of them.

The areas which have been most popular for outsourced services in recent years are information systems and technology, infrastructure management such as buildings and plant, distribution, administration, human resource management, financial and marketing functions.

What is the rationale for outsourcing?

The reasons for undertaking outsourcing may be many and varied. In the end though, they come down to the need to increase efficiency. Elmuti, Kathawala et al explain that executives of most corporations believe that successful global competitiveness stems from cost control rather than relying on increased revenue. The philosophy of outsourcing is that a specialist organisation may be able to carry out a particular service more efficiently than through in-house provision.

Outsourcing is mainly sought for those services that are regarded as supplementary to the core business activities. Elmuti, Kathawala et al identify three long-term and five short-term reasons for outsourcing. The long-term reasons are:

- freeing up resources for other purposes allowing the organisation to concentrate on its core activities;
- sharing risks and enabling the organisation to keep up to date with technological and legislative changes without committing internal resources and thereby becoming more adaptable in a rapidly changing environment;
- acceleration of benefits which may be generated from re-engineering following recognition that the in-house function is no longer performing to a high, even world class standard.

The short-term reasons for outsourcing include:

- increasing efficiency by outsourcing a function which is difficult to manage using resources which are simply not available internally;
- reducing the operating costs of supervision management and control through the purchase of economies of scale advantages enjoyed by the outsourcing organisation, generating cash by selling assets to an outsourcer who then provides the service to the organisation in accordance with the terms of the contractual arrangement established;
- making capital funds available with the organisation not having to supply the capital resources for necessary equipment, technology or buildings.

It should be made clear that some of these short-term reasons do have their limitations. If a function is problematic when performed in-house then these problems may still exist externally and be even more difficult to control after it has been outsourced. The non-availability of resources internally may lead to outsourcing a function in the short term, but in the longer time frame it may be more beneficial to bring the function in house. This may be as a result of the imposition of fixed costs and the determination of the break-even point. It may be more economic to provide the service in house if the volume of output exceeds this level.

What are the processes in outsourcing an internal service or activity?

First and foremost, it is necessary to be clear about the objectives of the outsourcing strategy. What does the organisation expect to achieve from the outsourced services and how will it measure the achievement of these expectations? It is also necessary to be clear about the cost and efficiency of the in-house function. This requires a good knowledge of basic cost accounting principles ensuring that such issues as non-controllable apportioned fixed overheads do not distort the cost of the service. Will these fixed overhead costs remain after the activity has been outsourced?

Stacey refers to 'lifecycle sourcing', which is a process of using management accounting techniques to assist in delivering overall organisational objectives. He identifies six phases of lifecycle sourcing:

- sourcing strategy;
- sourcing preparation;
- supply selection;
- transition;
- supply management;
- supply re-selection.

Sourcing strategy involves determining which activities are eligible for outsourcing. This follows the determination by the organisation of which generic strategy is to be pursued and identifying the resources needed to achieve it. The organisation will evaluate the competencies of the resources which are used and whether they are core to the business or operate in a support role.

Sourcing preparation involves obtaining detailed information on the function to be outsourced and determining the expected levels of improvement in quality, efficiency and effectiveness of performance.

Supply selection is the process of producing a tight service tender for the outsourced function and selecting an appropriate supplier. The organisation must satisfy itself on the quality of the outsourced service to be received from the supplier.

Transition involves establishing a plan to transfer the selected function to the chosen supplier. This often involves appointing a short life working group to organise and supervise the transition.

Once the function has been outsourced, the contract must be **managed** and the supplier monitored in terms of performance. This is where the detailed sourcing preparation and supply selection activity is critical as these provide the clear specification of the terms of the outsourced service.

Re-selection is concerned with reviewing the service provision and measuring the actual outcomes against those which were expected in order to determine whether the chosen supplier should be reselected at the end of the contract period.

Attention now turns to the benefits and problems of outsourcing.

Benefits of outsourcing

Use external expertise

Many businesses do not have the internal resources to carry out all essential activities. It makes sense therefore to make use of external staff who are experts in a particular field. Outsourcing also allows organisations to gain an outside perspective on complex issues and activities.

Concentration on core activities

Outsourcing allows internal staff to focus their efforts on the critical tasks of the core business in order to increase competitive advantage. As Elmuti et al suggest,

'Outsourcing allows companies to return to their most successful work and enjoy the benefits of allowing their outsourcing partners to do the same'.

Access to world-class capabilities

Organisations can take the opportunity to utilise external resources which are world class in their field. This may mean access to a larger pool of more flexible, specialised staff who are highly trained in this particular activity.

Shared risks

Organisations face enormous risk in the investments that they make. Outsourcing may enable them to be more flexible, dynamic and more able to adapt to changing business opportunities.

Problems of outsourcing

The reasons for outsourcing and the potential benefits it can offer have been quite clearly argued above. Implementation of an outsourcing strategy may lead to reduced costs and increased productivity, quality and profitability. However, it is also important for organisations to recognise the potential problems associated with outsourcing.

Reduction in control

Organisations may lose some control over the delivery of outsourced services and may find themselves overly dependent on the supplier.

Staff issues

Outsourcing may lead to low morale and reduced performance of the remaining staff. Employees will be concerned about the safety of their own positions in the organisation, which is likely to affect their motivation and subsequent performance.

Exploitation

Outsourcing can potentially be seen as exploitation, with many companies choosing to establish themselves in under developed countries where labour remuneration is relatively cheap. Publicity about exploitation of cheap labour can be severely damaging for business with loss of goodwill and the inevitable damage to an organisation's reputation.

Loss of skills/expertise

By outsourcing functions such as IT or personnel, the organisation may be losing internal skills from which it could benefit in the long term.

Information security

Outsourcing commercially sensitive activities may bring with it the possibility of risk to security of information.

Reasons for failure of outsourcing

The following have been put forward as the main reasons for failure of outsourcing initiatives.

- Inappropriate partners chosen for outsourcing;
- Poor cost assessment prior to outsourcing and unsatisfactory sourcing preparation;
- Unclear expectations;
- Over-emphasis on short-term benefits.

Conclusion

Outsourcing requires an objective analysis of organisational core competencies and the correct mix of in house and outsourced activities to ensure long term success. To succeed in today's business environment, companies need to be resourceful, innovative and productive in order to achieve a competitive advantage. *(Continued overleaf)*

Mariotti's Ten Myths of Outsourcing (1998) are worth repeating here:

	MYTH	FACT
1	You can outsource whatever service you want with no investment	When you make no investment, you usually have no ownership or equity in what you get
2	If you don't have the necessary knowledge, you can buy it	You aren't buying it, you are just renting it. The competition can also buy the same knowledge
3	You can buy market share or entry more cheaply by using an outsource contractor's capabilities	Again, you are just borrowing the capability, until the competitors rent the same market
4	Outsourcing makes it easier to deal with fluctuating staffing needs	Only if the contractor can find someone with counter seasonal needs. If the contractor cannot balance the demand you will have to pay for the down time
5	There is no need for day to day management involvement when you outsource	True, but there is no control over the day to day results
6	An easy way to solve a difficult problem is to outsource to a specialist	Only if the problem is not a structural one that your company causes. Outsourcing may move the problem further away and harder to solve
7	The outsource contractor needs to know all about your business to be most effective	If the contractor knows too much about your business there may be a chance that they will steal your business away. There is a fine line between sharing relevant information and giving too much away
8	Everyone says it's the thing to do	You should ask 'everyone' what their motives are. Many of those quoted in the media are those selling outsourced services
9	The cost is lower if you outsource	This is only true if the contractor is significantly better at the task than you. The contractor will have their own costs to cover and a profit margin
10	'They promised they would do things for us that they won't do for the competition'	If they will do it for you, they will do it to you!

Outsourcing can be a very effective strategic tool to gain competitive advantage, which involves the whole organisation, from senior management down to the line worker.

Strategic outsourcing is a critical aspect in the search for increased productivity and performance. External experts can bring advantages of expertise, cost and efficiency over in house activities.

Focusing on activities in which organisations have expertise along with implementing strategic outsourcing will allow organisations to remain flexible and focused on those processes which will achieve long term profitability and productivity.

1 ELMUTI, D., KATHAWALA, Y. *et al*: 'Outsourcing to gain a competitive advantage', *Industrial Management*, May 1998.

2 STACEY, M.: 'Outsourcing—how organisations need to prepare in order to realise the full benefits', *Management Accounting*, May 1998; 'Outsourcing—how to differentiate supplier offerings in order to realise the full potential benefits', *Management Accounting*, June 1998; 'Outsourcing—how to deliver the full benefits through expert supply management teams', *Management Accounting*, July/August 1998.

3 MARIOTTI, J.: 'Ten myths of outsourcing', *Industry Week*, 20 April 1998.

EXAMINERS' INSTRUCTIONS

The examinations department of the CIMA has asked the Institute's examiners to be precise when drafting questions. In particular, examiners have been asked to use precise instruction words. It will probably help you to know what instruction words may be used, and what they mean. With the Institute's permission, their list of recommended requirement words, and their meaning, is shown below.

Recommended requirement words

Advise/recommend	Present information, opinions or recommendations to someone to enable that recipient to take action
Amplify	Expand or enlarge upon the meaning of (a statement or quotation)
Analyse	Determine and explain the constituent parts of
Appraise/assess/evaluate	Judge the importance or value of
Assess	See 'appraise'
Clarify	Explain more clearly the meaning of
Comment (critically)	Explain
Compare (with)	Explain similarities and differences between
Contrast	Place in opposition to bring out difference(s)
Criticise	Present the faults in a theory or policy or opinion
Demonstrate	Show by reasoning the truth of
Describe	Present the details and characteristics of
Discuss	Explain the opposing arguments
Distinguish	Specify the differences between
Evaluate	See 'appraise'
Explain/interpret	Set out in detail the meaning of
Illustrate	Use an example - chart, diagram, graph or figure as appropriate - to explain something
Interpret	See 'explain'
Justify	State adequate grounds for
List (and explain)	Itemise (and detail meaning of)
Prove	Show by testing the accuracy of
Recommend	See 'advise'
Reconcile	Make compatible apparently conflicting statements or theories
Relate	Show connections between separate matters
State	Express
Summarise	State briefly the essential points (dispensing with examples and details)
Tabulate	Set out facts or figures in a table

Requirement words which will be avoided

Examiners have been asked to avoid instructions which are imprecise or which may not specifically elicit an answer. The following words will not be used.

Consider	As candidates could do this without writing a word
Define	In the sense of stating exactly what a thing is, as CIMA wishes to avoid requiring evidence of rote learning
Examine	As this is what the examiner is doing, not the examinee
Enumerate	'List' is preferred
Identify	
Justify	When the requirement is not 'to state adequate grounds for' but 'to state the advantage of'
List	On its own, without an additional requirement such as 'list and explain'
Outline	As its meaning is imprecise. The addition of the word 'briefly' to any of the suggested action words is more satisfactory
Review	
Specify	
Trace	

SYLLABUS

The syllabus contains a weighting for each syllabus area, and a ranking of the level of ability required in each topic. The Institute has published the following explanatory notes on these points.

Study weightings

A percentage weighting is shown against each topic in the syllabus; this is intended as a guide to the amount of study time each topic requires.

All topics in a syllabus must be studied, as a question may examine more than one topic, or carry a higher proportion of marks than the percentage study time suggested.

The weightings do not specify the number of marks which will be allocated to topics in the examination.

Abilities required in the examination

Each examination paper contains a number of topics. Each topic has been given a number to indicate the level of ability required of the candidate.

The numbers range from 1 to 4 and represent the following ability levels:

Appreciation (1)
To understand a knowledge area at an early stage of learning, or outside the core of management accounting, at a level which enables the accountant to communicate and work with other members of the management team.

Knowledge (2)
To have detailed knowledge of such matters as laws, standards, facts and techniques so as to advise at a level appropriate to a management accounting specialist.

Skill (3)
To apply theoretical knowledge, concepts and techniques to the solutions of problems where it is clear what technique has to be used and the information needed is clearly indicated.

Application (4)
To apply knowledge and skills where candidates have to determine from a number of techniques which is the most appropriate and select the information required from a fairly wide range of data, some of which might not be relevant; to exercise professional judgement and to communicate and work with members of the management team and other recipients of financial reports.'

Syllabus overview

Set in a planning environment, this syllabus is essentially forward and outward looking, draws upon a broad content of knowledge and is designed to be integrative. It emphasises the dynamic yet unstable nature of the environment within which organisations, both profit seeking and 'not for profit', operate. This requires the management accountant to evaluate alternative courses of action to promote a more adaptive stance for the organisation and be aware of professional ethics, and the possible personal conflicts of interest that may arise.

Aims

To test the candidate's ability to:

- relate the organisation to its environment(s)
- formulate strategies and recognise the importance of flexibility within the organisation as a prerequisite to achieving organisational objectives
- understand the principles of strategic management accounting and its application within the organisation
- appreciate the role of the management accountant in the servicing of the marketing and other functions in a competitive environment

Content and ability required

14(a) Appraising the environment *(study weighting 20%)*

		Ability required
(i)	Impact on the organisation of changing national and international influences: demography; technology (professional alternatives/acceptability); economic resources; social attitudes and aspirations; legislation and regulation; political forces; government and other agencies, including pressure groups	2
(ii)	Use of renewable and non-renewable resources including the ethical implications of such use; the effect of the environment on corporate performance	2
(iii)	External sources of information, including data bases, both private and public, and their usefulness to the organisation	2
(iv)	Impact of innovation, substitution and obsolescence on business processes (including marketing and production)	2
(v)	Impact of international market integration on the transfer of goods, services and labour	2
(vi)	Comparative organisational performance: market share; production capacity	4

14(b) Establishing the corporate objectives *(study weighting 10%)*

		Ability required
(i)	Organisational missions, aims, goals and objectives	2
(ii)	Long-term (strategic) and short-term (operational) objectives: quantitative and qualitative evaluation	3
(iii)	Application of decision theory	4
(iv)	Problems of achieving balanced growth and development	3
(v)	Internal and external factors affecting decisions; implications of 'short-termism'	4

14(c) Position appraisal and analysis *(study weighting 30%)*

(i)	Identifying the organisation's strengths and weaknesses, opportunities and threats	3
(ii)	Identification and quantification of the planning gap	3
(iii)	Closing the planning gap through the identification and evaluation of alternative courses of action: improved efficiency; improved product(s) or services(s); introducing new products; entering new markets; merging with or acquiring other organisations	4
(iv)	Use of alternative strategies	3
(v)	Quality as a strategic variable; its implementation and management	4
(vi)	Performance against operational and strategic targets: flexibility, economy, efficiency and effectiveness	4
(vii)	Performance against that of competitors; benchmarking; use of inter-firm comparisons; the limitations of external data	4
(viii)	Performance of cost, profit and investment centres using financial and non-financial measures	4
(ix)	Problems of measuring divisional and subsidiary company performance	3
(x)	International and multinational trading; transfer pricing of goods and services and their impact on trading results	4
(xi)	Impact of changing price levels on current performance and future projections	3
(xii)	Customer outlets, including customer profitability analysis	3

14(d) Strategy in the market place *(study weighting 30%)*

(i)	Assessing threats and opportunities to the marketing plan; determining the need for change in the planning area	3
(ii)	Development of marketing strategies to meet organisational objectives	4
(iii)	Assessing the nature and size of the market using internal records, market intelligence, market research	2
(iv)	The processes of creating, reviewing, selecting and marketing the right product in the right place, to the right customer at the right time, while achieving the right price; relevance of the product life cycle	4
(v)	The product portfolio; formulation, management, the relevance of branded merchandise	3
(vi)	Consumer power within the marketing environment	2
(vii)	Strategic management of markets through mergers, acquisitions and divestments	4
(viii)	Problems associated with the acquisition of foreign subsidiaries especially in respect of performance appraisal	3

14(e) Corporate social responsibility and professional ethics *(study weighting 10%)*

(i)	Disclosure and confidentiality	4
(ii)	Profit motive versus other corporate objectives	4
(iii)	Goal congruence and corporate performance measurement	4
(iv)	The role of professional bodies in regulating the activities of members	2
(v)	Stakeholders in business and the obligations of the organisation	2

CIMA SYLLABUS GUIDANCE NOTES 1999-2000

The following Guidance Notes were published by the CIMA in the August 1999 CIMA Student as an aid to students and lecturers.

'The following guidance notes have been drafted by the Chief Examiner for each of the subjects. They are intended to inform candidates and lecturers about the scope of the syllabus, the emphasis that should be placed on various topics and the approach which the examination papers will adopt.

Most of these guidance notes are applicable immediately, insofar as they provide general guidance on each subject. Guidance specific to changes effective from the May 2000 examination will be applicable from that examination.

General guidance note (Stage 4)

As the final test of professional competence in management accountancy, Stage 4 has certain unique characteristics. It is the culmination of the whole examination and requires from candidates the highest level of ability.

From Stage 2 onwards, candidates should remember that the syllabus content of subjects at earlier Stages is re-examinable. This does not imply that a Stage 2 question will appear in a Stage 4 question paper. However it does mean that candidates need the ability to build on knowledge and skills learned originally for an earlier stage.

Candidates will be required to integrate new material with that learned earlier, and to use the combined knowledge at a higher level of ability. Revision of earlier material, particularly by those who have been credited with exemptions, must form part of the studying process. The majority of the topics in the four papers is ranked at ability level 4 (Application). This means that candidates must not only be able to select the relevant data and apply the appropriate technique; they must also be able to communicate to others the results obtained. There is thus an emphasis on the practical application of knowledge and skill. To test this, the examiners rely heavily on case study questions and scenario-based questions.

A case study is simply a history or description of an organisation, firm or industry facing a particular set of circumstances, which could be a problem of some sort, or perhaps an opportunity. There is usually some discussion of how the organisation's current situation developed, and there is often one or more central characters charged with the task of resolving the problem, or exploiting the opportunity. Such characters are invariably senior members of management, for example the managing director, because it is at this level where strategic decisions are made.

Cases will be between one and three pages long. They may be based around activities of real people and organisations (although candidates do *not* require any specialist knowledge of any particular organisation), or they may be fictitious.

The essential function of the case study is to test a candidate's ability to resolve relatively complex, unstructured problems. It is characteristics of a case study that there may be several feasible solutions and candidates should not necessarily expect there to be a single definitive answer. The solution will involve the use of techniques which have been learned, but usually also requires the exercise of judgement and creative thinking. This means that study and examination techniques which might have been suitable at earlier Stages need to become more sophisticated and directed when preparing for the Stage 4 papers. Preparation to answer case incident/scenario-based questions cannot rely on reading alone, but must be heavily supplemented by question practice under examination conditions.

It is important to realise that in case study questions marks are earned by the quality of the reasoning and exposition displayed. The ability to structure a coherent report which leads logically to its conclusion is regarded as essential. Recommendations are often required. Acceptable recommendations may vary but must be sensible and fully justified.

As candidates advance through the examination Stages, their career progress can restrict their available study time. Fewer find it possible to maintain contact with a teacher or tutor as part of a class. Yet the nature of the examination makes that contact highly desirable - perhaps more so than at earlier Stages. However, candidates will be gaining a greater breadth of experience in the workplace. This valuable practical experience can be drawn on when answering practical-based questions.

Candidates' chances of success will be significantly enhanced if they are familiar with the current business environment. An easy way to achieve this is to read selectively from the *Financial Times* which analyses companies' published accounts, comments on marketing and strategy, and also publishes a weekly management page. There are also other international newspapers which carry out the same sort of analysis. It is quite clear that examination answers are enhanced by examples drawn from press articles and that such answers are given credit by markers.

Stage 4 involves the integration of all subjects. There is inevitably and deliberately some overlap between papers as topics are dealt with from the different perspectives of strategy, marketing, information management, control and financial management. The following guidance notes give more information on the syllabuses for the four subjects, but candidates should be continually aware of the integrative nature of Stage 4 and should not view each of the syllabuses in isolation.

Strategic Management Accountancy and Marketing

Candidates are reminded of the aims of the syllabus.

'To test the candidate's ability to:

- *relate the organisation to its environment(s)*'

  Candidates should appreciate that questions in this area will require structured answers that relate to the circumstances as described. The tendency to produce lists of factors without relating these to the circumstances should be resisted.

  What is likely to be examined is the candidate's appreciation of the environment, the forces that influence it and how all this impinges upon the organisation. Another important aspect which is likely to be tested is the extension of management accounting techniques into the public sector.

- '*formulate strategies and recognise the importance of flexibility within the organisation as a prerequisite to achieving organisational objectives*'

  This will be achieved within the context of the contribution which can be expected from the Chartered Management Accountant. Candidates should be aware of the procedures used by and the techniques available to the strategic planner, and that the role of the Chartered Management Accountant is likely to be one of ensuring that any plan proposed is feasible and consistent with management policy.

  The topics examined here reiterate those of other papers, although in this paper they will be applied at the strategic level. The topics may require both numerical and discursive answers.

- *'understand the principles of strategic management accounting and its application within the organisation'*

  This aim is fundamental to this paper and is likely to influence most questions.

- *'appreciate the role of the management accountant in the servicing of the marketing and other functions in a competitive environment'*

  Candidates will need an appreciation of the marketing philosophy and also of marketing techniques. An understanding of the relationship between marketing and other functions of the organisation and the Chartered Management Accountant is also required.

  Candidates should be aware of planning procedures and should be able to demonstrate an appreciation of the factors to be taken into account when compiling strategic and marketing plans.

Each constituent section of this syllabus addresses the aims as set out above. Although the syllabus is divided into sections, the student must recognise that, in reality, there are no barriers existing between each section. Thus, for example, environmental appraisal will inevitably form a part of the other sections. The syllabus contents should not be seen as existing within watertight compartments and therefore candidates should be prepared to draw on their knowledge of relevant aspects of the syllabus when tackling any question on the paper. For example, the establishment of a strategy to close the planning gap (section (c)) must have regard to corporate objectives (section (b)) and an understanding of the environment in which the organisation is situated (section (a)).

The examination paper

The examination paper will be divided into two sections.

Section A will contain compulsory question(s) based on a case study which may embrace any or all aspects of the syllabus. This will have a weighting of up to 60% of the paper.

Section B will offer candidates a choice of questions.

Appraising the environment

Syllabus reference 14(a)

Study weighting 20%

This section forms the basis for the whole syllabus and a thorough understanding of the corporate environment is essential.

In the examination, candidates may be required to:

- analyse the different requirements of stakeholders, draw appropriate comparisons and identify areas where potential conflict may arise;
- demonstrate a general appreciation of the value of databases;
- demonstrate an understanding of the principles of new product and market development and the use of renewable and non-renewable resources.

The following items are *not* examinable:

- detailed understanding of cultural or economic factors that affect only the UK;
- detailed knowledge of the impact of international market integration.

Establishing the corporate objectives

Syllabus reference 14(b)

Study weighting 10%

In the examination candidates may be required to:

- apply decision theory in certain and uncertain conditions. The emphasis in Stage 4 is weighted towards the technique's application and the interpretation of the information which it provides. This does not necessarily mean however that any questions on this topic will be exclusively discursive;
- analyse the process for determining and evaluating long and short term organisational objectives.

Position appraisal and analysis

Syllabus reference 14(c)

Study weighting 30%

In the examination, candidates may be required to:

- answer questions of a numerical and/or discursive style relating to international and multinational trading and transfer prices;
- answer questions of a numerical and/or discursive style relating to the impact of changing price levels on current performance and future projections;
- apply techniques and strategic planning models previously studied within the OMD syllabus and consolidated within this syllabus.

Strategy in the market place

Syllabus reference 14(d)

Study weighting 30%

Marketing is not an activity which is separate from strategic planning and management. Candidates are expected to recognise that marketing is central to the development of strategic plans. Marketing as a subject area could feature either as part of, or as the sole focus of, a question within the paper.

In the examination, candidates may be required to:

- apply marketing planning models such as McCarthy's Marketing Mix and the Boston Consulting Group Growth Share Matrix.

The following is *not* examinable:

- preparation of a detailed marketing plan appropriate to any particular undertaking.

Corporate social responsibility and professional ethics

Syllabus reference 14(e)

Study weighting 10%

Any strategic planning and management decision has ethical and social considerations associated with it. This does not relate only to ethical environmental issues, such as pollution.

This area relates to the obligations of an organisation and of the individuals associated with it, in carrying out their business and professional activities. It is essential that the organisation should recognise its obligations within the community, at a local, national or international level. This is specifically applicable in this section, but it may also apply in any other section of the syllabus.

In the examination, candidates may be required to:

- demonstrate an appreciation of the fact that business and strategic policies and decisions have ethical and social implications that may not only be of an ecological nature;
- show an awareness of the need for these issues to be considered by organisational management before deciding on any particular course of action.

The following is *not* examinable:

- detailed understanding of the role of professional bodies in regulating the activities of members. Emphasis is placed here on the word 'detailed'. Candidates are required to have a general appreciation of the regulatory activities of the professional bodies in respect of their members.

PRESENT VALUE TABLE

Present value of 1 = $(1+r)^{-n}$ where r = discount rate, n = number of periods until payment

This table shows the present value of £1 per annum, receivable or payable at the end of *n* years.

Periods (n)	1%	2%	3%	4%	5%	6%	7%	8%	9%	10%
1	0.990	0.980	0.971	0.962	0.952	0.943	0.935	0.926	0.917	0.909
2	0.980	0.961	0.943	0.925	0.907	0.890	0.873	0.857	0.842	0.826
3	0.971	0.942	0.915	0.889	0.864	0.840	0.816	0.794	0.772	0.751
4	0.961	0.924	0.888	0.855	0.823	0.792	0.763	0.735	0.708	0.683
5	0.951	0.906	0.863	0.822	0.784	0.747	0.713	0.681	0.650	0.621
6	0.942	0.888	0.837	0.790	0.746	0.705	0.666	0.630	0.596	0.564
7	0.933	0.871	0.813	0.760	0.711	0.665	0.623	0.583	0.547	0.513
8	0.923	0.853	0.789	0.731	0.677	0.627	0.582	0.540	0.502	0.467
9	0.914	0.837	0.766	0.703	0.645	0.592	0.544	0.500	0.460	0.424
10	0.905	0.820	0.744	0.676	0.614	0.558	0.508	0.463	0.422	0.386
11	0.896	0.804	0.722	0.650	0.585	0.527	0.475	0.429	0.388	0.350
12	0.887	0.788	0.701	0.625	0.557	0.497	0.444	0.397	0.356	0.319
13	0.879	0.773	0.681	0.601	0.530	0.469	0.415	0.368	0.326	0.290
14	0.870	0.758	0.661	0.577	0.505	0.442	0.388	0.340	0.299	0.263
15	0.861	0.743	0.642	0.555	0.481	0.417	0.362	0.315	0.275	0.239

Periods (n)	11%	12%	13%	14%	15%	16%	17%	18%	19%	20%
1	0.901	0.893	0.885	0.877	0.870	0.862	0.855	0.847	0.840	0.833
2	0.812	0.797	0.783	0.769	0.756	0.743	0.731	0.718	0.706	0.694
3	0.731	0.712	0.693	0.675	0.658	0.641	0.624	0.609	0.593	0.579
4	0.659	0.636	0.613	0.592	0.572	0.552	0.534	0.516	0.499	0.482
5	0.593	0.567	0.543	0.519	0.497	0.476	0.456	0.437	0.419	0.402
6	0.535	0.507	0.480	0.456	0.432	0.410	0.390	0.370	0.352	0.335
7	0.482	0.452	0.425	0.400	0.376	0.354	0.333	0.314	0.296	0.279
8	0.434	0.404	0.376	0.351	0.327	0.305	0.285	0.266	0.249	0.233
9	0.391	0.361	0.333	0.308	0.284	0.263	0.243	0.225	0.209	0.194
10	0.352	0.322	0.295	0.270	0.247	0.227	0.208	0.191	0.176	0.162
11	0.317	0.287	0.261	0.237	0.215	0.195	0.178	0.162	0.148	0.135
12	0.286	0.257	0.231	0.208	0.187	0.168	0.152	0.137	0.124	0.112
13	0.258	0.229	0.204	0.182	0.163	0.145	0.130	0.116	0.104	0.093
14	0.232	0.205	0.181	0.160	0.141	0.125	0.111	0.099	0.088	0.078
15	0.209	0.183	0.160	0.140	0.123	0.108	0.095	0.084	0.074	0.065

CUMULATIVE PRESENT VALUE TABLE

This table shows the present value of £1 per annum, receivable or payable at the end of each year for *n* years.

Periods					Discount rates (r)					
(n)	1%	2%	3%	4%	5%	6%	7%	8%	9%	10%
1	0.990	0.980	0.971	0.962	0.952	0.943	0.935	0.926	0.917	0.909
2	1.970	1.942	1.913	1.886	1.859	1.833	1.808	1.783	1.759	1.736
3	2.941	2.884	2.829	2.775	2.723	2.673	2.624	2.577	2.531	2.487
4	3.902	3.808	3.717	3.630	3.546	3.465	3.387	3.312	3.240	3.170
5	4.853	4.713	4.580	4.452	4.329	4.212	4.100	3.993	3.890	3.791
6	5.795	5.601	5.417	5.242	5.076	4.917	4.767	4.623	4.486	4.355
7	6.728	6.472	6.230	6.002	5.786	5.582	5.389	5.206	5.033	4.868
8	7.652	7.325	7.020	6.733	6.463	6.210	5.971	5.747	5.535	5.335
9	8.566	8.162	7.786	7.435	7.108	6.802	6.515	6.247	5.995	5.759
10	9.471	8.983	8.530	8.111	7.722	7.360	7.024	6.710	6.418	6.145
11	10.368	9.787	9.253	8.760	8.306	7.887	7.499	7.139	6.805	6.495
12	11.255	10.575	9.954	9.385	8.863	8.384	7.943	7.536	7.161	6.814
13	12.134	11.348	10.635	9.986	9.394	8.853	8.358	7.904	7.487	7.103
14	13.004	12.106	11.296	10.563	9.899	9.295	8.745	8.244	7.786	7.367
15	13.865	12.849	11.938	11.118	10.380	9.712	9.108	8.559	8.061	7.606

Periods					Discount rates (r)					
(n)	11%	12%	13%	14%	15%	16%	17%	18%	19%	20%
1	0.901	0.893	0.885	0.877	0.870	0.862	0.855	0.847	0.840	0.833
2	1.713	1.690	1.668	1.647	1.626	1.605	1.585	1.566	1.547	1.528
3	2.444	2.402	2.361	2.322	2.283	2.246	2.210	2.174	2.140	2.106
4	3.102	3.037	2.974	2.914	2.855	2.798	2.743	2.690	2.639	2.589
5	3.696	3.605	3.517	3.433	3.352	3.274	3.199	3.127	3.058	2.991
6	4.231	4.111	3.998	3.889	3.784	3.685	3.589	3.498	3.410	3.326
7	4.712	4.564	4.423	4.288	4.160	4.039	3.922	3.812	3.706	3.605
8	5.146	4.968	4.799	4.639	4.487	4.344	4.207	4.078	3.954	3.837
9	5.537	5.328	5.132	4.946	4.772	4.607	4.451	4.303	4.163	4.031
10	5.889	5.650	5.426	5.216	5.019	4.833	4.659	4.494	4.339	4.192
11	6.207	5.938	5.687	5.453	5.234	5.029	4.836	4.656	4.486	4.327
12	6.492	6.194	5.918	5.660	5.421	5.197	4.988	4.793	4.611	4.439
13	6.750	6.424	6.122	5.842	5.583	5.342	5.118	4.910	4.715	4.533
14	6.982	6.628	6.302	6.002	5.724	5.468	5.229	5.008	4.802	4.611
15	7.191	6.811	6.462	6.142	5.847	5.575	5.324	5.092	4.876	4.675

Question bank

LONG CASE STUDIES

1 G PLC: OBJECTIVES AND ENVIRONMENT (5/96) *90 mins*

Introduction

G plc is a long-established divisionalised company with its origins in shipping. The company has been in existence for nearly 160 years and has developed a reputation for reliability and quality of service. Whilst the company obtains the majority of its turnover from various forms of shipping, its subsidiary interests extend into transport, construction and property.

The shipping activities in which G plc is engaged comprise four divisions - Cruise, Ferries, Containers and Bulk Shipping. The Cruise Division is engaged entirely in the carriage of passengers and the Ferries Division carries passengers and vehicles. The vehicles carried by the Ferries range from motor cars to articulated lorries and single-deck buses. The Containers and Bulk Shipping Divisions are engaged in the carriage of freight only and do not carry any fare-paying passengers.

Organisational aims

The company had stated over recent years that it aims to achieve the following goals:

1. Increase its emphasis on international businesses to achieve long-term profitability.
2. Provide those businesses with the necessary capital investment to achieve their development.
3. Continued development and training of the company's employees to achieve the organisational objectives.

Environmental policy

The company has established an environmental policy which is monitored through an audit system in an effort to ensure that its policies are being achieved. It is the aim of the company to have operational standards which at least equate with the best industry practice. Training of management, staff and specialist auditors is seen as a priority within the organisation's environmental policy. This has become a major concern of the company which is aware of customer anxiety about travelling on roll-on roll-off (RORO) ferries following public debate about their safety.

Financial results

In the last financial year, earnings per share totalled £0.353 (35.3 pence) producing a dividend cover of 1.15. The dividend per share paid by G plc has remained at the same level for five years. Comparative values for divisional turnover and operating profit of each of the shipping divisions are as follows.

	Turnover			*Operating profit*		
	This year	*This year adjusted for inflation*	*Last year*	*This year*	*This year adjusted for inflation*	*Last year*
	£m	£m	£m	£m	£m	£m
Divisions						
Cruise	856	815	735	96	91	88
Ferries	667	635	626	90	86	80
Containers	1,262	1,201	1,051	42	40	40
Bulk shipping	125	119	112	(5)	(5)	(3)

During the year, general inflationary levels in the shipping industry were approximately 5% per annum.

Chairman's statement for the financial year

In his statement, the Chairman of G plc commenting on turnover and profit before the inflation adjustment, said the company achieved encouraging results, particularly in the Cruise Division. The company has taken delivery of a new cruise liner, at a cost of £200 million and has two more on order. The Chairman believes that this is an expanding market and considers the company to be in a good position to take advantage as it is one of the world's largest cruise companies. With regard to the Ferries Division, the Chairman expects continued growth, although there is an expectation of a sharp decline in the number of routes across the English Channel due to the opening of the tunnel link between the United Kingdom and France. Economic recovery a continual reduction in costs and increased cargo volumes were all cited by the Chairman as reasons for the improved performance of this division. This contrasted with his view of the depressed Containers and Bulk Shipping market which contributed to these divisions' continuing disappointing results.

Market information

G plc commissioned some marketing research into its passenger shipping activities. The results of this research indicate that, in recent years within the cruise liner industry, there has been a change in customer appeal. Traditionally, the main customer base has comprised wealthy retired people. In the last five years, the Cruise Division has experienced a increase in younger customers. This stemmed from the late 1980s, when the world's largest cruise company shortened the length of some cruises to appeal to American passengers who have only a short vacation period. This resulted in more affordable prices: other cruise companies, including G plc, followed the market leader. This, in turn, resulted in even more affordable prices and the market expanded, with a younger age range of customer being identified.

By contrast, the research shows a 15% increase in passengers crossing the English Channel, but G plc's market share actually reduced by 4%. In its other ferry services, G plc has seen the market holding steady.

The report indicates that the probability of the cruise market continuing to grow for the next five years at the current rate is 0.6, and that a growth rate of half of that which it currently enjoys over the same period has a probability of 0.3. There is no expectation of a decline in this market over the next five years, and the probability of the market remaining static is 0.1.

The report concludes that, in respect of the Ferries Division, the passenger market across the English Channel is expected to reduce by a further 5% over the next year and then remain at this level for the next four years. This is given a probability of 0.7, whilst there is a 0.1 probability that the market will remain at its current level, and a 0.2 probability that it will fall by a further 10% next year and then remain static. The report concludes that the other ferry routes should maintain their current market levels.

Required

(a) With reference to the organisational aims set out above state what G plc's corporate objectives should address. **5 Marks**

(b) It has been argued that an organisation which operates in a turbulent environment should include flexibility as an objective in order that it can be responsive to changing environmental conditions.

Explain how G plc could achieve flexibility in its operations, and discuss potential areas of stakeholder conflict which may occur in satisfying its organisational objectives. **15 Marks**

(c) Discuss the change in turnover and profit of the shipping divisions within G plc in the last financial year, and state, with reasons, whether you consider the chairman's statement reflects the divisional results achieved. **10 Marks**

(d) With reference to Porter's five competitive forces model, assess the nature of the Cruise and Ferry shipping market in which G plc is engaged, and discuss what opportunities and threats exist in respect of its market share. **15 Marks**

(e) Discuss how monitoring through an audit system can be implemented to ensure that G plc's environmental policy is being achieved. **5 Marks**

Total Marks = 50

2 MYRIAD PLC: STAKEHOLDERS AND DIVERSIFICATION (SPECIMEN PAPER)

90 mins

Myriad plc was founded in 1962 and its original business was as a manufacturer of metal castings. It became a listed company in 1977. Myriad plc has always traded profitably, but by 1987 the directors had become very concerned about the volatility of its earnings. Consequently, they commissioned a review from a firm of consultants which specialised in advising on corporate strategy. Following this review, Myriad plc announced that it would 'aggressively pursue a policy of conglomerate diversification, by external acquisitions, to promote growth and reduce risk'.

By 1993 Myriad plc has achieved the following structure. There is a group headquarters based in London and three divisions - Leisure, based in Oxford, Light Engineering in Coventry and Office Equipment in Birmingham. Each division has its own executive management team which has responsibility for earning a criterion rate of return on the funds invested in it by the group.

Group headquarters has the responsibility for raising capital and operates a group treasury function. The group headquarters has a staff of 25 which includes the main board directors. The costs of running the group are charged out to the divisions by means of a management charge.

Divisions

Leisure

This division operates fitness centres inside hotels; it developed from a personal interest in fitness of one of Myriad plc's directors. Profit growth has been 25% per annum in the two years that the division has been in operation and it is forecast to continue at this rate following the recent signing of a five year contract with a national hotel chain. The division's managers believe that the prosperity of their business is dependent on growth in consumer spending which is forecast to grow by 5% per annum for the next five years.

Light engineering

This activity formed the original basis of Myriad plc's business. The division's management has characterised its business as '...mature, stable, offering the prospect of modest but sustainable growth'.

Office equipment

This division was established immediately after the review in 1987. This was done by buying three separate companies which were then consolidated into one.

Its managers regard it as operating in a mature market but the forecast target profit growth rate at 10% per annum is higher than for Light Engineering. This division has a diverse customer base. Many of its customers are government agencies. This means that there is no danger of default and they also pay their bills promptly.

Financial characteristics

Myriad plc had the following earnings in 1993.

	£ million	*Stock market earnings ratios at 31.12.1993**
Leisure	3	18
Light engineering	5	6
Office equipment	2	10
Group	10	8.6

*As the divisions are not separately listed they do not have P/E ratios. However, P/E ratios are given above for sectors to which the divisions are most closely related. The group P/E ratio is the actual ratio at 31 December 1993.

The consortium's proposal

An informal consortium of institutional shareholders, who hold around 15% of Myriad plc's equity, has been pressing the Board for a review of strategy. Its members have indicated that if their wishes are not granted, they will raise the matter at the forthcoming AGM.

Their main concern is that Myriad plc has underperformed during the period 1987 to 1993 and this is based on the fact that Myriad plc's share price increased by 16% whilst share prices in Myriad's sector increased by 23%. Other information relating to the period 1987 to 1993 is given below. All the data are in real terms.

	Myriad's sector	*Myriad plc*
Average dividend yield	5%	3%
Average dividend cover	2	4
Average gearing**	60%	20%
Beta factor range	1.1 to 1.5	0.75 to 0.83

** Gearing: defined as Total borrowings/Total capital in issue plus reserves.

The consortium believes that Myriad plc should take the opportunity offered by current market conditions to rationalise its portfolio. Its members suggest disposing of the Leisure division, using half the proceeds to pay a 'once and for all' dividend to the shareholders and retaining the other half to strengthen Myriad plc's balance sheet.

The consortium has also suggested that after the Leisure division has been sold, Myriad plc could reduce its costs by closing its group headquarters and the treasury operation. After the consequent redundancies, the remaining staff could be relocated to either Coventry or Birmingham where labour costs and accommodation costs are significantly cheaper than in London.

Required

(a) Assess the implications of the strategic decision of 1987 on Myriad plc's shareholders and management. **10 Marks**

(b) Assess the extent to which the diversification has been successful. **4 Marks**

(c) Discuss the extent to which the Board of Myriad plc should attempt to identify the wishes of the different interests affected by the forthcoming decision about Leisure. Explain how the Board could implement a strategy for communication with the different interests. **15 Marks**

(d) Describe the conflicts of interest which exist for Myriad plc in the 1993 situation. **6 Marks**

(e) Advise the Board on its response to the consortium. You should include in your advice any recommendations which you feel are appropriate and explain why you make them. **15 Marks**

Total Marks = 50

3 HESTER BATEMAN: COMPETITIVE, MARKETING AND PRODUCTION STRATEGIES *90 mins*

Hester Bateman plc (HB plc) is a manufacturing cutler: that is, the company makes knives, forks and spoons. HB is based in Sheffield in the United Kingdom which has been the centre of the UK cutlery industry for at least one hundred years. When the industry was first established, it was very fragmented and there were many small entrepreneurial businesses making cutlery. often, these businesses were organised around a family and they usually employed between six and ten people. Hester Bateman was one such entrepreneur. The industry began to consolidate, in the late nineteenth century and early twentieth century, as a series of mergers were effected.

HB plc was constituted in its present form in the 1920s when it obtained its market listing on the Stock Exchange. It now consists of a large factory which employs 500 people and a Head Office employing 200 people. These are both in Sheffield.

In 1981 HB plc made a rights issue to finance a modernisation programme in its factory. At that time the Board reviewed the company's objectives. A statement was issued by the Board which said:

> HB plc is a UK manufacturing cutler based in Sheffield, the home of the cutlery industry. Our success is due to harnessing local skills in production and design and using these to deliver the finest quality product to our customers across the world. They know that the finest cutlery in the world is stamped "Made in Sheffield". We intend to continue with our fine traditions.

HB plc has always made all its cutlery in Sheffield and attaches great importance to the fact that it can, therefore, be marked 'Made in Sheffield'.

HB plc usually spends approximately £150,000 a year on research and development. 5% of this spending is on new designs for the export market and the remainder is evenly split on designs for the home market and on improvements in production systems.

BQ plc

There is another UK manufacturing cutler of a similar size to HB plc, BQ plc, which is based in Birmingham.

Since 1985 BQ plc has followed a different production policy to HB plc. Approximately half of its cutlery is made in Korea and imported to the UK and marketed under BQ plc's brand names.

Markets

From the date of its formation until the early 1980's HB plc did very good business with countries across the world.

Since 1981 HB plc has experienced increasing competition from countries of the Pacific Rim - Korea, Taiwan, Hong Kong and Singapore. This competition has been conducted on the basis of cost. This has been possible because the production technology involved in making cutlery is a mature one. It is also comparatively cheap and readily available. Further, for many users cutlery has become a generic product.

> Generics are unbranded, plainly packaged, less-expensive versions of products, purchased in supermarkets, such as spaghetti, paper towels and canned peaches.(Kotler, *Marketing Management,* Prentice-Hall)

HB plc has experienced a growing loss of market share in the UK to imports from the Pacific Rim. HB plc's export markets have largely disappeared. The only export business which it does is an annual sale of about £200,000 of very high quality cutlery to a department store in New York. HB plc makes a gross margin of 45% on this business.

Estimated market data at December 1993:

	UK market share	
	by quantity %	*by value* %
HB plc	35	45
BQ plc*	30	35
Imports	35	20

* These percentages include all cutlery sold by BQ plc whether made in the UK or in Korea.

Financial performance

The increasingly competitive environment has had a marked effect on HB plc's profitability and stock market performance. After the publication of its latest annual results the following comment was made in an influential UK financial newspaper:

> HB plc's latest results which show a profit after tax of £2.25 million look deceptively good. However, these are flattered by the fact that HB plc has not made any major investments since the 1980s.
>
> Its ROCE is about 4% and this could be beaten by any fixed return risk-free deposit investment. There seems to be little prospect of growth in any direction. These shares are really only a HOLD for the sentimental; otherwise SELL.

Required

(a) Explain how Porter's classification of generic strategies could be used by HB plc to analyse its current competitive position. **8 Marks**

(b) Discuss the extent to which you believe that the statement of objectives made in 1981 is still applicable in 1994. **7 Marks**

(c) Recommend possible marketing strategies for HB plc. Discuss the advantages and disadvantages of your recommendations. **11 Marks**

(d) Recommend possible production strategies for HB plc. Discuss the advantages and disadvantages of your recommendations. **11 Marks**

(e) Explain how the interests of the stakeholders of HB plc will be affected by your responses to parts (b), (c) and (d) above. **13 Marks**

Total Marks = 50

4 SJM PLC: EVALUATION, JOINT VENTURE (11/95) *90 mins*

Organisational background

SJM is a long-established retail organisation operating 227 supermarkets nationally. It is a listed company which has expanded over its 60-year history. The company has attained distinctive competitive advantage by stocking and selling only high-quality products. SJM plc has enjoyed profitable trading and now ranks as one of the leading retailers in the country. It has not been affected by restructuring of the retailing industry and its Board is intend on maintaining the company's independence.

The Board of the company has set a clear aim of achieving profitability with efficient consumption of resources, whilst maintaining the sale of high-quality goods and delivering a courteous and efficient service to customers. This overall aim has been incorporated within the mission statement and forms a central part of the company's promotional advertising.

Financial characteristics of the company

The following information is supplied in respect of SJM plc for the last financial year.

	£million
Turnover,	2,400
Earnings attributable to ordinary shareholders	220

There were 1,200 million ordinary shares in issue at the end of the last financial year and the company's share price was £4.03.

SJM plc has established that its cost of capital is 12% per annum. Over the last year, the company's share price has varied between £3.30 and £4.05. SJM plc paid a dividend of £0.12 (12 pence) per share in the last financial year and has achieved steady dividend growth of 8.4% per annum over the last five years.

'Out-of-town' stores

The company has recognised that its customers are increasingly using personal transport and value the convenience of 'out-of-town' locations. 'Out-of-town' means that a store is located on a city's fringes rather than in the centre. The object of building stores in such a location is to provide customers with easier access to shopping facilities as this is often difficult within the busy city environment. Typical of the out-of-town location is a large car parking facility and good public transport links.

SJM plc established a plan five years ago to build a number of out-of-town superstores to an original design near four major cities. The first of these superstores has now been in operation for one year. The other superstores are in various stages of completion.

SJM has followed its competitors in developing out-of-town sites and is considering a partnership initiative with another retailer whose merchandise would not be a competitive threat. This would involve joint development of superstores on out-of-town sites. The only commitment to this initiative by SJM plc, so far, is a feasibility study of a single joint project with the other retailer. This will be completed before entering any contractual obligations.

The superstore strategy

SJM aims to provide a satisfactory return to its shareholders. The superstore which is already operational has achieved a high level of profitability in its first year of operation. The company has also experienced a simultaneous reduction in return obtained from other stores which it operates within the vicinity of the superstore. SJM plc is aware of growing governmental concern at the impact out-of-town developments are having on city centre retailing. These two factors have caused the company planners to pause before approving any other out-of-town developments. In addition, public transport provision has been established to service the operational superstore, but the transport providers are now objecting that there is insufficient demand to maintain frequent services as most customers travel to and from the site by car.

Superstore developments

The superstore developments are all built to a standard specification which comprises 40,000 square metres. The life of the project is fifteen years. Typically, the development takes place over a three-year period from planning stage to final commissioning. Each superstore is assumed, for investment appraisal purposes, to have a life of 12 years following completion. The cost of the first superstore development was £25 million with approximately 20% being incurred in the first year. The remaining costs are split evenly over the second and third years. Included within these costs was £500,000 for architects' fees which have reduced by half in subsequent developments. The architects' fees can be assumed to fall due for payment in direct proportion to the building costs.

The superstore developments are targeted to achieve a net cash inflow of £250 per square metre per annum from the commencement of operations. Experience has shown that the first superstore has achieved this target during the first year of operation. A total reduction in net cash inflow over the same period has occurred in other SJM plc stores which trade within the surrounding areas. This has been calculated as having the effect of reducing the superstore net cash inflow by £40 per square metre per annum.

Each superstore is assumed to have a net residual value of zero. All cashflows can be assumed to occur at the end of the year to which they relate. The cashflows and discount rate are in real terms. Taxation should be ignored.

Required

(a) Prepare and comment on the financial appraisal which justified the investment in the first superstore. Assume that twelve equal annual net cash inflows commence in the first year following completion of the superstore, which takes three years to construct. **8 Marks**

(b) Identify the market opportunities and threats which SJM plc will confront if it develops more out-of-town superstores. **12 Marks**

(c) Describe and comment on the impact of the out-of-town developments by SJM plc on each of five groups of stakeholders. **10 Marks**

(d) Discuss whether SJM plc should pursue other out-of-town developments completely on its own or jointly with the other retailer. Pay particular attention to potential planning and operational difficulties which may arise from these initiatives. **10 Marks**

(e) Describe the contribution a management accountant may make to the planning processes of SJM plc in the areas of project feasibility, evaluation, monitoring and post audit. **10 Marks**

Total Marks = 50

5 LINDLEYS PLC: STAKEHOLDERS AND PERFORMANCE (5/95) *90 mins*

Background

Lindleys plc (the Bank) is a United Kingdom clearing bank. It has 2,000 retail branches. It categorises its business as retail and corporate. Each category currently accounts for half of the Bank's turnover.

The Bank defines retail business as 'banking for customers in their own right and small businesses where lending would not exceed £1,000,000 in any one year'.

Corporate business is defined as ' ... where lending would exceed £1,000,000 in any one year'. Corporate lending includes international lending.

Traditionally, corporate lending has been the most profitable business, yielding 70% of profit before taxation. Corporate lending has been carried out by six regional offices and a department at head office in London. The London office is also responsible for international lending. There are 200 staff employed in corporate lending.

Retail banking has operated in the following way.

The number of retail and small business customers at each branch has ranged from 1,000 to 10,000, although 5,000 is typical. The bank has employed the following Mission statement for its retail banking.

'Our Mission is to deliver a high-quality service to customers based on our managers' personal knowledge of customers' affairs.'

The bank recognised that retail banking was relatively unprofitable. It was willing to operate a policy of cross-subsidisation between corporate and retail as it hoped that some retail customers would become corporate ones. It saw its branch managers as assisting in this process because of their financing expertise and deep knowledge of their customers.

The bank has operated each branch as a cost centre. Managers have been provided with a three-monthly expenditure report which compared committed expenditure to budgeted expenditure. The bank had not operated an accrual accounting system as regards branch expenditure for these three-monthly reports. However, year-end adjustments reconciled committed, actual and budgeted expenditures. These accounting operations were carried out by management accounting staff based at head office.

The managers' remit was to operate within their expenditure budgets. In addition to this, they were set targets, for example, number of new accounts opened, amount of holiday insurance sold, level of bad debts.

The managers were not consulted about the size of their budgets or their targets. These were imposed by head office.

Proposals for change

The bank is reappraising its corporate posture. Its corporate lending has declined in profitability because of problems with third-world debt and movements in foreign exchange rates. The bank has also become concerned about the attitudes which it believes have become dominant in retail banking. Most of its managers have found their targets relatively easy to achieve. They have been criticised for a lack of entrepreneurial awareness and for being too inward-looking. The managers have retorted that 'as soon as a customer gets to be interesting we lose them to corporate, so why bother?' Because of these factors, the bank has decided upon the following changes.

(a) Retail banking must, in future, earn 50% of the bank's profit before taxation.

(b) There will be a programme of branch rationalisation in which half the branches will close.

(c) New 'superbranches' will be established. These will be at the centre of a network of six to eight existing branches. The superbranch will contain the manager, who will make all the major decisions for the network of branches. He will be assisted in this by two assistant managers who will probably be drawn from the existing managers in the network.

(d) Each superbranch will be designated as an investment centre and must earn a return of 15%. No target has been set for residual income, although the bank intends to set such targets after it has gained some experience of the superbranches' operations. (Residual income should be taken as pre-tax profits less an imputed interest charge for net assets.)

Each superbranch has been given an expenditure budget which equates to that of the cumulative total spent by its network branches in the previous year. No extra funds have been allocated for the establishment of the superbranches. The manager of the superbranch has discretion as to where the superbranch will be located. This could be inside an existing branch or in new premises.

(a) The manager of the superbranch will be responsible for the design and operation of all of the network's information systems. These will be capable of being interrogated by head office, which will continue to draw up the statutory accounts.

(b) The manager of the superbranch has discretion as to the number of employees working in the network. If there are to be any redundancies, head office will negotiate nationally to determine the terms for redundant staff. The superbranch will be charged with the costs, if any, of redundancies in its network.

The managing director of the bank has described the new philosophy for retail banking thus:

'We are operating in a very competitive environment and in order to survive, we must change. We must never forget that we are a profit-seeking organisation. Retail banking has been subsidised in the past and had become inefficient. Our proposals will enable us to deliver an efficient, low-cost service. However, I am afraid the days of the bank manager being a personal friend and adviser are over.'

Required

(a) Explain the implications of the new philosophy for retail banking upon staff, customers and shareholders of the bank. You should contrast the new philosophy with the old mission statement. **12 Marks**

(b) Discuss the advantages and disadvantages of the proposal to make superbranches investment centres. **8 Marks**

(c) (i) Describe the reports you believe will be necessary for the manager of a superbranch to manage successfully. Your answer should include the reasons for your suggestions. **12 Marks**

(ii) Suggest, and fully justify, three qualitative performance indicators you consider would be of assistance to a superbranch manager. **12 Marks**

(d) State three stakeholders who should have been involved in the determination of proposals by the bank to reorganise retail banking. Explain the reasons for each of your recommendations. **6 Marks**

Total Marks = 50

6 PK LTD: PERFORMANCE AND ACQUISITION (5/97) *108 mins*

Introduction

PK Ltd is jointly owned by two United Kingdom-based conglomerates which manufacture mainly electrical products. In its own right, PK Ltd is regarded as a world leader in the installation and maintenance of railway transport signalling systems. The company is based in Europe, where most of its manufacturing units are located, but it has established other plants and marketing facilities in the USA, Latin America, Asia and Australia.

Activities of the company

The company specialises in the supply of railway signalling and control systems and employs over 15,000 staff worldwide. In addition to these systems, PK Ltd also supplies advanced electronic equipment for safety signalling applications which can be added to systems which have already been installed. Passenger information systems are also manufactured and supplied by the company, which uses advanced technology to provide full displays on railway platforms and stations.

Over the last two decades, PK Ltd has experienced increasing competition within its European and North American markets.

Recent international activities

In addition to carrying out major signalling work for the Channel Tunnel rail link between the United Kingdom and mainland Europe, PK Ltd has recently equipped a high-speed rail line in Asia with electronic equipment. Within Europe, the company succeeded in winning the tender to build, equip, operate and maintain a rail link between a major Scandinavian city and its airport.

Research and development

The Chief Executive of PK Ltd has stated that the market-oriented approach of the company requires that it should maintain and develop its position as leader in 'state of the art' technology. This is facilitated by a large established Research and Development unit which aims to improve product reliability and develop advanced computer software solutions in its business activities, all at lower cost, without compromising quality.

The reduction of life cycle costs and environmental damage, whilst at the same time pursuing technical developments, have been stated by the Chief Executive as key objectives of the company.

Financial position of PK Ltd

The latest Report and Accounting Statements declared that the financial year just ended produced results which were 'disappointing'. The Chief Executive indicated that the company had experienced difficult trading conditions and encountered strengthening international competition. Whilst turnover increased, operating profit after tax and overall orders were lower than the previous year. At the year end, the number of orders in the order book was 8% below the level achieved at the previous year end.

Abridged comparative accounting information for the last and previous financial year are as follows.

	Last year	*Previous year*
	£'000	£'000
Value of orders	3,750	4,600
Turnover	4,400	3,900
Operating profit after taxation	310	320
Shareholders' equity	935	850

PK Ltd had achieved on average a 20% growth in turnover and a 10% increase in operating profit after taxation over the preceding five-year period until the last financial year. The Chairman of one of the parent holding companies has expressed his concern regarding PK Ltd's results in the last financial year. In response, the Chief Executive of PK Ltd has outlined his company's strategy of international acquisition and joint ventures as a means of returning to sustained growth and profitability.

Proposed acquisition

A number of acquisitions and joint venture arrangements have been considered by the Board of PK Ltd, aimed at increasing the company's profile outside Europe. In particular, the acquisition of a small South African electronics component manufacturer (RA Ltd) is being actively pursued. If acquired, RA Ltd will provide the basis for PK Ltd to increase its range of products in what is considered to be an expanding market with high growth potential.

This acquisition would enable advantage to be taken of the opportunities for development in South Africa. In addition, RA Ltd would provide a base for further market penetration of other African countries. RA Ltd is unquoted and owned by a diverse group of shareholders, with family interests in the company controlling 40% of the voting shares.

PK Ltd considers that RA Ltd is under-capitalised. It is currently achieving a 2% return on turnover after interest and tax despite working at full capacity. RA Ltd employs 2,000 people, who possess mixed abilities and skills. Mostly, however, the employees are unskilled or at best very poorly trained. As many as 25% of RA Ltd's products are returned by customers because of faults and this proportion has steadily increased over recent years.

The directors of PK Ltd are mindful that the South African currency (the Rand) is continuing to depreciate in value compared with the English currency (pound Sterling). The Rand has continually fallen in value compared with the pound over a long period and currently stands at an exchange rate of 7.6 Rand to £1 whereas a year ago the exchange rate was 6 Rand to £1.

Required

(a) Explain the difficulties with which the parent companies may be confronted in assessing PK Ltd's performance. **12 Marks**

(b) Recommend and justify what financial and non-financial measures may be applied to assess the performance of PK Ltd. **10 Marks**

(c) Discuss the strategic objectives and market opportunities available to PK Ltd which will be created by its acquisition of RA Ltd. **15 Marks**

(d) Discuss the managerial, cultural and financial considerations PK Ltd will need to examine before undertaking the acquisition of RA Ltd. **15 Marks**

(e) Explain the difficulties PK Ltd may encounter in objectively assessing the performance of RA Ltd post-acquisition. **8 Marks**

Total Marks = 60

7 HAULAGE: COMPETITION, POSITION AND MARKETING (11/96) *90 mins*

Background

M is the Managing Director of H Ltd, a small haulage contracting company which he founded twelve years ago. Originally, M was a heavy goods vehicle driver himself, working for other contractors, but he was intent on establishing his own haulage business. Having obtained a loan, M acquired a heavy goods vehicle and began to work from home. Over time the business expanded and now H Ltd operates a fleet of 24 heavy goods vehicles (tractor units as they are called) and 48 trailers which are hooked on to the tractor units. A quarter of the current fleet of tractor units was acquired in the last financial year, replacing older units which were becoming too expensive to maintain. H Ltd now employs 20 full-time and a varying number of part-time drivers. The part-time staff work as and when required.

M acquired a small plot of land six years ago and built a house on it which he and his family occupy. In addition, he built a garage with facilities for minor servicing and repairs on the same site. Living on site has enabled M to offer a 24-hour service to clients. Consequently, movement of tractor units and trailers in and out of the site occurs at all times of day and night. There have been objections raised by local residents and administrative officials to the disturbance, and the local newspaper has at various times reflected this criticism.

Business development

In addition to haulage, H Ltd obtained a licence to undertake fork-lift truck training. This has proved to be a successful diversification as there is a regular stream of customers. This training takes place mostly in H Ltd's own garage facilities.

It became clear to M that the land on which the garage facility is built was inadequate for the needs of his growing business. In addition to the inadequacy of the maintenance provision for a growing fleet, it became impossible to house all the tractor units and trailers operated by the business. This problem was compounded when, as frequently occurs, the client's own trailers were attached to the tractor units and parked overnight on H Ltd's land.

Acquisition of land

One year ago, M entered negotiations to lease some land which would more than satisfactorily accommodate all the tractor units and trailers. The land is situated on an industrial estate 5 km from the existing facility. In addition, there is room to build a repair and maintenance facility which would be adequate for the needs of the fleet. M believes that surplus land on the site can be used for storage of trailers for local companies. Following agreement of a lease arrangement, which was concluded just before the completion of the last financial year, H Ltd occupied the land on which there were no buildings erected or utilities supplied. Since taking possession of the land, a large security fence has been erected and a small portable cabin placed on site. Water, sewerage and electricity utility services have been supplied and negotiations are taking place for the installation of a large diesel tank adequate to service other vehicles besides those of H Ltd.

Accounting provision within H Ltd

M recruited J, a part-time book-keeper, four years ago. Prior to J's arrival H Ltd applied a policy of paying all invoices immediately on receiving them. As debtors were frequently taking over and above the credit period allowed, H Ltd suffered a cashflow shortage which resulted in a large bank overdraft.

J introduced some basic financial accounting procedures into the company. In addition to exercising some control on H Ltd's expenditure, J has reduced the debtors' collection period to about half its former level. Creditors are now paid when the invoices fall due rather than immediately upon their receipt. Such control had been lacking prior to her arrival at the company. The bank manager has praised J for her efforts and informed M that in his opinion the control measures now introduced have saved the business from liquidation. As a consequence of the improvement in financial control, the bank has been willing to fund additional loans for the development of the new land. In making its decision, the bank required H Ltd to supply its statutory financial statements and a cashflow forecast for the development.

J has persuaded M of the need to provide information which will be useful for strategic management purposes. Her own background and experience have been focused on the provision of a bookkeeping service, but she is enthusiastic about the challenge of obtaining and presenting strategic management accounting information.

Customer base

The company faces strong competition for haulage contract work. Typically, haulage contractors operate on a low-margin basis and smaller companies often sub-contract from large-scale hauliers.

H Ltd carries haulage for a variety of customers as well as undertaking some sub-contracting. Much of the haulage work the company carries out is seasonal. Approximately 70% of its turnover is derived from C Ltd, a local company which manufactures soft furnishings such as cushions and pillows.

Following the recent appointment of a new transport manager, C Ltd has begun to employ other hauliers besides H Ltd. Over the last two months, the haulage work H Ltd has received from C Ltd has reduced by about a third.

Required

(a) Assess the nature of competitive forces to which H Ltd is subject. **12 Marks**

(b) Present a position appraisal for H Ltd, separating the internal and external factors to which the company is exposed. **10 Marks**

(c) (i) Explain the use which H Ltd could make of internal and external sources of information in establishing its marketing strategy. **6 Marks**

(ii) Advise M on the strategic management accounting information of a financial and non-financial nature should be provided to assist future decision making and cost control. **10 Marks**

(d) Recommend and justify a marketing strategy for H Ltd which emerges from an analysis of its marketing mix. **12 Marks**

Total Marks = 50

8 T PLC: PEST FORCES, INVESTMENT AND THE PLANNING GAP (11/97)

108 mins

Introduction

T plc is a well-established company providing telecommunications services both nationally and internationally. Its business has been concerned with telephone calls, the provision of telephone lines and equipment, and private telecommunication networks. T plc has supplemented these services recently by offering mobile phones, which is an expanding market world-wide.

The company maintains a diverse customer base, including residential users, multi-national companies, government agencies and public sector organisations. The company handles approximately 100 million calls each working day, and employs nearly 140,000 personnel.

Strategic development

The Chairman of T plc stated within the latest Annual Report that there are three main areas in which the company aims to develop in order to remain in a world leader in the telecommunications market. He believes that the three main growth areas reflect the evolving nature of the telecommunications market, and will provide scope for development.

The areas in which development is planned are:

(1) Expansion of the telecommunications business in the national and overseas markets, both by the company acting on its own and through partnership arrangements with other suppliers.

(2) Diversification into television and multi-media services, providing the hardware to permit telephone shopping from home and broadcasting services.

(3) Extension of the joint ventures and strategic alliances which have already been established with companies in North America, Europe, India and the Far East.

The Chairman explained that the company is intent on becoming a world leader in communications. This will be achieved through maintaining its focus on long-term development by improving its services to customers, developing high-quality up-to-date products and being innovative, flexible and market-driven. His aim is to deliver a world-class service at competitive cost.

Financial information

Comparative statistics showing extracts from the company's financial performance in its national telecommunications market over the last two years are as follows:

	Last year	*Previous year*
	£ million	£ million
Turnover	16,613	15,977
Profit before interest and tax	3,323	2,876
Capital employed	22,150	21,300

The company estimates its cost of capital to be approximately 11%.

The Chairman expressed satisfaction with the increase in turnover and stated that cost efficiencies were now being generated following completion of a staff reduction programme. This would assist the company in achieving a target return on capital employed (ROCE) in this market of 20% over the next three years.

Business opportunities

The Chief Executive of T plc has stated that the major opportunities for the company lie in the following areas:

- encouraging greater use of the telephone;
- provision of advanced services, and research and development into new technology, including the Internet and systems integration;
- the increasing freedom from government control of world-wide telecommunication services.

An extensive television and poster advertising campaign has been used by the company. This was in order to penetrate further the residential market by encouraging greater use of the telephone with varying charging incentives being offered to residential customers.

To further the objective of increasing long-term shareholder value, the company is actively considering investment of £200 million in each of the next three years in new technology and quality improvements in its national market. Because of its specialist technical nature, the investment is not expected to have any residual value at the end of the three-year period.

Following the investment, the directors of T plc believe that its rate of profit before interest and tax to turnover in its national telecommunications market will remain constant. This rate will be at the same level as last year for each of the three years of the investment.

Markets and competition

The company is currently experiencing an erosion of its market share and faces increasingly strong competition in the mobile phone market. While T plc is the leader in its national market, with an 85% share of the telecommunications business, it has experienced a reduced demand for the supply of residential lines in the last five years as competition has increased.

The market for the supply of equipment in the national telecommunications market is perceived to be static. The investment of £200 million in each of the next three years is estimated to increase T plc's share of this market to a level of 95%. The full improvement of 10% is expected to be received by T plc next year and its market share will then remain at this level for the full three-year period. It is anticipated that unless further investment is made after the three-year period, T plc's market share will revert to its current level as a consequence of the expected competitive response.

Industry regulation

The government has established an industry regulatory organisation to promote competition and deter anti-competitive behaviour.

As a result of the activities of the regulator and aggressive pricing strategies, it is anticipated that charges to customers will remain constant for the full three-year period of the new investment.

All cash flows can be assumed to occur at the end of the year to which they relate. The cash flows and discount rate are in real terms.

Required

(a) Explain the nature of the political, economic, social, and technical forces which influence T plc in developing its business and increasing its market share. **10 Marks**

(b) (i) Apply Ansoff's Product/Market Growth Vector matrix to assess the extent of the potential market development opportunities available to T plc. **15 Marks**

(ii) Explain how this matrix may be incorporated into the strategic planning process to determine the extent of the planning gap. **5 Marks**

(c) Evaluate and comment on T plc's proposed investment in new technology and quality improvements in its national telecommunications market.

Assume that variable costs are 80% of the incremental revenue, and that fixed costs will not increase. Ignore working capital. **15 Marks**

(d) (i) Assess to what extent the investment in new technology and quality improvements in T plc's national telecommunications market contributes towards the closure of the company's planning gap in respect of its target ROCE.

Note: You may assume that the entire capital investment is written off at the end of the three-year period. **5 Marks**

(ii) Recommend a strategy which T plc could employ to close the planning gap and achieve the strategic development aims identified by the Chairman. **10 Marks**

Ignore taxation. **Total Marks = 60**

9 B PLC: APPRAISAL, ANALYSIS AND STRATEGIC AIMS (5/98) *108 mins*

Background

Over 20 years ago, B plc was established to manufacture and sell naturally-based cosmetics and skin products. The first shop was opened in the Untied Kingdom (UK) in 1976. Since then, B plc has successfully expanded and now trades in over 40 countries world-wide through more than 1,000 retail outlets, 75% of which are located outside the UK. The ecologically-friendly aims of B plc have not changed since it was first established. The company campaigns against animal testing in the cosmetics industry and for human rights all over the world. It seeks to establish trade relations with overseas countries, and to integrate itself into the local communities in which it trades so that it can be more aware of the specific needs of its customers. B plc prides itself on its achievements in educating staff and customers through providing information on its products and methods of manufacture.

Corporate activities

B plc is intent on preserving the environment by promoting the efficient use of energy, keeping waste to a minimum and using only renewable resources whenever possible. These basic principles have been challenged by some observers who suggest that, in the aggressive corporate climate which currently prevails, B plc will need to abandon its environmentally-friendly aims in order to compete. The company's Chairman is determined that this shall not be the case and is proud of the fact that B plc was one of the first companies within the UK to publish environmental audit reports. Activities which B plc carries out include sourcing high-quality raw materials directly from producers throughout the world and extensive product research and development, both in the UK and Latin America. The results of successful research are converted into innovative products which are manufactured by B plc in its modern production facilities. The products are then transferred to its retail outlets. In addition, B plc is active in health education promotion throughout the world and, some years ago, initiated a newspaper designed to help the homeless, which sells throughout major cities in the UK.

Market share and financial review

The ecologically innovative approach adopted by the founders of B plc resulted in it initially attaining 100% share of what was a niche market in the UK when the company first started. Since then, competition has developed to the extent that B plc now has 90% of the naturally-based cosmetics and hair-care market. In terms of profitability, B plc achieved in the last financial year an operating profit of £26 million (previous year £29 million) on a turnover of £175 million (previous year £154 million). The Chairman of B plc attributed the reduction in profit to difficult trading conditions, particularly in the UK, and an increase in overheads due to the enlargement of its head office facilities. It is clear to B plc's directors that the increasing level of competition is now threatening its niche market domination.

Strategic development

The directors of B plc have considered a number of strategic options and have identified two possible courses of action. They could either invest more in quality improvement and further differentiate the company's products from its competitors, or increase the level of promotion and attract a higher market share. Capital constraints on the company prevent it from doing both in the next year.

Quality improvement

B plc's previous experience of improving quality has resulted in optimism about its potential success. The company estimates that it has obtained good results 70% of the time by following the strategy of quality improvement. Unsatisfactory results have been experienced from the remaining 30% of the time in which the strategy has been applied. The cost of carrying through the improvements in the next financial year would be £50 million. Over a four-year period it is estimated that in present value terms, a net cash inflow of £100 million would be made if the market response was strong, and £60 million if it was weak. (Both of these values are before deduction of the capital cost of the improvements.) To assess the likelihood of a strong or weak market response, the directors have engaged a firm of consultants who have in the past been proved right on 80% of occasions when they predicted a strong market response. The consultants have also been proved right on 90% of occasions when they have predicted a weak market response.

The management accountant for B plc has carried out some decision analysis on this information and has concluded that the most likely outcome is a net cash inflow of

£37.996 million. The management accountant's working to arrive at this value are shown in the table below.

Increased promotion

The directors believe that by investing £10 million in promotional activities in the next financial year, the net cash inflow, before deducting the cost of the initial investment, over a four-year period in present value terms would be £40 million.

Competitive reaction to proposed strategies

B plc's directors believe that the current competitors are likely to react to either of these strategies. The most likely reaction is to increase their own promotion activities; it is also likely that efforts will be made by competitors to identify and exploit areas where B plc is not able to maintain its high standards of ecological protection. It is very clear that improved information on its activities in order to counter this threat is an essential requirement for the directors to maintain customer confidence.

From the start, B plc has grown in size organically. The directors are keen to ensure that the company continues to develop and at the same time maintain its principles of ecological protection. They further recognise that organic growth is not the only route they could take and are seeking other potential forms of strategic development.

	Higher return £100 million	*Lower return* £60 million
Strong response	$0.8 \times 0.7 = 0.56$	$0.1 \times 0.3 = 0.03$
Weak response	$0.2 \times 0.7 = 0.14$	$0.9 \times 0.3 = 0.27$

- Probability of a high return given a strong response is $\frac{0.56}{0.59} = 0.95$
- Probability of a low return given a strong response is $\frac{0.03}{0.59} = 0.05$
- Probability of a high return given a weak response is $\frac{0.14}{0.41} = 0.34$
- Probability of a low return given a weak response is $\frac{0.27}{0.41} = 0.66$

The expected value of the proposal is:

Response	*Return*	*Probability*	*Return* £m	*Expected value* £m
Strong	Higher	0.95	100	95.0
	Lower	0.05	60	3.0
				98.0
Weak	Higher	0.34	100	34.0
	Lower	0.66	60	39.6
				73.6

However, there is a 59% probability of a strong response and a 41% probability of a weak response. The expected outcome of the investment is:

Strong	59% of £98.0 million	57.820
Weak	41% of £73.6 million	30.176
		87.996
Less: cost of quality improvement		50.000
Expected outcome		37.996

Required

(a) Present a corporate appraisal for B plc. **12 Marks**

(b) Comment on the two options evaluated. Your answer should:

- include an assessment of the best and worst outcomes from the quality improvement option;
- express any reservations you might have about the results; and
- take into consideration the likely potential reaction of competitors if B plc implements either strategy. **21 Marks**

(c) Recommend what information the management accountant should provide to the directors of B plc to assist them in assessing the company's progress towards the achievement of its strategic environmental aims. **15 Marks**

(d) By reference to potential future market opportunities and threats, recommend a strategy which B plc may adopt in order to pursue its strategic environmental aims. **12 Marks**

Total Marks = 60

10 WG PLC: PRODUCTS, OBJECTIVES, PROFITABILITY AND STRATEGY (11/98) *108 mins*

Introduction

WG plc was formed four years ago following the merger of two large pharmaceutical companies. Prior to the merger the two companies had been competitors: they believed that by combining forces the shareholders of each company would benefit from increased profits arising from the rationalisation of manufacturing facilities, distribution networks, and concentration of resources towards more focused research and development.

With operating outlets in Europe, Asia, the United States of America and Africa, WG plc regards itself as a global company. It employs approximately 50,000 people worldwide and has developed a wide portfolio of products. Its profits before tax last year increased by 20% and represented approximately 35% of turnover. The company declared that its earnings and dividends per share in the same period increased by 15% over the previous financial year.

All manufacturers of pharmaceutical products claim that their pricing policies need to be set at a level to achieve high profitability in order to attract funds from investors. They argue that this is necessary to meet their high research and development commitments. In recent years, WG plc and other pharmaceutical manufacturers have encountered public and governmental challenges to their high levels of profitability.

WG plc encounters strong competition from other world-class pharmaceutical manufacturers but these are few in number. High research and development costs present a major obstacle to potential competitors tempted to enter the industry.

Mission and objectives

The directors of WG plc have defined their overall corporate mission as being to 'combat disease by developing innovative medicines and services and providing them to healthcare organisations for the treatment of patients worldwide'.

The directors have confirmed their main objective is to sustain profitability while achieving the company's overall mission. They have also explained that WG plc aims to work towards eliminating those diseases for which the company is engaged in providing treatments. Achievement of the profitability objective is continually threatened by patents coming to the end of their lives. Patents give the sole right to make, use and sell a new product for a limited period.

Product development

A large proportion of the company's turnover in recent years has been derived from one particular drug. The patent for this drug expires next year and it is expected that its sales at that time will represent no more than 10% of total turnover. Four years ago, the sales of this drug produced almost half the company's entire turnover.

A new product, *Coffstop*, has now completed its rigorous development phases and is being marketed to pharmaceutical stores throughout the world by WG plc. It is in competition with a similar drug, *Peffstill*, produced and marketed by a direct competitor of WG plc. Medical research and opinion has concluded that *Coffstop* is generally more effective than *Peffstill* in treating the condition for which they are intended. Both drugs are available over the counter from pharmacies. The directors of WG plc are optimistic that *Coffstop* will become very popular because of its improved effectiveness over other market products.

The retail market price of *Coffstop* is £1.50 per bottle, compared with £10 per bottle of *Peffstill*. However, the recommended dosage of *Coffstop* is 6 times more than that for *Peffstill*. The bought-in costs per bottle to the retail pharmacist are £0.50 and £7.40 for *Coffstop* and *Peffstill* respectively. Initial indications to the management of WG plc are that retail pharmacists tend to prefer to stock *Peffstill* on the basis that it achieves 2.6 times the level of gross contribution per bottle compared with *Coffstop*.

It is estimated that the cost to the retailer of holding *Coffstop* is £0.40 per bottle and £0.80 for *Peffstill*. The availability of shelf space is a limiting factor for most retailers. The shelf area occupied by each bottle of *Coffstop* is 18 square centimetres and 60 square centimetres for each bottle of *Peffstill*. Early indications show that the average weekly sales volume for retail outlets stocking both products are 120 bottles of *Coffstop* and 20 bottles of *Peffstill*.

Market development

WG plc has experienced slow growth in its mature markets of Western Europe, North America and Japan. These markets contribute 80% of overall turnover but their governments have reduced expenditure on pharmaceutical products in recent years. The company has encountered a rapid sales increase in its expanding markets of Eastern Europe, South America, the Asia Pacific region, India, Africa and the Middle East. The directors of the company hold the view that increasing population growth in these markets is likely to provide substantial opportunities for the company over the next two decades.

Research and development

Almost 15% of WG plc's turnover last year was spent on research and development. WG plc has the largest research and development organisation of all pharmaceutical companies worldwide.

Much research is sponsored by national governments and world health organisations. A major piece of research which has recently been undertaken relates to new treatments for malaria as the disease is now demonstrating some resistance to existing treatments. WG plc has established a 'donation programme' for the new drug in virulent areas for the disease. This means that the company is donating batches of the drug to the health organisations in these areas. The cost of this programme is offset by the sales of the new drug in other areas of the world by making it available to people proposing to travel to the regions where malaria is widespread.

Required

(a) Assess the nature and importance of the market threat which WG plc would face if it failed to provide sufficient resources for product development. **12 Marks**

(b) WG plc's main objective is to sustain profitability through developing innovative medicines and services for treating patients worldwide. The company also aims to eliminate disease.

Discuss the nature of the five competitive forces (identified by Porter) which are exerted on WG plc in satisfying both these objectives at the same time. **16 Marks**

(c) (i) Demonstrate whether *Coffstop* can provide a higher contribution to the retailer than *Peffstill* by using:

(1) Cost Volume Profit analysis, taking account of the gross contribution per limiting factor; **4 Marks**

(2) Direct Product Profitability analysis after charging holding costs. **6 Marks**

(ii) Explain how WG plc can market *Coffstop* to improve its competitive position. **10 Marks**

(d) Discuss the practical issues which the directors of WG plc would need to consider if the company entered a strategic alliance with a competitor for the joint development of future pharmaceutical products. **12 Marks**

Total Marks = 60

11 BSN: STRATEGIC PLANNING, STAKEHOLDERS AND SUBSIDIARY PERFORMANCE (5/99) *108 mins*

Introduction

BSN is a public service radio and television broadcasting organisation. Its Board of Directors stated in its latest annual report that the main objectives of the organisation are to:

- remain a public service broadcaster;
- provide a comprehensive range of distinctive programme and to give excellence in providing a public broadcasting service;
- make and broadcast television and radio programmes which inform, educate and entertain.

BSN is mainly funded through television licence fees which are paid by the residents of the country in which it is based. The television signal is currently broadcast through transmitters located on the surface of the land rather than via a remote satellite. The Board of Directors is held responsible by the government for ensuring that best value is obtained by the licence-fee payer.

Competition

The main competition for BSN comes from commercial broadcasters which are funded through advertising revenue. Some of these broadcasters use transmission media for both television and radio programmes which are earth-bound and others transmit via satellite. BSN has achieved an improvement in its market share of the viewing and listening audience in recent years despite this competition. One of the most distinguished services provided by BSN is its world radio service, which is renowned for its unbiased and uncensored news broadcasts relating to national and international events. None of its competitors is able to provide a parallel service of the same quality and reputation.

Accountability and editorial policy

BSN is accountable through its Board of Directors to the licence-fee payers and to the government. It regularly consults with representatives of its audience for both television and radio programmes and has established independent panels of viewers and listeners to review and advise on programmes.

In terms of editorial policy, the Board of Directors tries to ensure that there is as little interference as possible on the creativity of programme makers. Nevertheless, the Board aims to ensure that programmes are fair, accurate, impartial and meet the highest standards of good taste and decency.

New developments

Recently, BSN has introduced a 24-hour television news service. In addition, the organisation has entered a joint venture with a television subscription channel provider which allows the subscriber to access television programmes at any time to suit themselves rather than when they are broadcast. The additional income earned through subscriptions to this facility is re-invested by BSN in its main public service. Another potential development is the connection of the television to the telecommunications network, which would allow greater efficiency in the delivery of programmes.

Financial efficiency

The Board of Directors has entered a four-year licence-fee agreement with the government. The terms of this are that the licence fee will increase at a compound rate of 2% per annum both this year and next year. The licence fee will then remain at this level for the remaining two years of the agreement. The total licence fee income received in the last financial year as $2,147 million. The Board of Directors expects the number of licences sold to remain at the same level as last year for the full four-year period.

The Board of Directors is proud that BSN exceeded the efficiency savings target set by the government by 2% in each of the last three years. Over this period, BSN has out-sourced its financial processing functions and sold its transmission service to an independent company which has guaranteed the maintenance of a high-quality service at a reduced cost. The Board of Directors has placed much emphasis on the elimination of duplication of effort and reduction in waste from surplus capacity or over-staffing. An internal market has been introduced into BSN with programme-makers given the freedom to buy from producers who may be employed by the organisation or who may be external and completely independent of it. The savings achieved have been re-invested in programmes and services.

Despite these efficiency measures, BSN has experienced a steady average compound rate of growth of 3.7% in its expenditure over the last five years, and this is expected to continue at the same level over the next four-year period.

The following estimated levels of income and expenditure for the four-year period of the licence fee agreement are as follows:

	Income	*Expenditure*
	$ million	*$ million*
Year 1	2,190	2,114
Year 2	2,234	2,192
Year 3	2,234	2,273
Year 4	2,234	2,357

Future targets and developments

The government has congratulated the Board of Directors on its record of achieving efficiency savings and has set a Return on Capital Employed (ROCE) target of 6% per annum. Its current ROCE is 9%, and has been calculated as follows:

$$\frac{\text{Excess of income over expenditure x 100}}{\text{Average capital employed}} = \frac{\$108\text{million}}{£1{,}195\text{million}}$$

with average capital employed here equalling $\frac{\$1{,}250 + \$1{,}140\text{m}}{2}$

It is assumed that the value of capital employed by BSN will change only by adjustments in its operating reserve.

There has been continuing debate on the funding mechanism used for BSN through the licence fee. Some members of the government have questioned the fairness of this. They argue that commercial broadcasters cannot rely on a regular and guaranteed source of income and that the licence itself is a form of tax giving no discretion to the fee payer. One suggestion being considered by the government, to reduce BSN's dependence on the licence fee, is to separate the radio and television services. The radio services may then be financed by advertising revenue but would remain within the overall group alongside the television service. The rationale for this is that the licence fee is charged only on television receivers and therefore BSN does not obtain any direct income to support its radio services.

Financial extracts

Extracts from BSN's accounts reveal an increase in the overall surplus transferred to the operating reserve in the last financial year. Comparative extracts from the accounts over the last two years are as follows:

	Last year *$ million*	*Previous year* *$ million*
Income and expenditure account		
Excess of income over expenditure	108	82
Balance sheet		
Total assets less current liabilities	1,355	1,240
Long-term creditors and provisions	105	100
	1,250	1,140
Represented by:		
Capital reserve	700	698
Operating reserve	550	442
	1,250	1,140

BSN's total expenditure in the last financial year was $2,039 million, compared with $1,700 million five years ago. The breakdown of these costs in the last financial year was as follows:

	Last year *$ million*
Broadcast expenditure:	
Television services	1,265
Radio services	423
Non-broadcast expenditure	351
	2,039

Required

(a) Summarise the contents of a rational planning model which should be applied by BSN when formulating its strategic plan. **8 Marks**

(b) BSN's major stakeholders are the public, the government, its employees and management. Explain how the Board of Directors can obtain the views of BSN's major stakeholders in determining the future strategic development of the organisation. **7 Marks**

(c) (i) Calculate BSN's ROCE for each of the four years of the licence fee agreement.

(ii) In the light of your findings, discuss what action BSN's management could take. **15 Marks**

(d) Discuss the implications for BSN's objectives if the television and radio services are separated. **10 Marks**

(e) Explain what financial and non-financial information should be provided to the Board of Directors of BSN on the performance of the radio subsidiary following its separation from the television service. **10 Marks**

(f) Discuss how a research programme may be carried out by BSN to determine how the radio service should be marketed to attract listeners and advertising revenue. **10 Marks**

Total Marks = 60

DO YOU KNOW? - ESTABLISHING CORPORATE OBJECTIVES

- *Check that you can fill in the blanks in the statements below before you attempt any questions. If in doubt, you should go back to your BPP Study Text and revise first.*
- A .... can be defined as a course of action, specifying the resources required, to achieve a given ....

  TRY QUESTION 13
- The rational model suggests a number of stages in a 'top-down' logical sequence:
  - o .... (objectives are defined, the environment is analysed, and position audits and corporate appraisal are conducted);
  - o .... (alternative strategies are developed, analysed and compared);
  - o ...., whereby the strategy is enacted.
- Other models of strategy include:

  .... (whereby opportunities are seized when they arise)

  .... (strategies develop from small adjustments to existing practices)

  ...., whereby decisions are shaped by managers and given direction.

  TRY QUESTION 16
- Operational goals can be quantified as objectives according to SMART criteria;

  S .... R ....

  M .... T ....

  A ....
- For businesses, a prime corporate objective might be ...., or .... on investment or increase in .... value. Public sector organisations generally have limited .... and so are seeking the most effective use of them.

  TRY QUESTIONS 13 & 14
- Corporate strategies also have the interests of other .... in mind.
- Objectives are achieved through .... processes, ... control and .... control. Strategic planning is concerned with the .... Management and operational control are concerned with ensuring that .... performance is in line with the plan.

  TRY QUESTIONS 17 & 20
- Resources have to be .... according to strategic needs, through .... and operating ....
- A criticism of management accounting information is that it has been too geared to reporting .... performance and is not always a good guide to strategic ....

  TRY QUESTIONS 19 & 22
- You should be aware of the use of costs for strategic decision-making.
  - o .... costs (eg lease payments) are costs which will have to be incurred whatever management decisions are taken.
  - o .... costs reflect physical relationships between inputs and outputs.
  - o .... costs are those under managerial control.

  TRY QUESTION 18
- *Possible pitfalls*

  Write down the mistakes you know you should avoid.

DID YOU KNOW? - ESTABLISHING CORPORATE OBJECTIVES

- *Could you fill in the blanks? The answers are in bold. Use this page for revision purposes as you approach the exam.*
- A **strategy** can be defined as a course of action, specifying the resources required, to achieve a given **objective**.

  TRY QUESTION 13
- The rational model suggests a number of stages in a 'top-down' logical sequence:
  - **strategic analysis** (objectives are defined, the environment is analysed, and position audits and corporate appraisal are conducted);
  - **strategic choice** (alternative strategies are developed, analysed and compared);
  - **implementation**, whereby the strategy is enacted.
- Other models of strategy include:

  freewheeling opportunism (whereby opportunities are seized when they arise)
  incrementalism (strategies develop from small adjustments to existing practices)
  crafting strategy, whereby decisions are shaped by managers and given direction.

  TRY QUESTION 16
- Operational goals can be quantified as objectives according to SMART criteria:

  Specific **Measurable** **Attainable** **Results-orientated** **Time-bounded**
- For businesses, a prime corporate objective might be **profit**, or **return** on investment or increase in **shareholder** value. Public sector organisations generally have limited **resources** and so are seeking the most efficient and effective use of them.

  TRY QUESTIONS 13 & 14
- Corporate strategies also have the interests of other **stakeholders** in mind.
- Objectives are achieved through **strategic planning** processes, **management** control and **operational** control. Strategic planning is concerned with the **long term**. Management and operational control are concerned with ensuring that **short term performance** is in line with the plan.

  TRY QUESTIONS 17 & 20
- Resources have to be **allocated** according to strategic needs, through **budgets** and operating **plans**.
- A criticism of management accounting information is that it has been too geared to reporting **historical** performance and is not always a good guide to strategic **decision-making**.

  TRY QUESTIONS 19 & 22
- You should be aware of the use of costs for strategic decision-making.
  - **Committed** costs (eg lease payments) are costs which will have to be incurred whatever management decisions are taken.
  - **Engineered** costs reflect physical relationships between inputs and outputs.
  - **Discretionary** costs are those under managerial control.

  TRY QUESTION 18
- *Possible pitfalls*
  - **Inability to perform simple (eg DCF) calculations when required**
  - **Lack of attention to the long term v. short term trade-off when discussing corporate strategy**
  - **Confusion as to how 'strategic management accounting' can help realise corporate objectives.**

12 TUTORIAL QUESTION: MISSION AND OBJECTIVES

(a) List five or more possible overall goals of a public limited company.
(b) List three or more possible overall goals of a local government authority.
(c) Describe the differences between mission and objectives.

Approaching the question

Remember that the crucial difference in (a) and (b) is profit orientation.

13 MANAGEMENT ACCOUNTING AND THE PUBLIC SECTOR *45 mins*

In recent years there has been a considerable extension of management accounting into the public sector, eg hospitals and schools.

At the same time as management accounting was being introduced into these areas, many governments were specifying goals for the public services, eg:

(a) Hospital - 'to improve the standard of patient care'
(b) Schools - 'to improve the quality of education'

Governments have also laid stress on the efficient use of resources in these areas.

Required

(a) Comment on the above goals and to assess the contribution that management accounting can make towards their achievement in the public sector. **15 Marks**

(b) Explain how activity based costing could be used in public sector, non-manufacturing environments. **10 Marks**

Total Marks = 25

14 PUBLIC SERVICE OBJECTIVES (11/98) *36 mins*

A company engaged in the supply of water for public and industrial consumption operates in a service industry. It is subject to external influences when establishing its objectives and formulating strategy. The nature of this industry is that new technology is constantly being developed in treating and supplying water of sufficiently high quality for customer use. The organisational culture of such a company needs to reflect the nature of the industry in the provision of a reliable service to the public.

Required

As a member of the company's strategic planning team, advise the board of directors on the extent to which external influences may affect the formulation of organisational objectives and strategies. Your advice should recognise the public service nature of the industry and the way this affects the company's organisational culture.

Note: No specific knowledge of the water supply industry is required to answer this question.

20 Marks

15 PUBLIC SECTOR PLANNING *45 mins*

DocCent is a government department which issues licences to road users. It employs 2,000 people. The costs of the department gave two main elements: Staff and Information Technology. DocCent's funding has been provided by the government and this determined the spending on Staff and on Information Technology.

The licences issued by DocCent have to be paid for by the road users. However, DocCent did not benefit from the revenues raised from the sale of licences as these were passed directly to government. DocCent has no tradition of management accounting and it has never prepared a profit and loss account.

The government has a policy of reducing the size of the public sector. Other government departments, similar to DocCent, have been turned into Agencies. Although the government retains ownership, the Agencies are very similar to private sector companies. Their managers are set profitability targets and receive salaries similar to those in the private sector. The Agencies are able to raise loan capital in the open market. It is not thought that DocCent will be made into an Agency imminently. However, there is a feeling that such a change is very likely within the next five years.

In order to improve efficiency, the government has decided to introduce 'modern business practices' into DocCent. In the case of DocCent, the government intends to introduce management accounting and strategic planning, which were previously not carried out at DocCent.

Required

(a) Describe how DocCent could prepare for the implementation of management accounting and strategic planning. **6 Marks**

(b) Discuss the extent to which management accounting and strategic planning are applicable in:

   (i) a government department;
   (ii) an Agency (as described above). **11 Marks**

(c) Explain approaches which DocCent could use in the planning of its allocation and control of its resources. Distinguish (where necessary) between approaches which are applicable in a government department and those which are applicable in an Agency. **8 Marks**

Total Marks = 25

16 INTRODUCING STRATEGIC MANAGEMENT (11/96) *45 mins*

N Ltd is a small family-controlled manufacturing company. In its 40-year history, the company has grown to the extent that it now employs 35 staff, producing a wide and diverse range of household goods and utensils. The company has increased in size from its small original base. However, it has never employed a strategic management approach for its development and has relied on operational decision-making to determine priorities. N Ltd has never gathered any information relating to its markets. In recent years, the company has experienced a reduction in turnover and profitability and is assessing how it might redress the situation.

Required

(a) Explain how strategic management differs from operational management. **10 Marks**

(b) The directors of N Ltd have now decided to introduce a strategic management approach which will assist in the selection of appropriate strategies for future development of the company.

   Required

   Discuss the cultural and organisational changes which N Ltd will need to implement in order to successfully introduce strategic management. **15 Marks**

Total Marks = 25

17 BZ: NEW OBJECTIVES (5/97)

36 mins

BZ Ltd is a service company which was founded by L, its proprietor, who invested his redundancy payment to establish the business. In addition to his own capital, L obtained a bank loan, and these were the only two sources of finance used to start the business. The company has achieved success by providing a very differentiated service. L has personally carried out the full range of planning and operational management activities required to develop the business ever since it began.

It has become apparent to L that in order to continue growing, further capital needs to be injected. Additionally, it is clear to L that he needs to appoint other senior managers to maintain the operational side of the business. He believes this will leave him free to pursue BZ Ltd's strategic development.

L's strategic objective has been to exploit market opportunities, and he has achieved a high level of return on his investment. However, L now considers that in order to continue growing, BZ Ltd needs to raise more capital than he personally is able to introduce.

L is actively considering raising the new capital by a public issue of shares.

Required

(a) Explain in what ways the strategic objectives of BZ Ltd may change if it obtains new capital from the public issue of shares. **10 Marks**

(b) Describe and comment on the appropriate strategic planning processes which BZ Ltd should adopt in order to satisfy its organisational objectives following the public issue of shares. **10 Marks**

Total Marks = 20

18 TUTORIAL QUESTION: STRATEGIC COSTS

What are the critical success factors of any strategic management accounting system?

Approaching the question

Firstly determine the type of information a strategic management accounting system is supposed to provide.

19 INTRODUCING STRATEGIC MANAGEMENT ACCOUNTANCY (SPECIMEN PAPER)

45 mins

'One important observation which has been made about Japanese organisations is that although a more direct link exists between management accounting practices and corporate goals in Japan than in the West, marketing objectives are more important than manufacturing factors in establishing product costs.'

Management Accounting: Evolution not Revolution
Bromwich and Bhimani, CIMA 1989

Required

(a) Explain what you consider to be the significance of the above observation. **8 Marks**

(b) Discuss the extent to which you feel the situation described by Bromwich and Bhimani has been caused by a lack of appreciation of strategic management accountancy in the West. **9 Marks**

(c) Describe a strategy to introduce strategic management accountancy into an organisation of your choice. **8 Marks**

Total Marks = 25

20 INFORMATION FOR STRATEGIC DECISION MAKING (11/95) *45 mins*

You have recently been appointed to lead the management accounting department of W Ltd, which is a small engineering company engaged in the manufacture of precision parts. The market in which the company sells its products is small and W Ltd faces severe competition. Due to the production facilities available, the company is able to undertake only small-scale engineering work. Large-scale engineering jobs are turned away as the company does not possess the manufacturing facilities to undertake them. At best, it can act only as agent for another contractor to do the work.

The board of W Ltd is aware that the volume of work which is being turned away is increasing. This is particularly frustrating as the company is unable to utilise its capacity to the fullest extent all the time. W Ltd has achieved a steady increase in profit over the last few years. Nevertheless, the board of the company believes that it could increase profitability still further by expanding and thus being able to carry out the larger scale work which is currently being turned away.

Budgetary control and standard costing information has, for many years, been provided as the sole output of the management accounting department. The previous management accountant prided himself on the punctuality and comprehensiveness of the reports produced. Each job is priced by adding a percentage to its total cost calculated in accordance with the company's standard costing procedures. The annual cost budget is split into monthly parts and flexed to take account of a particular period's actual production. Monthly cost variances, comprising those for direct materials, direct labour, variable and fixed production overheads, are produced and provided to the relevant manager. In addition, sales price and volume variances are produced by the management accounting department each period.

The company does not have a marketing department although new customers are obtained from advertising within professional engineering journals and by attendance at trade shows. At one such recent trade show, the managing director was introduced to the concept of benchmarking. He believes that there may be advantages in W Ltd undertaking benchmarking.

Required

(a) In consideration of the need for the board of W Ltd to be provided with information which assists its strategic decision making, comment critically on the management accounting reports currently provided. **6 Marks**

(b) State and justify what changes you, as management accountant, would make in providing information which facilitates strategic planning in the company.

Within your answer, describe what financial and non-financial information you would supply which is different from that already provided. **12 Marks**

(c) Explain the concept of benchmarking and suggest how it might be applied to information for strategic planning in W Ltd. **7 Marks**

Total Marks = 25

21 PUBLIC SECTOR PERFORMANCE (5/97) *36 mins*

In recent years, there has been growing pressure to reduce the financial resources allocated to government-funded organisations. Increasingly, these organisations are being required to provide an effective service while making more efficient use of scarce resources. Comparative performance indicators are being applied by the providers of resources to organisations which operate within the same sector, such as health-care provision. These performance indicators provide statistics on expenditure and service delivery and frequently attempt to portray levels of efficiency by producing league tables which rank the organisations being compared.

Required

(a) Discuss the limitations of assessing performance by using comparative data drawn from organisations operating in the same government-funded service sector.

8 Marks

(b) In recognition of the requirement for reduced reliance on government financial support, recommend how a government-funded organisation may develop the effectiveness of its services whilst simultaneously demonstrating improved economy and efficiency in the use of its resources. **12 Marks**

Total Marks = 20

22 INFORMATION FOR ACHIEVING CORPORATE OBJECTIVES (11/97) *36 mins*

Management accounting practice has traditionally focused on techniques to assist organisational decision-making and cost control. In concentrating on the internal environment, the management accounting function has been criticised for not addressing the needs of senior management to enable effective strategic planning. In particular, the criticism has focused on inadequate provision of information which analyses the organisation's exposure to environmental change and its progress towards the achievement of corporate objectives.

Required

Explain how Strategic Management Accounting can provide information which meets the requirements of senior managers in seeking to realise corporate objectives.

20 Marks

DO YOU KNOW? - APPRAISING THE ENVIRONMENT

- *Check that you can fill in the blanks in the statements below before you attempt any questions. If in doubt, you should go back to your BPP Study Text and revise first.*

- One purpose of strategy is to enable the organisation to secure a fit with its .... This means anything outside an organisation's ....

  TRY QUESTION 23

- Strategic planners must be aware of:

  - general environmental influences, such as changes in ...., the ...., ..., and .... (PEST);
  - the specific .... environment of the firm and industry structure.

  TRY QUESTIONS 24 & 29

- .... factors include a country's general stability or instability, government control over the ...., and .... (eg on Health and Safety, and Employment Rights).

- .... factors include the rate of growth, interest rates, exchange rates and so forth. These affect the level of demand and the cost of capital.

- .... factors include trends in the population as a whole: its size, where people live, the age distribution and so on. Culture affects people's ....

  TRY QUESTION 26

- .... issues include the rate of change of new .... technology, new .... technology, and how this impacts on the business.

- Pressure and interest groups aim to get .... to encourage a change in public policy, and influence .... or .... directly.

- The impact of a firm's activities on the physical surroundings by considering costs and corporate liabilities is measured by .... management accounting.

  TRY QUESTION 30

- An important environmental trend for world trade is ....: this has seen the dismantling of trade barriers between different countries.

- Porter's Five Forces model features the following influences on competitiveness:

  ....

  Bargaining power of ....

  Bargaining power of ....

  ....

  ....

  TRY QUESTION 27

- Porter's competitive advantage of nations model suggests that .... circumstances can affect a firm's capacity to compete globally.

- *Possible pitfalls*

  Write down the mistakes you know you should avoid

DID YOU KNOW? - APPRAISING THE ENVIRONMENT

- *Could you fill in the blanks? The answers are in bold. Use this page for revision purposes as you approach the exam.*
- One purpose of strategy is to enable the organisation to secure a fit with its **environment**. This means anything outside an organisation's **boundaries**.

  TRY QUESTION 23
- Strategic planners must be aware of:
  - general environmental influences, such as changes in **politics**, the **economy**, **society and culture**, and **technology** (PEST);
  - the specific **competitive** environment of the firm and industry structure.

  TRY QUESTIONS 24 & 29
- **Political** factors include a country's general stability or instability, government control over the **economy**, and **legislation** (eg on Health and Safety, and Employment Rights).
- **Economic** factors include the rate of growth, interest rates, exchange rates and so forth. These affect the level of demand and the cost of capital.
- **Social and cultural** factors include trends in the population as a whole: its size, where people live, the age distribution and so on. Culture affects people's **attitudes**.

  TRY QUESTION 26
- **Technological** issues include the rate of change of new **product** technology, new **process** technology, and how this impacts on the business.
- Pressure and interest groups aim to get **publicity** to encourage a change in public policy, and influence **government** or **companies** directly.
- The impact of a firm's activities on the physical surroundings by considering costs and corporate liabilities is measured by **environmental** management accounting.

  TRY QUESTION 30
- An important environmental trend for world trade is **globalisation**: this has seen the dismantling of trade barriers between different countries.
- Porter's Five Forces model features the following influences on competitiveness:

  Barriers to entry
  Bargaining power of **suppliers**
  Bargaining power of **customers**
  Substitute products
  Competitive rivalry

  TRY QUESTION 27
- Porter's competitive advantage of nations model suggests that **national** circumstances can affect a firm's capacity to compete globally.
- *Possible pitfalls*
  - **Not being able to apply Porter's Five Forces, or indeed any model, to a given situation. You must be able to use the basic models.**
  - **Forgetting the importance of cultural factors when discussing international operations.**
  - **Environmental factors are all important. They will usually figure in the case study, so do not neglect them.**
  - **Failing to bring in knowledge from the rest of the syllabus. For example, technological factors may be influenced by IT, so your IFM studies may be relevant.**

23 TUTORIAL QUESTION: GENERAL ENVIRONMENTAL ISSUES

(a) 'Strategic management .... is considered to be that type of management through which an organisation tries to obtain a good fit with its environment.' (P McNamee) Explain briefly how forecasting can assist an organisation to obtain 'a good fit' with its environment.

(b) In talking about turbulence, P McNamee has said: 'Each organisation's unique environment is not static but is constantly changing due to the continuous variation in the intensity and mix of forces in it'.

- (i) List four factors which give rise to such turbulence.
- (ii) Briefly explain the segments into which the business environment can be analysed.

(c) Discuss in what sense government, as a segment of the environment, may be regarded both as an *aid* and as an *impediment* to business.

24 TUTORIAL QUESTION: COMPETITIVE FORCES

Identify five competitive forces in the environment of a firm and discuss the threat posed to the firm by each of these forces.

Approaching the question

A 'threat' is something that affects a firm's capacity to act in, and react, environmental conditions. The competitive forces can also be a source of strength.

25 TUTORIAL QUESTION: MANAGEMENT ACCOUNTING AND COMPETITOR ANALYSIS

Explain how a petroleum retailer can make use of management accounting to evaluate the likely response of local competition were he to be offered a five pence per litre reduction in the price charged by his supplier for premium road fuel provided he increases throughput by 10%.

Approaching the question

Competitor analysis is an example of the external and forward-looking perspective that the management accountant is increasingly required to consider. The question might appear to revolve around pricing, but competitor analysis deals with the competitor's ability and willingness to respond.

26 OVERSEAS ENVIRONMENT (11/95) *45 mins*

A clothing company based in the United Kingdom believes that its domestic market is limited and is proposing to expand by the manufacture and sale of its products abroad. At this stage, it has not identified where it will locate its manufacturing facility. The company believes that there are major advantages to be gained by setting up a factory in a country with a low-wage economy.

The company recognises the need to understand the marketing environment of the country within which it establishes its manufacturing facility. It appreciates that besides labour, there are other local environmental issues which need to be fully considered before entering negotiations to build a factory.

Required

(a) Compare and contrast the environmental factors which apply in both the UK and the other country. **15 Marks**

(b) Explain the possible cultural influences on the effectiveness of the workforce in respect of local education and training, technology, working hours and domestic amenities. **10 Marks**

Total Marks = 25

27 THREAT OF NEW ENTRANTS (5/96) *45 mins*

In order to achieve sustained profitability, a company engaged in a low-technology industry must continually assess the threat posed by the entry of new competitors.

Required

(a) Explain how new competitors entering a low-technology industry can pose a threat to established companies. **6 Marks**

(b) State, with reasons, the information you consider a company in low-technology industry requires to assess the extent of the threat posed by potential new competitors. **10 Marks**

(c) Discuss how a company in a low-technology industry can counter the threat posed by the entry of new competitors. **9 Marks**

Total Marks = 25

28 STRATEGIC PLAN FOR CHANGED ENVIRONMENT *45 mins*

BG plc is a defence contractor faced with a changing environment. In the past, all the work done by BG plc was for its own National Government, and it was performed on a 'cost-plus' basis. That is, BG plc was paid on the basis of its costs, plus a profit percentage. The company was exposed to minimal competition.

The existing government believes that the 'cost-plus' system encouraged inefficiency. In the future, BG plc will be required to quote fixed prices for government business. Government defence contracts are being increasingly given to BG plc's foreign competitors, who have been undercutting BG plc's prices. In addition, BG plc is faced with a general contraction of defence expenditure by its home government.

BG plc's existing costing system is aggregated, that is, all overheads are recovered on direct labour cost. BG plc has to have confidence in its costs, in order to get the government orders at an economic price, and to compete internationally.

Required

(a) State the factors that would influence BG plc when it formulates a strategic plan to meet the new situation. **8 Marks**

(b) State the strategic responses that are available to BG plc in the new environment. **9 Marks**

(c) State what BG plc's management accounting response should be. **8 Marks**

Total Marks = 25

29 COMPETING UNIVERSITY *45 mins*

PG is a university. It is a 'not for profit-making' organisation. PG earns its income from charging fees to its students, and these are set by central government.

PG is not the only university in the market, and there are other educational institutions, whose prices are also controlled by the government. These institutions are competing with each other, as they all search for a bigger market share.

Required

(a) Describe the ways in which PG can compete against the other institutions. **10 Marks**

(b) Describe how PG can establish the extent to which its users are satisfied with its services. **7 Marks**

(c) Describe how PG could measure the effectiveness of its use of resources. **8 Marks**

Total Marks = 25

30 ENVIRONMENTAL MANAGEMENT ACCOUNTING (5/97) *36 mins*

The depletion of scarce natural resources in production processes is increasingly being recognised by governments, environmentalists and industry. It has been stated that the availability of natural resources needs to be considered alongside capital and production capacities in assessing limiting factors in the global economy. Chartered Management Accountants have a major contribution to make towards the improvement of industrial practices so as to reduce environmental damage and depletion of scarce natural resources. This may be achieved by extending their traditional techniques into environmental cost reporting and control or providing information and control systems which integrate economic and environmental criteria.

Required

Discuss how the Chartered Management Accountant can provide information for the purposes of managing the utilisation of scarce natural resources.

20 Marks

31 GENERIC STRATEGIES AND THE EXPERIENCE CURVE (5/98) *36 mins*

The concept of Generic Strategies was established by Professor Michael Porter during the 1980s. He stated that a company must choose one of these strategies in order to compete and gain sustainable competitive advantage. In addition to assessing the source of competitive advantage, Porter also explained that it was necessary to identify the target for the organisation's products or services. This involved distinguishing between whether the target was broad and covered the majority of the overall market, or narrow and concentrated on a small but profitable part of it.

Required

(a) Critically appraise the value of Porter's Generic Strategy model for strategic planning purposes. **12 Marks**

[illegible] the theoretical principles of the Experience Curve may be applied to [illegible] generic strategy for a company. **8 Marks**

Total Marks = 20

DO YOU KNOW? - POSITION APPRAISAL AND ANALYSIS

- *Check that you can fill in the blanks in the statements below before you attempt any questions. If in doubt, you should go back to your BPP Study Text and revise first.*
- A .... audit examines the current state of the entity in respect of assets, finance, products, brands and markets, operating systems, internal organisation, current results and returns to shareholders.

  TRY QUESTIONS 32 & 34
- A position audit might include such issues as follows.
  - A .... audit. This can include customer profitability analysis whereby the costs of servicing individual customers or classes of customers are assessed.
  - A .... audit of the organisation's material and human resources etc. This can include limiting factor analysis and .... analysis, whereby a firm's ability to add value to its inputs can be assessed.

  TRY QUESTION 38
- The .... and .... analysis suggest that products and markets have different cost/profit profiles, which change over ....

  TRY QUESTIONS 36 & 37
- .... denotes how well resources have been utilised. .... denotes whether resources have been used in the best possible way.
- .... analysis is the analysis of the revenue streams and service costs associated with specific customers or customer groups.

  TRY QUESTIONS 35 & 39
- .... assesses the organisation's internal strengths and weaknesses in relation to the opportunities and threats offered by the environment.
- .... identifies the gap that should be filled by new strategies to meet objectives.
- Three strategic choices exist:
  - How to ....: this is the choice of generic strategy (overall cost leadership; product differentiation; focus).

  TRY QUESTIONS 40 & 42
  - The .... of growth: in new or existing markets, with new or existing products, using the .... matrix.

  TRY QUESTION 43
  - The .... of growth: acquisition vs organic growth.

  TRY QUESTIONS 44 & 46
- Performance is measured in a variety of ways. .... reports measure the organisation's success in passing certain strategic milestones. Non-financial performance indicators cover variables such as ....

  TRY QUESTIONS 52 & 53
- The .... aims to integrate performance indicators, so that strategic realities are taken into account, as well as .... performance.
- Performance measures must be designed carefully, so as to promote ...., especially in divisionalised organisations which use transfer pricing, and to .... managers.

  TRY QUESTIONS 47 & 50
- *Possible pitfalls*

  Write down the mistakes you know you should avoid

DID YOU KNOW? - POSITION APPRAISAL AND ANALYSIS

- *Could you fill in the blanks? The answers are in bold. Use this page for revision purposes as you approach the exam.*
- A **position** audit examines the current state of the entity in respect of assets, finance, products, brands and markets, operating systems, internal organisation, current results and returns to shareholders.
  TRY QUESTIONS 32 & 34
- A position audit might include such issues as follows.
  - A **marketing** audit. This can include customer profitability analysis whereby the costs of servicing individual customers or classes of customers are assessed.
  - A **resource** audit of the organisation's material and human resources etc. This can include limiting factor analysis and **value chain** analysis, whereby a firm's ability to add value to its inputs can be assessed.

  TRY QUESTION 38
- The **product life cycle** and **BCG** analysis suggest that products and markets have different cost/profit profiles, which change over **time**.
  TRY QUESTIONS 36 & 37
- **Efficiency** denotes how well resources have been utilised. **Effectiveness** denotes whether resources have been used in the best possible way.
- **Customer profitability** analysis is the analysis of the revenue streams and service costs associated with specific customers or customer groups.
  TRY QUESTIONS 35 & 39
- **SWOT analysis** assesses the organisation's internal strengths and weaknesses in relation to the opportunities and threats offered by the environment.
- **Gap analysis** identifies the gap that should be filled by new strategies to meet objectives.
- Three strategic choices exist:
  - How to **compete**: this is the choice of generic strategy (overall cost leadership; product differentiation; focus).

  TRY QUESTIONS 40 & 42
  - The **direction** of growth: in new or existing markets, with new or existing products, using the **Ansoff** matrix.

  TRY QUESTION 43
  - The **method** of growth: acquisition vs organic growth.

  TRY QUESTIONS 44 & 46
- Performance is measured in a variety of ways. **Strategic control** reports measure the organisation's success in passing certain strategic milestones. Non-financial performance indicators cover variables such as **quality**.
  TRY QUESTIONS 52 & 53
- The **balanced scorecard** aims to integrate performance indicators, so that strategic realities are taken into account, as well as **financial** performance.
- Performance measures must be designed carefully, so as to promote **goal congruence**, especially in divisionalised organisations which use transfer pricing, and to **motivate** managers.
  TRY QUESTIONS 47 & 50
- *Possible pitfalls*
  - **Being unfamiliar with the theories of Porter and Ansoff. They help you to analyse a scenario and provide frameworks for developing strategies. Learn them.**
  - **You have to be able to assess areas that are not easy to quantify, such as cultural problems. Do not be thrown by this. Non-financial performance indicators are very relevant at strategic level.**
  - **Do not hesitate to bring in your performance appraisal knowledge from MCS where this is relevant.**
  - **Do not forget that strategic management accounting has an external focus.**

32 TUTORIAL QUESTION: CORPORATE STRATEGY DEVELOPMENT

In the context of the development of a company's corporate strategy, you are required to explain the composition and the function of:

(a) a position audit;

(b) a corporate appraisal.

Approaching the question

This question is to drive home the fact that these procedures are different. If in doubt, consult CIMA's Official Terminology

33 TUTORIAL QUESTION: GAP ANALYSIS AND VALUE CHAIN

(a) Define and explain gap analysis. Consider how gap analysis might be applied to a product/market situation.

(b) Draw a diagram of the value chain and describe its components.

34 IMPERIAL TRADERS *45 mins*

Imperial Traders plc was established in 1785 and its head office has always been in London.

Currently, most of its business takes place in and around the 'Pacific Rim', ie in Japan, Korea, Malaysia and Australia.

Required

(a) (i) Explain what a Position Audit is (as defined in CIMA's *Official Terminology*).

(ii) Describe the benefits to Imperial Traders plc of conducting a Position Audit in respect of a possible move of the head office from London to a Pacific Rim country. **10 Marks**

(b) Discuss the effects of a relocation to a Pacific Rim country on the various aspects considered by the Position Audit. **10 Marks**

(c) Describe briefly the cultural differences that Imperial Traders plc may encounter in its new domicile. **5 Marks**

Total Marks = 25

35 ORIENTATION AND CUSTOMER PROFITABILITY (5/96) *45 mins*

Marketing has been defined as identifying customer needs and wants and finding ways to satisfy them profitably. Selling has been described as supplying existing products or services to customers, paying little regard to their particular needs and requirements. Whilst the marketing-oriented organisation recognises the value of satisfied customers, the sales-oriented organisation tends to have little understanding of the importance of customer satisfaction. As a consequence, the organisation which focuses on sales rather than on marketing is likely to have difficulty in analysing profitability derived from its different customer groups.

Required

(a) Discuss the benefits which an organisation may obtain from carrying out customer account profitability analysis. **10 Marks**

(b) Compare the management accounting information required to assess customer account profitability in a sales-oriented organisations with one which has a marketing orientation. **15 Marks**

Total Marks = 25

36 BCG MATRIX I (5/97) *36 mins*

The Boston Consulting Group (BCG) Growth Share Matrix is a model which identifies the positioning of a Strategic Business Unit (SBU) indicating its market growth rate and relative market share. It has been stated that the matrix is useful as it illustrates the strengths a portfolio possesses and helps in providing a guide for the strategic direction of each SBU. However, the matrix has also attracted criticism with regard to its use and interpretation.

Required

(a) Explain how the market growth rate and relative market share are employed in establishing the position of an SBU on the BCG Growth Share Matrix.

You are not required to describe the contents of the four quadrants contained within the BCG Matrix but should confine your answer to the market growth rate and relative market share. **6 Marks**

(b) Critically appraise the BCG Growth Share Matrix as a model for strategic planning purposes. **14 Marks**

Total Marks = 20

37 BCG MATRIX II (11/98) *36 mins*

The Boston Consulting Group (BCG) Growth Share Matrix is a model which plots Strategic Business Units' (SBUs) market growth and market share relative to their largest competitors.

The model was established to analyse the balance of a company's product portfolio and has been adopted by many commercial organisations.

Many public sector organisational are now experiencing increasing levels of competition for the supply of their services. This competitive environment has resulted in the need for such public sector organisations to develop analytical techniques which previously operated mainly within the private sector.

Required

(a) Explain how the BCG Growth Share Matrix could be used to analyse, for the purpose of improving overall market share, the cash flows expected from the activities of different SBUs. **10 Marks**

(b) Discuss whether application of the BCG Growth Share Matrix can make an effective contribution to the strategic development of a public sector service which is mainly government-funded, but is subject to increasing levels of competition. You may refer to any public sector service with which you are familiar. **10 Marks**

Total Marks = 20

38 VALUE CHAIN ANALYSIS (11/97) *36 mins*

Analysis of the 'added value' achieved by an organisation will reveal how much has been contributed by each of its primary and support activities. The object of the analysis is to identify those activities undertaken by the organisation which contribute the most to the total value added. This is so that strategies may be established to increase their contribution still further in order to meet organisational objectives.

Required

Explain how Value Chain analysis may help a company:

(a) to assess the value added by each of its primary and support activities; and
(b) to determine its priorities for strategic resource allocation.

20 Marks

39 CUSTOMER ACCOUNT PROFITABILITY (5/99) *36 mins*

It has been stated that companies do not have profitable products, only profitable customers. Many companies have placed emphasis on the concept of Customer Account Profitability (CAP) analysis in order to increase their earnings and returns to shareholders. Much of the theory of CAP draws from the view that the main strategic thrust operated by many companies is to encourage the development and sale of new products to existing customers.

Required

(a) Briefly explain the concept of CAP analysis. **5 Marks**

(b) Critically appraise the value of CAP analysis as a means of increasing earnings per share and returns to shareholders. **15 Marks**

Total Marks = 20

40 TUTORIAL QUESTION: GENERIC STRATEGIES

Michael Porter suggests that there are three generic strategies for creating and sustaining superior performance. These strategies are overall cost leadership, differentiation and focus.

Describe each of these strategies and indicate how each will result in competitive advantage.

Approaching the question

Remember that focus strategies can involve an element of the other two.

41 TUTORIAL QUESTION: TO BUYOUT OR NOT TO BUYOUT?

A management team in the subsidiary company of a large group have been told that the group's board of directors plan to sell off the subsidiary. The management team meets together to discuss the possibility of offering to buy out their company. List the issues that they should address.

Approaching the question

Three broad categories are: the parent firm, the business itself and the interests of the managers.

42 STRATEGIC MODELS (5/95) *45 mins*

It has been suggested that the logical start point for the strategic planning process would be to review the current situation of the organisation in terms of its internal resources and the external environment.

Required

(a) Explain what you regard as a logical start point for the strategic planning process. **6 Marks**

(b) Describe how the following could be used by an organisation wishing to generate strategies:

(i) Porter's model of generic strategies;
(ii) Ansoff's (product-market expansion) matrix.

You should supplement your descriptions with diagrams. **10 Marks**

(c) Explain the limitations of the two models which you have described in your answer to (b). **9 Marks**

Total Marks = 25

43 DIVERSIFICATION AND THE PLANNING GAP (11/95) *45 mins*

Diversification may be achieved by internal growth or through pursuing a policy of acquisition and mergers. Whether the diversification is related or unrelated to the organisation's existing business activities, it is a high-risk strategy for closing the planning gap because it takes the organisation into the development of new products and markets simultaneously.

Required

(a) Explain why diversification may be adopted as a strategy to close the planning gap. **6 Marks**

(b) Discuss the potential advantages of diversification to a company in pursuing the strategic management of markets. **8 Marks**

(c) Explain and discuss the statement that diversification is a high-risk approach to closing the planning gap. **11 Marks**

Total Marks = 25

44 TUTORIAL QUESTION: ACQUISITION VS INTERNAL GROWTH

Most companies intending to enter a new market with a product that is materially different from their current outputs generally prefer to acquire or invest in existing businesses. This strategy has inherent costs, eg goodwill has to be paid for, and inefficiencies existing in the acquired firm supported until any necessary reorganisation has taken place: this could entail possible losses in production and a lowering of worker morale. Despite these factors, the acquisition strategy is preferred to internal growth, ie developing one's own production expertise or marketing channels.

Required

(a) Explain what advantages are likely to accrue to the purchaser of an established brand-name from an under-capitalised supplier of consumer products.

(b) Explain how far the choice of operational strategy after an acquisition needs to take account of policies implemented by previous managements.

Approaching the question

A brand can often have a life that is 'independent', in consumers' eyes, of its owner.

45 UNBUNDLING *45 mins*

Until quite recently many firms pursued a policy of conglomerate diversification. This was usually linked with the strategic objective of growth, and often effected by mergers. However, a contrary form of policy has now become popular, that of 'de-merger' or 'unbundling'.

Required

(a) Assess the appropriateness of growth as a strategic objective. **6 Marks**

(b) Explain why a company might follow a policy of conglomerate diversification. **13 Marks**

(c) Explain why a company might follow a policy of demerger. **6 Marks**

Total Marks = 25

46 DF EXPORTERS (5/99) *36 mins*

DF has been engaged in exporting from its home base for many years. Rising shipping costs have led DF to increase its prices. The Board of Directors is also aware of the view held by many customers that the company is too remote from its overseas market. Reduced turnover and profitability in DF's overseas market have resulted from these two factors.

In order to address this steady decline in its foreign customers, DF is now seriously considering the establishment of a manufacturing and distribution base overseas rather than relying on exporting. The new overseas manufacturing and distribution base will be located in the country to which DF currently sends most of its exports. It would operate as a subsidiary of DF with the parent company continuing to service its home market.

Required

Discuss the strategic issues of organisational management, finance and potential government regulatory requirements that must be considered by the Directors of DF in converting from an exporting company to one which operates an overseas subsidiary.

20 Marks

47 DIVISIONAL PERFORMANCE MEASUREMENT (5/98) *36 mins*

(a) Briefly explain how the measurement of divisional performance differs when assessing the achievement of strategic targets as distinct from operational targets. **5 Marks**

(b) J is a hospital which supplies a wide range of healthcare services. The government has created a competitive internal market for healthcare by separating the function of service delivery from purchasing. The government provides funds for local health organisations to identify healthcare needs and to purchase services from different organisations which actually supply the service. The service suppliers are mainly hospitals.

J is a service supplier and has established contracts with some purchasing organisations. The healthcare purchasing organisations are free to contract with any supplier for the provision of their healthcare requirements.

Previously, J was organised and controlled on the basis of functional responsibility. This meant that each specialist patient function, such as medical, nursing and pharmacy services, was led by a manager who held operational and financial responsibility for its activities throughout the hospital. J now operates a system of control based on devolved financial accountability. Divisions comprising different functions have been established and are responsible for particular categories of patient care such as general medical or general surgical services. Each division is managed by a senior medical officer.

J's Board recognises that it exists in a competitive environment. It believes there is a need to introduce a system of divisional appraisal. This measures performance against strategic as well as operational targets, using both financial and non-financial criteria. The Board is concerned to develop a system which improves the motivation of divisional managers. This will encourage them to accept responsibility for achieving strategic as well as operational organisational targets. In particular, the Board wishes to encourage more contractual work to supply services to healthcare purchasing organisations from both within and outside its local geographical area. It is a clear aim of the Board that a cultural change in the management of the organisation will result from the implementation of such a system.

Required

Discuss the issues which the Board of J should take into consideration in establishing a system of performance measurement for divisional managers in order to ensure the attainment of its strategic targets. **15 Marks**

Total Marks = 20

48 PERFORMANCE INDICATORS AND QUALITY (11/95) *45 mins*

The introduction of indicators to measure operational and managerial performance has grown within organisations over recent years. It has been argued that managers will concentrate only on the indicators upon which their performance is measured. As a consequence of this, they disregard the impact on quality of service which is not subject to a performance indicator.

Required

(a) Discuss the view that managers will pay attention only to the indicators upon which their performance is measured to the detriment of quality of service. State, with justification, whether you agree or disagree with this argument. **8 Marks**

(b) Many organisations believe that the introduction of total quality management (TQM) is a method of achieving distinctive competitive advantage.

Discuss the possible impact of performance indicators on the behaviour of operational managers when introducing TQM as a competitive strategy. **8 Marks**

(c) In the light of your answers to parts (a) and (b), explain how an organisation can ensure that TQM is successfully implemented. **9 Marks**

Total Marks = 25

49 TRANSFER PRICING ISSUES (5/96) *45 mins*

Transfer pricing is a widely debated and contested topic within management accountancy. Much of the literature tends to concentrate on the selection of a transfer price which will maximise profits in the short tun when relating to organisations operating within a domestic market. In practice, however, such organisations often ignore this theoretical economic approach and establish a transfer price which focuses on other considerations besides marginal cost and marginal revenues. Transfer pricing is also undertaken by organisations whose activities cross national boundaries.

Required

(a) Discuss the validity of the traditional economic theory of short-run profit maximisation in the determination of transfer prices in the domestic market situation. **10 Marks**

(b) Compare and contrast the objectives of a transfer pricing system established by a company operating solely within its domestic market with that operated by a multi-national company. **15 Marks**

Total Marks = 25

50 CENTRALLY DETERMINED TRANSFER PRICES (11/97) *36 mins*

P plc is a multi-national conglomerate company with manufacturing divisions, trading in numerous countries across various continents. Trade takes place between a number of the divisions in different countries, with partly-completed products being transferred between them. Where a transfer takes place between divisions trading in different countries, it is the policy of the Board of P plc to determine centrally the appropriate transfer price without reference to the divisional managers concerned. The Board of P plc justifies this policy to divisional managers on the grounds that its objective is to maximise the conglomerate's post-tax profits and that the global position can be monitored effectively only from the Head Office.

Required

(a) Explain and critically appraise the possible reasoning behind P plc's policy of centrally determining transfer prices for goods traded between divisions operating in different countries. **10 Marks**

(b) Discuss the ethical implications of P plc's policy of imposing transfer prices on its overseas divisions in order to maximise post-tax profits. **10 Marks**

Total Marks = 20

51 EXPERIENCE CURVE AND LIFE CYCLES (5/99) *36 mins*

The theory of the experience curve is that an organisation may increase its profitability through obtaining greater familiarity with supplying its products or services to customers. This reflects the view that profitability is solely a function of market share.

Required

Discuss the extent to which the application of experience curve theory can help an organisation to prolong the life cycle of its products or services. **20 Marks**

52 QUALITY AND ADDED VALUE (11/98) *36 mins*

The introduction of improved quality into products has been a strategy applied by many organisations to obtain competitive advantage. Some organisations believe it is necessary to improve levels of product quality if competitive advantage is to be preserved or strengthened.

Required

Discuss how a management accountant can assist an organisation to achieve competitive advantage by measuring the increase in added value from improvement in its product quality. **20 Marks**

53 RUS PLC: SERVICE QUALITY *45 mins*

RUS plc operates a chain of hotels. Its strategy has been to provide medium-priced accommodation for business people during the week and for families at weekends.

The market has become increasingly competitive and RUS plc has decided to change its strategy. In future, it will provide 'a high-quality service for the discerning guest'.

Required

(a) Explain the relevance of a programme of 'total quality management' for RUS plc in the implementation of its new strategy. **10 Marks**

(b) Summarise the financial and organisational implications of RUS plc's new strategy. **5 Marks**

(c) Discuss the contribution that RUS plc's management accountant could make to the new strategy. **10 Marks**

Total Marks = 25

54 SALES TEAM BENCHMARKING (11/96) *45 mins*

A company which manufactures and distributes industrial oils employs a team of sales people who work directly from home and travel around different regions in the country. Each member of the sales team has his or her own geographical area to cover and they visit clients on a regular basis.

The sales team staff are each paid a basic monthly salary. Each member of the team is set an identical target for sales to be achieved in the month. A bonus payment in addition to the basic salary is made to any member of the team who exceeds his or her monthly sales target.

Generally, experience has been that the members of the sales team succeed in improving on their targets each month sufficiently to earn a small bonus. However, the managers are unclear whether all the team members are achieving their maximum potential level of sales. Consequently, the managers are considering introducing a system of benchmarking to measure the performance of the sales team as a whole and its individual members.

Required

(a) Explain the objectives of benchmarking and how it may be used to assist the managers in evaluating operational performance. **9 Marks**

(b) Describe how a system of benchmarking could be introduced to measure the performance of the sales team:

(i) as a whole; **8 Marks**

(ii) as individuals in comparison with each other. **8 Marks**

Total Marks = 25

DO YOU KNOW? - STRATEGY IN THE MARKET PLACE

- *Check that you can fill in the blanks in the statements below before you attempt any questions. If in doubt, you should go back to your BPP Study Text and revise first.*
- .... is the management process which identifies, anticipates and supplies .... requirements efficiently and ....
- Markets are often .... to provide a .... market which can then be the focus of a specific campaign.
- A marketing .... involves a focus on the ...., as opposed to the ....
- The customer for a good or service may not be the end .... of the good or service.
- Markets can be broadly classified between .... and .... markets.
- .... behaviour is influenced by a variety of factors, social and psychological. .... behaviour is influenced by the defined needs of the .... but also by the characteristics of the .... (DMU) or buying centre.

  TRY QUESTIONS 55, 56, 58 & 59
- .... research is the obtaining of information relevant to marketing decisions, covering, products, sales, distribution etc.
- .... is research directly undertaken on behalf of the researcher.
- .... is a review of other data, such as government statistics.

  TRY QUESTION 65
- Marketing .... is very relevant to corporate plans, although it deals with specifically marketing activities. It can involve assessing the market .... of a product (how it is perceived by customers in relation to other products).
- The marketing ...... , which is the set of controllable variables a firm uses to influence a target market, includes the following 4 Ps: .... ; ....; ....; ....

  TRY QUESTION 61

  For services, 3 extra Ps are added: ...., ... and ....
- The management accountant is interested in a product's .... (introduction, growth, maturity, decline) as different phases have different ....

  TRY QUESTION 64
- .... is a way of creating an .... for a product. It is a name, term, symbol or design which .... a product from those of competitors.

  TRY QUESTIONS 57 & 63
- Pricing issues are also of concern to the management accountant: prices can reflect ...., or, as in the case of .... costing, costs are reduced in line with an estimated target price.
- .... suggests that a firm should have a mix of old and new products, with different cash generating characteristics.

  TRY QUESTIONS 62 & 66
- There are three main modes of entry to overseas markets: .... exports, ... exports and ....
- *Possible pitfalls*

  Write down the mistakes you know you should avoid

DID YOU KNOW? - STRATEGY IN THE MARKET PLACE

- *Could you fill in the blanks? The answers are in bold. Use this page for revision purposes as you approach the exam.*
- **Marketing** is the management process which identifies, anticipates and supplies **customer** requirements efficiently and **profitably**.
- Markets are often **segmented** to provide a **target** market which can then be the focus of a specific campaign.
- A marketing **orientation** involves a focus on the **customer**, as opposed to the **product**.
- The customer for a good or service may not be the end **consumer** of the good or service.
- Markets can be broadly classified between **consumer** and **industrial** markets.
- **Buyer** behaviour is influenced by a variety of factors, social and psychological. **Industrial buyer** behaviour is influenced by the defined needs of the **organisation** but also by the characteristics of the **decision-making unit** (DMU) or buying centre.
  TRY QUESTIONS 55, 56, 58 & 59
- **Marketing** research is the obtaining of information relevant to marketing decisions, covering products, sales, distribution etc.
- **Primary research** is research directly undertaken on behalf of the researcher.
- **Secondary research** is a review of other data, such as government statistics.
  TRY QUESTION 65
- Marketing **planning** is very relevant to corporate plans, although it deals with specifically marketing activities. It can involve assessing the market **positioning** of a product (how it is perceived by customers in relation to other products).
- The marketing **mix**, which is the set of controllable variables a firm uses to influence a target market, includes the following 4 Ps: **product; place; price; promotion**
  TRY QUESTION 61
- For services, 3 extra Ps are added: **people** , **process** and **physical evidence**.
- The management accountant is interested in a product's **life cycle** (introduction, growth, maturity, decline) as different phases have different **financial characteristics**.
  TRY QUESTION 64
- **Branding** is a way of creating an **identity** for a product. It is a name, term, symbol or design which **differentiates** a product from those of competitors.
  TRY QUESTIONS 57 & 63
- Pricing issues are also of concern to the management accountant: prices can reflect **cost**, or, as in the case of **target** costing, costs are reduced in line with an estimated target price.
- **Portfolio analysis** suggests that a firm should have a mix of old and new products, with different cash generating characteristics.
  TRY QUESTIONS 62 AND 66
- There are three main modes of entry to overseas markets: **indirect** exports, **direct** exports and **overseas production**.
- *Possible pitfalls*
  - **Confusing marketing research with market research. The latter is one aspect of the former, which is fairly wide in scope and can also include product and price research.**
  - **Paying inadequate attention to industrial markets. The customers here are very different and strategies will need to reflect this.**
  - **Strategic management accounting is future-orientated. Customers may include 'future' customers as well as existing ones.**

55 TUTORIAL QUESTION: SEGMENTATION

Segmentation is often described as a 'rifleshot' approach to marketing. What do you understand by segmentation? What are the criteria for effective segmentation and what are the benefits?

Approaching the question

A fairly straightforward revision question. If you have any difficulty with this question, you need to do a lot more work.

56 BUYER BEHAVIOUR (11/96) *45 mins*

(a) Kotler states that the factors which influence a consumer's purchasing behaviour are cultural, social, personal, and psychological.

Required

Explain how each of these factors may influence a consumer's purchasing behaviour. **16 Marks**

(b) Kotler, by reference to Webster and Wind's definition of a buying centre, also states that in an industrial marketing environment the buying decision results from the influence exerted by the individual roles played by different categories of employee who have an interest in the purchase.

Required

Discuss how the roles of those categories of employee who have an interest in the purchase may affect buying decision within an industrial marketing environment. **9 Marks**

Total Marks = 25

57 BRAND STRATEGY APPROACHES (5/98) *36 mins*

H plc is a leading manufacturer of food products and has for many years successfully developed a corporate brand name. The company has achieved high profitability following its success in creating the image that its brand name stands for good quality. The company has successfully established a corporate brand, in which all its products are clearly recognised under one corporate identity.

Until now the company has concentrated its efforts in manufacturing food products which are packaged in cans and distributed through supermarket chains world-wide. The company is increasingly being exposed to strong competition, with other manufacturers developing their own rival brands. H plc's directors are concerned to ensure that it at least retains its current market share and have determined the need to review its brand strategy. In carrying out this review, the directors are considering pursuing one or a combination of the brand strategy approaches of line extension; brand extension; multi-branding; new branding.

Required

Discuss the benefits and advantages to H plc of applying each of the brand strategy approaches, and recommend which of these the company should develop. **20 Marks**

58 NOT FOR PROFIT MARKETING *45 mins*

The Smalltown Horticulture Society is a not-for-profit organisation with 300 members. It is owned by its members who each pay an annual subscription of £7 a year, and it has £12,000 in the bank. It has no debts and its only assets are a typewriter and some stationery. It rents its premises. The society's purpose is to 'promote a greater understanding of Horticulture'.

Note. Horticulture: 'the art or science of cultivating gardens' *(Collins English Dictionary)*

The society has held an annual flower show since 1905. Until 1970 the show was very well supported. It was held on the Wednesday and Thursday of the final week in September and attracted an attendance of around 8,000 people. Such a level of attendance enabled the society to cover the costs of the show and also to make a surplus. It used the surplus to finance its other activities, for instance providing free seeds to local elderly people.

Since 1970 the attendances have declined, and in 1990 the show was put on to a single-data basis as the admission receipts were insufficient to pay for the hire of the premises for two days. However attendances have continued to decline and the latest show was 'very disappointing' (Society Chairman).

Following this, the chairman made a statement in which he called for 'the ladies of Smalltown to become involved with the show like they used to be'. He observed that at the same time as the Smalltown show was being held, another society held a much bigger show in a town some sixty miles away. This show made a profit and was very well attended. Some Smalltown residents travelled to the other show but did not attend the Smalltown one.

The chairman concluded that 'unless we get better support in future, we will not be able to continue with the show and the people of Smalltown will lose out'.

Required

(a) Describe the fundamentals of the marketing concept. **4 Marks**

(b) Provide a report for the members of the Smalltown Horticulture Society, which comments on the extent to which the marketing concept has been utilised by the Society. **8 Marks**

(c) Recommend strategies which would enable the society to fulfil its purpose in the future. Your recommendations should include a consideration of the role of market research for the society and be drafted to respect the culture of the society. **13 Marks**

Total Marks = 25

59 RR CONTRACTORS (5/99) *36 mins*

RR is a contractor which specialises in roof repairs for commercial and domestic buildings. The company obtained most of its work from local customers. This was because the prices charged by RR for its work were lower than those of its local competitors. RR was able to achieve low prices by cutting its own costs, and using sub-contracted labour and competitively-priced roofing materials.

RR has found over the last year that its customer base is reducing, resulting in a loss of profitability. It has also discovered that guarantees which it issued on the work it carried out three years ago are being exercised, and the renewal of its own insurance indemnity policy has proved to be very costly.

The initial response of RR to this situation has been to increase its promotion and reduce its prices still further. This has removed the company's margin and has not increased the number of orders.

The situation for RR is now serious. Few orders are being taken. Fixed overhead costs are increasing and are not being covered by contribution because of the need for the company to follow a policy of distress pricing.

Required

(a) Suggest reasons why RR has experienced a reduction in the number of its customers. **5 Marks**

(b) Recommend an appropriate marketing strategy which RR might employ to overcome its serious reduction in profitability, and discuss potential difficulties which may be faced in its implementation. **15 Marks**

Total Marks = 20

60 MARKET ATTACK STRATEGIES (11/98) *36 mins*

It has been stated that increase in market share is the strategic objective of most market challengers. The reason for this is their belief that higher market share will lead to increased profitability. Companies which do not hold the highest market share may attack the market leader, but this is often viewed as a high-risk strategy. The attack strategies are usually identified as frontal, flanking, encirclement, by-pass and guerrilla.

Until last year, A Ltd was the market leader in the production of a specialised component. Recently, A Ltd has lost its leadership position in the supply of the component to B plc, a competitor which has recently entered the market. It is clear to the directors of A Ltd that B plc is continuing to erode the company's market share in the production of the component. This is viewed as a serious threat as manufacture of the component represents the majority of A Ltd's total turnover. B plc is a conglomerate: in the financial year it attained approximately six times the turnover and levels of profitability that A Ltd achieved.

Required

Discuss each of the attack strategies, and advise the directors of A Ltd which would be most suitable for it to try in order to recover its market share from B plc.

20 Marks

61 TUTORIAL QUESTION: MARKETING MIX

The term 'the marketing mix' was first used in 1952. Discuss the principal elements in the mix and identify the elements in the marketing mix that would be particularly relevant to:

(a) a manufacturer of domestic washing machines; and
(b) a manufacturer of heavy commercial vehicles.

Approaching the question

You are dealing with both consumer and industrial markets in this question.

62 TUTORIAL QUESTION: PRODUCT DEVELOPMENT AND PRICING

(a) Describe the role of product development as part of an overall marketing strategy.

(b) Explain why a direct relationship between the costs of production and a selling price may be inappropriate as a pricing strategy.

(c) How might customer benefits be taken into account when prices are set?

Approaching the question

Remember the role of the product life cycle here and the need to take market conditions into account when setting prices.

63 PRODUCTS AND BRANDS (5/95) *45 mins*

It has been argued that products have life cycles whereas brands do not.

Required

(a) Discuss the validity of the above argument. **6 Marks**

(b) Explain the role of brands in the construction of barriers to entry. **8 Marks**

(c) Recommend some suitable financial criteria which could be used, at the different stages of the product life cycle, for the purposes of financial control. **5 Marks**

(d) Discuss, with reasons, the advantages and disadvantages of capitalising brands on the balance sheet. **6 Marks**

Total Marks = 25

64 SPORTS CENTRE: MARKETING MIX AND LIFE CYCLE (5/96) *45 mins*

A local administrative authority allowed a supermarket development to go ahead providing that the company concerned built an extension to the authority's sports centre on an adjoining site.

In recent years the sports centre has encountered a growth in competition from local commercial recreation organisations. Simultaneously, the authority had experienced a reduction in its central funding, and has steadily increased its charges for the use of its sports centre facilities.

In reviewing its services at the sports centre, the authority has applied the product life cycle (PLC) model. It has identified the stage within the life cycle at which each of its sports centre services is positioned, as follows.

Introductory stage: Martial arts, with little take up as yet.

Growth stage: Squash playing facilities, which have required capital investment from the authority and on-going maintenance costs of the courts and equipment.

Demand for the facilities is increasing rapidly.

Maturity stage: Gymnasium facilities, which require little maintenance expense and experience steady demand which generates surplus cash.

Swimming, which incurs a continual increase in maintenance and water purification costs.

Decline stage: Badminton, with a continual reduction in demand.

Required

(a) Recommend how the local authority could market its sports centre services. **8 Marks**

(b) Comment on the strategic resource allocation implications of each stage of the product life cycle when applied to the sports centre facility.

You are *not* required to describe or draw the product life cycle model. **12 Marks**

(c) In the light of your answer to parts (a) and (b), and paying particular attention to the increasing competitive threat, recommend what services the authority should offer in the future within its sports centre. **5 Marks**

Total Marks = 25

65 MARKETING RESEARCH PROGRAMME (11/97) *36 mins*

The sales and profitability of D Ltd have declined in recent months. Until six months ago, one particular product range always achieved a high level of sales, representing 40% of D Ltd's overall annual turnover. The Managing Director has expressed extreme concern regarding the decline in popularity of this product range, which is now projected to achieve only half its previous sales level. The Sales Director (Q) has been asked to establish a marketing research programme for this product range. The Board of Directors insists that strict financial control should be exercised in carrying out the research: it has set a budget for the programme which must not be exceeded without prior approval by the Board.

No previous marketing research has been undertaken by D Ltd, and Q is unsure whether the budget set by the Directors is sufficient to allow a full marketing research programme to be implemented. Q has now approached the company's Management Accountant (M) for assistance in planning the marketing research programme.

Required

(a) Explain how the Management Accountant (M) can assist the Sales Director (Q) to plan the marketing research programme. **12 Marks**

(b) Recommend what advice M should provide to Q if the budget set by the Board is found to be insufficient to permit the programme's full implementation. **8 Marks**

Total Marks = 20

66 PHARMIA PLC: NEW PRODUCTS *45 mins*

Pharmia plc is a drugs manufacturing company. It is operating in an intensively competitive market and prices are being forced down all over the world.

To maintain its position, Pharmia plc utilises the concept of the product portfolio. Currently, there are 34 new products in the portfolio, at various stages of development. Pharmia plc cannot predict if any of these will become a major product. However, its belief is that 'There are a number of runners in the race and the more you have the greater the chance there is of picking a winner'.

The company has also stated that it is a 'Research and Development (R&D) driven company'. Therefore Pharmia plc always tries to ensure that there is adequate investment in R&D. The other major aspect of its corporate strategy is a belief in aggressive marketing, occasioned by the circumstances of the global market.

A product manager of Pharmia plc has been unexpectedly given £5 million extra funding and has the following options available.

(a) Tyrix is a drug in the early stages of development. If £5 million is invested now, it will reduce the time required before the drug is ready to be sold.

(b) Medvac has been successfully introduced into the market. It is having to compete against two rival products. An investment of £5 million would pay for an advertising campaign which it is thought would increase its market share.

(c) Sonprex is a mature product and is probably going to be superseded in the near future. An investment of £5 million would enable it to be repackaged and allow some promotional activities to be undertaken.

The following information has been provided by the marketing department.

Investment	*Product*	*Outcome*	*Probability*	*Discounted payoff* £ million
£5m	Tyrix	Success	3%	150
		Failure	97%	Nil
		Market share		
£5m	Medvac	+30%	1/6	48
		+15%	1/3	27
		+10%	1/2	(10)
£5m	Sonprex	Success	1	14

The options are mutually exclusive and must be undertaken completely or not at all. The payoffs are calculated before the cost of the investment.

Required

(a) Discuss the significance of the concepts of product portfolio and product life cycle for Pharmia plc. **7 Marks**

(b) Present the expected values of the outcomes of the three options in the form of a decision tree. **5 Marks**

(c) Evaluate the appropriateness of the use of expected values and subjective probabilities for this decision. **4 Marks**

(d) Advise the product manager as to which drug should receive the investment. **9 Marks**

Total Marks = 25

67 PRICE COMPETITION *45 mins*

Traditional economic theory asserts that in a situation of perfect competition where there is perfect knowledge and perfect substitutes are available, price is the primary basis of competition and the primary determinant of demand. (P McNamee, *Strategic Planning and Marketing*).

Required

(a) Discuss the applicability of this argument in a capitalist economy. **8 Marks**

(b) Discuss the advantages and disadvantages of seeking competitive advantage through price competition. **7 Marks**

(c) Explain what other roles a pricing strategy could play apart from seeking competitive advantage through price competition. **10 Marks**

Total Marks = 25

DO YOU KNOW? - SOCIAL RESPONSIBILITY AND ETHICS

- *Check that you can fill in the blanks in the statements below before you attempt any questions. If in doubt, you should go back to your BPP Study Text and revise first.*
- A firm's impact on society is sometimes analysed through .... analysis, which holds that a firm is a pool of activities in which society as a whole, and different groups within it, have an interest.

  TRY QUESTION 70
- .... stakeholders include the government and the general public.
- .... stakeholders include employees and management.
- Shareholders, customers and suppliers are all .... stakeholders.
- Corporate .... is the extent to which an organisation demonstrates concern for society or groups in it.
- Examples of corporate social responsibility can include ...., sponsorship, involvement in .... affairs, as well as .... good practice.

  TRY QUESTION 68
- Some argue that a firm's only responsibility is to its ...., and that the state or democratically elected institutions are best able to deal with social problems.

  TRY QUESTION 69
- Elaine .... suggests that the defining purpose of a business is the maximisation of ...., and that .... and .... are the two main ethical concerns involved in business decisions.
- .... ethics describes the impact of moral issues on business problems.
- .... ethics refers to specific codes of conduct for people with professional expertise, such as accountants.
- *Possible pitfalls*

  Write down the mistakes you know you should avoid.

DID YOU KNOW? - SOCIAL RESPONSIBILITY AND ETHICS

- *Could you fill in the blanks? The answers are in bold. Use this page for revision purposes as you approach the exam.*
- A firm's impact on society is sometimes analysed through **stakeholder** analysis, which holds that a firm is a pool of activities in which society as a whole, and different groups within it, have an interest.

  TRY QUESTION 70
- **External** stakeholders include the government and the general public.
- **Internal** stakeholders include employees and management.
- Shareholders, customers and suppliers are all **connected** stakeholders.
- Corporate **social responsibility** is the extent to which an organisation demonstrates concern for society or groups in it.
- Examples of corporate social responsibility can include **charitable donations**, sponsorship, involvement in **community** affairs, as well as **ecological** good practice.

  TRY QUESTION 68
- Some argue that a firm's only responsibility is to its **shareholders**, and that the state or democratically elected institutions are best able to deal with social problems.

  TRY QUESTION 69
- Elaine **Sternberg** suggests that the defining purpose of a business is the maximisation of **long-term owner wealth**, and that **ordinary decency** and **distributive justice** are the two main ethical concerns involved in business decisions.
- **Business** ethics describes the impact of moral issues on business problems.
- **Professional** ethics refers to specific codes of conduct for people with professional expertise, such as accountants.
- *Possible pitfalls*
  - **Do not confuse stakeholders and shareholders. The latter is just one example of the former, although it is true that many regard them as the most significant example.**
  - **If you find questions on ethics difficult to address, you may like to approach your answer using the basic rule of thumb that if a business is acting legally, and in accordance with Sternberg's model, then it can be said to be within its ethical obligations.**
  - **Do not, however, be too dogmatic. There are many different approaches to making ethical judgements.**
  - **Finally, do not neglect this area of the syllabus. It is topical, has a study weighting of 10% and will be examined regularly.**

68 OPERATIONALISING SOCIAL RESPONSIBILITY (5/95) *45 mins*

An increasing number of companies have expressed their willingness to consider their wider social responsibilities. This often involves them in voluntarily undertaking extra responsibilities and costs, for example:

(a) in order to reduce pollution, they made decide to treat waste products to a higher standard than required by legislation;

(b) they may decline to trade with countries whose governments they find objectionable;

(c) they may pay wages above national minimum levels.

Required

(a) Discuss:

(i) whether the pursuit of a policy of social responsibility *necessarily* involves a conflict with the objective of shareholder wealth-maximisation;

(ii) the extent to which the existence of a conflict between a company's objectives is acceptable. **9 Marks**

(b) Discuss the extent to which it is feasible for a company to 'operationalise' its social responsibility aspirations, that is, whether it is possible to bring these considerations into strategic decision making in a programmed or systematic way. **9 Marks**

(c) Discuss whether it is feasible for companies to include the requirements of their stakeholders when they seek to recognise their wider social responsibilities. **7 Marks**

Total Marks = 25

69 FORWARD LOOKING DISCLOSURES (5/98) *36 mins*

Companies have an obligation to provide information to their stakeholders. The financial information provided tends to be of a historical nature. It has been argued that shareholders in particular should be entitled to receive forward-looking information. Some companies wishing to communicate selectively with a sub-group of shareholders are often prevented from doing so as all shareholders should receive the same financial information.

Required

(a) Explain why a company may wish to disclose forward-looking information to its stakeholders and in particular to its shareholders. **10 Marks**

(b) Discuss the competitive issues a company must consider before disclosing forward-looking information to its shareholders. **10 Marks**

Total Marks = 20

70 ACQUISITION: ETHICS AND STAKEHOLDERS (11/96) *45 mins*

C plc, a quoted chemical manufacturing company, has until recently achieved a steady increase in profitability over a number of years. It faces stern competition and the directors are concerned about the disquiet expressed by major shareholders regarding performance over the last two years. During this period it has consistently increased dividends, but its share price has not grown at the same rate as it did previously.

K plc, a direct competitor, is similarly experiencing a reduction in profitability. Its shareholders are diverse, with the majority being financial institutions. K plc has been criticised for under-investment and has achieved no product development over the last two years. Following a concerted media campaign, K plc is facing prosecution for discharging untreated pollutants into a river.

C plc is seriously considering making a bid to acquire K plc. The directors of C plc, however, are divided as to whether K plc should be closed down or permitted to continue production post-acquisition if a bid is made. In either situation, significant staff redundancies would follow.

Required

(a) State the strategic factors which C plc would need to consider before making a bid to acquire K plc. **10 Marks**

(b) (i) Discuss the social and ethical implications for the managers and staff of both C plc and K plc if the acquisition goes ahead. **8 Marks**

(ii) Discuss the environmental issues which would face the directors of C plc if it proceeds with the acquisition of K plc. **7 Marks**

Total Marks = 25

Answer bank

1 G PLC: OBJECTIVES AND ENVIRONMENT

Pass marks. This is a wide ranging question, which only goes to show how the elements in the syllabus relate to each other: for example, objectives can sometimes crop up again as performance measures. The wording of Part (a) was slightly confusing.

Examiner's comments. In general candidates related well to the scenario. Part (a) caused some confusion, probably because the question referred to goals and then asked students to derive objectives from them. The distinction to bear in mind is that of operational goals - which can be expressed as objectives - and non-operational goals which cannot. Note that you were not expected to design a *specific* set of objectives for G plc, but were expected to discuss the nature of objectives in more general terms. In their answers to part (b) on flexibility and stakeholder conflict, many candidates failed to mention the need for internal flexibility (eg organisation structure). Candidates might usefully have applied portfolio analysis. Part (c) generated reasonable analyses of the financial data, although in many cases, more use should have been made of the chairman's comments. Short-termism should have been mentioned. In Part (d), separate five force, opportunities and threats analyses were required for each of the two divisions mentioned; surprisingly, some candidates confused Porter's five forces analysis with PEST. Answers to Part (e) omitted the need for a supportive corporate culture.

(a) **Organisational aims and corporate objectives**

Deficiencies in the current aims are as follows.

(i) There is **no mission statement,** outlining in broad terms how the firm sees its business, what its key competences are, how it aims to satisfy its clients and the required corporate values. Although some mission statements are little more than public relations exercises, they can be useful in focusing management attention on the essentials.

(ii) **G plc's aims confuse 'goals' with strategies.** The only goal mentioned is long-term profitability; the increased emphasis on international business is the strategy to achieve it.

(iii) **G plc's aims confuse strategies with tactics at corporate level**. Arguably, capital investment and training are, from the corporate level, tactical issues, although they are undeniably important.

A statement of corporate objectives will address the following issues.

(i) They will be set within the overall framework of the mission, and will embody the operational goals outlined to fulfil the mission.

(ii) Objectives have the following characteristics:

(1) Specific
(2) Measurable
(3) Attainable
(4) Realistic
(5) Time-bounded

For example, if the goal is long-term profitability, this can be quantified as, for example, earnings per share growth of 5% per annum over the next three years.

(iii) **Objectives should be expressed in a hierarchy,** clearly identifying primary and secondary objectives.

(1) The primary corporate objective relating to profitability can be supported by objectives for market share, for example, or the increase in revenue and profit from overseas operations.

(2) There will be objectives for each division.

(iv) **Non-financial objectives are needed.** Most genuinely corporate goals are financial - but G plc's environmental policy, which covers the firm as a whole, requires objectives to support it, and these are expressed in performance standards for safety.

(b)

> **Pass marks**. This part of the question seems to cover two, only distantly related issues, flexibility and stakeholder conflict, but we are not given any indication of the marks allocated between them.

Flexibility as an objective

Flexibility is the ability to respond swiftly and effectively to external circumstances, in other words to deploy resources quickly, efficiently and effectively to cope with changing needs and competitor challenges.

Strictly speaking, flexibility is not an objective, as such, according to the definition in (a) above, rather it is a **characteristic** of a firm developed from several features of its organisation, resources, culture, strategies, positioning and management.

Ansoff identifies two type of flexibility, internal and external.

External flexibility

Ansoff suggests this can be achieved by:

(i) **having many customers**, none of whom are too powerful;

(ii) operating in as **many different markets** as possible;

(iii) using different kinds of **technology**;

(iv) by implication, having a **portfolio of products**/markets each of which has different risk/return or marketing or financial characteristics (the Boston Consulting Group's matrix is an example).

It appears, however, that what Ansoff describes as external flexibility is very similar to **diversification**. The advantages of diversification are the spread of risk, and that resources can be easily transferred from one part of the group to another. G plc is applying its shipping expertise to a number of markets. External flexibility seeks to avoid becoming dependent on any of them.

However, the extent to which this strategy is appropriate to G plc must be questioned. It can lead to a **misallocation of resources**, under-investment (resources spread too thin) and lack of focus.

G plc currently maintains a **diversified portfolio**, although it is concentrated in shipping. Its other transport interests are relevant (as shipping is a transportation business), but property and construction expose G plc to risks unrelated to its core markets. These subsidiary businesses are not sufficiently large, we might assume, to offer any real flexibility or comfort.

As for shipping, the financial data shows that Cruise and Ferries are far more profitable than commercial shipping - arguably, the **performance of the group as a whole** is being dragged down by poor profitability of Containers and losses on Bulk Shipping.

Internal flexibility

Internal flexibility relates to the characteristics of the organisation in broad terms and the resources it can deploy. Flexibility can be essential to a firm's survival, its ability to maximise long term owner wealth, as measured in shareholder value, and its ability to respond to short-term, immediate pressures. Areas where flexibility can be useful are as follows.

(i) **Strategic planning processes**

(1) **Content**. A review of environmental conditions and the firm's ability to respond to them can indicate where flexibility might be needed, and what changes have to be made.

(2) **Process**. There is a danger, as highlighted by Mintzberg, that strategic planning processes become a substitute for genuine strategic thinking, in that managers' basic recipe for business success is unchallenged and becomes divorced from operations.

(ii) **Organisation structure and operations**

The organisation structure relates to reporting lines and communication patterns, and also matters of operating detail such as job descriptions.

Job descriptions: seafarers. Many firms are seeking to make employees 'multi-skilled' and able to work on a number of different jobs as and when this is required. Such operational flexibility could cut costs. In the sailing fleet, there is no reason why seamen should not be transferred between divisions.

Job flexibility: service personnel. The experience of airlines (such as BA) has shown that empowering 'front-line' service personnel to take decisions improves customer service. This is relevant for the Ferry and Cruise divisions.

Communication mechanisms are also a feature of organisation structure. Divisions could exchange information - particularly Bulk Shipping and Containers who similarly have business customers.

(iii) **Culture**

Underpinning flexibility in organisation structure is the culture of the organisation, the basic assumptions under which people work. Of course, there will be a professional culture in the shipping division, but there may also be a corporate culture. This will particularly effect the flexibility of the service staff, as mentioned above.

(iv) **Resources**

Finance. Ansoff suggests that a measure of internal flexibility is having sufficient liquid resources and cash to react to a situation. Effective contingency and scenario planning may reduce the need for standby funds (which are effectively unproductive). G plc probably does not need to hoard a cash pile - shareholders will not like it - when it could develop relationships with banks and obtain standby lines of credit for emergencies.

Human resources can be transferred between the different divisions; it is most unlikely that the ships themselves can be easily converted to other uses. For the carrier businesses, the firm should have the flexibility to outsource for special contracts.

Services. Presumably repairs and maintenance facilities are already shared.

G plc should be able to deploy its resources to meet the new demand for short-cruises.

(v) **Technology**

Technology can be used to enhance flexibility and customer responsiveness. For example, it can be used to track cargoes and build a customer database.

Flexibility: summary

Two approaches to flexibility are implied above.

(i) Have resources to spare - they do not earn a return, and this is uneconomic. This is not an objective worth pursuing.

(ii) Make flexible and imaginative use of resources available - it is in this sense that G plc should be flexible, in line with many other service firms.

Conflict

Stakeholders are all those who have an interest in the business. G plc has many stakeholders: shareholders; customers (freight and passenger transport); employees (professional seamen, customer service personnel, marketing staff) and their unions, governments (eg public safety), and other suppliers.

(i) **Conflict between objectives**

Strategic planning should solve any conflict between objectives. In a business, such conflict is normally resolved so that shareholders' objectives ultimately prevail, simply to keep the business going at all. However, there are occasions when the objectives themselves conflict.

(1) **Short term/long term**. For example, an objective to maintain/increase dividends may conflict with the need to retain funds for capital investment. Short-termism is a problem if managers are judged and rewarded on short term results alone.

(2) **Other:** a desire to maintain/increase dividend payments may lead to higher than anticipated cash outflows, which may conflict with a desire to reduce borrowing.

(ii) **Conflicts of interest between stakeholders**

(1) **Managers and employees/shareholders**. Managers' perceptions of risk and reward differ from shareholders perceptions, and managers may pursue goals that further their careers rather than the shareholders' interests. However, growth in profits should benefit shareholders.

(2) **Inter-managerial conflict**. All divisions fight for scarce resources. The loss making divisions, in particular, will have to fight for resources.

(3) **Managers/employees**. In any case of downsizing, managers and employees have different objectives. As far as **unions** are concerned, some managers are side-stepping them completely by going to other countries for cheaper non-unionised labour. Whilst managers want operational flexibility, workers want job security.

(4) **Customers/shareholders**. Safety measures are expensive and to boost profits, some firms tend such measures less than wholeheartedly. In the long run, however, safety is a prerequisite for staying in business at all.

(c) **Financial results and the chairman's report**

> **Pass marks**. It is an easy exercise to calculate the figures for cost, cost as a percentage of sales, and net profit as a percentage of sales. Ability to comment on the figures is more important. We have made several observations. You may have thought of others.

The table below is based entirely on the inflation-adjusted figures.

Division	*Sales increase*	*Cost increase*	*Profit increase/ (decrease)*	*Net profit percentage (this year)*	*Net profit percentage (last year)*
Cruise	10.9%	11.9%	3.4%	11.2%	11.9%
Ferries	1.4%	0.5%	7.5%	13.5%	12.8%
Containers	14.3%	14.8%	0.0%	3.3%	3.8%
Bulk shipping	6.3%	7.8%	(66.7%)	(4.2)%	(2.6)%
Total	9.7%	10.3%	3.4%	7.6%	8.1%

(i) **General comments on the chairman's report and financial data**

(1) **Not adjusted for inflation.** Inflation is high enough to make an inflation adjustment worthwhile, especially when net profit margins are low. Before inflation growth in profits (£223m/£205m) is 8.7%. After inflation, this improvement in real terms amounts to 3.4% as in the table above.

(2) **Future-orientated.** The chairman's report addresses the future, and is the main information we have about investment plans.

(3) **No sector comparisons**. Before we judge we need to see the extent to which G plc is better than other firms in the market, if a comparison can be made.

(4) **Only two years**. Whilst some trend information is published elsewhere in the scenario for Ferries and Cruises, none is given for Containers, the largest business in terms of revenue. More data, going further back, would indicate how cyclical this business is.

(5) **Asset utilisation**. Arguably, a better measure of efficiency than net profit is return on investment and asset utilisation - but we cannot calculate these figures from the data provided.

(6) **Cost structure**. A breakdown of fixed and variable costs for each division would help us to assess efficiency.

(7) **Performance comparisons**. The chairman has not drawn attention to the basic faultline in the business. Passenger services (cruise and ferries) generate 52% of the revenue but 83% of profit.

(ii) **Cruise**

The chairman says that Cruise results are 'encouraging'. Whilst **revenue and profits growth before inflation** of 16.4% (£856m/£735m) and 9% (£96m/£88m) are impressive, the figures are less flattering after inflation (10.9% and 3.4%).

Costs have risen higher than revenue (11.9% as opposed to 10.9%) which means that the **net profit percentage,** adjusted for inflation, is down to 11.2% from 11.9%. With a £200m cruise liner already delivered and two more (assuming they also cost £200m each) costing £400m the depreciation and/or leasing charges will eat into profits more, unless these modern ships can be operated more efficiently, and their capacity can be fully utilised.

The chairman is painting too favourable a picture.

(iii) **Ferries**

(1) The chairman has not commented at all on last year's performance, the best in the group.

(2) Although revenue growth is limited (1.4% after inflation), costs have been controlled so operating profit adjusted for inflation is up 7.5%.

(3) Perhaps he does not want to highlight the fact that Ferries division earns 40% of group profit on 23% of group revenue, and is the *only* division to have improved its profit percentage in the year.

(iv) **Containers and Bulk Shipping**

The chairman rightly points out these divisions 'continuing disappointing results'. However, he has not mentioned the fact that Bulk Shipping's losses have increased: they are worse, after inflation, than last year. In both cases, costs have risen more than revenues.

(v) **Summary**

The chairman's statement is too kind to Cruises, not kind enough to Ferries, and is reasonably accurate about Containers and Bulk Shipping. In no case does he **justify** the fact that, in every division but Ferries, costs have increased more than revenues.

(d)

> **Pass marks**. Again, this part of the question covers two distinct topics - Porter's five forces analysis and Opportunities and Threats analysis - without any indication of the split of marks between them. Be sure to provide separate analyses for Ferries and Cruises, as their markets are very different.

The **five competitive forces** underlying the structure of an industry are: the threat of new entrants; substitute products/services; customer bargaining power; supplier bargaining power; and the current intensity of competition.

Cruise division

Five forces analysis

(i) **Barriers to entry**. These are high given the £200m capital cost for a ship, the need to keep ships seaworthy and, operationally, the need to have experience in managing a service business. As many countries develop their tourism industries, more firms will enter the market (eg from Russia, Eastern Europe etc).

(ii) **Substitute products**. Cruises are competing with other package holidays, whose prices are low, and this might set an upper limit on price - however, cruises are highly differentiated as a product.

(iii) **Customer bargaining power**. This is exercised not by any individual customer but by the firm's reputation and the ease by which customers can choose other holiday providers.

(iv) **Suppliers**. There is no shortage of shipbuilders or oil-firms (for fuel) and no shortage of attractive destinations for docking and tourism. In a service industry, the most important supplier day-to-day is the service labour force, but it is probably fairly easy to find cooks, actors (for entertainment) and other seafaring staff, who can be appropriately trained.

(v) **Intensity of competition**. High fixed costs mean that pressure might be put on prices to earn contribution and cover capacity.

To summarise, the industry is characterised by high entry barriers, intense competition owing to high exit barriers, low customer and supplier bargaining power. Substitute products are an important influence, despite the high product differentiation.

Cruises: Opportunities and threats

Although we are given no figures for market share, we know that G plc is not the market leader. G plc's weak profitability does cast a shadow over its future in the market, but the new liners should address this, providing capacity can be exploited.

Opportunities

(i) **Continued and growing demand from wealthy retired people** - in demographic terms, the proportion of elderly people in the population is increasing. With early retirement, better pension provision than in previous generations, and people's greater experience of overseas travel, this affluent segment should continue to be targeted.

(ii) **Demand from young people**. This is specifically identified in the case material. Younger people want shorter holidays. A problem here is that they are less lucrative a market than the wealthy retired, and higher volume will be necessary to cope with the higher customer turnover. This might have something to do with G plc's costs rising more than its revenue. Although the market is growing, everybody is competing in it.

(iii) **Demand from new markets.** The case study mentions that some cruises were targeted at American passengers who have short vacations. There may be other groups of customers (eg from eastern Europe, Russia) who could be targeted.

Threats

(i) **Continued intense competition.** G plc is investing perhaps £600m in new ships, to take account of the new market; perhaps other firms are doing the same.

(ii) **Less than anticipated market growth.** The profitability figures are slightly less enticing than they appear. Whilst there is a 60% chance of continued growth at current levels, there is a 40% chance of this not happening.

(iii) **Downward pressure on prices**. Competition in the package holiday industry might make substitute products more attractive.

These are threats because of the implications they have for capacity. Fixed costs are probably high, so it is important to run at full or high capacity. This is one reason why the **traditional** cruise market should not be ignored: ships are at sea for longer, customers spend more, and less effort is needed to attract new customers.

Ferries division

Five forces analysis

(i) **Threat of new entrants**. This is probably low. There are high entry barriers, and there is plenty of existing capacity.

(ii) **Substitute products**. The Channel Tunnel is the most important substitute product, which offers some significant advantages over the ferries in terms of speed and convenience. The Channel Tunnel does not substitute for all ferry routes, however, and there have been some media concerns regarding safety.

(iii) **Supplier bargaining power**. This is low, for reasons similar to the cruise division.

(iv) **Customer bargaining power** is low on an individual basis.

(v) **Intensity of competition**. Over the English Channel, competition is intense. As well as the substitute product of the Channel Tunnel, there are capacity surpluses as firms build bigger and faster ships to compete for custom.

Despite the increased market for cross channel travel, the industry might be plagued by overcapacity, as firms will seek to avoid being the first to quit the market. Of course, it may be possible to sell the ships.

Opportunities

(i) **Increased trade and tourism**, arising from the continued economic growth of the EU, should lead to increased numbers of total channel crossings (including the Channel Tunnel), particularly for freight. Furthermore, there are still routes where the Channel Tunnel is neither cheaper nor quicker (eg to Scandinavia, Holland).

(ii) **New shipping technology**. Bigger and faster ships can be built.

(iii) **New markets**. There may be other opportunities to run ferries, perhaps in the Mediterranean. With the single European market, G plc should be able to compete elsewhere in Europe.

(iv) **New services**. The firm could run day trips to France - mini-cruises for leisure travellers.

(v) **Asset sales**. G plc can probably sell its older ferries.

(vi) **Synergies**. G plc has other transport interests, although these are not detailed. G plc may be able to add value in some way by integrating ferries and other transport services.

Threats

(i) The **Channel Tunnel** could continue to eat into Ferries' cross channel business. Eurotunnel has to pay high interest charges, so this could lead to price competition.

(ii) **Safety**. In recent years, shipping accidents have led doubts as to the safety of RORO ferries. Increased safety might result in higher costs.

(e) **Implementing monitoring through an audit system**

(i) Appoint **specialist staff**, versed in industry best practice to be responsible for running the audit system.

(ii) Set up an **independent department for safety**. The safety auditors should report to the Board as a whole, not the operations managers who might influence their report. The department needs to be independent.

(iii) Carry out a thorough **review of existing procedures and practices**, to assess how safety issues are actually dealt with.

(iv) **Participation**. Enlist the support and expertise of seafaring staff. They may be aware of safety problems, but have not reported them for fear of reprisals or punishment. The firm might have the best procedures, but they will be useless if they are not implemented. The support of the staff - making them be responsible for improving safety - is essential.

(v) **Culture change**. The corporate culture should highlight safety issues, and safety issues should be incorporated in the reward system. Major breaches of safety procedures, for whatever reason, must be documented.

(vi) **Benchmarking**. G plc seeks to equate, at least, with best practice. This implies that it seeks to be a leader in terms of safety - it will probably be benchmarked itself by other firms.

(vii) **Training programmes**. Staff should be trained in the new procedures and should go on refresher courses every so often, especially where new equipment is introduced.

(viii) **Suppliers safety assurance**. New ships must be designed with the highest safety standards in mind, and these should be incorporated with any tender document.

(ix) Safety should be considered as part of a **wider policy of best practice** - eg avoiding waste.

(x) There should be regular **inspections** of safety equipment - but each ship's captain should know that it is his/her responsibility to ensure that safety is maintained.

2 MYRIAD PLC: STAKEHOLDERS AND DIVERSIFICATION

(a) **Strategic implications of 1987 decision on shareholders and management**

Myriad is unusually averse to risk

Myriad plc, a small conglomerate, is slightly unusual when compared to the rest of the sector in which it operates. Dividend yield (dividend plus tax credit divided by market value of the share) is 3% compared to the industry norm of 5%. The reason for this would appear to be a combination of **lower risk** (as identified by a beta factor of less than one), a relatively **low dividend payout** (dividend cover of 4 as opposed to 2 for the industry as a whole) and a **conservative attitude** to borrowing (gearing being 20% as opposed to 60% in the industry as a whole). It would appear that the company is **risk averse,** to the extent that it might not have invested in viable projects which other companies in its sector might have taken an interest in. Minimising earnings volatility was, after all, the reason for diversifying in the first place. Moreover, the low gearing has meant that Myriad was not so badly hit by the period of high interest rates during sterling's membership of the ERM.

Low risk means low returns

This conservative strategy has been a success on its own terms, but it is possible that investors have a different opinion to the managers as to the most desirable mix of risk and reward in this sector, hence the complaints about the underperformance of the share price.

Growth has rewarded managers

The decision to become a diversified conglomerate was taken to reduce earnings volatility and promote growth. Growth is an interesting objective. Henry Mintzberg suggests that growth can be a system goal of an organisation, of limited relevance to the organisation's basic mission and perhaps of limited value to investors. Growth, after all, secures **managerial careers** in a number of ways.

(i) Running a large company is likely to lead to greater executive rewards, in terms of basic pay. Reduced earnings volatility also benefits managers with share option schemes.

(ii) Reduced earnings volatility also means that managers' jobs are secure. A sudden fall in profits, and hence share prices, can make the firm more vulnerable to a takeover, which can put managers out of a job.

(iii) There are psychological satisfactions to be had from running large companies.

It is harder to see how **shareholders** have gained.

Shareholders have benefited less than they might

(i) **'Asset stripping' opportunities have not been exploited.** Conglomerates, like Hanson (in the 1980s), have been able to divest themselves of many of the assets purchased in pursuit of a **diversification policy**, at a substantial profit, realising assets for more than they were purchased for. It is hard to see how individual groups of shareholders would be as well placed as experienced managers, to make a success of such a policy. However, Myriad plc does not seem to be in 'the business of buying and selling businesses' and so the conglomerate diversification policy must be assessed on its own merits.

(ii) **Management synergies are non-existent**. An argument against conglomerates is that, from the investor's point of view, they contain many different businesses with different **risk and return** profiles: in other words a conglomerate might be considered to be a **portfolio** of very different investment projects. Investors are perhaps able to make up their own minds as to a proposed portfolio, by buying and selling shares directly, rather than through the medium of a conglomerate. The only merits of a conglomerate are if the managers bring a special expertise to the acquired companies, thereby increasing the return that an acquired company was making before the takeover by an injection of new managerial skills, insights and disciplines but there is little evidence of any shakeup in this respect.

Shareholders can sell, but choose not to

It is almost certain that managers have gained more than shareholders. Two qualifications have to be made to this statement however.

(i) Shareholders always have the option of **selling their shares** if they do not like the strategy. Myriad's situation is quite unusual in that institutional shareholders are taking an **active role** in suggesting management and commercial changes.

(ii) Not all shareholders are in a position to acquire a **portfolio** of their own, owing to transactions costs and the expense of acquiring information. Personal investors, (eg through schemes such as PEPs) with small holdings might value a company with low earnings volatility, especially if they are more interested in income than capital growth.

(b) **Estimating the success of diversification**

The success of the diversification must be measured by how far it has reduced volatility and promoted growth. Volatility has certainly been reduced, to the extent that **Myriad's beta factor is lower than the sector norm.**

Head office subtracts value (from the investor's view point)

The market value of the group is £86m (based on a p/e ratio of 8.6 and earnings of £10m).

(i) Myriad's original business was in **metal castings**, the basis of the light engineering division, which offers modest but sustainable growth. This is clearly a mature market, which can be milked for cash. Earnings of £5m, and a p/e ratio of 6, imply a market capitalisation of £30m for this business. However the p/e ratio is lower than for the other two divisions, suggesting that they have better growth prospects.

(ii) **Leisure** accounts for 30% of earnings but with a p/e ratio of 18 (and earnings of £3m), if the business stood on its own, it would have a market capitalisation of £54m.

(iii) **Office equipment** tells a similar story to leisure, but future growth prospects are not spectacular. The p/e ratio implies that earnings are likely to improve in this business. On its own the business have a market capitalisation of £20m (earnings of £2m applied to a p/e ratio of 10).

In short the businesses **individually** would have a total market capitalisation of £104m (£30m + £54m + £20m), as opposed to £86m for the group. This reflects the conservative approach, in relation to risk and gearing, that Myriad's management have taken. Lower risk would be expected to result in a lower reward.

However, from the point of view of **management**, Myriad is performing better after the diversification. From the **shareholders**' point of view, we do not have enough information to assess whether Myriad's management injected new and better management to the new divisions: would they have performed just as well on their own?

Myriad's shareholders perhaps could have done even better if they had made their own investment decisions rather than invested through a conglomerate.

(c) **Interest groups**. The identification of different interest groups implies the concept of stakeholder analysis. A stakeholder is a person, group or institution that has an interest or concern in the running of the organisation. The main stakeholders in a business are shareholders, managers and employees. However, bankers, the Government, the European Commission and the public also have an interest in its activities in certain circumstances.

Shareholders

Institutional shareholders hold about 15% of Myriad's shares, and hence it must be assumed that the remaining holdings are held by personal shareholders. We have no idea whether these are small investors, or whether a significant proportion is held by one individual. Shareholders own the company, and the Board is accountable to them, so their interests must be considered.

It has been suggested already that the requirements of small investors and personal shareholders on the one hand, and institutional investors on the other, might differ. Institutional investors are much better able to trade their shares, and invest in a variety of companies, than are private investors. Information for institutional shareholders is less expensive, and transaction costs are probably lower.

Arguably, the proposal is rather extraordinary.

(i) Myriad's balance sheet, with its low gearing, **does not appear to need strengthening**. The company already has a lower risk profile than other companies in the sector, and its financial risk is also low.

(ii) If the institutional shareholders wished to release their capital, they could **sell their shares** in the group as a whole. However, the sale of Leisure would realise the most valuable part of the group.

(iii) Smaller investors may take a different view: they may prefer the ease and safety of Myriad's different businesses, especially as Leisure is a good prospect.

The management, therefore, have to consider the needs of all shareholders, not only the most powerful.

Communication with the different shareholders can be achieved through a number of different approaches.

(i) The **annual report** must be published. It is an opportunity for the board to indicate its wider objectives and strategies to investors. Many annual reports can be used as part of a wider communications strategy, not only to contain the annual results. In the non-audited sections, the management can put whatever gloss they like on the results, and can indicate future plans.

(ii) **Public relations.** Many firms employ a communications officer to deal with the media, or, at the very least, appoint a PR agency to deal with the media, and to generate publicity to interested parties. Shareholders might be targeted in this way.

(iii) **Advertising.** TV advertising is of limited usefulness, as it would be a very expensive way of reaching shareholders. Some conglomerates have used TV to publicise the firm but the benefits for Myriad, which is relatively small, would be limited. Newspaper advertising might also be used.

(iv) **Circulars.** The board can send newsletters to shareholders every so often.

(v) **Brokers' briefings.** The Board can communicate with investment analysts, journalists etc to propose its plans and justify its strategy.

(vi) **Non executive directors** can be appointed, if there are none already, to review the company's operations from the shareholder's point of view.

The Board does not necessarily have to consult shareholders in this decision, unless the ramifications have Companies Act implications.

Employees

Employees are another important stakeholder group. The effect of the divestment would be to sell Leisure to another company and also to render redundant some of the head office staff. Employees' interests should be taken into account, in the light of the following.

(i) **Employment law** (eg appropriate selection for redundancy).

(ii) **Existing contracts** (eg if Myriad runs an occupational pension scheme, there might be liabilities to consider).

(iii) **Morale** might be adversely influenced by the decision. This might affect the attractiveness of Leisure to an investor.

A **communications policy** can include such matters as a company newsletter explaining the strategy, dispelling any rumours, etc. Bad news is preferable to uncertainty. Also **team briefings** might be employed to explain the proposed changes. It is unlikely that employees in the other metal castings and office equipment divisions will be affected, so the communications will be directed to head office staff and staff in Leisure.

(d) **Conflicts of interest**

(i) **Managers and shareholders.** The potential conflict of interest between management and investors has already been identified. Reducing the size of the company will involve some executive dismissals, and a loss in prestige for managers. Disposing of the division with the best growth prospects would lead to more volatile earnings and lower growth, thus increasing the personal risk to the managers remaining.

(ii) **Institutional shareholders and small investors.** Small investors and institutional shareholders might have different objectives and needs. Small shareholders might welcome the conglomerate, as it removes from them the onerous task of diversifying against risk. A large one-off dividend might also be unwelcome for reasons of **personal income tax.**

The supposed rationale for the sell-off, the strengthening of a balance sheet which is already strong, is hardly a priority for the company.

(e) **How the Board should deal with the issues raised**

The Board has a number of options. It does not need to go through with the plan, but it might consider other ways of quelling shareholder dissatisfaction. A firm with a low share price might be attractive to a bidder, and the institutional investors might be inclined to support such a bid.

(i) **Canvass the opinion of all shareholders.** This will indicate the extent to which there is a demand for changes to the firm's policies.

(ii) **Communicate with the institutional investors** to persuade them as to the strength of the existing strategy; or, at the very least, discover if the institutional shareholders could be satisfied in some other way than the course they outline.

(1) **Incorporate Leisure as a limited company,** and offer some of its shares to investors. Myriad would still benefit from growth, and cash would be realised to satisfy some of the demands of the institutional investors.

(2) **Increase the company's annual dividend.** There seems to be ample resources for this. However, it is perhaps more important to indicate a **change in dividend policy** which will raise the share price. A one-off payment, with no promise of future growth, will make little difference.

(3) **Share buyback**. Some firms purchase and cancel their shares. This will only be of any use if the price offered to institutional investors exceeds that available on the market. In other words, it must reflect the hidden value of Leisure.

(4) **Rights issue**. Institutional investors could be enabled to dilute their holding by way of rights issue.

All these suggest that the company has **adequate resources of cash**. Although gearing is currently low and profits are good, the company may not necessarily have the resources to pay out a substantial sum without borrowing and increasing its gearing. At the moment, the company pays less interest than others in the industry as its gearing is low. It has thus the flexibility to finance its projects from retained profits, a less risky form of financing than borrowing.

Some investors may not wish the risk of investing in the company to be increased and might possibly look adversely on increased borrowing.

3 HESTER BATEMAN: COMPETITIVE, MARKETING AND PRODUCTION STRATEGIES

> **Pass marks**. This is a very broad question, searching your knowledge of several different areas of the syllabus. However, it enables you in a way to stand back and look at the problem from first principles, discussing Porter's theory of competitive strategy to begin with and its implications. You must ensure that your answers to parts (c) and (d) are consistent with each other (and of course relevant to Hester Bateman's situation). You are also required in part (e) to relate your answer to the other parts of the question, so you should not simply rattle off lists of stakeholders and their interests in general; you need to be specific.

(a) **Generic strategies**

Michael Porter states that there are three broad competitive strategies any organisation must pursue.

(i) **Overall cost leadership**. This means becoming the lowest cost producer in the market. Such a firm is always able to compete on price for a given level of quality. Even if the firm does not compete on price, its cost efficiencies will ensure that it will make the highest profits (or the least losses). This might be relevant to cyclical businesses. By definition there can be no more than one cost leader in any industry.

(ii) **Differentiation**. For firms which do not aspire to overall cost leadership a strategy of differentiation, by which a firm's goods and services are made different in some way from its rivals, can be pursued. The product can have special features of its own, or, on the other hand, the firm's marketing and promotional strategies can give it a unique position in the market.

(iii) **Focus**. A firm concentrates on a segment of a market, or a particular subgroup of customers. Within each segment, however, the firm will pursue a strategy of cost leadership or differentiation.

Porter argues that a firm must choose one of the strategies, or go under. This latter point has been disputed on theoretical grounds and empirical fact: many firms pursue **stuck-in-the-middle strategies** successfully (as outlined by Johnson and Scholes), but the model is still a useful one.

Applying generic strategies to HB

In Hester Bateman's (HB's) case, the issues are not particularly clear cut. The size of the market is changing. From being strictly demarcated on national lines, the market has become global. This trend is certain to continue. In this new global market, what choice is HB offered?

(i) **Cost leadership** would seem out of the question, in the short term at least. This is because cutlery-making technology can be easily imitated by countries in the Pacific. At the moment, their labour costs are much lower; how long this will remain is a different question.

(ii) **Differentiation**. HB could differentiate the product on a global basis:

(1) on the basis of quality (by using special alloys); or
(2) by designing products that are attractive to users; or
(3) by introducing a range of new designs.

(iii) **Focus**

(1) HB could decide to serve the UK or European market only, but it will still be vulnerable to cheaper competition.

(2) HB could position itself as a luxury brand to serve wealthier consumers.

Clearly, **differentiation or focus** are the way forward; HB will always be vulnerable to **lower-cost competition**, from Pacific rim countries first of all, and then from other countries as they industrialise.

(b) **Statement of objectives: applicability in 1994**

(i) **Objectives are vague and backward looking**

The statement of objectives contains remarkably few of them! Nothing has been **quantified**. As a mission statement it addresses the past not the future, on the assumption that past traditions can be preserved as a guarantee for future success.

(ii) **Objectives explain past success**

The date at which the statement was drawn up, 1981, throws an interesting light on the problem. Many UK manufacturing firms closed down in the recession that characterised the first years of the Thatcher administration. The value of the pound sterling on foreign exchange markets was very high, pricing UK exporters out of their markets, and sucking in cheaper imports. Yet HB was confident enough, in the depth of that recession, to make a rights issue, and investors supported it. Clearly, managers saw their survival as a result of concentrating on their existing skills.

To some extent, having survived the recessions of the early 1980s and 1990s, HB is in a strong position, having obviously taken steps to maintain its competitiveness. It is still able to trade on its quality image, as it has 45% of the market by value, as opposed to only 35% by volume. This is still significantly more than its competitors from overseas, suggesting that they are fighting over a niche that is relatively unprofitable for UK companies. Concentrating on the higher end of the market, rather than battling over market share for cheap generic items has been a sound strategy.

(iii) **The future holds new challenges which the statement of objectives does not address**

However, can this strategy be continued? It is possible that competitors will do their best to raise quality and HB's premium position will no longer be secure. Furthermore, the lack of investment will begin to tell. Although the firm has maintained its market position in the short term, it has lost the confidence of investors in its ability to deliver long term improvements.

(iv) **Action: new objectives are needed**

(1) HB therefore needs to update its objectives with a proper **mission statement** to satisfy the needs of its various stakeholders. This will identify:

- the extent it can continue to trade on its quality image;
- the customers it is looking to satisfy;
- what it intends to do to address the concerns of its investors.

(2) Clearly, the **survival of the firm** itself as an independent entity is in doubt. Investors are being advised to sell, yet the firm is still profitable and has a large share of the UK market. It has failed to capitalise on the competitive strengths it has.

(3) **Exports**. If it is exporting to a New York department store, it is clear that there might be further export opportunities which are not being satisfied, in the luxury goods market.

(4) Finally, **objectives need to be developed for dividends** and the growth in **shareholders' wealth.**

Summary

HB's position is therefore confused. It has survived two recessions, no mean feat. It has a commanding position in the British market, and its designs satisfy choosy US customers. Investors however have another viewpoint. The firm seems vulnerable to a takeover.

(c) **Competitive and marketing strategies**

(i) HB must first of all decide which **generic strategy** it is to pursue. We have suggested that cost leadership is out of the question, and so either differentiation or focus should be pursued. Only once this is decided, a suitable **marketing mix** must devised.

(ii) **Choose differentiation-focus**. We can suggest a focus strategy, exploiting product differentiation (ie a differentiation-focus strategy). HB already produces ranges of cutlery at different levels of quality (eg the highest quality is exported to the US). In order to improve profits, HB first of all needs to identify which product markets are the most profitable, and how to deal with them. Different strategies might be suggested for different market niches.

(iii) The firm needs to undertake a programme of **market research** to find out what its customers (both retailers such as the New York department store, and the end-consumer or user) think about HB, and how it can better satisfy their needs.

(iv) **Product**

Quality and design should be the position for exports. 'Made in Sheffield' goods enable the firm to charge a premium price. The firm should concentrate on exploiting the international luxury market for high quality 'designer' goods. For example, scotch whisky is exported to Japan, and HB can skew its R and D towards producing a variety of innovative designs that can combine premium prices at the high end of the market.

Import a cheap brand for the lower end of UK market to deter competitors. At the same time it needs to enhance the profits earned from the UK market where it is facing cheap generic competition. It has little scope for cutting prices, and so it might be a good idea to maintain its position but at a lower price. It could set up, therefore, a brand of cheap imported cutlery, to compete with BQ and the other importers. This would release resources to concentrate on higher quality premium-priced products which could still have the Made in Sheffield tag.

HB can therefore set up two brands. There are obviously profits to be earned from the generic end of the market, and HB still has the opportunity to deliver. Many firms sell low and high-quality versions of a product under different brand names. It is not so much the **company** that has to be positioned appropriately in the market, as its **brands**.

Expand the range. The firm could also use its expertise in quality metal work to expand its product range (using Ansoff's product development strategy) into the same market. Suggestions might include:

(1) related products such as silver (soup tureens, trays, silver goblets);
(2) less plausibly, perhaps, ornaments, jewellery, even cufflinks.

(v) **Price**

Premium prices for quality. The price element of the mix is implicit in the product. To increase its profitability, HB is to manufacture premium products at **premium prices**. This is in order to increase the ROCE: the New York business earns a gross margin of 45%.

Penetration price for cheap brand. Under a different brand name, HB is to import cheap generic products from Pacific Rim or cheaper countries, and use its existing networks to take on the competition. This will hopefully generate more profits, or at least cover costs, as the expensive manufacturing capability will be directed elsewhere. HB will be able to compete more effectively.

(vi) **Place**

The **distribution system** is an important element of the marketing mix. HB has obviously no problem in the UK, but perhaps it needs to consider whether it is as effective and efficient as it could be. We are told little about HB's existing distribution and logistics systems.

However, the twin pronged strategy does require some new **expertise**.

(1) **UK**. If the company is importing its generic products from overseas, it will need to have suitable warehousing and storage facilities, and to have systems which can predict likely demand, so customers do not have to wait too long.

(2) **Overseas**. It is hoped that many of the premium priced products will be exported. The US department store is a model of strategies that can be adopted in other countries in the EU and over the world. HB will need assistance, perhaps from one of the UK government's export advisory services, to find distributors for its product. The distributors will inevitably have a significant say in how the goods are to be positioned and sold. In a market such as Japan, HB will need a suitable partner to negotiate the thickets of the distribution system; in a country that uses chopsticks, demand for cutlery will be limited, but it can be sold as a luxury item. However, the main markets would be the US where further expansion is obviously possible and the EU.

(3) The company might consider offering an enhanced service to customers, for example a **just-in-time** delivery system.

(vii) **Promotion**

To **customers**. Promotional strategies will be an essential feature of HB's repositioning itself as a premium priccd quality product. This means finding a suitable advertising agency, and researching the communications messages the company wishes to pursue. It might mean advertising in media it has not used before (eg magazines promoting luxury goods, or lifestyle magazines).

To investors. The firm needs to promote itself to another audience: investors, who have to be convinced that the new strategy will work. At the moment they are critical, and will sell to a bidder. To keep their jobs, the existing managers must work to convince investors that the company's existing and potential strengths can be better exploited in future.

(d) **Production strategies**

(i) **Plant**. We are told that cutlery making is a mature technology and that HB has made no investment since the 1980s.

(1) If the rate of **technological advance** in the industry is slowing this is not a problem.

(2) If HB is at the **premium** end of the market and trading on a craft image (rather like Rolls Royce, many of whose cars are hand painted and hand finished), then for some of its most profitable businesses, investing in high technology production is perhaps not a priority.

(3) On the other hand, investing in design **technology** and metallurgical research, to find new alloys to produce ever sharper blades with a variety of sheens and finishes, is probably a 'must'. Getting hold of the money to do so, given investors' existing attitudes, might cause problems. Costs will have to be cut elsewhere, if expenditure on R and D and on design is to increase.

(ii) **Make or buy**. The production technology must be tailored to the generic strategy.

(1) Production of the **premium**-priced product must not be subcontracted, especially as the firm is trading on a quality image. It might even be appropriate to introduce total quality programmes.

(2) As the firm is going to import cheaper products to sell as generics, it will not need to invest in new equipment to make them. However, if the strategy is successful, it might be sensible to make generic cutlery in the UK eventually, as this will enable greater responsiveness to customers: if JIT is required then importing the generics may not be the most efficient option in the long term.

(3) A compromise can be made though. BQ both imports and makes its own cutlery. In the short term, production capacity for cheap generics could slowly be run down, as the firm builds up its premium product business, and becomes experienced in importing. Hopefully, there will be a slow changeover. Once the premium business develops, margins will improve, and so the firm will be able to afford further investment.

(e) **Stakeholder interests**

A stakeholder is any person or group or organisation with an interest in the organisation's activities. Any company has a variety of stakeholders. Stakeholder responses are likely to be as follows.

(i) **Investors**. Shareholders have to be won over. At the moment, the company is being criticised for its inertia, and its low ROCE. Further growth is regarded as improbable. The strategy of the company addresses these problems, by concentrating the firm's efforts on increasing the premium product area of the business which promises high profits and gross margins. The strategy also addresses the business's need to grow.

Investors will need to be convinced that it is worth their while continuing to support the firm. The low share price makes a firm vulnerable to a predator, and makes it hard to raise any necessary capital.

Provided the strategy is sound, and its effects are communicated to shareholders, investors in the firm should benefit. After all, shareholders are more concerned with future performance than with past growth, and if HB's management outline a convincing case, shareholders should support it.

(ii) **Suppliers.** The firm is still profitable, and we are not informed about any problems with cash flow. Suppliers will be concerned. A strategy of imports of generic goods will mean lower demand for metals. However, suppliers of special metals are likely to benefit.

(iii) **Bankers**. We are not informed of any substantial bank borrowings, and so we can only assume that at present the firm has no difficulties with cash flow. In fact HB may need to borrow money to finance some of its activities in the short term. Also, as HB becomes more export orientated in its premium quality division, and imports more to compete in the generics market, the bank will be able to offer fee-based services such as export finance, documentary credits, foreign exchange and treasury services. The bank can thus benefit from the strategy.

(iv) **Customers**. End-users will still be able to buy British made quality cutlery. Those satisfied with generics will have a greater choice available to them if these are imported. Retailers will be happy, as long as their margins are preserved and HB is able to deliver goods which customers want.

(v) **Employees.** The strategy envisages a slow build up of imports as existing production capacity is switched over to the premium end of the market. It should be possible to keep employees adequately trained, especially as they are likely to support the quality driven culture. Some worries are certain, however. These should be allayed by a proper programme of change management.

(vi) **Local government.** The local council will be concerned about the effects on employment, but if the strategy is to deliver long term growth and security for local residents, they are likely to be supportive.

(vii) **National government.** The government will be concerned with the effects on tax revenues if material is imported and also the effect on employment. However HB is not really big enough for government at a national level to care too much. That said, the government will be in a position to offer specialist advice through the export programmes and initiatives supported by the Department of Trade and Industry.

4 SJM PLC: EVALUATION, JOINT VENTURE

Pass marks. In part (a), the preparation of the financial appraisal itself should be fairly straightforward. The discount factor for years 4 to 15 is determined by deducting the sum of the first three years from the 15 year figure. You could also do an IRR calculation. You can comment both on the results of the calculation and on its scope. Did the appraisal take all relevant factors into account? Could it have been improved?

Examiner's comments. Most candidates related well to the scenario - but some misunderstood the question and felt that a *merger* was in the offing, not just a *joint development* of a common site. In part (a), many candidates seemed unable to calculate a simple net present value for the store, and many of those who did failed to use the present value tables provided. There was no need to use Gordon's Dividend Growth model. Part (b) was answered better, especially those which linked the different opportunities and threats: a list of strengths and weaknesses was *not* required. Part (c) was well answered. Part (d) caused problems, as candidates failed to develop the planning and operational issues. In part (e), candidates should have focused their discussion of the management accountant's role on the planning issues mentioned.

(a) **Financial appraisal of the first superstore**

Net present value

Year	£'000	*Discount factor @ 12%*	*Present value* £'000
Cost of development			
1 £25m × 20%	5,000	0.893	(4,465)
2 (£25m – £5m) × 50%	10,000	0.797	(7,970)
3 (£25m – £5m) × 50%	10,000	0.712	(7,120)
Total	25,000		(19,555)
		Cumulative discount	
Revenue over 12 years	£'000	*factor (W1)*	
Gross £250 × 40,000 sq metres	10,000		
Less £40 × 40,000 sq metres	(1,600)		
Net annual revenue per annum	8,400	4.409	37,035
Net present value			17,480

Working

The superstore will generate revenue for 12 years, in other words years 4 to 15 inclusive.

Cumulative discount factor for	15 years (12%)	6.811
	3 years	(2.402)
Cumulative discount factor for years 4 - 15		4.409

Assumption

It is not clear from the question as to whether the fall in sales at the other stores (equivalent to a £40 per sq metre fall at the superstore) was *predicted* when the initial appraisal was made. However, a well established and experienced firm such as SJM would almost certainly have considered the impact on neighbouring sites, and this answer assumes that this was predicted.

Clearly, the NPV is overwhelmingly positive for the firm.

The **internal rate of return (IRR)** of the store can also be calculated, as follows. We will take 20% as the rate used for comparison. (This is the maximum rate in the mathematical tables you have been given.)

At 20% the cash flows are these.

	£'000	*Discount factor 20%*	*Present value* £'000
Year			
1	5,000	0.833	(4,165)
2	10,000	0.694	(6,940)
3	10,000	0.579	(5,790)
			(16,895)
Years 4 - 15 £10,000 – £1,600	8,400	(4.675 – 2.106)	21,580
Net present value at 20%			4,685

Applying the formula:

$$20\% + \left(\frac{4,685}{17,480 - 4,685} \times (20\% - 12\%)\right) = 22.9\% \text{ IRR}$$

Clearly the superstore has a high IRR.

Comments on the financial appraisal

The financial appraisal does appear to justify the investment. However, it has a number of deficiencies.

(i) **Residual value.** It is unlikely that a superstore would have a residual value of nil. The land alone would be worth something for **redevelopment,** and its value might be high. Of course, this increases the attractiveness of the project still further.

(ii) **Inflation.** As the cash flows and discount rates have been expressed in real terms, inflation has presumably been considered. The problem lies not so much in the discount rate but the fact that net cash inflow in real terms is supposed not to change. In fact, inflation rates differ on retail products, and so the **sales mix** of the superstore will have a significant impact.

(iii) **Risk.** The calculation seems to take no account of the risk that revenue might be less than expected. With an IRR of nearly 23%, the project does not appear risky.

(1) Were a **competitor** to open a similar store nearby, the sales per square metre could fall significantly. Many UK supermarkets have faced competition from discounters recently, which has forced price cutting.

(2) **Political factors** have been mentioned in the question; possible curbs on car usage suggested might reduce the stores' attractiveness as a destination. With current plans to revitalise high streets, customers might want a number of stores to visit.

(iv) **Marketing strategy**. No account has been taken of major changes in retail formats, and additional construction costs that these might incur.

(v) **A lack of strategic management accountancy information.** There seems little external orientation or consideration of wider issues of the business environment. A scenario building approach could have integrated strategic and financial issues.

(vi) **Cash flows and dividends**. The current price/earnings ratio is £4.03/(£220m/£200m)= 22. Shareholders are expecting consistent dividend growth. In the last financial year, £144m (12p per share × 1,200 million shares) was disbursed in dividends to shareholders. In the next year, assuming 8.4% growth, this will rise to £156m. The firm has to ensure sufficient resources of cash for this, as well as to fund its investment programmes, with dividend cover of 1.5.

(b) **Market opportunities and threats**

Opportunities

The need to increase volume. Supermarkets make their profits on a high volume of transactions. (Earnings of £220m are 10% of revenue.) Any increase in the volume of transactions will bring significantly increased profits. The new superstores have been designed to increase the volume of transactions.

Attract new customers (market development). New customers might:

(i) have cars and like to do all their shopping in one go;

(ii) defect from competitors with no out of town stores in the area;

(iii) move from the city centre (in the USA, where out of town shopping has become more developed, some suburbs are said to have developed into 'edge cities' of their own);

(iv) come from other outlying areas, as the store's location will be convenient for people who are further afield;

(v) be found in other parts of the country, if SJM's geographical coverage is not evenly spread. This is a long term consideration.

Generate additional sales to existing customers. This can be achieved by:

(i) extending the range of products on offer (**product development** eg petrol retailing, banking);

(ii) providing facilities which make shopping convenient (eg a crèche or a tea shop);

(iii) introducing loyalty card schemes which discourage customers from defecting to competitors;

(iv) introducing other innovations to make shopping more pleasant (eg trolley attachments so that customers can key in their own purchases).

Benefits for other stores. It is possible that there will be knock on effect. Some customers may visit the superstores only rarely but, if they are favourably impressed, they might use SJM's other stores at other times.

Economies of scale. SJM's new stores offer an opportunity to save money, in that the logistics of stocking them are probably better than the city centre sites. They are probably more profitable. SJM already seems quite large; any increase in market share might enable the firm to strike even better bargains with suppliers.

Customer databases. Many firms are using loyalty schemes to generate customer databases so that customer needs can be assessed more precisely.

Threats

(i) **Saturation and overcapacity**

In the UK, supermarkets have been expanding at the expense of smaller grocers and weaker chains, but there might come a point when the market is unable to support any more stores.

The danger is that SJM and its competitors may thus saturate the market, in which case SJM will be left with a large fixed capital investment with limited opportunity for growth.

However, competition in any area is partly restricted by planning regulations, in that most local authorities would not want too many out of town developments next to each other. Paradoxically, better transport links, especially roads, would enable customers to go even further afield, thus increasing competition.

(ii) **New entrants**

New firms can enter the industry. In the UK, discount retailers have established useful niches, by concentrating on price. SJM might have to segment its stores differently. For example, people might change their habits and go to discount stores for essentials and specialist stores for other items.

City centre revival. The government is hoping to revive the city centres, although it is not clear what form this policy will take. If city centre shopping becomes more attractive, for whatever reason, out of town developments will suffer. (A number of the supermarket chains have returned to city centre sites; an example is Tesco Metro.) A problem might be that customers will visit a site with a *number* of stores, not just one.

(iii) **Opportunity costs**

The heavy use of funds might mean that other ways of increasing profitability (eg by investing in IT or making other service improvements) are not exploited.

(iv) **Transportation problems**

(1) Any curtailment on car usage (eg through road pricing, whereby people pay per mile travelled) will decrease the centre's attractiveness.

(2) Decreased bus services will discourage some shoppers (eg the elderly) from using the centre.

(v) **Demographic change**

(1) The superstore's success is determined by the size of its catchment area and suburban growth. If city centres revive, they will be less attractive.

(2) With an **ageing population**, many shoppers might prefer home delivery if they can afford it (**increasing affluence**) or if they are unable to travel.

(c) **Impact on stakeholders**

A stakeholder is a person or group with an interest in the activities of a business. The affect on stakeholder groups (five only required) is outlined below.

(i) **Shareholders**

Shareholders expect **dividend growth,** and they probably hope that the 8.4% annual growth will be continued. In this they may be disappointed in the long term, as there are government restrictions on out of town shopping developments and there is the risk that the market will be saturated and that cheaper stores will take over. Furthermore, any investment programmes will need more resources. However, given management's track record so far, they should have no cause for concern. The short term prospects seem bright, and given slow rises in living standards, customers will have more to spend.

Ratios can be calculated from the data.

(1) The **price earnings ratio** of 22 (£4.05 × 1,200m/£220m) has already been mentioned.

(2) **Earnings per share** is £0.183p (£220m/1200m).

(3) The firm is already paying 12p per share in **dividends,** so dividends account for 65% of earnings.

(4) Based on a share price of £4.05p the **earnings yield** is around 4.51%, and **dividend yield** is 2.96%.

However, there is not much we can make from these figures; each industry has its own characteristics, and we would need **comparative figures** from other quoted firms in the industry, and indeed the sentiment in the investment community as a whole, to draw any firm conclusions.

(1) The **low dividend cover** (1.5) does suggest limits in future dividend growth.

(2) **The higher the P/E ratio, the greater investors' confidence**. The prospect of enhanced profits and cash flows should raise the share price, and might enable SJM to raise more capital more cheaply to fund its programme.

(ii) **Customers**

Serving customers more effectively is the rationale for the whole business. Their interests will be served by the convenience the store offers, its size and range of goods, the easy parking, and the possibility of one-stop shopping.

However, if city centre shops close, customers might feel forced to use the out of town site. The problems with public transport suggest that some customers might eventually be disadvantaged by the move. SJM must hope that the increased business deals with this problem.

(iii) **Suppliers**

The out of town developments affect two groups of suppliers.

(1) **Builders**. The investment will be a boon to construction firms which will be building the new developments. Firms which provide infrastructure (eg electricity and water) can expect increased revenue from the development.

(2) **Suppliers of the goods** that SJM retails will welcome the opportunity for increased sales. Much of the immediate impact will depend on delivery arrangements: most supermarkets have central warehouses from which

deliveries are made. The new store programme might involve improvements to SJM's existing logistics networks.

Suppliers might be concerned at increased concentration of **bargaining power** in the hands of a smaller number of large retailers, and to this extent such developments may not be entirely welcome in the long term. Retailers can more or less dictate terms to suppliers (especially small firms).

(iv) **Employees** (as suppliers of labour) will benefit from available jobs, and the new sites may be more pleasant places to work. However, such jobs are not paid too well, and employees may have to rely on a decreasingly reliable public transport service. That said, if the firm was consistently loss making they may lose their jobs anyway, whereas if the firm expands, this gives further opportunities for promotion.

Many firms have employee share ownership schemes (ASDA is an example); if SJM has one, employees will benefit from increased profits.

(v) **The local community**

Local people will benefit from a major employment opportunity nearby, and better shops. It is local government's job to ensure that planning regulations are adhered to, but there may be drawbacks:

(1) **Traffic**. A massive change in traffic patterns may result, causing inconvenience and noise in previously quiet areas, and pressure on existing infrastructure.

(2) **Environment**. A loss of 'countryside' (although this is in theory protected by green belt policies) will spoil the environment.

(3) **Local businesses**. Some local businesses will suffer, both competitors and other firms in the city centre which benefited from passing trade.

(vi) **Central government**

The government aims to promote economic growth, and this economic activity will be welcome, as will the concomitant tax policy. Government policy covers many areas, however, including transport and the environment, and central government does not always speak with one voice. More controls on out of town developments are anticipated.

(d) **Joint ventures**

The first store was effectively an experiment which has succeeded well. Even if all future developments are going to do as well, there are still reasons for favouring joint ventures.

(i) **Risk can be shared.**

(ii) **Flexibility and buying power**. Sites are not always easy to find, and will become more difficult if new developments are becoming less acceptable. A joint venture might afford more flexibility.

(iii) **Attractiveness to customers**. Customers are probably familiar with shopping malls which contain a large number of major stores. Both stores would benefit from trade from each other's customers. In other words, as well as customers who drove specifically to shop at SJM, customers of the partner firm might also drop in.

(iv) Cost savings (sharing the costs regarding any roads that had to be built such as construction and legal advice).

(v) Economies of scale in managing the development.

Criteria for assessing a joint venture: planning and operational issues

If a joint venture with a supplier of non-competing products is attractive to SJM's customers, it should be attractive to SJM. Whether SJM should go ahead or not will depend on the results of the feasibility study.

(i) **Complementary businesses.** The relationship between the partners' businesses should be **genuinely complementary** for both to benefit. The mere fact that they do not compete is not enough. A clothes retailer and a food retailer might go together. A food retailer and, say, a firm selling car spares is a less logical mix if both hope to benefit from being near to each other. This will be established at planning level.

(ii) **Joint management** of the site this includes matters such as delivery times (so their respective delivery lorries do not get in each others' way) and opening hours. They may appoint a site manager to look after the entire operation.

(iii) **Basic design issues** (eg number of floors) need to be decided at planning stage.

(iv) **Common policies** for security, fire safety and so forth become more pressing the larger the site.

(v) **Joint marketing arrangements** might be needed to entice people to the site. For this to have maximum effectiveness, the partners will need to co-ordinate promotions. This implies that any incompatibilities in their business aims should be kept to a minimum.

(vi) **Colour schemes**, signage and so forth need to be acceptable to both parties. SJM might have to give the site a separate identity of its own.

(vii) **Running expenses** (eg lighting).

(e) **The management accountant's contribution to the planning process**

(i) **Project feasibility**

(1) **Revenue estimation.** The management accountant will need to discuss with marketing personnel the various trends in the industry in order to arrive at an approximate figure for revenue.

(2) **Cost forecasting.** The purchasing department should indicate likely trends in costs.

(3) **Construction costs.** This will give an approximate indication as to whether the idea is worth pursuing at all. Although the information will not be precise, a properly supported feasibility study is essential if money is not going to be wasted later.

(ii) **Project evaluation**

(1) **Estimates of cash flows,** capital costs and so forth are required for the investment appraisal (see part (a)). The management accountant will be involved in obtaining such information. The accountant will have to model any changes to the costs of logistics.

(2) **Breakeven.** The costs of **running the new developments** should also be assessed, to ensure that the stores break even and provide a contribution.

(3) In assessing the **building cost,** the management accountant might be involved in preparing estimates, and reviewing submissions from architects and construction firms. This is to avoid the *risk* of the project being late and over budget. Also, a realistic view is needed of the costs for control purposes.

At this stage more detailed estimates of likely business is needed, to assess cash inflows.

The accountant might be asked to do a **financial evaluation of alternative proposals**, whereby NPV and cash flows are compared. The evaluations should in theory take account of:

(1) **risk;**
(2) **competitor behaviour;**
(3) the **effect on shareholders' funds**, gearing etc.

Various **decision techniques** can be employed (eg maximax etc, probability analyses) to support the conclusions.

(iii) **Monitoring of the project**

(1) **During construction**, the building project involves a large disbursement of funds, according to a fairly tightly defined project deadline. All builders require some sort of progress payment. The accountant may assist in verifying this sum.

The accountant will be responsible for detailed monitoring of expenditure against budget and against contract. Year-end evaluations must also be prepared for financial reporting purposes.

(2) **The project will have a budget**. Many **cost overruns** should be borne by the contractor, but there may be cases where this does not happen, and the accountant should identify any variances, and prepare forecasts of likely outcomes.

Cash flows. As well as monitoring the costs in profit and loss account terms, the accountant must factor in the cash flows related to the forecast in the overall cash flows of the firm, to ensure that SJM does not fail to meet its obligations and funds are arranged.

(iv) **Post evaluation**

(1) The management of the project itself can be assessed by examining what went well and what went wrong, so that future savings can be made. The information should be detailed enough for lessons to be learned for the management of future projects.

(2) Similarly, the actual performance of the completed stores can be compared with plan, to see if they are doing better or worse than expected. The insights obtained can be used to improve the planning process for future projects.

5 LINDLEYS PLC: STAKEHOLDERS AND PERFORMANCE

Pass marks. Particular problems appeared in part (b), as candidates got sidetracked into discussing the pros and cons of the plan as a whole, or of decentralisation as such, rather than the proposal to make the branches investment centres required to make a 15% return: this part of the question demonstrates the syllabus's emphasis on the role of management accounting in strategic management. Candidates should also explore the uses of return on capital for comparative performance measures. Other comments by the examiner suggested that many candidates failed to read the question.

(a) **New philosophy and old mission statement**

The bank's new philosophy is to 'deliver an efficient, low-cost service' dedicated to profit, but without the 'bank manager being a personal friend and advisor'. The old mission was 'to deliver a high quality service to customers based on our managers' personal knowledge of customers' affairs.'

Staff

(i) **Redundancies**

In the **short term**, there will be the pain of the change process itself, especially with the redundancies. We are not told of staff numbers but, with half the branches closing, the number of redundancies will be considerable. This has an adverse effect on **morale**, even of those who have escaped. **It is also costly**.

The 1,000 branches remaining will be serviced by between 125 and 166 superbranches, with a manager and two assistants, all three being former branch managers. Between 375 and 500 managerial jobs will thus be retained, whereas 1,000 managerial jobs will be lost from the closure of existing branches. Whether more will be axed from the branches which remain is not stated: many of the remaining branches will be supervised by super-branches, and so high level managerial posts could go.

Thus, one reading of the data would suggest that around 75% of the managerial staff, with all their detailed customer knowledge, will leave the bank.

(ii) **Changing job content**

In the **long term**, the job of many staff members will change.

(1) As banks automate their processes, already there has been a shift towards front office and selling activities.

(2) The super-branch approach will change staff roles. Staff will be expected to be more productive, especially as retail banking activities are expected to become more profitable.

(3) Greater uniformity of approach may be encouraged. The bank will look for further automation, even though customers tend to like the human interface.

Customers

Each branch has approximately 5,000 customers. It is most unlikely that any branch manager would have detailed knowledge of all of these and, applying the ABC principle, much of his time would be spent on a small number of customers. Some of the businesses the bank serves will be fairly large.

(i) **Business customers**. Arguably, the bank's definition of **retail business** is strange, as it includes a significant proportion of **business lending**.

(1) **Advantages**. The new super-branch approach might in fact improve services to business customers. The super-branches will be in a better position to offer contacts and facilities for networking.

(2) **Disadvantages**. The team of three might be overworked, dealing with accounts from a catchment area formerly covered by eight branches.

(ii) **Personal customers**. As far as personal customers are concerned the situation is more complex. Many use the branch for basic account maintenance, such as paying in money and so forth. The branch is where many of a banks' automated teller (cashpoint) machines are found. Some use the branch for more complex transactions such as arranging mortgages and so forth. The branch network is an opportunity to sell services.

Closing half the network could have a detrimental impact on personal customers, as it will make basic bank services, such as paying in facilities or ATMs, harder to locate and less convenient to use, unless other provision is offered (eg ATMs in shopping centres or supermarkets). Given the intensive competition in banking services, with the building societies muscling in, the bank may be denying itself a vital marketing opportunity. Customers can easily take their accounts elsewhere.

That said, a philosophy focusing on **efficiency** and **low cost** will certainly be popular with those customers that remain, if it means fewer errors in banking procedures and cheaper services.

Shareholders

This brings us to shareholders, and their expectations of increased profit, and how the bank hopes to achieve it.

(i) The objective of increasing retail's share to 50% of pre-tax profit is **meaningless**; a fall in corporate's pre-tax profit would achieve this with no change in retail's activities at all. Retail cannot influence corporate, especially as corporate's earnings are becoming more volatile.

(ii) The figures for the relative profitability of corporate and retail divisions are misleading.

(1) Many of the costs of nurturing corporate customers have been incurred by the branches, and so arguably the retail side's input to the bank's overall success in the **long term** is actually higher than it appears. This is because a bank account is a long term **relationship** in which profits can be earned at various stages (a **sort of customer life cycle**).

(2) With big business clients, the retail side has been lumbered with the high costs of nurturing future profit makers, and the risk that these high costs will reap no reward; such seems to be the managers' view.

(iii) **Improving productivity** in the retail business is bound to increase the bank's profitability as a whole, and shareholders will welcome it.

(1) They might be concerned at the tendency to **short-termism** the new philosophy might encourage.

(2) **Risk.** They will also be keen on any measures which reduce the risk profile of the bank, and if the bank becomes not only safer but more profitable the shareholders will welcome it. At least some of corporate's high returns have come from riskier business.

(iv) The **costs of restructuring** might be considerable.

(1) Not only are there **redundancy** costs to consider, but the superbranches will need to be set up.

(2) However, some of these costs might be met by the **sale of the properties** where the old branches are currently situated, but with many high streets losing out to out-of-town shopping centres, disposing of high street property might not be easy or particularly profitable.

(b) **Super-branches as investment centres**

The CIMA defines an **investment centre** as 'a profit centre with additional responsibilities for capital investment and possibly for financing and whose performance is measured by return on investment'. (A profit centre is 'a part of a business accountable for costs and revenues'.) In an investment centre as so defined, the manager has control over controllable costs, sales prices, output volumes and investment.

(i) **Investment centres in principle**

Generally, the advantages of investment centres are held to be these.

(1) The **quality of the decision** should be improved since investment centre managers (those taking the decisions) have good knowledge of local conditions affecting their investment centre and should therefore be able to make more informed judgements.

(2) With the personal incentive to improve the investment centre's performance, **managers ought to take decisions in the investment centre's best interests**. The personal responsibility for investment, revenues, costs and profits of a business segment should act as a motivator to investment centre managers.

(3) **The speed of the decision should be improved** because information does not have to pass along the chain of command to and from top management.

(4) Investment centre organisation **frees top management** from detailed involvement in day-to-day operations and allows them to devote more time to strategic planning.

(5) Investment centres provide valuable **training grounds** for future members of top management by giving them experience of managerial skills in a less complex environment than that faced by top management.

(6) In a large business organisation, the central head office will not have the management resources or skills to direct operations closely enough itself. Some authority must be **delegated** to local operational managers.

A disadvantage of **investment centres** is that the business organisation will divide into a number of self-interested parts, each acting at times against the wishes and interests of other parts. A task of head office is therefore to try to prevent dysfunctional decision making by individual investment centre managers. To do this, head office must reserve some power and authority for itself so that investment centre managers cannot be allowed to make entirely independent decisions.

(ii) **Investment centres in Lindleys bank**

(1) **Cost control is limited.** In practice branch managers will not have the freedom identified in (i) above, so calling the new arrangement an 'investment centre organisation' is perhaps an exaggeration. For example, redundancy and employment costs will be negotiated nationally, with obviously little regard for local labour market conditions. Furthermore while managers have some control over costs, they cannot influence the cost of the **funds** they receive from deposits.

(2) **Control over revenue limited**

- The investment centre will probably have little say over key sources of revenue, such as charges for overdraft interest or **mortgage interest rates**. Standard **credit scoring procedures** may offer branch managers less flexibility than before to influence revenue from loans.
- Nor is it likely that each branch will be able to determine the **fees** of any insurance policies it sells.

- All the branch can do to increase revenue is to **scout for new customers** and try and sell as many different services as possible to those that exist already.

(3) Finally, it is not certain how much control they will have over capital spending. The bank will wish to maintain consistent levels of service at all its branches, and some head office control will be necessary to minimise costs.

(iii) **The use of ROCE for purposes of comparative performance**

(1) How will the **capital employed** side be determined? After all, each superbranch will be running 6 to 8 satellite branches. These properties will have a value, but property values vary widely over the UK. Branches with lower value properties will have a lower capital employed, and will find it easier to earn the 15% return.

(2) **Treatment of relationship costs**. As indicated in section (a), many banking profits come from the long term relationship a bank has with its customers, which is why banks offer costly promotional incentives to recruit student customers. The bank sells insurance products and loans but much of its profit comes from taking in customers' money and reinvesting it, over the customer's lifetime. It is not clear how that 15% return on capital can reflect this long term relationship.

(3) **Demography**. Different branches may be situated in catchment areas with peculiar demographic profiles. The costs and revenues of a branch in a university town with a large student population will differ from a town in which there is an unusually large proportion of retired people.

(4) **Risk** To maintain the return, the bank might indulge in over-risky lending to reach the targets it has set itself. In itself, ROCE is pointless unless some assessment as to **acceptable risk** is offered. After all, much banking income is interest income, and capital employed includes debtors and loans, some of which are riskier than others.

(c) (i) **Management reports**

The **old system** offered:

(1) **simple management reports** for expenditure, with a three monthly report, and an annual report adjusted for accruals.

(2) **reports related to specific aspects** of the bank's business including sales of insurance, and bad debts.

Under the **new system**, with responsibility being delegated downwards, the management information requirements are likely to be more onerous. Although at the moment, residual income is being considered, the main performance indicator is **return on capital**. The general problems with this approach were outlined in part (b)(iii).

In order to control costs effectively, the reports may need to be **analysed for each branch** as well as for the superbranch as a whole.

Period and timescale

Some aspects of banking business are **seasonal**, such as purchase of holiday insurance. The reports must therefore enable an analysis over regular periods, to allow comparison with previous periods. Ideally, the report would contain:

(1) **actual, budget and prior year figures** for the current month and the year to date;

(2) perhaps supplemented by a **twelve month rolling forecast**.

Standard format. Each superbranch should prepare reports for income, expenditure, assets and liabilities to assess capital employed. It is important to realise that these reports will have to be standard across the bank if they are going to be much use to senior managers comparing the performance of different branches.

Content of report: income and expenditure

(1) **Net interest income over capital employed: Interest received** (from loans to customers) less **interest paid** (eg on deposit accounts) should be compared with the size of loans and deposits. The net interest income will be the first component of the report. The key measure here will be the spread between borrowing and lending costs.

(2) **Other income** can be analysed, for example bank charges, commissions on sales of insurance and pension policies, commission on share dealing services, foreign exchange transactions and so forth.

(3) Operating expenses

- **Staff costs**: many banks have been trying to reduce headcount to improve the ratio of costs to income.
- The new arrangement may involve **additional expenses in travel** and perhaps entertainment.
- In addition, if each superbranch is an investment centre it will probably have to **depreciate the fixed assets** of each branch. Clearly, the initial property valuations will have a serious impact on profit.

Content: assets and liabilities

In order to calculate **ROCE, a statement of assets and liabilities** is needed.

(1) For banks, the loans they make to customers are assets (debtors) and deposits from customers are liabilities (creditors). How this will be incorporated into the reporting framework is uncertain. Traditionally, banks have tried to increase their lending, as a proxy for growth. This will have to be included in the superbranch management reports somehow.

(2) Other aspects of the balance sheet include **property and equipment valuation** mentioned earlier.

(3) On its own ROCE is not a suitable measure, because it makes no allowance of the degree of **risk** the bank is taking on. The urge to increase profits may encourage risky lending, to increase the level of interest income in the short term. The level of **bad debts** will only become apparent later. For banks, therefore, the **quality of earnings** is important and banks might reduce lending to certain sectors.

Other indicators

A number of other performance indicators are therefore necessary to get an overall picture of the health of the branch. They might include an analysis of loans by **sector** (eg personal loans, business loans) or **industry** (loans to builders, shops etc), levels of arrears and doubtful debts.

(ii) **Qualitative performance indicators** will not be financial but they will relate to the operations of the business, and include the following. (Three only were required by the question.)

(1) The **number of new bank accounts opened**. Customer bank accounts are an important resource for the bank: money which can be loaned to borrowers. Many accounts offer interest, and there is significant competition from other providers.

(2) **The number of accounts closed**. As a corollary of the above, the bank should seek to minimise accounts lost to competitors. However, in many banks, competition policy is set centrally.

(3) The **number and size of loans advanced,** with suitable indications for risk. This will feed back directly into the interest income statement.

(4) **Efficiency measurement**. The bank's mission is to provide an efficient low-cost service. Efficiency measures include the speed of processing loan applications or customer queries, the number of errors, and the level of complaints. This is especially important in the transitional period. Some of the super-branches may undertake quality management initiatives to ensure greater productivity and efficiency.

(5) In the branches themselves, performance indicators are needed to assess **quality of service** and also to monitor **customer usage. Queuing times** can be monitored, and **customer satisfaction surveys** can be set up (eg to monitor staff courtesy). The **availability of cash** in cashpoint machines should also be monitored.

The long term: customer profitability

(1) Many banks are developing customer databases, so that the bank's entire **relationship** with the customer can be mapped. Once the superbranches have become established, the banks can develop their marketing practices using this technology. For example, banks can try to persuade their existing account customers to buy additional products from them (eg by mailshot). The bank should have enough information to try a basic segmentation approach.

(2) Arguably, banking is not like a manufacturing business, in that much of the profits are built up over a long term life time relationship with a customer, who lends his money to the bank for the bank to invest. Only part of the profit derives from sales of products such as insurance. With this in mind, the bank should consider analysing its customers in order to assess **relative customer profitability**. The superbranches, covering a wider catchment area than the old branches, may be able to segment customers more effectively, and identify target segments for particular levels of service. **Segment profitability measures** can be drawn up, suggesting further marketing opportunities.

(d) **Stakeholders involved in the determination of the reorganisation**

The stakeholders were identified in part (a) of the question. They have varying degrees of influence on the reorganisation.

(i) **Shareholders**

(1) The re-organisation is taking place in order to increase profitability and to satisfy shareholders. The recent problems have arisen less out of retail than corporate and overseas lending, which have been riskier. Increasing retail profitability should reduce the **risk profile,** making it more attractive to shareholders.

(2) Shareholders can exert various degrees of pressure. If they choose, they can sell the shares, perhaps lowering the price. The share price indicates

shareholders' confidence in management. Major investors or the investor community as a whole can signal to management the need for change, but the precise nature of change is what managers are paid to determine. Only rarely will shareholders depose an existing board, although it is possible that shareholder activism is increasing.

(ii) **Staff.** Staff are greatly affected by the changes as there may be many **redundancies**. Almost certainly this will be opposed by unions and staff associations initially. Staff have negative power in that refusal to co-operate could prove very costly. Severe disruption would damage **customer service**. With the scale of the redundancies, severance packages will be negotiated, and perhaps voluntary redundancies will be offered first. This will be costly, but the disruption will have to be minimised. Their active co-operation will be needed.

(iii) **Customers** are the final group affected by the change. **Marketing research** should identify whether customers consider the existing arrangements appropriate or worth paying extra for. The marketing research might discover that not all customers regard the personal touch as being all that important; those that do might be easily serviced from the new superbranches.

6 PK LTD: PERFORMANCE AND ACQUISITION

Examiner's comments. Some candidates assumed that PK was not a UK based company, because the question stated that the company is based in Europe; the examiner said that 'candidates who made this assumption may reflect on the fact that the UK is within Europe'. Many answers lacked detail despite the generous time allocation. Part (a) was well answered, although many answers missed the potential for conflict between objectives. Part (b) saw a number of rehearsed answers, not applied to the case. Although there were good answers to part (c) many needed further elaboration and lacked detail. Many candidates provided only one side of discussion whereas two or three would have been more appropriate. Part (d) was well answered, with candidates using their knowledge of Organisational Management and Development at Stage 3 – oddly, many missed discussing the cost of the acquisition and the currency risk. Part (e) was intended to focus on the peculiar issues of monitoring performance post-acquisition – a link with (d) would have helped.

(a) **Difficulties parent companies have in assessing PK's performance.**

(i) **The parent companies are based in the UK whereas PK has more international exposure**. They may be less exposed to overseas conditions and less able to interpret PK's performance for this reason. Furthermore, PK is exposed to substantial risks.

(1) **Currency risk**: PK's results are reported in sterling, whereas revenue, costs and cash flows are in a variety of currencies. Recent turmoil in Asian currency markets highlights this concern.

(2) **Business/political risk.** The type of infrastructure project PK is involved in is often subject to changes in public expenditure requirements.

(ii) PK's business is probably **more complex** than that of the parent firms.

(1) **A great deal of PK's work is project-based**, work on the Channel Tunnel being a good example. This requires a different set of skills and competences than perhaps the parent companies use or appreciate.

(2) PK is also involved in **servicing** equipment, which requires building up customer relationships over time to develop a long term income stream. Its **parents are in manufacturing**. Cash flows and profits are different for service businesses, where **customer account profitability** can be used.

(iii) **PK's parents report directly to the capital markets** and have their own objectives for shareholder value and performance. **PK's management** are, because they **report directly to the management of the parent companies, partly insulated** from these developments.

(iv) PK requires heavy **investment in R&D** to sustain its position. R & D is commercially focused – towards cost, reliability and quality – but it is hard to measure, year on year, the success of the R & D function. R & D is a long term investment.

(v) **PK has two parents, who are joint owners**. Being similar companies based in the UK they face similar capital market disciplines. It is **not clear how much autonomy** PK has: PK's management may be able to play the parent companies off against each other, making it harder for the parents to assess and control PK's performance.

(b) **Financial and non-financial performance measures to assess the performance of PK**

PK is not listed on the stock market, so its performance cannot be easily measured in terms of price/earnings ratios. Similarly, other shareholder based measures such as dividend yield cannot really be appropriate given the parent companies can probably force PK's management to pay a level of dividend. It is possible, however, that techniques such as shareholder/economic value analysis can be used for investments.

PK's parent firms are able, however, to extract more management information from their subsidiaries than if PK was quoted on the stock market.

(i) **Return on capital employed (ROCE**). PK's parents can quite easily calculate this simple accounting measure. They know how much they have invested and PK's audited profit figures should provide details for this calculation. The limitations of ROCE are well known – PK requires a lot of up-front investment in R&D, which is unlikely to be capitalised. Similarly, ROCE can be inflated by delaying investment – it **encourages short-termism,** whereas PK, with its need to build customer relationships and R & D, needs to think long-term.

(ii) Other **accounting measures** such as profit margins (gross and net) also give an indication of how successfully PK has managed its activities over the year.

(iii) Arguably, **cash flow** is more important. PK incurs substantial costs in building and installing the signalling networks over a number of years. These projects can have cost overruns. Cash flow is often an **indicator of future growth in value of the firm,** in particular its ability to fund future investment and to pay out dividends.

(iv) **Turnover**: turnover **reflects PK's past success** in winning contracts, and its ability to penetrate current markets (by selling extensions to systems already installed). To be useful, however, turnover (and profits) should be analysed by class of business. Manufacturing and installation/service have very different cost, revenue and profit characteristics.

(v) Profit on **individual customer relationships (customer account profitability)** and contracts (**contract profitability**), if they can be measured. Were PK a quoted company, this information would not be in the public domain and PK would probably wish to keep this information from its customers and competitors. PK's parent companies can legitimately obtain this internal management information.

(vi) **Purchase costs of subcomponents**. Many of PK's products and systems are developed internally and, presumably, protected by patents and copyright. Other components might be outsourced. PK to minimise its risks will have to spread its purchase costs in different markets.

Non-financial indicators

(i) **Order book size**. Boeing and Airbus routinely announce the size (if not the value) of the order book. This can be used as a **proxy of future market share and revenues**, if not profits. There is a finite number of railway companies in the world and a limited number of firms able to do the signalling installation work. Of course, not all competitors release such information.

(ii) **Quality** can be measured internally, in terms of **delays and defects in the production** process, and externally in the systems' **safety and reliability** in use. This has a direct **impact on the cost of the service contracts** over time and **customer satisfaction**. The company's reputation will suffer if its signalling systems are faulty. Hence, complaints, warranty costs and so forth give an idea of performance in this respect – they do not capture, of course, the effect on PK's reputation and brand.

(iii) **'Innovation and learning'**. PK is a technological and world leader. It has to be able to sustain this position. The firm can use measures from the balanced scorecard. This could include the number of new product developments, the number of **patent registrations** and software copyrights and so forth.

(iv) **Environmental impact**. Railways are more environmentally friendly than motor vehicles, so the firm has a good record in this respect. Environment measures can refer to the **short term local impact of installing the new signalling systems** and **construction work**, as well as measures concerning the factory (**pollution**) **and wastage of material**. The components of signalling systems may require the use of rare metals and alloys, so the firm will have an incentive to control costs.

(v) Other **marketing objectives** include contract renewals and industry perception of PK (as evidenced by the results of industrial market research).

(c) **Strategic objectives and market opportunities created by the acquisition of RA Ltd**

Objectives

(i) **Improve profit and ROCE?**

(1) **Disappointing current performance**, with difficult trading conditions and increased competition. Clearly the firm had not met its profit objectives despite an increase in turnover of almost 13%. Similarly, return on capital (calculated as operating profit over shareholders' funds) has fallen to 33% from 37%. Most worrying is the 18% fall in the order book, which will translate into lower turnover later on unless this can be made up. Operating profit percentage has fallen from 8.2% to 7.0%.

(2) We do not know how far these are affected by **falling volumes, price cuts** or **exchange differences. We do not have information** regarding

accounting policies leading to the ROCE and profit calculations. An artificially high figure for capital leads to higher depreciation and lower profits – perhaps useful for tax purposes.

(ii) The **acquisition offers some help** in dealing with these issues, **but only in the long term**. PK's group accounts will benefit from the increased turnover even though PK's return on capital will fall. To a degree, however, the fall in the value of the Rand may make any gain dependent on accounting policies adopted and there are clearly opportunities to improve the performance of the company.

Market opportunities

(i) The African market may offer scope for **expansion in the long term**.

(1) RA's **lower cost base will enable it to expand** into African markets, because components manufactured in Europe, say, would be too expensive.

(2) Future reductions in **political risk**. Such markets, given the current political climate, offer high political risk. On the positive side, state control of the economy has been reduced in those countries, whose governments with limited resources are trying to rebuild their infrastructures.

(ii) Providing that RA improves its quality of output to something approaching world class, PK can use the firm as a relatively **low-cost source of components** for its operations elsewhere, and also for export to other firms **especially in developing countries.**

(iii) PK can use RA as a vehicle to **introduce advanced technology** into the African market, depending of course on quality improvements.

(iv) The first opportunity, closer to home, is to **turn round the performance of the company** to re-establish its reputation.

(d) **Managerial, cultural and financial considerations**

Financial considerations

(i) **The cost of the acquisition**. RA is a private, unquoted company (as indeed is PK), with a family ownership large enough to form a blocking minority. Relations between family shareholders in businesses of this nature tend to be fraught, and family members might wish to drive a hard bargain. As the firm is **not quoted on a stock exchange** in South Africa, there is **no readily available means of assessing its value**; PK's financial staff and advisors will have to work out what they regard as an appropriate price.

(ii) **Currency affects costs and profits**. Clearly, the fall in the Rand makes the acquisition far cheaper – snapping up the company now may therefore seem like good sense as, eventually, growth and a stronger exchange rate can be expected in the South African economy. Currency risk will also affect PK's reported profits and cash flows which will clearly be lower because of the exchange rate. There may be a source of profits, if RA provides components for PK's operations elsewhere.

(iii) **RA is under-capitalised, but what type of investment is needed?** Importing large amounts of machinery and computer equipment from outside South Africa would entail no reduction in the size of the investment in sterling terms arising from the weakening Rand. If the investment involves locally produced material, on the other hand (eg new buildings), currency falls would reduce the amount of the investment required in sterling terms.

(iv) **Profits and financial regulations**. PK needs to ensure that there are no problems arising from repatriation of profits or cash flows. Many countries have liberalised capital flows recently, but there still exist restrictions in some developing countries.

Cultural considerations

(i) **Cultural differences within South Africa: legacy of apartheid**. South Africa contains people of many different ethnic and language groupings, and until the end of apartheid these differences were rigidly policed. For example PK probably conducts its business in English. This is now one of several official languages in South Africa. Perhaps the low level of training and quality is related to **communications problems** arising out of linguistic differences. Successful and sensitive management of these issues is vital to the long term success of the company.

(ii) **Cultural differences between countries.** PK's organisation culture might conflict with the South African context. In other respects, there may be cultural similarities: South Africa's legal system might have similarities with the UK's.

(iii) **PK is already a multi-cultural company** with manufacturing plants and projects in progress world-wide, not only in the wealthier industrialised world. PK therefore is experienced in dealing with these problems.

Managerial considerations

(i) **Legacy of apartheid**. Nothing is said about the internal management of RA at the moment, and about how the abolition of apartheid has changed the system. In the past, some management positions might have been reserved solely for the white minority. There might thus be a legacy of **mistrust and thwarted aspirations** which the arrival of PK's expatriate managers, perhaps, would do little to dispel, without consciously addressing the problem.

(ii) **Total quality requires teamwork** and initiative from the workforce. It is probable that command and control management methods were used. It might be harder breaching the cycle of distrust. PK's involvement will probably be welcomed given the investment in the business and the security this should offer the company over the long term.

(iii) **Shareholders.** PK would be best advised to buy a controlling interest. A significant minority interest would create problems in PK's exercise of control over the company.

(iv) **Local or expatriate managers.** PK will be keen that its investment is worthwhile and will lead to improvements within the company. To do so, PK may have to make the existing management redundant if they are unable to adapt to new conditions.

(v) **Organisation structure and culture.** RA will have to be re-organised to facilitate PK's control, and also to act as a spring board for an expansion into other African markets. The marketing department, if one exists, will have to be reorganised to cope with the expansion. There will be stronger role for human resources management, as the workforce will require training and the firm will have to build a corporate culture.

(e) **Difficulty in measuring performance under new ownership**

(i) The **management information systems may have been poor,** so accurate and detailed information may not have been available.

(ii) There will be a **period of transition**. On taking over the company, PK will be introducing many changes to management, systems, training, organisation structure (possibly) and management information. This will complicate performance measurement which always depends on comparisons.

(iii) **Accounting policies**. PK may have to write down some of RA's assets: RA's ROCE may have been manipulated to produce artificially low profits. This immediately will improve ROCE and, because of lower depreciation, profitability. From that time on, the firm will not be comparing like with like. Attention to cash flows will be most important.

(iv) **Attention to quality**. We already know the defect rate, and levels of performance in this regard can be monitored easily. As well as crude measures of the defect rate, there may be other aspects of waste which can be accounted for. Attention to avoiding defects in production should in the long term improve quality, providing that enough training is given.

(v) **Productivity**: comparisons of labour and capital productivity are slightly misleading.

Labour is cheap in developing countries because, compared with the developed world it is relatively unproductive. So comparing RA with a plant in Germany, say, is not appropriate as Germany has an infrastructure of training and so forth which developing countries do not have. Levels of literacy and numeracy tend to be lower in many developing countries.

7 HAULAGE: COMPETITION, POSITION AND MARKETING

Pass marks. Competitive forces and competition have featured in a number of sittings of the exam, so part (a) should not be too problematic.

Examiner's comments. Although a small, low margin business, the case offered a good test of a number of competitive models. Some candidates were aware neither of Porter nor the marketing mix - such candidates should not be presenting themselves for this examination. In part (a), many grasped the five forces model, but failed to apply it. The SWOT or position audit in (b) was well answered. Surprisingly, candidates had difficulties with (c)(i), as there were many obvious sources. Part (c)(ii) is fundamental to the syllabus, but answers were disappointing. Part (d) saw many candidates unable to apply the marketing mix. Some candidates discussed generic strategies, but this was only acceptable if supported by consideration of the mix.

(a) **The nature of the competitive environment faced by H Ltd**

The competitive environment can be outlined using Michael Porter's five forces framework.

(i) **New entrants**. Road haulage is a fairly **easy industry to get into**. All that is needed is an HGV licence and a bank willing to lend money to buy a lorry. Other regulatory requirements raise the cost of entry somewhat, but even so all that is needed is a friendly bank and some initial capital. Customers have few switching costs, and can easily contract to another distribution firm. Some firms, such as TNT, benefit from economies of scale, and others (eg Eddie Stobart) are able, by product differentiation, to promote a brand image.

(ii) **Substitute products** to road haulage are the railways, air and water transport. Air freight tends to be very expensive. Rail only becomes economic beyond certain distances and even then relies on lorries for delivery from the railhead to the customer. Canal freight is very specialised.

(iii) **Suppliers** are van manufacturers, oil companies, garages and suppliers of other general business services such as accountancy. Their **bargaining power is low**. The government is a supplier of a kind, in that it builds roads and the necessary infrastructure. As suppliers of labour, drivers have low bargaining power in the long-term as they can be replaced but in the short-term they can cause severe disruption.

(iv) **Customers have relatively high bargaining power**. In most cases, switching costs are low, although distribution is vital for many businesses - but if necessary, some firms can do their own distribution in-house. This is exacerbated by the fact that C accounted for 70% of turnover. Unless H can win back the business, this revenue will inevitably fall. Furthermore, H is not big enough only to be a contractor - as an occasional subcontractor, it is near the bottom of the pile.

(v) **Competition is fairly intense.** There is a large number of firms, both small and large. Barriers to entry are therefore pretty low, and the road haulage industry is populated by relatively small outfits.

(b)

> **Pass marks**. The phrasing of the question suggests a more wide ranging approach could be adopted than CIMA's own definition of position audit would suggest. The position audit impacts on the corporate appraisal, or SWOT analysis, which is why our review of external factors is slightly more extensive than a position audit would be on its own.

According to CIMA a position audit is 'part of the planning process which examines the current state of the entity in respect of resources of tangible and intangible assets and finance, products, brands and markets, operating systems such as production and distribution, internal organisation, current results and returns to stockholders'.

Internal factors

Tangible assets

(i) The **fleet of lorries** has been partly upgraded. Only 25% of the tractor units are brand new, but the policy indicates a rolling programme of replacement to keep costs under control. The units are obviously serviceable.

(ii) M is in a good position regarding its **land,** as it is able to move to an industrial estate. However facilities on the new site are fairly primitive and more money is needed to be spent. The new repair facility remains to be built. Stricter safety regulations may lead to increased costs.

Intangible assets: none, apart from its reputation. (Personnel issues are covered under 'internal organisation'.)

Operating systems such as production and distribution are not really identified, other than maintenance. The new facility should address this weakness, but there are still problems related to maintenance and parking.

Internal organisation. For a firm this size, H has done fairly well, especially with regard to its finance department which is successfully collecting and reducing the credit period. Financial systems are a strength, in the short term.

Human resources are both a strength and a weakness. M himself is obviously an experienced manager. There is a slight downside risk however that the business depends too much on him. Were he to suffer a heart attack or a prolonged period of sickness, the business would not survive; the firm suffers from a lack of management depth - the business is small of course, but this makes it more vulnerable unless there are systems of people in place able to develop the strategy. Given that the firm has lost 33% of its business with a major customer, M can be expected to be suffering from stress.

External factors

Products, brands and markets

H operates in two product-market areas, both in service industries, haulage and training. Training is an example of **diversification,** supported by synergies in the use of the site and in the expertise needed. Although training is a successful business, it will remain local and small scale, although it is an effective use of facilities.

The **threats** are of new competition and the further reduction in business from C. Opportunities include extending the 24-hour service.

Of course, whilst C Ltd offered security and useful sales revenue, no information is given as to relative profitability of this particular customer. In the short term at least, this customer is important nonetheless.

Opportunities include developing the market for training - but this is a sideline, however successful, and it would not replace the main haulage business. However, it can be developed further, especially when the main parking and maintenance facilities are transferred to the new site. The maintenance is an example of related diversification based on existing competences and equipment. The 24 hour service could be introduced at the new site, which is on the industrial estate.

Other external stakeholders

The local community is increasingly agitated about noise. This should reduce at the old site, when the new site is fully operational. The nature and timing of any actions the local council and residents will take are still uncertain.

The bank. Finance is a possible area of vulnerability. Although the Bank has funded additional new loans for the development of the land, the financial risk to the bank is low (because of the security), but the firm has to meet the **cash outflows** of both interest and loan principal. The bank requires statutory financial information and a forecast.

Summary

The firm has many strengths, and in the long term it should be able to diversify successfully (training and maintenance) as well as building the core business. The firm has a strategy even though it is not explicit.

The main worry is in the short to medium term. Having taken on new debt, the firm's existing and dependable source of cash (C Ltd) is turning bad. The firm may be faced with a rough ride as it tries to deal with building up a new business and increasing cash flows whilst facing greater demands from the bank.

(c) (i) **Use of information, internal and external in marketing strategy**

Marketing strategy and the corporate strategy are intimately linked. The main subjects of marketing strategy are the needs of the customer and how these can be satisfied with an appropriate marketing mix, in other words products and markets. With the possible defection of C Ltd, and the new diversification opportunities, customer needs will become increasingly important.

The purpose of external information is to find out about existing and future customers and what will affect them, as well as other matters which relate to industry structure.

External sources of information include the following.

(1) **Public databases**

(2) The **trade press,** for product and service innovation and intelligence regarding trends in the industry as a whole.

(3) The **local press** (trends in the local environment).

(4) **Local government planning offices** (eg there may be planning applications held by the county or district council for review for new industrial developments in the immediate locality). H Ltd will be able to exploit proximity as a competitive weapon (**place**) and advertise its presence (**promotion**) to local businesses.

(5) **Highways agency and local government roads department** for details of any schemes to improve the local road infrastructure.

(6) **EU and government directives** about lorry size and capacity and safety standards.

(7) **Competitor intelligence** (eg their prices).

Internal sources of information relevant for marketing include the following.

(1) Records of existing customers, level of demand, trends in demand.

(2) Records of complaints, and whether these resulted in lost business (seasonality).

(3) Enquiry records (especially if no business resulted).

(4) Business refused (and why - eg if customer asked for a service which H Ltd was unable to provide).

(5) Payment history.

(6) Price list, if any

(7) Past advertising and promotion expenditure (and its success).

It is quite possible that H Ltd's internal records are deficient, as they seem based on accounting. The information above can be used to analyse H's customers and their needs, and how the firm has met them in the past. Furthermore, the firm should be able to glean some information about its marketing expenditure.

(ii) **Strategic management accounting information**

> **Pass marks**. The question asked for the use of strategic management accounting information both for decision making and for cost control, two separate, if interrelated, uses.

Strategic management accounting information should assist the strategic decision-making of the business. It is not designed merely to track costs throughout the accounting system for the purposes of financial reporting, important though this is (for companies house filings, tax computations and the bank). The bank's demands for information are of strategic importance given they are relevant for the loan approval. So conventional accounting information remains relevant to the firm's strategic objective, in satisfying a major stakeholder, the bank.

Ward cites a number of **aims of a strategic management accounting system.** These include: decision-relevance; identifying the type of decision; comprehension by managers (not just accountants); the ability to distinguish between discretionary and engineered costs, and discretionary and committed costs; the use of standard costs strategically; and allowance for changes over time.

H does not have a sophisticated costing system, as the business itself is not terribly complex. The need for **strategic** management accounting information is however very important as the company is effectively diversifying from its core haulage business into maintenance and training. These are strategic decisions with a long term effect on the profitability of the firm.

Strategic management accounting information (SMAI) also has to have an **external focus** and a **future orientation**.

Decision-making

Decision making should follow the general principle of **ignoring sunk costs**; Ward goes further than this to say that **committed costs** should be ignored for decision making processes as they cannot be avoided. Ward suggests that three types of decision are particularly pertinent: entry to a new business area (eg servicing other firms' vehicles, training their drivers), changing the balance of resources and exit decisions. H is not considering exit.

What to do with the new land. This involves a decision to **enter a new business area**. Currently, the new site is a sunk and committed cost. For decision making purposes, the firm should decide whether it is worth building the maintenance facility or whether more contribution could be generated by using it as a parking space.

(1) SMAI implications would be the need to **model future cash flows** for a number of uses of this site, with a realistic element of how much could be made from it.

(2) An external orientation would suggest that H reviews what **other firms** charge for similar facility or indeed what other haulage businesses pay.

(3) A **break-even analysis** would suggest the necessary **economies of scale**: once H knows its customers' costs, it can offer a cheaper service.

This is strategic as it involves awareness of customers' value chains: H Ltd can use its own haulage business as a model.

The firm has a strategy for the site but it does not appear to have been costed. Some options are still open - the diesel tank negotiations have not been concluded; therefore this potential cost is still discretionary.

Resource allocation decisions. Ward identifies that SMAI should ignore sunk costs, as we have already suggested, and consider **opportunity costs**. For example, the resources directed at the training business in terms of space and personnel might be better employed elsewhere and might earn a higher contribution if redirected. SMAI should be provided to indicate these opportunity costs.

The planning process. The sorts of decisions above appear throughout the planning process. Supporting data needed to provide the analyses above include the following

(1) **Environment analysis**. Market size/market share analysis will determine the availability of economies of scale.

(2) The customer's own costs (modelled on customers' value chains).

(3) **Product life cycle/BCG analysis.** This will enable H to model its future costs (eg with learning and scale economies, the cost of providing a service will come down).

(4) **SWOT**. Competitors' costs (eg garages) and prices are important as a strength is only **relative** to competition (and is only perceived by the customer).

(5) **Strategy evaluation**. SMAI will include DCF models to evaluate different strategies. This means that something equating to the **cost of capital** needs to be established. H is a privately owned firm, and so M can more or less determine what profit he wants to make - but the bank's interest charges can be a good basis for estimating an interest cost.

Cost control

Too often, **cost control** has been an issue of reconciling standard costs to budget. Variance analysis has been a means of tracking costs rather than using them for any strategic purposes. Cost control implications of SMAI could include the following.

(1) **Avoidable/unavoidable costs**. Avoidable costs can be controlled easier than unavoidable costs.

(2) **Discretionary/engineered costs**. Some costs, such as petrol, are engineered in that they are necessary for the business to survive at all, and they have a direct relationship with the amount of work done. Discretionary costs can be avoided in the short term. Both suggest different approaches to control. Engineered costs can be reduced in some cases, for example, by switching to low taxation fuels. (The UK government is encouraging the use of liquid natural gas for fuel, as opposed to diesel.) Discretionary costs can be cut more easily. An example is the trade off between maintenance and new products. Poor maintenance increases the risk of failure.

(3) **Customer profitability analysis**. This should be relatively easy to prepare.

- The firm has few administrative overheads and the cost of each journey in terms of driver hours, overtime and so forth can be easily logged. One question will be how to account for **depreciation** and wear and tear of the lorries.
- The costs of the journey can easily be compared to the profit and a margin assessed.
- Some customers can be offered discounts to encourage further use.
- The number of journeys commissioned by a customer is also important.

This information should be easily prepared from the existing accounting data - the firm might need to consider the interest cost of slow payers.

(d) **Marketing strategy**

The marketing strategy is based on the marketing mix. We can employ the services marketing mix, in the context of diversification, for H. The marketing mix must maximise capacity usage (of vans and the time of any training and maintenance staff).

(i) **Product**

H is providing three types of product: road haulage (directly for customers or as a subcontractor); maintenance and overnight parking for other firms in the business; and forklift truck training.

(1) For haulage, a speedy and reliable service should be provided.

(2) Maintenance has a higher level of risk; the firm might be sued if a customer's lorry is poorly maintained. In maintenance speed is necessary, so that customers' vans need be off the road for as little time as possible: as H is a haulier itself, it knows the customers' business very well and should be able to devise service packages that customers will like.

(3) Forklift truck training is a separate business whose output is measured by results (good drivers, and better operated warehouses): for training, speed is less the essence than reliability.

Each service should have its **own marketing mix.**

(1) Haulage is forced to compete on price: reliability is necessary to be in business at all and margins are low, but the firm can offer guarantees as an additional inducement to customers (provided these do not offer unnecessary risk). It is unlikely that the firm could charge much more. however different haulage deals could be offered (eg same day delivery etc.)

(2) Maintenance packages can be designed around H's experience of customer needs, taking seasonality into account. 24-hour shift working - although expensive as a result of unsocial hours and overtime - might be an attractive service innovation for some customers.

(3) For forklift truck training, the firm needs to get itself certified as an approved trainer.

(ii) **Price**. Price strategy is determined by the wider conditions of the business.

(1) There is little scope for premium pricing for haulage, but the firm can offer discounts for repeat business, and premium prices for a premium service in some cases.

(2) For maintenance, again there is plenty of competition, but H does offer a 24-hour service, for which a premium could be charged.

(3) For forklift truck training, the price can be set at what the market will bear, as there seem few competitors in the vicinity. Again it should encourage customer retention.

(iii) **Place**. Place is largely a given: the firm's two sites. The leased land has yet to be developed. Its location on the industrial estate is convenient. The existing site is probably crowded and has encountered opposition for night time movements. With two sites, H is able to be flexible with regard to place.

(iv) **Promotion**. Little promotion at all has been done so far - H has been content to rely on one main customer, C, and to wait for offers from other firms to arrive. With C's partial defection, H will have to promote itself more efficiently and effectively. Obviously, TV is out of the question. Advertising in trade and local papers - conceivably on local radio - combined with direct mail to existing and potential customers might be useful. As part of a promotional campaign, some thought might have to be given to the company's **name and logo**, so that it is recognised and distinctive.

(v) **Physical evidence** includes the environment of the service encounter, and is intimately involved with place - but it also concerns the appearance of the lorries (cleanliness) and their drivers (eg clear identification of the firm, badges and so forth) as well as the design of documentation (for ease of use). As the firm is trying to attract new business, such matters are important in creating the right impression and giving the firm a distinct image.

(vi) **Processes**. In a logistics business, efficient processes are intimately bound up with the product and service offered. For example, the most efficient maintenance techniques enable this service to be provided cheaply, quickly and to the right standard. The same is true of the haulage business. Processes are also part and parcel of training to ensure that every aspect is covered methodically.

(vii) **People**. Appropriately qualified personnel (eg with HGV licences) are essential for the business to function at all. The firm could have a policy of enhancing the skills levels (eg of its garage maintenance staff) by only employing those with appropriate qualifications.

To summarise, the marketing mix will need a heavier accent on promotion, especially to widen the customer base and to advertise the new services, but fairly inexpensive methods can be used. Although a low margin business, a number of service innovations can be introduced to maximise capacity usage enabling some differentiation on a premium basis.

8 T PLC: PEST FORCES, INVESTMENT AND THE PLANNING GAP

Pass marks. This question incorporates most of the syllabus areas, particularly section (c) Position Appraisal and Analysis. The case is a topical one, in that the telecommunications market in Europe is undergoing substantial change. Note the requirement for a calculation in parts (c) and (d). Be prepared for these in the exam. You may need to undertake them in order to support your arguments and commentary. This paper presupposes your ability to perform calculations such as DCF.

It may seem obvious, but time management is crucial in the case study. Be sure to give it enough time, yet also be strict with yourself on each question part. Never be tempted to spend longer on a section worth five marks than on one worth fifteen marks, even if you know more about the topic.

Other points. Some confusion may have been caused by the precise wording of the question in part (b). In Ansoff's terms 'market development' has a precise meaning, the sale of the existing/product service range to new markets. It seems likely that the examiner wants you to examine all the options on the grid, otherwise the question would not have been phrased in terms of the Ansoff matrix as a whole. Similarly, the scenario mentions 'diversification' – we would suggest that this is more accurately described as product development, selling new products/services to current markets. The key is to look at the issues and make clear what you mean.

Examiner's comments. It was disturbing in part (b) to see how many candidates confused Ansoff's Product/Market Growth Vector matrix with the Boston Consulting Group Growth Share matrix. In section (ii) of part (b) candidates were not expected to quote the CIMA definition of the planning gap, but they should have been able to say what the planning gap is. It is unacceptable to enter this examination without the basic underpinning knowledge.

Many candidates displayed evident weakness in their ability to perform calculations when the requirement does not come presented in the form of a traditional question.

The last part of the case study had ten marks attached to it. Too many candidates either failed to answer this part at all, or paid it very little attention.

(a) **Political and legal factors**

Everybody has access to a phone and thus there are **many stakeholders**. As a major service provider, employer, economic force and public company, T has to deal with customers, employees, the government representing the public interest and, as T is a profit-orientated business, **shareholders.**

With an 85% share of the market, T is dominant. As T is no longer under public ownership, consumers' and competitors' interests are protected by a **regulator**. Ultimately, the effect of the new competitive environment, enforced by a regulator, will be to **reduce market share.**

As T is central to the communications infrastructure, its activities are relevant to the **government's own objectives**. The government may wish to improve communications in education. This influence may eventually ensure market growth.

Economic factors

The UK is T's **home market,** which currently provides the bulk of its revenues. A healthy economy means that consumers have more money to spend on communications. This affects the **total size and growth of the market**.

T is not market leader in any **overseas markets,** so T can only grow here. T has the opportunity in markets which are rapidly growing to increase revenues and share. Of course, many developing markets are able to 'leap-frog' some of the old technology and so T can install the newest technology.

There is also a market for services on a **global scale,** hence the various merger discussions and strategic alliances in the telecommunications industry. International economic integration offers a major opportunity.

Wider economic trends influence T's **cost of capital** (eg interest rates). T is also seeking a target **return on investment**.

Social factors

Most households in the developed world have a phone. T will try to encourage greater usage. Social trends include:

(i) Increased use of the **internet** as a leisure activity
(ii) **Home**working, home banking and home shopping
(iii) The demand for **mobile phones**

Technological factors

These are most uncertain because of the ways in which technology develops and changes.

(i) **Convergence** between telecommunications, computing and broadcasting. For example, the telephone cable can be used to carry TV.

(ii) Technological developments enable a **reduction in the cost base** as new systems are brought in.

Clearly, to offer the service to business and domestic users, T should be at the forefront of **technological developments**.

(b) (i) The **Ansoff matrix** enables companies to consider product/market issues in a systematic way, and offers four options to T plc:

Penetration: more of the same product or service to existing customers

Market development:

Domestic markets. T has 85% of its home market and there is a regulator whose job it is to ensure that the market is a competitive one. The only hope for a **penetration strategy** is by an increase in the size of the market, but this does not seem to be likely. T cannot increase prices, because of the regulator's **price cap.**

Mobile phone communications is an expanding market in the UK and overseas, and so is a useful option for penetration strategies.

Overseas markets. As a new entrant, T is in a better position to pick up customers, especially if overseas governments are keen to promote competition.

Product development:

(1) **Internet**-based services can be offered, in tandem with other suppliers
(2) **Cross-selling.** Mobile telephony can be sold to the same customer base.

T should be able to exploit its knowledge and R & D. Examples in recent years have been caller-identification, call-waiting, voice mail. T is also able to offer business users a wide range of communications service needs.

Market development

T can enter countries which are already developed through the use of joint ventures (as BT has established throughout Europe), enabling it to benefit from local knowledge and lower risk.

Diversification

The chairman intends to diversify. Given that new services will be marketed to the existing customer base, this is more characteristic of product development.

True diversification involves a more radical shift but T is only considering selling more hardware.

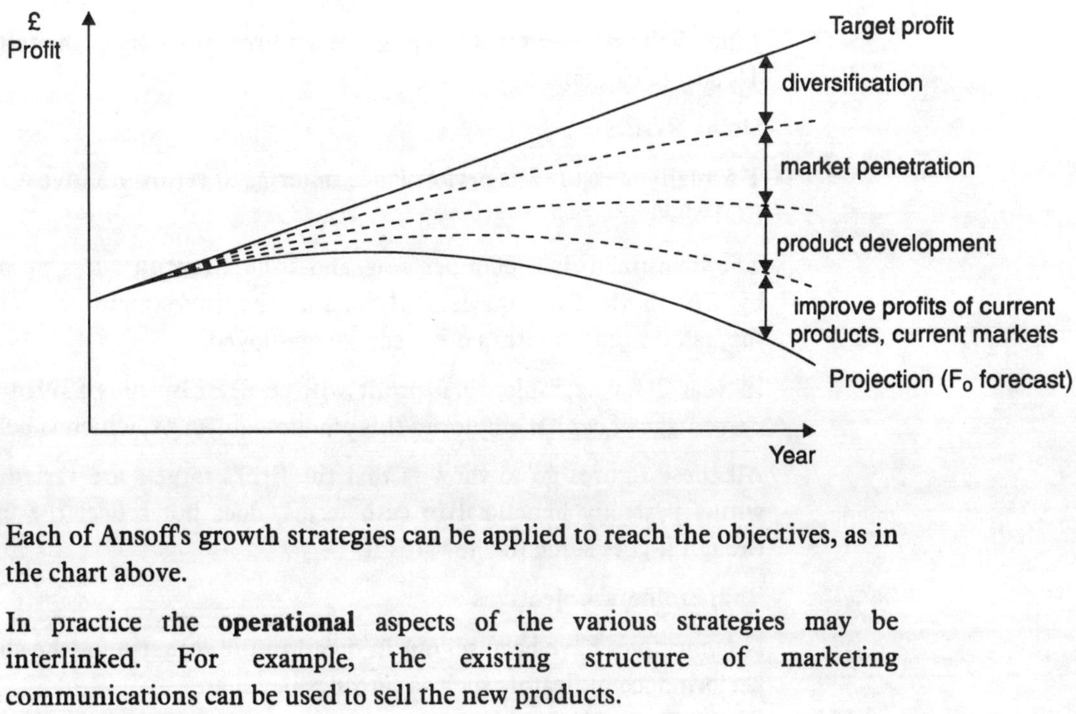

Each of Ansoff's growth strategies can be applied to reach the objectives, as in the chart above.

In practice the **operational** aspects of the various strategies may be interlinked. For example, the existing structure of marketing communications can be used to sell the new products.

(ii) **Gap analysis** is the identification of the difference between the firm's objectives (profit, sales revenue, or return on capital) and the likely outcome of continuing with current activities.

(1) **Ansoff** suggests that the gap can be filled by one or more of the strategies identified above. Provided the organisation has the **resources,** they are not mutually exclusive.

(2) **Strategies of withdrawal are excluded from the Ansoff matrix**. Withdrawing from a market might have a very healthy effect on profit and ROCE.

(3) Applying Ansoff to gap analysis also ignores other **techniques** for increasing profits and ROCE, such as cutting costs or making better use of capacity.

(4) Finally, the Ansoff matrix takes no account of **risk**.

(c) T's proposed investment in technological improvements

Using DCF

Investment outflows are £200m per year for three years. The discount factor for three years at 11% (cost of capital) of 2.444 gives a present value of these cash outflows of £488.8m.

Revenue inflows. The assumption is that market share will increase from 85% to 95%. Currently, turnover, for 85% of the market is £16,613. This will increase to £18,567m, an inflow of £1,954m pa. Applying the discount rate this gives a present value of £4,767m over three years.

Variable costs are 80% of the incremental revenue. This amounts to £1,954m × 80% = £1,563.2m or, applying the discount factor, £3,814.2m over three years.

Net present value calculation

	£m
NPV of investment	(488.8)
Revenues	4,767.0
Variable costs	(3,814.2)
Net present value	464.0m

Thus the investment yields a positive net present value, as the return is higher than T's cost of capital.

Using ROCE

T actually measures its performance in terms of **return on investment,** with a target ROI of 20%.

The investment is £200m per year, and annual revenues less variable costs increase by £391m (ie £1,954m less £1,563m). The investment should perhaps not be separated from the firm's other capital employed.

In year 1 for example, total profit will be £3,323m plus £391m = £3,714m. As a percentage of capital employed this amounts to 16.7%, which is below target.

All these figures go to show is that the firm's targets are varied. The investment, whilst perfectly beneficial in cash terms, does not reflect the target ROCE even though it goes some way towards it.

Shareholders' objectives

No objectives have been set out in detail in the scenario for the share price or other performance indicators such as earnings per share.

Further considerations

Aside from using DCF and ROCE to measure the benefits of investment in technological improvements, other considerations will impact upon the decision to invest. These may include the following.

(i) **Competitor response** to the initiatives. Technology is often a barrier to entry, but it may also be easily copied and improved upon. Quality improvements have to be real to be a source of competitive advantage – if customers perceive no difference between T plc and its competitors, then the investment may not lead to increased market share.

(ii) **Strategic direction**. Are the improvements in quality, and investments in technology, in tune with T plc's strategic objectives? Will they lead to increased long-term shareholder value, as the directors hope?

(iii) **Cost of inaction**. T plc may not be able to afford to stand still. Technological development in the telecommunications market occurs at a fast pace, and failure to keep up now will mean that much greater effort is needed in the future simply to maintain market share. Loss of market share to more innovative competitors could be disastrous and very difficult to recoup. With deteriorating performance, the return required from investment in new technology would be greater if T plc were to close the planning gap and achieve growth objectives.

(d) (i) **Closing the planning gap**

The chairman hopes to achieve a target ROCE of 20%.

On capital employed of £22,150, this suggests a target annual profit of (£22,150 × 20%) £4,430m. In other words, annual profit will have to increase by £1,107m.

The new investment, providing £391m per annum, amounts to 35% of the planning gap. Additional profit of £716m is needed to close this gap.

The calculation ignores the following issues.

(i) The risk of **regulatory** response
(ii) **Competitor** reaction
(iii) The need for expenditure to **maintain** market share.

(ii)

> **Pass marks.** Ideas for suitable strategies are flagged throughout the question. Remember that this part of the question does not address market share objectives or innovation objectives but is directly focused on increasing reported ROCE and hence profit over the next three years. Any strategies you suggest must, whatever else they do, be profitable and not require huge investments no matter how large the 'long-term' benefits will be.

To close the planning gap, T has to generate annual profits of £716m. Any new investment might affect the capital employed figure. Projects will be chosen which offer the **highest possible return**.

(1) **More cost cutting**? To chose the remaining gap, T could cut its costs further by approximately 5% (being £716m /(£16,613m - £3,323m). A 1% cut in costs would achieve savings of £143m.

(2) **Penetration (domestic)**. T can encourage customers to make more use of the phone, simply to generate revenue, for the same level of fixed costs. (Friends and Family discounts are an example.)

Penetration (overseas) This is a big opportunity, but not at the expense of a massive investment, which would decrease return on capital, and take time to generate profits. It seems likely that T should concentrate its efforts on alliance with local firms.

(3) **Market development**

New markets can include new overseas markets or new consumer markets.

A genuinely global market is, in a way, a new market. A problem is that prices will almost certainly fall, so T has to position itself to get revenue from increased volume or offer higher value-added services such as network management.

From the chairman's point of view, such alliances can take time to develop. They are also subject to heavy regulatory pressure.

(4) **Product development**. The chairman has already indicated new services, such as home shopping and internet services. T can gain more of the potential revenue by acting as a service provider in its own right.

(5) **Diversification** may offer the highest rewards providing it is **related.** As owner of the hardware and the communications system it stands to profit from the increased traffic.

Summary

Most of the chairman's suggestions offer the prospect of significant wealth – but they seem to be **long-term investments** rather than the focus on the relatively short-term profit and ROCE targets. Cost cutting and market penetration, in the UK and overseas, is the best way to deliver the targets.

9 B PLC: APPRAISAL, ANALYSIS AND STRATEGIC AIMS

Pass marks. Make sure that you devote enough time to the question and have a go at all parts. The examiner recommends that you answer the question parts in order, so that you maintain a logical sequence as you progress through the question. Bear in mind throughout that the company has environmental objectives which will colour all its strategic decisions. So long as you can justify your answers in this light, you will gain marks, so if your approach and conclusions are not the same as ours, don't worry.

Other points. You may have used PEST in your answer to part (a). This model is quite general and the question wanted a specific corporate appraisal, so we have not used it here. Corporate appraisal involves a SWOT analysis. You would have around 20 minutes to plan and answer part (a) in an exam, so if you have not covered as many points as us that is understandable. You should aim to make two or three points under each SWOT heading. In part (b), the examiner was looking above all for the ability to provide a logical answer to a question involving decision theory, so if your conclusion as to favoured strategy is different from the one presented here, that would not have cost you marks. Our answer to part (c) contains some industry examples. These would impress the examiner and show that you have read around the subject, but you would not need such extras to pass.

Examiner's comments. Unfortunately many candidates failed to appreciate how B plc's environmental stance should be kept in mind throughout their answer. Most candidates quite rightly applied SWOT analysis in their answers to part (a). Alternative approaches to SWOT gained credit *where appropriate*. In part (b), the numbers were often poorly analysed. Most candidates addressed the likely reaction of competitors after quality improvements by B plc, but few related the need to ensure that the quality improvements were compatible with the organisation's environmental objectives. In part (c), many candidates applied principles of environmental management accounting techniques, but often did not relate these specifically to B plc's environmental objectives. Much has been written about environmental management accounting techniques in *Management Accounting* over the last couple of years. The requirement for a recommended strategy in part (d) was reasonably answered, and again it was important to relate such a strategy to B plc's environmental objectives.

(a) B plc is being increasingly threatened by competitors and so needs to undertake a review which will help it to achieve its desired performance. This review encompasses the company's strengths, weaknesses, opportunities and threats (**SWOT analysis**) and is otherwise known as **corporate appraisal**. The appraisal draws on information about objectives, current position, its expected position and forecasts about both the internal and the external environment.

Strengths

The company is fairly **long established** with a strong worldwide presence and hence **brand recognition**. Management is likely to have a broad range of **experience** ranging from international operations to public relations. The chairman strongly believes in the company ethos and this is likely to be shared by all employees.

The company still has **strong profits** (although they are under threat) and a **market share** of 90%, which is likely to have few equals in any private sector market.

Along with strong brand recognition, the company has a good **public image**. Ecological issues are at the forefront in the 1990s, and the UK government recently (November 1998) announced a blanket ban on the testing of cosmetics on animals. This has underlined the company's stance. Being one of the first companies to product an environment audit report will have also made a positive contribution to the company's standing.

Investment in modern production facilities and a well established research and development function are also strengths possessed by B Plc, as are its evident optimism and ability, despite being such dominant players for so long, to come up with **new ideas and options** for the company to promote its objectives still further.

Weaknesses

The company is potentially hidebound by its strategic objectives of **ecological purity**. It may be **restricted** in the products it can be associated with, which would limit growth and inhibit its long term ability to compete. On balance, however, the strategy works well, attracts customers and has enjoyed spectacular success to date. Customers may not be happy with any dilution of its ecological aims, leaving the company worse off if they desert it.

Control of overheads could be a weakness. Enlarging head office is an unusual move, on paper at least, in these days of rationalising and cutting down administrative costs. The full justification for head office expansion is not given by the scenario so it is difficult to comment any further.

Opportunities

Most of B plc's outlets (750 out of 1,000) are located outside the UK, so there may be an opportunity to **expand** on the 250 outlets covering the **domestic market**, given the recent ban on cosmetics testing on animals by the UK government which could conceivably affect some competitors. This strategy may not be viable as the UK market may be saturated by B plc branches and incapable of supporting more (no information is given in the scenario on geographical segmentation of sales and profits - the overseas outlets may only account for 30% of sales, for example). **International expansion** may also be a goal.

Opportunities exist for more **promotion** of the company, by giving out more information on its activities to counter threats by competitors. **Further research** could be undertaken to find new products still within the company's ecological framework.

The company has outlined two different strategic options (increased quality and increased promotion) and opportunities for **cash inflows** as outlined by the management accountant would help the company defend its position against competitors, and maybe investigate the possibility of **acquisition** of a competitor to consolidate market share. It is clear that the company has no intention of standing still.

Threats

A company with such a strong ecological stance as B plc is always open to the attack that it is not living up to its ethical principals and competitors may jump in to fill the gap. This charge was levelled against The Body Shop in the UK.

Market share may be eroded if a competitor finds a new ecological cause to champion before B plc has time to jump on the bandwagon - it cannot become complacent and regard itself as the only company with an ethical conscience. The high standards maintained to date have to be consistently applied to avoid charges of trading falsely on the public's faith in the company as an environmental advocate.

Difficult trading conditions are referred to in the scenario and this will impact on trading as perceived 'luxury' items are the first to go from the shopping list. Despite its ecological concern the public may become **price sensitive** and not pay the extra for a B plc product (information on prices is not given in the scenario, although it may be reasonable to assume that, using The Body Shop as a reference point, a jar of B plc moisturising cream is more expensive than a supermarket own brand equivalent).

Finally, **operating profit margins** have declined from 18.8% to 13.9% in the space of a year. Difficult trading conditions and increased overheads have been blamed, but the company may have cause to review its entire cost structure and make changes to restore profitability.

(b) The options evaluated involve a choice between improving quality and increasing levels of promotion.

Quality improvement is aimed at enhancing the product in the eyes of consumers, and therefore encouraging them to buy both the improved products and also other products in preference to those of a competitor, who may have an equally strong ecological ethic. It must be noted that the quality improvements should be in line with B plc's aims.

The management accountant has done the calculations and the **expected value** of pursuing this option is just under £38 million. This is not an **actual** value that would be achieved as the result would be somewhere between £50 million cash inflow in the case of a positive response, and £10 million in the case of a weak market response, after deducting the cost of the investment.

Increased promotion will bring a net cash inflow of £30 million after deducting the cost of the initial investment. This strategy is aimed at increasing already strong customer awareness and clawing back some of the 10% market share that has been lost to competitors.

There is therefore a range of expected outcomes: varying from £10 million to a £50 million benefit under the quality improvement plan, or a £30 million benefit under the plan for increased promotion. Given that both projects are being assessed over a four year period, it is relevant to consider the **initial cost of the investment**.

The increased quality program will yield an **expected** benefit of almost £38 million after an investment of £50 million. Increased promotion yields net inflows of £30 million after investing £10 million, and clearly provides the better return and net benefit, moreover involving the company in committing less money. This is not necessarily the end of the story, however.

The **attitudes** of B plc's managers will be of significance in making the decision, as some may want to aim for the return of £50 million if they perceive that it is a **risk** worth taking. It is difficult to predict with certainty what will be customer and competitor reaction to the improved quality, so **risk averse** managers may on the other hand prefer the relative certainty of a £30 million return via increased promotional activity.

The decision will also depend upon the validity of the forecasts and estimates that have been prepared. **Sensitivity analysis** would usually be conducted to see how the decision would change if certain parameters were varied. For example, if net cash inflows from a strong and weak response were reduced to £80 million and £55 million respectively, the expected value of the quality improvement programme would reduce to £22.5 million after deduction of the initial investment. The costs of carrying through either of the improvements may increase if B plc delays its decision and costs of such commodities as advertising space begin to creep up.

Competitors, as noted in the scenario, are bound to react to either strategy. A recent advertising campaign by The Body Shop in the UK eschewed traditional selling of cosmetics, which uses what could be seen as impossible ideals of beauty. It tried to do this by employing realistic images of women. Competitors fought back by claiming that their advertising was designed to appeal on an aspirational level, which was enjoyed by most customers. The Body Shop's campaign was possibly less effective as a result.

Promotional campaigns are therefore always capable of being **imitated** if not openly attacked, and there will not be a significant time frame within which to enjoy an advantage.

Launching improved quality products may take competitors by surprise, but it is always possible that competitors could exaggerate their own quality improvements to try and stay in line with B plc. **New packaging** could be introduced relatively quickly and give competitor's products a fresh edge, which could be enough in the customer's eyes to make the product appear of equal quality. Publication of **specific information** on quality improvements which the competitor will find it hard to match is therefore desirable, either in the accompanying promotional literature or on the packaging.

It must be remembered by B plc that the quality enhancements will have to be **communicated** to the customer. It is not clear from the scenario whether this cost has been built into the £50 million investment, or whether it would be an **additional factor** to consider.

Assuming that the **financing** for either of the options is available, either from external sources or B plc's own reserves, the favoured strategy is not clear-cut, and depends upon the variables outlined above. Quality improvements are a true investment in the **longer term** future of the company which may generate benefits for the whole product range. They are likely to be longer lasting in their effects than specifically targeted promotional campaigns, so for this reason the £50 million invested may have a longer 'life' than the four years currently associated with it.

(c) B plc pursues an avowedly environmental strategy which is key to an understanding of the company. The management accountant should be seeking to provide information which can assist in **promoting these aims**. Taking the business environment as a whole, few organisations have the full picture of the implications of the environment for their long term business. This is largely because accountants, environmental managers and others with **relevant information** are seldom brought together to consider it. B plc may be an exception to this rule, but it is likely that even it could make improvements to the environmental information that management receives from the **planning and accounting** functions. If they have not done so already, the designation of an environmental 'champion' in those departments, who could develop a checklist for addressing and understanding key environmental and energy issues, would be a significant contribution.

An ecologically friendly company might aim, among other things, to use less energy, produce less waste, recycle, emit less harmful by-products into the atmosphere and promote trading with less developed economies which avoids exploitation of their comparatively underdeveloped status. Such policies have attendant **costs and benefits,** and may also be regulated by **legislation.** Infringement of anti-pollution legislation, for example, would involve B plc in heavy fines and, perhaps more significantly, be disastrous for its corporate image. Pressures in this area are likely to increase rather than diminish.

The management accountant should therefore be providing information and reports in areas such as the following.

(i) Trends of **energy costs** and usage. There are obvious savings to be made via waste minimisation and energy efficiency.

(ii) **Cost/benefit analysis** of alternative energy sources where this could be appropriate.

(iii) Trends of **waste** production and disposal, especially as regards the costs. To take an example, Zeneca Agrochemicals has saved million of pounds after identifying its 'costs of waste' through examination of process and product data. Similar savings may be available to B plc.

(iv) Analysis of **recycling** levels throughout the company, from waste paper at head office to recycling of by products from one production process by using them as inputs to another. Sites may be compared and encouraged to improve where possible.

(v) **Press comment** on company activities and details of any **pressure group activity,** and analysis of its impact on corporate image and environmental aims.

(vi) The management accountant may want to assess whether **new data sources** are needed, such as the establishment of new account codes for recording the costs of **different energy sources** to enable comparisons to be made.

(vii) Monitoring of government **policies** on emissions, and effects of **legislation** in environmental rates, such as the UK landfill tax or more severe taxation on carbon emission, whenever these apply to B plc.

(viii) Analysis of sales revenues from its newspaper.

(ix) **Competitor analysis**, where they are undertaking similar environmentally benign activities to B plc, to enable B plc management to better understand its **position in the industry**.

(x) Ideas and cost/benefit analysis for ecologically sound **promotional campaigns** (perhaps with the involvement of the marketing department).

(xi) **Segmental analysis**, on a regular basis, of the international trading being undertaken by B plc, with relative profitability of each segment. Trading with a particular area may be far less profitable than other areas, but B plc may have made it a policy to trade with them due to some particular environmental objective.

Management will want to see how much its particular choices are costing the company and assess progress towards the ultimate objective. An example may be setting up a small production facility (at considerable initial expense to B plc) in a far-flung area, which provides employment for a very poor community, with the ultimate aim of developing a much larger production site. Such a policy would need to be continually monitored for its **effectiveness** and **comparison to budgets**.

Even though it is driven by environmental concerns, B plc is a business with **shareholders** who must be sure that their value is being **well managed**. Therefore the strategic and financial imperatives driving any company will also be relevant to B plc. **Budgets and plans** must be set and monitored, different **cost centres** should be charged with achieving targets (on waste management costs, for example) and reports on company performance should be regularly produced. These are all likely to have an environmental slant.

Environmental policy will have impact on areas ranging from **project appraisal** to **setting prices**. A project that has the required return may be rejected because it has a damaging effect on the environment, or fails to live up to its initial promise.

Employees should also be encouraged to promote the environmental aims of the company, perhaps via internal competitions for new ideas, or 'suggestion boxes'.

(d) B plc uses it strongly environmentally conscious image as a source of significant **competitive advantage**. The opportunities and threats present in the market place should be explored from this standpoint.

Cosmetics testing on animals has been banned in the UK, so this presents an opportunity to promote B plc's virtues. It can exploit its stance as the 'only way', and convince customers that by supporting B plc they are fulfilling their **social responsibility**, in all sorts of other areas (such as fair trade with less developed economies).

Using **Ansoff's product/market growth** strategies model it is possible to formulate various strategies from the green perspective.

Market penetration, seeking higher sales in existing markets, by promoting its green ethics and stressing product quality.

Market development via opening up new markets for the existing products. This will involve significant promotional activity. It is not clear from the scenario whether there is room to expand the UK market or whether B plc must look overseas (to more countries, or the existing 40) to expand its customer base.

Product development would involve new research and investigation of new products, possibly in response to a new find by a competitor. New distribution channels may open with the discovery of new markets as outlined above.

Diversification may come from mergers, takeovers or joint ventures with local traders. This may bring B plc into contact with suppliers of goods which could form the basis for a new product range.

As described in part (a) one of the potential weaknesses of B plc is its possibly limited **product range**, which could be expanded to include related products such as clothes. **Expansion and diversification** makes this kind of strategic choice more likely, as the market for cosmetics and skin products is not limitless and is subject to competition. **Barriers to entry** are coming down (market share has fallen from 100% to 90%) and B plc may want to see off the threat of new entrants by **enhancing its offer** to customers in a way that competitors would find difficult to match. This would protect revenues (which have increased by 13.6% over the past year) and encourage future growth.

10 WG PLC: PRODUCTS, OBJECTIVES, PROFITABILITY AND STRATEGY

Pass marks. This case study is a relatively straightforward one, with some quite basic numerical analysis and an uncomplicated scenario. The key as always is to allocate your time correctly.

In our answer to part (a) we have referred to product development in connection with the Ansoff matrix. Part (b) calls for application of the five competitive forces, and the question even tells you it is Porter's model in case you need a memory jogger!. The numerical analysis in part (c) points you in the direction of contribution per limiting factor. Our answer includes a reference to the importance of stock turnover in the analysis, which is not addressed by CIMA's model answer. You should have few difficulties in applying the marketing mix for part (c)(ii). Part (d) requires a discussion of the practical issues surrounding strategic alliances. This does not necessarily call for an assessment of the advantages and disadvantages of such alliances, although an analysis along these lines may have been appropriate and would have earned marks if it clearly addressed practical issues.

Examiner's comments. There was a disappointing number of candidates who insisted on delivering a SWOT analysis when the question was clearly about threats only. Use was made of the Ansoff matrix or BCG analysis, but often not sufficiently directed to the question set.

(a) A successful business must develop its **products** and **manufacturing methods** on a regular basis if it is to maintain market share. This calls for strategic decisions on the part of WG plc. Its stated **objectives** include the develop **innovative** medicines and services, which it can only do by **investing** in development.

Product development has the advantage that it forces competitors to innovate and discourages newcomers with a significant **barriers to entry**. If WG's existing products were to fall in price and it did not have new products (such as Goffstop) to fall back on, its profitability would suffer. The **expiry of patents** and the opening up of a product and its market to competitors also highlights the danger of lack of innovation. Sales from previously central products will fall. In the case of WG, a product which previously accounted for nearly half its turnover is expected to contribute only 10% in future.

Failure to invest in research and development in such an innovative and **dynamic sector** is therefore of paramount importance. Nobody expects scientific or medical research to stand still while there are still diseases that need cures, or where existing cures are being resisted by new strains. A company that rests on its laurels, enjoys high profitability and seems to give little back will at the very least suffer a grave image problem.

Shareholders and investors in a pharmaceutical company should expect to see investment in research and development, but will also want to see more immediate profitability. The decision about the relative size of investment and payments for shareholders each year is a trade-off that the directors will have to make, when balancing **long and short term** performance issues.

WG does have significant production facilities, with much of its research being sponsored. The investment in research into malaria treatments has paid off, in that the company is able to donate supplies of the medicine to overseas areas. This will do a great deal to enhance WG's reputation worldwide.

Cash flows contributed by the products in WG's portfolio can be illustrated using the Boston Consulting Group **Growth Share Matrix.** This model demonstrates that, depending upon a product's individual **life cycle,** that product will go through stages of cash generating ability. Staple products are known as '**cash cows**' - they have a high market share in a stable market, and can provide the cash resources to invest in the development of '**stars**', which are those products which achieve a high market share in a high growth market. Coffstop may have the potential to become a star, and WG must make sure that there are others in the pipeline.

For the reasons outlined above, investment is crucial in maintaining market share and the appropriate resources must be allocated. The **expense** and the **risks** associated with significant investment in research and development must, however, be taken into account. It may take several years for the benefits of investment to be felt on sales and profits, so the products chosen for development must be carefully selected.

(b)

> **Examiner's comments**. Most candidates did pick up the clear contradiction in the objectives, although some seemed worried about presenting their view that disease eradication as an objective ran a poor second to profitability. If the evidence is there for such a view, then candidates should not be afraid to say so.
>
> This part of the question was concerned with *application* of Porter's five forces model, so a straight repetition of the model was not enough. Candidates needed to consider which of the forces were most applicable to the company and their effect on objectives.

The twin **aims** of sustained profitability through development of innovative medicines, and the elimination of disease, are **contradictory** when taken to the logical extreme. If all disease was eradicated, then WG would have no market in the long term.

The overall corporate **mission** aims to reflect a short term responsibility to **shareholders,** as well as recognition of wider **social responsibility**. Investment in developing markets overseas, such as the donation of the malaria treatment, will impact on profits. Public and government challenges to high levels of profitability reflect the fact that WG is expected to contribute to **furthering knowledge**, perhaps via **collaboration** with universities or research institutes. This will reduce WG's profitability while new products and markets are developed, but it will be aware of the latest developments and should be able to capitalise on them in the future.

Porter's model of the **five competitive forces** shows those factors which collectively determine the potential of the industry as a whole. Some industries have bigger profit potential than others. The pharmaceutical industry is one such profitable sector, because **competition** is relatively restricted by the significant levels of **research and development** that are required. The competitive forces outlined by Porter and their applicability to WG's objectives are as follows.

(i) **Threat of new entrants.** This is not a significant threat for WG. It is the product of a merger and enjoys significant **economies of scale** that a competitor is unlikely to be able to match. Manufacturing and research facilities operated by WG are amongst the largest in the industry and its **distribution network** is global. A new entrant would have to build up a large market share very quickly to be able to sustain its cost structure and hence profitability. World class pharmaceutical manufacturers are few in number.

    WG has built up a good **reputation** for its products and is likely to have strong customer **loyalty**. Its brands may crowd out the opposition, and **patent rights** give it breathing space to develop further products, as discussed above in part (a). Access to sources of raw materials on favourable terms may include a long-term low-price **supply** contract.

(ii) **Bargaining power of customers.** Customers usually want better quality products at the lowest possible price. If they are successful in getting this, WG's profitability will be affected. It has to concentrate its efforts on creating a strong **brand image** so that customers are not tempted to shop around, especially when patent restrictions are lifted. The **price awareness** of customers will vary. When product quality is important to the customer, as it is likely to be in the market for medicines, the customer is likely to be less price sensitive and so WG will be more profitable.

Customer demand for a long running profitable products may divert production resources from developing more innovative products, but if such long running products are 'cash cows' they may also be able to contribute towards development of disease-eradicating 'stars'.

(iii) **Bargaining power of suppliers.** WG can access supplies on a **global** basis and is therefore unlikely to be controlled by an individual supplier. A supplier is unlikely to be able to demand higher prices from WG. This depends on factors such as the **technical specification** of the products being supplied, and how important a particular supplier's products are for WG. Where there are just one or two **dominant suppliers,** they may be able to charge monopoly prices.

The development of innovative products and working towards the eradication of disease does depend very strongly upon an adequate supply of technical specialists and **expertise.** Research scientists are likely to be able to exert some bargaining power over WG when negotiating salaries. The few world-class companies will be competing for the best **human resources,** which could be limited in supply.

(iv) **Existing levels of competition.** There are only a few players in WG's market. Competitor activity usually means **price** competition. **advertising** battles, sales **promotion** campaigns, new **products,** improved levels of **service** and provision of **guarantees** or warranties. Competition can help an industry to expand by stimulating demand.

The level of competition found in the pharmaceutical industry is likely to be less intense than that found in other sectors, and firms will try to avoid competing on price. Competition is likely to be centred around innovation and research activities, as has already been discussed. This keeps WG ahead of the competition and moves it further towards the eventual eradication of disease.

(v) **Substitute products.** These are unlikely to come from another industry, but will arise when patents run out and competitors can start making their own version of a successful product. Again, the vital importance of research and development must be stressed.

(c)

> **Examiner's comments**. The calculations in this part of the question were very simple, but some candidates confused CVP and DPP. Many candidates were not able to perform CVP analysis, which is simply unacceptable at this level. A number of candidates did not apply marketing strategies at all in answering part (ii), although the marketing mix was an obvious model to use.

(i) (1) Retail pharmacists prefer Peffstill because they calculate that it achieves a £2.60 contribution compared to £1.00 for Coffstop. This analysis ignored the fact that Peffstill comes in a bigger bottle and so takes up more shelf space. **Cost volume profit analysis** demonstrates the contribution achievable with regard to the limiting factor (retailers' shelf space) as follows:

	Peffstill	*Coffstop*
	£	£
Selling price	10.00	1.50
Cost per bottle for retailer	7.40	0.50
Contribution per bottle	2.60	1.00
Sq cms shelf space per bottle	60	18
Contribution per sq cm in pence	4.33	5.56

Coffstop generates the most contribution per unit of limiting factor for the retailer. A retailer who stocks both products should give as much space to Coffstop as possible. Coffstop also sells more per week on average.

(2) Applying **direct product profitability** to weekly sales, thereby taking all costs into account:

	Peffstill	*Coffstop*
	£	£
Contribution per bottle as above	2.60	1.00
Holding costs	0.80	0.40
Net contribution per bottle	1.80	0.60
Contribution % of sales price	18%	40%
Shelf area required per week	60 sq cm × 20 bottles	18 sq cm × 120 bottles
=	1,200 sq cm	2,160 sq cm
The total weekly contribution	£36.00	£72.00
Per unit of shelf area	3.00p	3.33p

This analysis gives the same result for the retailer as cost volume profit analysis, indicating that Coffstop should still be the preferred product of the retailers. The shelf area required per week is the minimum that should be allocated to each product by reference to average sales.

It should be noted that **stock turnover** is also a relevant consideration - WG plc may offer to replenish the retailer's shelves twice a week, thereby halving the amount of space needed to support the same sales volume. This will increase the amount of contribution per scarce resource.

(ii) The marketing strategy of Coffstop can be planned with reference to the marketing mix.

Product

Medical research and opinion has shown the Coffstop is the more effective product, and therefore brings a better 'package of benefits' for the customer. WG plc has a strong reputation with a wide portfolio of products, which Coffstop should be linked with in the customer's perception.

Price

Coffstop is cheaper per bottle, which will encourage customers to purchase it, if only on a trial basis. The customer must have six times as much dosage of Coffstop and Peffstill, making the comparable prices £9 and £10 respectively. Therefore on price Coffstop has an advantage.

Peffstill may respond by dropping its price, or promoting the convenience of only having to buy only one bottle, but customers have come to expect discounts for buying in bulk. The fact that Coffstop is cheaper as well as being a better product than Peffstill would appear to give it a significant advantage.

Place

Coffstop is sold in retail pharmacies, who need to be taught that Peffstill makes less of a contribution. Retailers may decide to stock Coffstop instead of Peffstill, or at least reduce their stocks of Peffstill while Coffstop is introduced to the customers.

Both drugs are available over the counter from pharmacies and so it is possible to start selling Coffstop through supermarkets, who sell cough medicines (assuming that Coffstop is a cough medicine - the scenario is not specific) and often have their own in-house pharmacies. This will enable WG to reach an even larger market.

Promotion

The promotion campaign should highlight price and product benefits. Television advertising for cough and cold medicines is common, often on a seasonal basis, so this may be an appropriate product launch medium. Radio advertising, coupons, and free trial sizes are all possible promotional activities. Giving medicines away to the general public may be frowned upon, especially if Coffstop should be carefully administered, but free trial packs could be a suitable promotional tool when introducing the product to doctors.

Literature and posters detailing Coffstop's benefits could be distribution to doctors' surgeries and pharmacies. Making the packaging attractive while containing the expected safety features (child-proof caps, for example) will be a task for WG's marketing or design department.

(d)

> **Examiner's comments**. On the whole this question was reasonably well answered, although some candidates were tempted into stating the advantages and disadvantages of joint ventures.

WG is the product of a merger, which has enabled it to achieve economies of scale. Without going so far as another merger or takeover, a **strategic alliance** may offer benefits to WG, for example in the **value chain**. WG's expertise in production and research may be supplemented by the other's marketing and distribution facility. **Complementary competences** can be exploited to mutual advantage.

Alliances can also be a **learning exercise** for each partner. An alliance with a university would provide a good example, with WG taking on trainees or work experience placements from the science faculties. New technology offers many uncertainties as well as opportunities, so the funding of expensive research via an alliance can spared the **risks.**

Practical considerations include potential **conflicts of interest** between the parties. Disagreements may arise over **profit** shares, resources **invested, management** issues (including project management and resource management), **products** to be developed and **marketing** strategy. The alliance must be entered into on a **contractual** basis so that each party is clear about is **rights and responsibilities.**

Regulatory bodies may be concerned that a strategic alliance between dominant market players could be anti-competitive, and the venture may be subject to investigation before it is allowed to go ahead. The parties to the alliance must make sure that they have fully researched the implications of their venture for the industry to be able to present their case favourably to the regulator.

Resource investment includes consideration share of expenses and tangibles such as **capital** contribution, but also intangibles such as **expertise**. Joint ownership of patents for products that are developed by an alliance could be fertile ground for arguments about fair share of returns, unless the agreement is carefully and thoroughly worded. Such alliances may therefore involve significant legal bills.

Management issues also involve **staff** considerations. Staff loyalty may be tested, and **confidentiality** of individual business processes may be threatened. It may take a while for trust to be built up, but the benefits of such an alliance are likely to make the practical considerations a hurdle worth clearing.

11 BSN: STRATEGIC PLANNING, STAKEHOLDERS AND SUBSIDIARY PERFORMANCE

> **Pass marks**. The planning model required in part (a) would have presented most candidates with few problems, although it is very important to relate the planning model you describe to BSN's own circumstances. You may have chosen to draw a diagram, and CIMA's model answer indicates that is an acceptable approach provided you discuss the model's application. We have divided our answer into a consideration of strategic *analysis*, strategic *choice* and strategic *implementation*.
>
> **Examiner's comments**. This question addressed all four aims of the syllabus and required both numerical analysis and a discursive approach. Most candidates could relate to parts of the question very well although part (f) caused some problems, despite the topic having appeared in the November 1997 sitting.
>
> Part (a) was generally reasonably well answered, with most candidates able to apply a rational planning model. Few however explained which aspects of such a model were most appropriate to this type of organisation. The answer required a discussion of the model's application.

(a) Strategic planning divides into a number of different stages: strategic **analysis,** strategic **choice** and **implementation.** Providing a structure to the process serves to focus BSN management attention and make sure that all relevant factors are considered.

Strategic analysis is a consideration of BSN's overall strategic stance and the organisation's underlying values. This encompasses **mission, goals** and **objectives**. For BSN, this includes providing an excellent public broadcasting service and committing to 'inform, educate and entertain'. These are qualitative objectives. The government as a relevant stakeholder is concerned with 'best value' for the licence payer and has set an ROCE target of 6% per annum. This is a quantitative objective, based largely upon efficiency savings being made wherever possible.

A further component of strategic analysis is an assessment of 'where are we now?' for BSN. This can be addressed by a **corporate appraisal** (SWOT analysis) via environmental analysis and a position audit.

Environmental analysis should lead BSN to consider likely changes in communication technology and government policy on the licence fee agreement. If the basis for the licence fee changes, this would have a major influence on BSN's financial objectives. Competitors utilising satellite technology may begin to offer services that BSN cannot provide. A **position audit** will review BSN's current resources, and in particular the quality of its product offering compared with the competition, and its customer base.

Forecasting a likely future position for BSN after consideration of these factors will lead to identification of a **planning gap** that will need to be filled by appropriate courses of action. In other words, BSN will have to make **strategic choices**. Ideas have to be generated and evaluated for best fit with the organisation's objectives. The chosen strategy has to be **implemented** via appropriate marketing and production channels and ultimately **review and control** procedures must be in place.

(b)

> **Pass marks**. Part (b) is specific in its requirements, but do not lose sight of the fact that the examiner is interested in *strategic* developments. Asking employees for a report on their opinion of the staff canteen will not help BSN towards its strategic objectives.
>
> **Examiner's comments**. Part (b) saw candidates tending to focus on operational issues rather than on strategic development, but the question was reasonably well answered.

In determining the future strategic development of the organisation, a public service organisation dependent on licence fee income like BSN is well advised to consult with its **stakeholders**, both internal and external. In this case we are concerned with the viewing public, the government, employees and management. Their views must be represented by the Board when deciding on future strategy.

The viewing and listening public

BSN already consults regularly with audience representatives and independent review panels to ensure accountability. These stakeholders are likely to have valuable information and opinions, and BSN could back them up with further research covering the wider viewing and listening public in all areas of the country and overseas. Reactions to a new radio service could be predicted by conducting an opinion poll, or chairing a public meeting. BSN must be careful that the views it canvasses are representative of the population as a whole.

The government

The government, and its relationship with public service broadcasters, is an important factor in determining strategic direction. Government policy is a significant element of BSN's environmental analysis. Links with government officials and other politicians will ensure that BSN is included in discussions of relevant policy. Issues on which BSN, as a public service broadcaster, could be expected to contribute, will be fully discussed. New regulations on broadcasting standards may be planned, for example, which BSN would need to be aware of.

Employees and management

Employees of BSN may be expected to contribute ideas both formally at strategy-related meetings, and informally. Small working groups might be set up to look at different strategic initiatives, which then report to the whole organisation via newsletters or the company intranet. It is likely that senior management will have a greater role to play in strategy development than employees lower on the hierarchy, but no potential source of information or ideas should be rejected in the early stages of strategic analysis. It should be remembered that with jobs to defend, managers and employees often have negative power to impede implementation. Employees of the radio service may be concerned at the implications of separation of their division.

(c)

> **Pass marks**. Part (c)(i) is a very straightforward exercise and the case study scenario virtually tells you how to perform the calculations. There is very little reason for any candidate not to have scored heavily here. Your answer to the second part of the question should focus on ways of improving ROCE. Quality implications of cost cutting should be mentioned.
>
> *Other points.* You may not have questioned the validity of ROCE as a suitable measure of performance for BSN, but do not worry. So long as you had some sensible suggestions on improving ROCE, this would be enough for a pass mark.
>
> **Examiner's comments**. The ROCE calculation required in part (c) was a straightforward exercise which many candidates could not perform, despite the fact that the case itself provided an illustration! Average capital employed, according to CIMA's *Official Terminology*, is 'the average of the capital employed at the beginning and end of the year'. Candidates who did not apply this achieved little credibility and displayed a fundamental lack of knowledge. Numerous candidates concluded that as there was a deficit in years 3 and 4, an ROCE could not be calculated. That said, many candidates calculated the projected ROCE quite correctly and achieved full marks.
>
> The second part of (c) hinged on the fact that the organisation was going to fall short of its ROCE targets – options could have included reducing costs, increasing income, reviewing the asset base, quality considerations or demand generation. Few candidates questioned the validity of ROCE as an appropriate measure in the first place.

(i) The calculations of ROCE over the next four years of the licence fee agreement are as follows:

	Year 1	*Year 2*	*Year 3*	*Year 4*
	$m	$m	$m	$m
(1) Excess/(deficit) of income over expenditure (working 1) =	76	42	(39)	(123)
(2) Average capital employed (working 2) =	1,288	1,347	1,348.5	1,267.5
$\frac{(1)}{(2)}$ =	5.9%	3.1%	(2.9)%	(9.7)%

Working 1

Year 1 $2,190m - $2,114m = $76m
Year 2 $2,234m - $2,192m = $42m
Year 3 $2,234m - £2,273m = $(39)m
Year 4 $2,234m - £2,357m = $(123)m

Working 2

Year 1 $\frac{\$1,250m + \$1,326m}{2} = \$1,288$

Year 2 $\frac{\$1,326m + \$1,368m}{2} = \$1,347$

Year 3 $\frac{\$1,368m + \$1,329m}{2} = \$1,348.5$

Year 4 $\frac{\$1,329m + \$1,206m}{2} = \$1,267.5$

(ii) It is clear from the figures in (i) that BSN is heading for significant difficulties. The government **target ROCE** of 6% will not be met at all after this year, and in years 3 and 4 of the agreement BSN's expenditure will be in excess of expected income, generating a negative ROCE. As long as ROCE is the measure being used, ways to improve it will have to address either **increasing income, decreasing expenditure** or **decreasing capital employed.**

A strategy combining all three elements is likely to be the most effective. As it is unlikely that the government (or public) will countenance an increase in the licence fee, BSN will have to seek alternative sources of income. This may come from selling programmes and/or expertise to overseas organisations, merchandising, further subscription-based services (as described in the scenario) or educational services for schools and colleges. The **objectives** of the organisation in terms of 'excellence' and the vow to 'inform, educate and entertain' must also be kept in mind. The possible impact on comprehensiveness and **quality** of a rush to generate new sources of demand and therefore income must also be considered. Programmes must continue to be seen by the viewing public and the independent review panels as 'fair, accurate, impartial and [meeting] the highest standards of good taste and decency'.

Cutbacks in the asset base to improve ROCE (selling production facilities, for example) may also have adverse implications for quality. If quality is not maintained, a long term future for BSN could be unsustainable.

Reduction in costs may offer the greatest scope, but again quality may become compromised, although from the scenario presented, much emphasis has been placed on maintaining quality while reducing waste, surplus capacity and duplication of effort. The establishment of an internal market is very likely to have had a beneficial effect on quality, as programme makers have a wider choice of possible sources. The Board of Directors has a successful recent history of **efficiency savings**. Estimated expenditure is forecast to increase at a flat rate of 3.7% each year. How much realistic **analysis** has been put into these rather general forecasts, and is there any room for cutting costs, especially in the years when licence fee income is static? These estimates may need to be revisited.

It should be noted that return on capital employed is a performance measure with some **drawbacks**. Capital employed is notoriously suspect as a financial measure, since a book value on the balance sheet will probably bear little or no comparison with the 'true' value (replacement cost, net realisable value or economic value). **Long term** requirements for investment in BSN will be difficult to balance against **short term** ROCE targets, since longer-term projects will take more time to generate a return. BSN should try to persuade the government that other targets, more in keeping with objectives related to the **needs of viewers**, should be considered.

(d)

Pass marks. Make sure that you focus on the objectives of the organisation. Its public service nature will always colour its thinking, and the contrast (and potential conflict) between commercial advertising revenue and public service objectives should have struck you. We have taken that line in our answer.

Examiner's comments. Part (d) was not well answered, with many candidates failing to focus on objectives. Answering a question often requires more than stating the obvious – how does the obvious then relate to the circumstances of the case?

If the radio and television service are separated, the **objectives** for BSN are likely to become separated into two distinct streams: one for television and one for radio services, although the indications are that the organisation wishes to continue to be a public services broadcaster and this will be possible. While BSN's overall objective of remaining a high quality public service broadcaster could continue, the basis for obtaining revenue will have changed. Different funding mechanisms are very likely to impact upon content, and this is likely to impact on BSN's avowed public service objectives.

The vast majority of households in the UK own a television set. Households that only own radios are likely to be comparatively rare, and furthermore the possibility of charging for radio services separately as a way of subsidising possible lower television licence fees is likely not to be very lucrative. Radio services have not been specifically charged for in the past and the imposition of a fee is likely to be strongly resisted.

Financing the radio services by **advertising revenue** is a big step and is likely to be met with concern by a public that equates high advertising revenue with **commercial,** rather than **public service** broadcasting, objectives. The licence fee could be said to provide a stable funding mechanism allowing the production of distinctive programmes, while advertising revenue is likely to lead to a less distinctive service. Programme makers might start chasing advertising revenue on the back of tried and tested programme formats. We have seen in the UK a proliferation of television programmes based on veterinary practices, home improvements, garden 'make-overs', disastrous weather and dramatic rescues because if they prove popular once, they are likely to be produced and broadcast again and again.

Stakeholders in BSN, such as overseas listeners and politicians, may be concerned about the implication for editorial content if radio services are separated. Objective coverage of overseas events may be compromised if advertising revenue is to be sought. The **government** may be persuaded to provide some funding for this arm of the service.

It is unlikely that BSN's dependence on the licence fee as a stable source of funding can be reduced significantly. The opportunity to seek alternative sources of funding for the radio subsidiary, however, will open up BSN to **commercial pressures** that may have the positive effect of stimulating **innovative** ideas and services that could heighten its **reputation** and further its objectives of providing a comprehensive and distinctive service. Channel 4 in the UK could be said to have successfully met such a challenge. The licence fee as it stands will theoretically be able to 'go further' when producing television programmes, if radio services are attracting additional funding from previously untapped sources.

(e)

> **Pass marks**. Part (e) requires specific application to BSN's situation rather than general comments. How do the types and sources of information that you identify help management of the new radio subsidiary? What specific information might a radio service require?
>
> **Examiner's comments**. Candidates answering part (e) all too often provided general comments without specifically relating them to the separation of the radio subsidiary, or showing exactly how the items identified might provide appropriate information for management purposes. Questions of the relative importance of different types of information, the cost of collection and impact on existing systems were not addressed.

Performance measures enable an organisation to assess how far objectives are being achieved. **Financial performance indicators** concentrate on profitability, growth, liquidity, capital structure and market ratios.

From the point of view of the radio subsidiary of BSN, the management accountant should provide the Board with regular details of cost and advertising revenues (assuming that this is the agreed funding mechanism for the new service) to assess **profitability** against budgets. This provides a basic measure of both advertising **sales growth** and **operating income**.

The directors will be concerned to see that the new division is meeting its targets, and that it compares well to similar radio services which operate from advertising revenue.

Liquidity is measured by **cash flow**. Cash flow statements will have to be prepared for the new subsidiary, because adequate cash flow is key to survival. The pricing policy of BSN will be relevant here because if revenues (and hence cashflows) prove inadequate, the pricing of advertising 'slots' may have to be reviewed.

Return on capital employed has already been discussed as performance measure. It has its drawbacks but the directors may wish to see how the subsidiary is performing against government target ROCE, and in comparison to television services. Direct **comparison** of the profitability of radio and television services may no longer be meaningful because licence fee income and advertising income are different in nature. **Return on investment** as a measure may be more directly comparable.

Managers in the television subsidiary will have no control over licence fee income (at least for the next four years) while radio managers can influence advertising revenue via marketing initiatives. These initiatives will cost money, as will collecting the advertising revenue generally. New management accounting systems will have to be developed for the new funding system.

Details of the **market share** (both listening figures and share of advertising revenue) will also be highly relevant when assessing current performance and opportunities for future growth.

Performance measures can be both financial and **non-financial**. Non financial measures may give a more timely indication of the level of performance achieved, and for BSN's radio subsidiary would probably concentrate on audience-related factors. These are most likely to be the ones that can help further BSN's **objectives** of public service excellence. These would include the outcome of audience surveys on quality and enjoyment of programmes, listener rates and trends and (possibly) complaints received.

Major advertisers using BSN could be reported and reviewed each month, and this information used to generate repeat business and investigate possible new advertising clients.

Other performance measures may be **employee** related. The radio subsidiary will be highly 'people-based' and is likely to be characterised by highly autonomous production staff, so staff turnover, training costs and other personnel related matters will merit attention on a regular basis.

(f)

Pass marks. Marketing research was also examined in November 1997 (see question 65 in this Kit). Make sure you have set out a distinct framework for your research plan. Defining objectives is a key step. If you are properly prepared for this question, it is an easy task to slot in 'BSN-specific' issues to each stage. Collecting information is just one part of the process.

Examiner's comments. Part (f) was answered very badly indeed. It required an application of Kotler's theory. Few candidates explained the need to define objectives, develop the research programme, collect and analyse information, and present findings. Most concentrated solely on information collection, which is difficult if objectives have not been defined! Many candidates resorted to the Marketing Mix and AIDA, but these cannot inform how a programme should be carried out.

Marketing research involves the following stages of work.

(i) **Definition of the problem.** An individual marketing research project cannot be undertaken successfully until BSN's **research objectives** have been properly defined. BSN wants to attract listeners and advertising revenue – what information might be needed? Suggestions could include:

(1) analysis of **competitors**
(2) **demographic** information
(3) **market** analysis (size of likely advertising revenues)
(4) suggested new shows and features
(5) **financial viability** of the new subsidiary

(ii) **Definition of the objectives of the programme**

The research programme's **output** is likely to be a report with recommendations on attracting listeners and advertising revenue for presentation to the Board, and the likely overall viability of the new service.

(iii) **Design of the research and collection of the data**

The research data may be collected with the assistance of a **research agency** if BSN has no marketing research expertise of its own. The bulk of the data collected is likely to be from **external sources**. This may include **published research** of government or industry bodies, which may indicate overall trends in radio listenership and advertising revenues. The **internet** might provide some useful and up-to-date information.

After designing an appropriate **sample** a number of listeners and advertisers should be **targeted** with specific questions (either by postal questionnaire or personal interview) on their likely responses to programme content and advertising rates. Potential advertisers who have never used radio before may need convincing of the effectiveness of the medium. Published radio industry research would be greatly beneficial here.

(iv) **Analysis of the information**

Data will have to be **analysed** using appropriate **techniques**. Statistical consultants may need to be employed to interpret listener attitudes and convert these into likely outcomes for advertisers, as well as determining overall financial viability of the radio service itself. The statistical basis of the research must be understood so that accurate conclusions can be drawn.

(v) **Presentation of the research findings**

The report as presented to the directors should enable them to **reach a decision** as to the likely attractiveness of the new radio subsidiary to both listeners and advertisers, and the best way to market its services.

12 TUTORIAL QUESTION: MISSION AND OBJECTIVES

(a) **Public limited company**

We have listed seven possible objectives here. You may have thought of others.

(i) Achieving a certain level of **profitability**.
(ii) Achieving a certain return on **shareholder capital**.
(iii) Achieving a certain level of **EPS.**
(iv) Achieving **growth,** in profitability, return or EPS.
(v) Maximising **shareholder wealth** (capital gain plus dividends).
(vi) **Survival.**
(vii) Achieving a certain level of **return** without incurring more than a given amount of business **risk**.

(b) **Local government authority**

Here are four possible objectives.

(i) Providing certain **services** to the local **community,** at a certain standard of **efficiency,** and/or without excessive levels of local taxation.

(ii) To **develop the local area** to make it more desirable area to live in.

(iii) To **reflect the opinions** of the local community, and so bring a certain level of democracy to the running of local government.

(iv) To provide a **bridge** between the local community and central government.

(c) To be effective, a strategic planning system must be **goal driven**.

The components of the **mission statement** are as follows.

(i) '**What is our business and what should it be?**' The firm's business in terms of products and/or services and markets, and the identification of future directions.

(ii) The establishment of business **values, attitudes and beliefs**.

Once clarified, the business mission should then remain the focus of the firm's energies for a considerable time A well chosen mission statement can provide a powerful source of motivation for all company personnel.

Goals are general statements of intention which focus attention. These are not objectives as such because they are not **performance-specific** or **time related**. Objectives need to be capable of **measurement**.

Objectives should be **hierarchical, measurable, realistic** and **consistent**. Primary objectives relate to key factors for business success:

(i) **profitability** - ROCE increase;
(ii) **growth** - sales, market share;
(iii) **risk reduction** - increase product, customer, market base;
(iv) **cash flow**.

All functions are deployed strategically towards achieving these objectives. For example, the production function can reduce costs, the finance function can manage funds more efficiently, the personnel function can recruit better people at less cost and the marketing function can grow sales profitably.

Once **corporate objectives** have been established and translated into a co-ordinated corporate strategy the various functions can develop their **own objectives**. **Marketing objectives** are usually expressed in **sales terms** (eg market share, sales revenue, sales volume) and are then translated into objectives for product, pricing, promotion and distribution.

A corporate objective could be: 'to produce **net profits** of £1.8 million in 1995'; a related marketing objective could be: 'to achieve total **sales revenue** of £18 million in 1995 (a 9% increase from 1994)'; and the related promotional objective could be 'to increase **consumer awareness** of the brand from 15% to 30% in 1995'.

The key feature distinguishing missions, policies, aims and objectives are the **time scale** and the degree of **specificity**. They all, however, provide direction and focus, and the benchmarks against which performance can be measured. Missions are broad, corporate and long term in nature whereas objectives are specific, quantifiable and shorter term.

13 MANAGEMENT ACCOUNTING AND THE PUBLIC SECTOR

> **Pass marks**. A topical question, as market-like mechanisms are being introduced to the public sector. A question to avoid if you were not familiar with the subject matter as it is an encouragement to waffle.

(a) The political debate in the UK has shifted from slimming down the public sector, to ensuring that it works **efficiently**. Market forces, or pseudo-market forces are being introduced.

Comments

(i) **The goals quoted seem vague.** It would be difficult to find anybody who does not believe in good quality education and health care. However, they do indicate priorities, on quality as opposed to cheapness, and they seem to stress incremental improvement.

(ii) **The organisational goals embody social priorities.** Hospitals as a rule do not determine whether resources spent in treating illnesses could be used more cost-effectively on **preventative** medicine. That is a matter for government policy.

(iii) The objectives quoted must be translated into more **practical, measurable** objectives and targets. Objective setting and performance monitoring aim to ensure that public services are:

(1) **economical** (do not cost more than is necessary);
(2) **efficient** (get the most output for the level of input);
(3) **effective** (meet the wider objectives set).

(iv) In public services, it is not always easy to **measure the quality of output**.

(1) For example, league tables of exam results have been established for schools to identify which schools get the best results. However, this does not **necessarily** indicate the quality of teaching as results may be more closely linked to the social background of the pupils.

(2) Another example of the difficulty of assessing priorities is that some **resources are so scarce** that some people will not receive them. Some health economists have invented the concept of the Quality Adjusted Life Year (QALY): if only one treatment can be given, there are two patients who need it, and the treatment cannot be divided between them, a calculation can be made as to how long someone's life will be extended by the treatment, and this is multiplied by a factor supposed to represent the quality of that life.

Despite these difficulties, there are some useful performance indicators that can be developed for health care and education. In health care, the **length of waiting lists** for certain operations might be a performance measure.

As more sophisticated costing systems have been introduced to the public sector, so too there has been an increasing role for management accountants, who can provide information as to how those resources are **allocated**. They can then suggest savings.

Management accountants can provide an **accounting system** which can be used to **collect and review quantitative and budgetary information**. They can assess the cost of each treatment, and for each hospital suggest where operations can be contracted out or purchased from private sector health care operators.

(b) **Activity based costing** (ABC) was developed for manufacturing companies to address the problem of overhead absorption.

In capital-intensive industries, where the bulk of costs are **fixed costs**, it is inappropriate to allocate overhead costs by labour hours, which are of decreasing significance. ABC regards labour costs as fixed in the short run..

This cost profile also applies to many service industries. Labour is often fixed in the short run, there are few raw materials, and some items of capital equipment are very expensive. It may not be easy, for example, to allocate a ward sister's time over the patients in her care.

ABC recognises these problems. It tries to identify those **activities** on which the indirect cost is spent, referring to them as **cost drivers**.

The advantage of this approach is that it takes a **critical** financial view of work practices. High cost activities can be identified. An examination of the activities' cost drivers may result in those activities being better designed.

14 PUBLIC SERVICE OBJECTIVES

Pass marks. As the question says, a specific knowledge of the water industry is not necessary to produce a good answer to this question. It is true however that some awareness of industry issues, such as the existence of the water industry regulator, and the fact that some water companies have been criticised for the level of service they provide, would help you to gain very good marks. Without specific knowledge of the water industry, you would still be able to rely upon PEST forces as a framework for your answer, but, as always, remember to remain focused and relevant. The question unequivocally instructs you to do this, by saying that your answer should recognise the public service nature of the industry and its effect upon the organisational culture.

We have set out our answer in report format, although the CIMA model answer does not. Either approach appears to be valid, given the question wording.

Examiner's comments. There were two 'pegs' given in the question on which candidates could base their answers - the public service nature of the industry, and the impact of this on the organisational culture.

On the whole the question was answered satisfactorily, but too many answers did not relate to organisational objectives. Some failed to recognise that the organisation was a private sector company and therefore shareholders were an important consideration.

REPORT

To: Board of Directors
From: Management Accountant
Subject: External influences on objectives and strategies in a public service industry

Our organisation exists within an **environment**, which strongly influences what we do and whether we survive and develop. The strategic planning team must take account of **external influences** in order to produce plans that are realistic and achievable in a changing environment. Any strategy is made in conditions of partial ignorance, with external influences being a major area of uncertainty. These external influences can represent **opportunities** and **threats** to a company in any sector. These are expanded upon in the analysis below.

The **general external environment** includes all the political/legal, economic, social/cultural and technological influences. These are referred to using the acronym **PEST**. PEST factors relevant to our organisation are as follows.

(a) **Political and legal environment**. We are affected by the basic **legal framework** of parliamentary and European legislation, which will require us to supply water of appropriate quality. Any new strategic or technological developments will have to meet these requirements. The existence of **minimum quality standards,** for example pollution controls, will have an effect upon growth and profits.

Now that the water industry is privatised, we are free to borrow and spend as we wish, but the official **regulator** for the water industry, Ofwat, will reflect the government's stance on issues such as pricing. We would not be able to significantly increase our prices without attracting the attention of such agencies.

Similarly, a possible **strategic alliance** or merger with another water supplier may attract attention as being potentially anti-competitive. An adequate water supply is obviously vital for the country, and we can be sure that government attention will stay fixed on its suppliers. We must as a company be co-operative with all regulatory requirements and any investigations. Legislation can be seen as a threat to prospects but our strategy should aim to minimise it by trying to stay one step ahead.

The government's overall conduct of its **economic policy** also affects the company. Taxes and interest rates are an obvious example of where such influence will be felt.

(b) **Economic environment**. The state of the economy affects all organisations. **Demand** for water for **domestic use** is likely to remain fairly stable, subject to seasonal fluctuations, because water is a fundamental requirement rather than a product consumed out of choice. Growth in income levels will not necessarily affect individual demand for water, although increases in the housing stock will increase the number of connected customers. **Industry** demands will vary with the strength of the economy and the opening of new businesses.

For our organisation, our strategic challenge is to match demand to seasonal fluctuations and, in times of recession, be able to emphasise **cost-effectiveness** and continuing profitability against the background of service provision and regulation described above.

(c) **Social and cultural environment**. Businesses have to adapt to society, with the **household** as the basic social unit. Demand for water will be affected by the size of households and number of them in our catchment area.

The **culture** of our catchment area will also have an impact. For example, if there is a large number of parks and gardens then demand for water in the summer may increase more rapidly than it does for other providers. Leisure facilities (swimming pools, for example) will also consume water.

(d) **Technological environment**. Technology contributes to overall economic growth. It can enhance our offer to the customer, and our output, by enabling productivity gains, reduced costs and better quality water. New technology in the water industry is being constantly developed and it has to be a central factor in our strategy.

Quality control is vital and requires investment in facilities. Water quality **improvements** are likely to be finite, and there will be a point at which it is uneconomic to pursue tiny incremental improvements, because the gain to the customer will not be worth the expense of achieving them. As has been pointed out, our pricing policy is closely monitored.

The level of improvement that we want to see will be determined to an extent by the government regulations referred to above, but we may wish to exceed those requirements as part of our strategy. This is an opportunity for the company as it would be both a powerful public relations tool and also mean that we are well prepared for any future tightening of the regulations. It would also make it difficult for a new competitor to challenge our position. Technology is a powerful barrier to entry.

The company should also investigate other advances aimed at improving our service to customers, such as better storage methods to protect against surges in demand. This will help in the provision of a reliable service and will also sustain our public image. Negative publicity from water shortages has been very damaging for other water companies in the UK and has attracted criticism for their directors.

Investment in new technology is a significant expense which may take several years to produce a return, but the public service nature of our industry means that we will be expected to channel at least some of our profits into **service improvements**. This area needs careful management. Large profits and poor service levels will annoy regulators and customers. Our core strategy cannot be solely based on **maximising shareholder return**. It is up to the directors to decide how our company profits are used. A balance will have to be struck between investment in service improvement and returns for shareholders. The weighting given to each will reflect **long term and short term** strategic aims, and a trade off between them.

Other external influences might include **interest and pressure groups**. Environmentalists in particular will be concerned at the impact of our activities. Water treatment facilities have to meet certain standards. Consumers' associations campaign on issues of safety, quality and pricing. The health and safety of the community is a significant responsibility for management to bear in mind.

Some pressure groups are adept at **public relations** and we should always aim to be as transparent as possible so that there are no misunderstandings of our activities. The annual report and accounts is one way of communicating with the public, but we could also encourage visits from interested stakeholders.

The **task environment** relates to factors of particular relevance to a firm, such as its competitors, customers and suppliers. The level of **competition** is currently low due to significant technological barriers to entry referred to above, but we cannot remain complacent. Competitors may threaten to steal customers with a better service. Our **customers** are likely to view us as monopoly providers and for that reason the company must be careful to maintain healthy public relations. Our **suppliers** are also in a position to affect our strategy and profitability with variations in their own prices and service levels.

The conclusion to be drawn is that no organisation, be it a service provider or operating in any other sector, can ignore external influences when formulating strategy. Information about the environment is often uncertain and incomplete, but **external appraisal** of factors relevant to the organisation's current and future activities is vital. It will help a company analyse the opportunities available to it and possible threats to its position.

15 PUBLIC SECTOR PLANNING

(a) **Strategic planning** is a process whereby organisational objectives are set, and strategies for achieving them are identified and adopted. **Management accounting** provides management information for planning, control and decision making. In the past management accounting information has been criticised for not being entirely **relevant** to the strategic needs of management.

Simultaneous introduction of strategic planning and management accounting

(i) **Against:** these processes will be **new** to the organisation, and so it might be easier to plan and implement them one at a time.

(ii) **For**

(1) It will be helpful to know what strategic planning information will be needed when the management accounting system which will provide it is **designed.**

(2) Management accounting should provide data dealing with the firm's **critical success factors;** these will be identified in the first strategic planning process. Strategic planning and management accounting are therefore **complementary** in the current context.

The issues that have to be sorted out are as follows.

(i) **Technical and systems**

Public sector bodies used to prepare accounts on different principles to private sector bodies.

Systems

The introduction of modern business practices means that accounting data will be expected to enable management accounting information to be generated and strategic decisions taken. The type of data already available, and the type of data that should be available, should be identified and compared.

Classification

Balance sheets and profit and loss will need to be prepared, dividing ledger balances into capital and revenue items.

(ii) **Organisational**

(1) A **new strategic planning department** might be set up.

(2) **More accounting systems.** Additional staff might have to be recruited for the new accounting systems, converting data from the old to any new systems etc.

(3) **Training.** Existing staff will have to be re-trained and re-deployed as appropriate.

(4) **Management.** The management structure might also have to be redesigned.

(5) **Contracting out.** It is also possible that some of the agency's functions can be contracted out to alternative suppliers.

(iii) **Implementation**

DocCent needs to ask: 'Where are we now?' It should carry out a **position audit** and **SWOT analysis**. Although it is a monopoly supplier and therefore not subject to competition, it might be compelled by the Citizen's Charter and other initiatives to achieve demanding **performance targets.**

(b) (i) **Government department**

Government departments are **not commercial**. They are financed largely by **taxation.** They are not expected to cover their costs.

Government departments do not always have an **output**.

DocCent collects taxes and issues vehicle licences: its 'output' can be measured. In principle it is only a **cost centre**, but management accounting is still necessary to control costs, and to keep within overall expenditure limits.

(ii) **Agency**

Executive agencies are supposed to operate at arm's length from direct government control: for example, managers have more freedom over recruitment policies.
By setting up the department as an **agency**, and introducing the new accounting systems the government is hoping **to control its costs**, rather than make a profit.

The new managers have some opportunities for extra revenue, to mitigate the administration costs. They may be given the commercial freedom to sell database information, which would be of great interest to manufacturers, motoring organisations and insurers, subject to the requirements of the **Data Protection Act**.

The revenue collection side is not in itself a source of **profit**. Instead, there will be performance targets predominantly based on **cost**, such as cost per transaction processed.

A possibility would be for the agency's managers to agree an overall fee to the government for its revenue collection services and manage the costs itself. The Agency might be able to raise capital so as to generate a **return** for investors.

Although the agency will be managed autonomously, its special status means that it can never function exactly like a private business. However, it can use **strategic planning** to think further than the year ahead, and management accounting techniques to **deploy its resources** most efficiently.

(c) DocCent's planning and resource allocation procedures would be enhanced by conversion to agency status. In government departments the following might be used.

(i) **Annual cash targets**: there is an incentive for managers to spend money, as it cannot be carried forward to later years.

(ii) **Logical incrementalism** is often the mode for resource allocation. In other words, resources will be based on last year's allocation with some amendments.

(iii) Although **zero-base budgeting** (ZBB) systems have been tried, few governments have the time or money for such an exercise. (ZBB requires managers to justify their activities and expenditure from scratch.)

The techniques which might be included in an agency are as follows.

(i) **ZBB** might be employed, despite its cost, as a one off review of the Agency's operations and procedures.

(ii) **Management by objectives** or similar techniques might be introduced to ensure that the strategic plans are implemented.

(iii) **Activity based costing**. As a service organisation, the Agency might benefit from an analysis as to what drives its costs in the long run. ABC is relevant to service industries.

16 INTRODUCING STRATEGIC MANAGEMENT

> **Pass marks**. The answer follows the standard rational approach. You could possibly argue that N Ltd has followed, albeit unconsciously, an incrementalist approach, by small scale change when necessary. Strategic management does not only include the rational model - Mintzberg's crafting strategies approach might also be worth a mention, especially in part (b), to reduce the shock of the new approach - but the tone of the question suggests that the rational model was what the examiner is mainly interested in.
>
> **Examiner's comments.** This were the most popular question on the paper. Generally well answered, especially part (a), but some answers to part (b) were let down by a lack of focus on the specific organisational and cultural issues required by the question.

(a) CIMA defines **strategic plan** as 'a statement of long-term goals along with a definition of the strategies and policies which will achieve these goals'. A **strategy** is a 'course of action, including the specification of resources required to achieve a given objective'.

(i) For a manufacturing company part of its mission may be to produce products **technically superior** to the competition.

(ii) To do this a strategy might be to spend 15% of gross revenues on **research and development**.

(iii) Tactics would include **recruitment** from the best university courses.

(iv) Operational control would include participants feedback on all programmes attended and the integration of **training** needs with training programmes.

Strategic management

According to Ward, **strategic management** is 'an integrated management approach drawing together all the elements involved in planning, integrating and controlling a business strategy'. Johnson and Scholes characterise the concerns of **corporate strategic decisions** as follows.

(i) The **scope** of the organisation's activities, in other words the product and markets the organisation deals with.

(ii) The organisation's **'fit' with the environment** and the relationships it has with stakeholder groups.

(iii) Matching its **resource capability** with the environment.

(iv) **Resource allocation** (between divisions or functions of the business, and directed towards different product-market areas).

(v) The organisation's **long term direction**.

(vi) **Change.**

(vii) **Value systems.**

The implementation of a strategic management approach, according to the rational model, involves a three-stage process of **strategic analysis** of the organisation's current situation and the environment, **strategic choice** (the generation and evaluation of alternative strategic options) and **implementation** of the chosen strategy. Many strategic decisions are one-off, non-programmable decisions.

Operational management

The concerns of **operational management** are quite different.

(i) Its scope is **restricted** to the particular task in hand

(ii) Operational management is generally more **internally focused** - although day to day relationships with customers are an operational concern.

(iii) Operations managers have to work with the resource allocation decisions set by the strategy; their concern is the most **efficient** use of these resources.

(iv) Operations management is generally **shorter-term** than strategic management

(v) Operational decisions are often more **routine** than strategic decisions and are more likely to be programmed.

There are some cases when short-term decisions are of strategic importance, for example if the survival of the organisation is at stake. Moreover, poor performance at operational level can make or break a strategy.

(b) **Cultural and organisational changes at N Ltd**

In practice there are a variety of different approaches to strategic management. The extent of organisational and cultural change required will depend on the type of strategic management style adopted.

Current strategic management. Arguably the current style of strategic management is an incrementalist approach. There is little strategic review, and the underlying assumption of managers is that things will continue more or less as they are, any changes being coped with by incremental adjustment an operational level. The lack of market information is particularly worrying. The company appears to be reactive rather than proactive.

Introducing the rational model: organisational changes

(i) **Resources** must be diverted to strategic management.

(1) The strategic management system must be **designed for future use.**

(2) The initial stages of strategic analysis need to be done, and the directors will need some **guidance,** so management consultants may be employed.

(ii) Strategic management requires suitable **information systems**. This also requires resources. The scope of the strategic intelligence systems will almost certainly include **marketing research data**.

(iii) Changes to the **job descriptions** of existing personnel might be needed so that their new responsibilities, especially for information gathering, are outlined.

(iv) **The management accounting system,** if any, must be configured to provide information related **to product profitability**, so the firm can identify life cycle and portfolio issues.

(v) Strategic management involves the **setting of objectives,** and so new performance indicators will be needed to ensure that the strategies chosen are implemented successfully. The **balanced scorecard** approach could probably be adopted - given falling profitability, it is likely that financial indicators assume a great deal of importance. However other operational performance indicators need to be used so that managers do not become too short-termist in their outlook. A technique using some of the insights of management objectives might be employed.

To summarise, the organisational changes involve new information systems, changes to job descriptions and new performance indicators to encourage a strategic perspective and a more strategic approach to marketing.

Clearly, this involves a change in the **management style** of the company.

(i) **New approach to strategy**. There will have to be a cultural change at board level. Directors will have to consider strategic issues in an active way. This may involve challenging some of their assumptions as to how the business is run.

(ii) **Professional approach, not family management.** The company certainly needs professional management. Hopefully, the decline in profits and turnover provides a sense of urgency.

(iii) **A new approach to risk** is needed, especially with regard to products and markets.

(iv) Operational decision-makers who were used to doing more or less what they pleased will be faced with **objectives set by their managers higher up**. This is a resumption of **control,** and operations managers may feel that they are losing power and authority. It may be **demotivating.**

(v) **Innovation** will have to be addressed, both in products and in processes. The existing managers are probably technically aware in their own fields, but the firm needs a **marketing orientation** to ensure its continued success.

(vi) A programme of **education** will be needed to convince managers that it is necessary.

Arguably, strategic decisions have **emerged** from patterns of operational behaviour, but this mode of making strategy is obviously insufficient at the moment. Accepting some **bottom-up input** into the strategic decision making process will mean:

(i) the new system is accepted more **readily**; and
(ii) the **expertise** of operational decision makers is exploited.

17 BZ: NEW OBJECTIVES

Examiner's comments. This was a popular question and some candidates helpfully used their knowledge from the Stage 3 Organisational Management and Development paper. Many candidates spent too much time in part (a) speculating as to how strategy was made in the early days of L's business, but whilst this was valid as an introduction, candidates should have moved on to determining what those objectives should be. In part (b), many candidates rightly cited the rational model, but did not earn the marks they could have because they did not relate it to the scenario.

(a) **Changes in strategic objectives**

L's personal objectives have changed over time from **survival** to **growth**. The business, too, has changed. L's decision might relate to a **crisis of leadership**: growth has been powered by L's own creativity but the business needs specialist management skills. (This is Greiner's model.)

Although L may want the business to grow, another consequence of the flotation is that he may want to cash in his investment. At the same time, job satisfaction will lead him to continue his participation in the business.

L's personal objectives are now distanced from the objectives of the business.

Other **stakeholders** have to be considered.

(i) **External shareholders**: L will be accountable to the capital markets. Shareholders expect a return for a certain level of risk. They are also unwilling to defer this return to the future. Even so, the extent to which L has to devolve power will depend on the shareholding he retains himself.

(ii) So far, L has obtained **a high level of return** and presumably this is what he has promised shareholders. But shareholders want some returns now, and a mere **growth** in sales volume from new markets might reduce the overall profitability of the business.

(iii) L will concentrate on **strategic** rather than **operational** matters. The senior managers will have their own personal goals: financial reward and job interest. If they add value to the firm, L will be keen to retain them and he will have to learn how to **motivate** them to stay. The natural goals of the senior manager might be to make decisions at a higher strategic level and to have an overall say in the direction of the business.

(iv) In the past, the **bank** was a key stakeholder and, as a source of liquidity, remains so.

(v) For existing **employees**, the appointment of new senior managers will have an impact.

Summary: the main changes

(i) L's **personal objectives** will no longer dominate the decision-making process.

(ii) **External shareholders** will constrain what L can do with company funds and where he invests the profits

(iii) L will have to deal with the **aspirations** of the management team.

(b) **Appropriate strategic planning process for L Ltd**

There are several models of strategic management.

(i) **Freewheeling opportunism** – the exploitation of opportunities as they arise. This perhaps has been L's style to date – but we are not given data to comment. L has provided a highly differentiated service, suggesting that he targeted his markets and customers very precisely.

(ii) **Emergent strategies**. In the past, both strategy and operations were L's responsibility and concern. As Mintzberg says, operations can be of strategic significance and strategies can 'emerge' from them. Clearly, L is not interested in adopting this approach: his specific intention is to hand over operational issues in order to concentrate on what he considers to be 'strategic'.

The model usually applied to top-down decision-making is the **rational model,** which has the stages outlined below.

(i) **Mission**. This is the ultimate rationale and purpose of the business. L will want to establish a mission, if only for the benefit of the new senior managers brought in from outside. This should encapsulate profit-orientation, the values of the business and its underlying commercial approach.

(ii) **Aims and objectives** give voice to the mission. Satisfying shareholders can be quantified as a target for profit, earnings per share or whatever. Not all goals can be quantified, but they are still relevant. L should formulate targets carefully; he is appointing managers who will need direction.

(iii) **Position audit** identifies the existing strengths and weaknesses of the company in relation to products, markets and competences. Initially, L will be in a good position, with his detailed first-hand knowledge of operations.

(iv) **Environmental appraisal** is where L seems to be concentrating his attention, in order to identify new market opportunities.

(1) An environmental scan would cover all **PEST factors** relevant to the services L's firm provides, in terms of future demand, arising from

greater affluence and social change, or new technology which affects how the services are delivered or how customer relationships are maintained.

(2) L will want to look at existing and potential **competitors**. L already has a competitive strategy of **differentiation** but he needs to assess whether this is still relevant or profitable.

(v) **Corporate appraisal or SWOT** draws together the position audit and the environmental appraisal, so that L can match the firm's **Strengths** and **Weaknesses** with **Opportunities** and **Threats** in the environment. As a final model, gap analysis ties in the firm's objectives with what it is doing at the moment.

(vi) **Strategy development**. L will identify strategies to meet the objectives. He has already chosen **differentiation** as a means of selling his service. He will also need to decide whether growth can come from **penetration** of existing markets, applying the same service mix **to new markets** or applying a new service mix either to existing or to new markets.

(vii) **Implementation**. In many respects, this is a key issue because, as Mintzberg suggests, strategies can easily fail or get altered out of all recognition when they are implemented. The new managers are key to this process.

(viii) **Monitoring and control**. Actual performance is compared with planned performance, in order that control action may be taken. In the past L's operational involvement has ensured that there is no gap between strategy and its implementation. As he is taking a step back from operations, he may have to exercise control through performance measures.

18 TUTORIAL QUESTION: STRATEGIC COSTS

Most strategic decisions are **unique** as is the information needed to support them. However, the accounting system should identify the **type of information** needed.

(a) Decisions to enter or leave a business area, or to expand operations, should take account of **avoidable** and **opportunity** costs.

(b) The system should identify suitable **performance measures**.

(c) The system should be designed from the **perspective of strategic decision-makers**.

(i) **Maintenance and development** activities should be highlighted.

(ii) **Discretionary** costs can be distinguished from **engineered** costs.

Ward (**Strategic Management Accounting**) argues that a successful system of strategic-accounting will be judged on ten **critical success factors**. Here is a checklist.

- **Aid** to strategic decisions.
- **Close** the communication gap.
- **Identify** decision type.
- Suitable **financial performance** indicators.
- Economic vs managerial **performance**.
- Only provide **relevant** information.
- Separate **committed** from **discretionary** costs.
- Distinguish **discretionary** from **engineered** cost.
- Use standard costs **strategically**.
- Allow for **changes over time**.

19 INTRODUCING STRATEGIC MANAGEMENT ACCOUNTANCY

(a) The CIMA's **Official Terminology** (1996) defines **strategic management accounting** as: 'a form of management accounting in which emphasis is placed on information which relates to factors external to the firm, as well as non-financial information and internally generated information.'

The quotation from **Bromwich and Bhimani** would appear to suggest that Japanese management accounting practices take a more strategic approach than western ones. Bromwich and Bhimani develop this statement into a discussion as to how certain Japanese firms approach **product costing and pricing**.

Target costing. Japanese firms are able to apply cost control techniques to a product over its whole **life cycle**. The costs of the product are thus driven by its life in the market. Once a product has been designed and specified, the **price** at what the market will bear over the product's life cycle.

Cost control is directed at reducing the actual cost of production, by more efficient use of materials, labour and technology, to below the **target cost**, in order to secure long term **profitability**.

The significance of this approach is that cost control is determined by the **product's behaviour in the market**.

(i) This is the opposite of the **cost-plus** approach to pricing, whereby the sales price is determined as a **markup** on the cost of inputs. The target costing approach is the application of the **marketing concept** to product pricing decisions, whereas the cost plus approach denotes the application of the product, or at best the sales, concept.

(ii) The target cost approach necessarily leads to attempts to improve **productivity** and **manufacturing efficiency**, because costs have to be driven down.

(b) **Causes**

Bromwich and Bhimani point out that there are many reasons which have been given to explain the relative success of Japanese manufacturing companies since World War II.

(i) **Strategic management accountancy** might be a contributory factor, insofar as it reflects the ability of Japanese firms to deliver cheap products of high quality, and to sustain expensive investments in market share.

(ii) The case of western companies needs to be examined in more detail.

(1) Many western companies have had strategic planning systems for many years, and have learned to budget effectively.

(2) Many western companies have been able to compete successfully with the Japanese.

(iii) **Different focus.** To argue that Western companies lack an **external orientation** is to miss one of the differences between Western and supposed Japanese business arrangements.

(1) Until recently, Japanese companies could focus much more easily on the customer as they did not have to look so often over their shoulders at shareholders.

(2) Western companies are externally orientated, without a doubt, but this external orientation has to take in **shareholders** who, as **stakeholders,** are more powerful than in the Japanese system. Quarterly profit

reporting and concentration on the short term are the consequences of an external orientation, not a denial of it. Western managers, being so concerned to please shareholders, are less able perhaps to take strategic considerations relating to products, markets and competitors into decision making. Business cycles and financial reporting cycles do not necessarily go hand in hand.

There are difficulties in strategic accounting, not least the **uncertainty** of predicting the future, and the need to acquire information about **competitors**.

(c) **Introducing a system of strategic management accounting**

A strategic management accounting system will have an **external focus**, but will be able to shed necessary light on **internal processes** to provide managers with strategic information.

The nature of strategic management accounting information would suggest the need for a number of different models to be used and information sources to be tapped.

Most strategic decisions are unique: and hence is the information needed to support them. The accounting system should identify the **type of information** needed.

(i) Decisions to enter or leave a business area, or to expand operations, should take account of **avoidable** and **opportunity** costs.

(ii) The system should identify suitable **performance measures.**

(iii) The system should be designed from the **perspective of strategic decision-makers.**

(1) **Maintenance and development** activities should be highlighted (eg maintaining as opposed to increasing market share).

(2) **Discretionary** costs should be distinguished from **engineering** costs (ie those costs arising from a determinable relationship between outputs and the level of inputs).

Ward (*Strategic Management Accounting*) argues that a successful strategic management accounting system will be judged on ten critical success factors.

(i) **Aid to strategic decisions**. The system must recognise the links between objectives and strategies to achieve them. However, merely extrapolating from past data is unlikely to be a suitable guide.

(ii) **Close the communication gap**. The information must be helpful for strategic decision makers: in other words, it should not keep to technical formats only suitable for accountants. It should be user-friendly.

(iii) **Identify decision type**. Designing a system should identify the type of decision (eg increasing an allocation of resources, entering a new business area). The financial information should be based on the incremental costs incurred and the benefits derived, opportunity costs etc. Occasionally decisions have to be taken to cut losses.

(iv) **Suitable financial performance indicators**. These should be tailored to the particular strategies appropriate for the business.

(v) **Economic vs managerial performance**. With some projects 'the resulting ... career risk [to the senior manager] may not be matched by such an increased return, so that there is a lack of goal congruence between the manager and the organisation'.

In other words, the system should distinguish between **controllable** factors and **non-controllable** ones, so that managers are not judged on matters not under their control. However, it might be argued that strategy sometimes depends on an ability to 'read' the environment correctly.

(vi) **Only provide relevant information**. The system will have to facilitate the production of especially tailored reports, which show the future economic consequences of a decision, as the decision will affect the allocation of resources to specific products and markets.

(vii) **Separate committed from discretionary costs**

(1) The 1996 Official Terminology defines **committed costs** as 'costs arising from prior decisions, which cannot, in the short run, be changed. Committed costs incurrence often stems from strategic decisions concerning capacity, with resulting expenditure on plant and facilities. Initial control of committed costs at the decision point is through investment appraisal techniques.'

(2) **Discretionary** costs are easily altered. CIMA defines them as 'a cost whose amount within a time period is determine by, and is easily altered by, a decision taken by the appropriate budget holder. Marketing, research and training are generally regarded as discretionary costs. Control of discretionary costs is through the budgeting process. Also known as **managed** or **policy** costs.'

(viii) **Distinguish discretionary from engineered costs.** An **engineered cost** has a predictable input/output relationship (eg it takes 10 tonnes of steel to make one tank). This denotes a physical relationship. Once these relationships are identified, strategic managers can decide where discretionary resources are used effectively. CIMA (1996) defines **engineered cost** as 'a cost which varies in proportion to a measure of activity. Direct materials and royalty payments are engineered costs. Control is through flexible budgeting or standard costing.'

(ix) **Use standard costs strategically.**

(x) **Allow for changes over time.**

Other issues in operating a strategic management accounting system are as follows.

(i) **Use of IT**. Strategic decisions are one-off. IT can free accountants to do this type of work.

(ii) **Data collection and input**. Automation of transactions processing ensures a bank of internal data. However, the system should be expanded to include information not normally part of financial reporting (eg insurance valuations could be used as a basis for replacement costs). External data (eg the marketing department's on competitors) can be made available throughout the company.

(iii) **Information.** People are sometimes reluctant to share it.

20 INFORMATION FOR STRATEGIC DECISION MAKING

(a) Management accounting information should assist managers of a business exercise their functions of **planning, decision making** and **control**. Criticisms of management accounting information are that it is not relevant for many of these tasks in that it is historical and lacks external focus. Particular criticisms of the information currently provided are these.

(i) **Backward looking.** It is primarily historical, although the budgets probably contain a forecasting element. Strategic plans are future orientated. They also deal with uncertainties.

(ii) **Not relevant to decisions.** It is more concerned with allocating costs than taking decisions. Presumably W Ltd has an absorption costing system. This is inadequate for strategic planning, where a knowledge of competitors' costs can be important.

(iii) **It appears almost entirely financial**. Other performance indicators provide a valuable insight into the business. For example, it might be useful to know the value of the business turned away.

(iv) Jobs appear to be priced on a **cost-plus basis**. The firm is turning away customers; perhaps it is pricing its work too cheaply. A small firm in a competitive industry can price according to the market.

(vi) **The existing standard costing system is not appropriate for this type of production.** Different jobs require different machinery configurations, and the cost of set-up times does not seem to be dealt with in the accounting system. This indicates that an approach such as **activity based costing** would give a better idea as to real costs and real profits.

(vii) No **competitor information** is offered.

(viii) **Customer information** is skimpy. Customers now require larger orders. The firm should ask why.

That said, the reports are **timely, accurate** and **comprehensive.**

(b) The following suggestions can be made to improve accounting information at W Ltd.

(i) **New costing system.** The current costing system should be reviewed, to ensure it captures costs in an appropriate way. Some of the insights of ABC, in identifying the real costs of each job, may be useful here. Costs would include set up times for each order, administration costs and machine usage. Any product/job profitability analyses would therefore be more accurate.

(ii) **Non financial information** relating to costs could include quality information (eg on a TQM basis) such as wastage, reject rates and so forth. Statistical process control measures can be incorporated in management reports.

(iii) **The standard costing system can be used for strategic purposes.** For example, it can show trade-offs between using higher quality materials or more labour. Rather than use standard costing only to reconcile actual with budgeted costs, it can be used for decision making purposes (eg to take account of different materials prices, different mixes of materials, future costs).

(iv) **Marketing information.** At present, the firm has no marketing department. In an ideal world, marketing information would also be included in management reports.

(1) **The firm's market share,** if it is possible to assess it accurately and if it is a relevant indicator, can be provided

(2) **Customer profitability**. Such information can probably be provided from within the accounting system, which could be adapted to job costing where necessary. Segmentation analyses can be applied to identify groups of customers.

(3) **Customer value**. The firm can identify how its products fit into customers' value chains, by modelling customer costs. Such analyses should include the contractors for which it works, as well as the ultimate end-users. It can then suggest innovations which customers might value, but which could be fairly cheap to produce.

(4) **The cost of lost business**. The firm should estimate revenues it has sacrificed by turning away larger orders. This can then be input into a model to see whether investment in new capacity would be worthwhile. At present the firm cannot use all its capacity; would expansion, just to win a few larger orders, make this problem even worse?

(5) **Repeat business** from satisfied customers.

(6) If it did **marketing research** it might find new customers for its small scale engineering business.

(v) **Competitor information** should be provided as a matter of course. Some idea about pricing can be gleaned from the industry.

Competitor activity can be modelled in **industry scenarios**, identifying the future structure of the industry.

Finally, W needs to be aware of its own advantages in relation to competitors, with a view to pricing.

With these innovations, the accounting system will therefore provide information relevant to the **SWOT analysis** and **position audit**.

(c) **Benchmarking**

Benchmarks are goals of performance which an organisation wishes to achieve in particular value activities.

Benchmarks differ from other **performance indicators** in that many of them are derived from other businesses or other areas of the same firm.

(i) UK plants for overseas firms are often judged according to the levels of quality at the firm's other plants overseas.

(ii) Occasionally, a firm might benchmark its performance on that of **a selected competitor**. This might be part of a strategy of attacking that competitor, but is more likely to be a policy of **catching up**.

Benchmarks might include:

(1) **speed of new product development** (Japanese firms had expertise in this area, which European and American firms tried to copy);

(2) **productivity** (eg number of cars per worker per year);

(3) **quality** (eg rejected parts per million);

(4) **service** (eg delivery dates).

Benchmarking can be applied to W Ltd's strategic information in the following ways.

(i) W can fairly easily benchmark its **prices**, as that information should be available.

(ii) W can benchmark **quality and waste**.

(iii) W might find a firm of a similar size, but dealing with different markets, with which to enter an **alliance**, where information is jointly shared.

(iv) W can benchmark **productivity and efficiency**.

21 PUBLIC SECTOR PERFORMANCE

> **Examiner's comments**. This straightforward question was not very popular. It is relevant to a number of Stage 4 syllabuses. In part (a), whilst candidates validly identified on environmental factors causing difficulties of comparison, other themes, such as data collection methods, political influences and so forth, were ignored. In part (b), candidates should have defined economy, efficiency and effectiveness, and identified the need in practice for a balance between them. Too many answers relied on anecdotal evidence and sweeping assumptions.

(a) **Limitations of comparative performance data in the public sector.**

As part of the trend towards greater openness and accountability in government, many public sector organisations are required to publish **performance indicators** to assess how well they are doing in comparison with others in the same sector.

(i) **Schools,** for example, are assessed on league tables according to exam results.

(ii) **Hospitals** are assessed on waiting lists and so forth.

The purpose of these indicators is to give **choice** to members of the public and to **encourage under-performers** to improve their performance.

Problems with performance indicators, especially if applied in a simplistic way, are these.

(i) **Environment**. Schools have different catchment areas, and it seems certain that the schools are not solely responsible for educational performance. Schools in areas with profound social problems perhaps find it harder to score highly in league tables, despite high quality teaching.

(ii) **Service delivery**. Services might be delivered in **different ways** and so might affect the validity of any one performance indicator. That said, hospitals which score well may do so because their surgical/therapeutic techniques and/or management systems are genuinely better: identifying these differences is the purpose of performance indicators in the first place.

(iii) **Mix of indicators**. No one indicator is good enough, and public sector bodies need to be judged on a mix of indicators. Success in one might mean failure in others. For example, typical hospital performance indicators are turnover and waiting lists. Hospitals can reduce waiting lists by sending people home sooner. If this leads to a rise in emergency readmissions, then this policy is a failure.

(iv) **Information collection**

(1) A lot depends on the **quality of information** collected at operational level, and the integrity of the data and the people who deal with it.

Statistical information is prone to **manipulation,** and those who are judged on its performance many have an incentive to misclassify data, or make it impossible to collect. For example, some hospitals have different death rates, reflecting in part the quality of surgical procedures.

(2) Even ignoring the possibility of interference, the data collection systems need to capture the **right data for accurate indicators** to be prepared.

(v) **Government policy**. Improving the **cost-efficiency** and **effectiveness** of public services has been a key objective of recent government policy, for example with the Conservatives' promotion of the Citizens Charter, and the Labour Party's commitment to improving education and public health.

(vi) **Expenditure levels.** Public sector bodies are expected to provide a service for a given expenditure. (This is a criticism of Railtrack – in the private sector but receiving a large government subsidy – which has been accused of not spending enough money on investment.) There is also the problem of rolling budgets – institutions which have not spent their allocated funds by the year end lose the money.

(b) **Consequences of reduced funding**

> **Pass marks**. Many would assume that economy is an aspect of efficiency, but the examiner's comments on the paper described economy as being achieved by obtaining 'input resources at least cost'; clearly this should be better interpreted as 'value for money'. Least cost can easily mean least quality.

Effectiveness deals with the outputs of the system, **efficiency** with the process and **economy** with inputs.

(i) **Effectiveness:** have the resources of the organisation been deployed in the best possible way to meet the objectives of the organisation and to satisfy the needs of its chosen client groups, in other words 'doing the right things'?

(ii) **Efficiency:** have resources been utilised in the best possible way, irrespective of the purpose? This often measured as the ratio of outputs to inputs.

(iii) **Economy** is related to efficiency although it is perhaps concerned with ensuring that resources are purchased at the best ratio of cost to performance.

Economy, efficiency and effectiveness have to be balanced, especially when resources are in **short supply**.

(i) A cut in absolute (cash) terms in funds available.

(ii) Maintained funds in cash terms, but which mean a fall in real terms owing to general inflation.

(iii) Increases which do not meet even greater increases in demand or in specific supply costs.

The health sector has faced this problem. Demand is increasing, for example for geriatric care, as people live longer. Also, treatments become more sophisticated and expensive. Finally, wages and salaries have a tendency to increase at a rate faster than general prices.

In practice, the public sector has to make do the best it can with the resources available. Its managers have to make **satisficing** decisions rather than the **best** or **optimum** decisions.

Maintaining and developing effectiveness of services

(i) Such organisations need to ensure their **objectives and mission** are clear. There may be a danger that the organisation's right to exist is taken for granted by employees and management, and the **system goals** and/or personal goals of participants can take priority over the wider mission in the community.

(ii) **Research and develop** new ways of satisfying client needs, for example new drugs or therapies.

(iii) **Reconfigure the organisation** to satisfy the clients' changing needs. Resources in the organisation can be redirected to where they are needed. In many respects, however, this is influenced by decisions in the wider society. Schools for example have to deliver a national curriculum.

(iv) Investigate whether **other organisations** can be persuaded to assist the goals of the organisation.

Efficiency and economy

(i) Set up a management information system to monitor key **variables**, such as capacity usage, bed availability and so forth, to identify where resources are stretched or where they are free.

(ii) Use work study techniques to assess the **procedures** of the institution. For example, the geographical location of facilities in a hospital can be changed to avoid wasted time of people walking from site to site.

(iii) Drive down the **cost of supply**, for example by buying generic rather than branded drugs.

(iv) Try to obtain better **financing on purchases**, or try to obtain **discounts**, eg by combining purchasing with other hospitals.

(v) Efficiency and economy are not reached by one-off measures, normally, but by careful attention to costs.

Activity based management can be introduced to try to focus effort on activities which **add value** and **reduce the cost** of activities.

22 INFORMATION FOR ACHIEVING CORPORATE OBJECTIVES

Pass marks. A fairly straightforward question, but one which goes to the heart of the syllabus by identifying the importance of management accounting information. You must relate strategic management accounting to senior managers, as they attempt to achieve corporate objectives, to be able to answer this question properly. Ask yourself: "Why is strategic management accounting undertaken in the first place?"

Other points. You may have brought into your answer the long term v. short term trade-off, which is a favourite of this examiner. Long term shareholder value can sometimes be compromised by the short term demands of fund providers (such as the calling in of a loan by a bank). Information provided by the management accountant may need to take a long term view to support chosen strategies.

Examiner's comments. Far too many candidates relied on restating a list of activities learnt from a textbook, and did nothing to set them in context.

Traditionally, management accounting information was **inward looking**, concerned with **tracking costs** rather than identifying decisions and **looked backward**. Often, it was built around the **existing structure and responsibilities** of the company.

Strategy making, on the other hand, is about the organisation as a whole, its relationship with the wider **environment**, how it responds to **competitors** and its **long-term direction** in terms of the **products and markets** it operates in. It can deal with decisions concerning corporate **culture** which involves human resources management and marketing issues. The existing organisation structure can be re-aligned in accordance with business objectives.

Strategic management accounting (SMA) aims to match management accounting with the needs of strategic management in order to offer better **decision support**. SMA involves no new techniques, but instead requires the application of existing techniques to decision-making processes, exposing the potential **financial characteristics** of decision options.

According to the '**rational model**', strategic decision making involves a number of steps.

(a) Although SMA makes no contribution to determining **mission**, businesses express **objectives** in financial terms, such as earnings per share or profits. Clearly the management accountant can show whether these objectives are self-consistent. For example, a firm's profit objectives may be inconsistent with the costs and revenue budgets for individual departments.

SMA must also take into account **non-financial objectives**. For example, a firm may set itself quantified targets for output quality at functional level.

(b) SMA can assist **environmental analysis** in many ways. Ward cites many examples.

   (i) Strategic decisions are often taken with the likely **competitor response** in mind. By analysing the cost profiles of the competitors, SMA can identify the constraints on the competitor's performance, cost structures, and financial objectives. For example, decisions by competitors to build capacity may have an adverse effect on the cost/profit outlook of other firms in the industry.

   (ii) SMA can show how revenue, costs and profit can be affected by **different environmental conditions**. For example, the effects of economic growth on demand conditions can be modified.

(c) **Position audit** looks in detail in the firm's current positions and competences.

   (i) A certain level of **market share** might be necessary in order to break even. The SMA can identify this level.

   (ii) Sophisticated marketing firms treat **brands** as investments because they generate cash – brands are explicitly valued in determining acquisition prices. The SMA can assist in this by identifying **relevant cash flows** related to the brand.

   (iii) **Product and customer profitability analysis** – some customers generate less profit than others, and the SMA can provide this data.

(d) **Corporate appraisal** shows how existing **strengths** and **weaknesses** relate to **opportunities** and **threats** in the environment. SMA can quantify some of these issues, which may be specifically financial – for example is the Minimum Wage a threat which will drive up costs, or an opportunity because it will raise barriers to entry to low-cost competitors?

(e) **Strategy generation and choice**. Here, the SMA is mainly involved in **evaluation** issues. SMA must make a genuine distinction between these types of costs.

   (i) **Discretionary** and **committed** costs – committed costs are costs which the organisation has to incur (eg on a contract) even if not already sunk.

   (ii) **Avoidable** and **unavoidable** costs – for example the decision to cease selling an 'unprofitable' product should only consider costs that would genuinely be avoided by the decision.

   (iii) **Engineered** and **discretionary** costs – some costs are dependant on physical quantities of input and output.

Many investment projects will be subject to **DCF investment appraisal**. SMA will ensure that cash flows are identified correctly.

(f) **Strategic control**

Most performance measurement systems are **financially orientated**. The time horizons chosen in the past have been based on the needs of annual reporting to shareholders, rather than the **strategic cycles** of the business.

For example, Ward suggests that different measures are appropriate at different stages in the **product life cycle**. Normal considerations of profitability and ROI are only really applicable for products in the **maturity** stage. For products in the **decline** stage, for example, measures such as free cash flow are more suitable. In the introduction and launch phases, market share and marketing objectives are far more relevant than financial ones.

Variance analysis can also be adapted for cost modelling (eg using competitor costs, if known, as the basis for comparison).

23 TUTORIAL QUESTION: GENERAL ENVIRONMENTAL ISSUES

(a) A forecast is a 'prediction of future events and their quantification for planning purposes'. **Forecasting** involves the estimation of the trend in future variables such as sales, tastes or profit, using both quantitative and judgmental techniques. Whereas extrapolation is a purely statistical exercise, forecasting includes the assessment of environmental changes, and in this respect forecasting assists in obtaining strategic fit.

The strategic environment of the firm, discussed in more detail in part (b), consists of **economic, political, legal, social** and **technological** factors which influence the ability of the organisation to survive and make profits.

Examples of **environmental variables** with which a fit must be achieved include the following.

(1) The changing **tastes** of customers.
(2) Developments in the **market demand** for a product.
(3) The likely **trend** of interest and exchange rates.

Forecasting can be more than just a numerical exercise on estimated trends. Whilst trends in price, interest rates, market growth rates and margins will involve numbers, other forecasts do not:

(1) **values profiles** are long range forecasts of consumer and social attitudes;

(2) **geopolitical forecasts** consider changes in national economic power and can alert the firm to new markets or potential competitive threats.

The important role which forecasting plays in strategic planning is therefore to forewarn managers of possible changes in environmental factors.

The **long term** nature of strategic change means that effective forecasting is necessary to give the organisation time to adapt and obtain a good fit with its environment.

(b) (i) Turbulence can be defined as a disruption to the relationship with the environment in which the organisation operates. R Sykes has identified five levels of turbulence.

(1) **Repetitive** - little change, things happen as before.

(2) **Expanding** - efficiency gains allow for an organisation to expand its operations in the environment.

(3) **Changing** - turbulence is largely caused by changes in the competitive environment, so that an organisation's relation to the wider environment is mainly determined by market factors.

(4) **Discontinuous** - there are major changes in the wider environment, such as a change in the law, or some other shock (such as the quadrupling of the price of oil by OPEC in the early 1970s).

(5) **Surpriseful** - new technology, for example, means that a 'new environment' is created.

Examples of causes of turbulence includes the **speed** of technological innovation, the **complexity** of the environment and the **interrelationship** between the various elements in it (eg falling house prices depresses consumers' confidence leading them to defer expensive purchases). Specific causes include:

(1) the development of new technologies and materials;

(2) world political changes (eg the collapse of the Eastern bloc, the reunification of Germany);

(3) global exchange rate movements (eg those leading to sterling's removal from the ERM);

(4) cultural pressures (eg 'green' issues).

(ii) The environment of a business can be analysed into the following.

(1) **Politico-legal** factors include political changes (eg change in government, operation of the executive, openness of political institutions to business influence) and legal developments (eg health and safety legislation, developments in company law).

(2) **Economic factors** include overall economic growth levels, interest and exchange rates and the effects of the government's fiscal and monetary policies.

(3) **Social factors** include the country's demographic profile (eg age structure), the class system and trends in consumer tastes and wants.

(4) **Technological factors** include new product technologies, new materials and new techniques in production.

(c) The **government** can aid business by providing a more **stable** operating environment and by direct financial **assistance**. Examples of such assistance include the following.

(i) Setting or targeting appropriate **interest and exchange rates**.

(ii) Providing **education and training** relevant to business either directly through the state educational institutions or via grants to firms and local technical and educational councils.

(iii) Protection of **intellectual and physical property** through making the laws (eg patents, theft) and enforcing them.

(iv) **Economic planning** of key industrial areas, for example information technology.

(v) Acting as a **customer** to the private sector, for example when purchasing from the aerospace and defence industries.

(vi) Giving incentives for **capacity expansion**, for example capital allowances and investment grants.

(vii) Giving support to **emerging business**.

(viii) Creating **entry barriers** by restricting the activities of foreign businesses in the country, or by imposing import tariffs.

Conversely, the government can act as an impediment to business. Governments may be the source of **instability** and lead to costs, in addition to **tax**, being incurred on organisations. There is an argument that the commercial logic which drive competitors and markets can be learned by an adaptive organisation and hence allowed for. The government can be less easily anticipated.

Examples of the government acting as an **impediment** to business include the following.

(i) Creation of legal **regulations** which are costly to comply with.

(ii) **Distortion of markets** by the use of indirect taxation and discretionary production licenses.

(iii) **Uncertainty and volatility** in financial markets occur when governments change their policies in response to political pressure.

(iv) Imposition of **restrictions** such as monopolies and mergers controls and equal opportunities legislation may limit business activities.

(v) Putting **short term political advantages** before long-term national benefit.

(vi) Acting solely on behalf of **sectional interests.**

24 TUTORIAL QUESTION: COMPETITIVE FORCES

Porter categorises **five competitive forces** in the environment of a firm as follows.

- The threat of **new entrants** to the industry.
- The threat of **substitute products** or services.
- The bargaining power of **customers.**
- The bargaining power of **suppliers.**
- The **rivalry amongst current competitors** in the industry.

(a) **The threat of new entrants**

A new entrant will bring **extra capacity** into an industry and poses a threat to established firms because they may lose market share with a consequent potential loss of economies of scale.

The strength of the threat from new entrants depends on the strength of the **barriers to entry** and on the likely response of existing competitors to the new entrant. If prospective new entrants think that competitive retaliation will be strong then they might think twice before deciding to enter the market. The main barriers to entry are:

(i) economies of scale;
(ii) differentiated products;
(iii) capital requirements;
(iv) switching costs;
(v) distribution costs.

(b) **The threat of substitute products or services**

The products or services that are produced in one industry are likely to have substitutes that are produced in another industry. For example railway travel is a substitute for private motor travel.

Substitutes pose a threat because they limit the ability of a firm to charge high prices for its products and the firm is likely to find the demand for its products is relatively **price elastic.**

The strength of the threat from substitutes will depend on their price-performance characteristics. Indeed where the existing firms are unable to meet the challenge with similar offerings the market may degenerate into a **price war.**

(c) **The bargaining power of customers**

Customers require better quality products and services at lower prices. If they have the power to get what they want they will force down the profitability of the firms in the industry.

The strength of the threat from the bargaining power of customers will depend on a number of factors including the level of **differentiation** amongst products in the industry (including 'intangible' aspects such as customer service), the cost to the customer of switching from one supplier to another and whether a customer's purchases from the industry represent a large or small proportion of the customer's total purchases.

(d) **The bargaining power of suppliers**

Suppliers can influence the profitability of a firm by exerting pressure for higher prices or by reducing the quality of the goods and services which they supply.

The bargaining power of the supplier depends on a number of factors including the number of suppliers in the industry, the importance of the supplier's product to the firm, the cost to the firm of switching from one supplier to another and the ease with which the supplier could integrate forwards.

(e) **The rivalry amongst current competitors**

The intensity of competitive rivalry within an industry will affect the profitability of the industry as a whole. Although rivalry can be **beneficial** in helping the industry to expand, it might leave demand unchanged. In this case the individual firms will be incurring costs on sales promotion campaigns, advertising battles and new product development and they will be charging lower prices and so making lower profits without gaining any benefits except **maintaining market share**.

The **intensity** of competition will depend on a number of factors including the rate of growth in the industry and whether there is a large number of equally balanced competitors.

An example of competitive rivalry occurred in the car industry where the manufacturers made an issue of the longevity of cars and extended the corrosion protection in their products. The result was a drastic reduction in the total number of cars sold.

25 TUTORIAL QUESTION: MANAGEMENT ACCOUNTING AND COMPETITOR ANALYSIS

It is assumed that the retailer must initially buy fuel at the **full price,** and subsequently earn a refund of 5 pence per litre if he succeeds in increasing throughput by 10%.

This means that any **price reduction** by the retailer will affect his profits directly unless he can achieve the 10% volume increase.

The retailer could choose to reduce the price per litre of fuel by 5p, 4p, 3p, 2p, 1p or nil. A 5p reduction would bring him no extra profit unless the sales volume increased, or he might sell more 'non-fuel' items, such as goods in the on-site shop.

A nil reduction in price would oblige the retailer to seek ways of increasing volume of sales by 10% without any **price incentive to customers,** which is improbable.

If the retailer kept historical records of sales volume and prices, he might have sufficient data to estimate by how much volume is likely to increase or fall when the fuel price changes.

In order to evaluate the **likely response of competitors,** the retailer would also need corresponding historical information about the prices of local competitors at the time of these price changes. On this basis the probable increase in demand for the retailer's own fuel could be assessed.

In particular, do local petrol retailers follow each other when one makes a price change, or are they often willing to allow a price differential of 1p, 2p or even 3p per litre between a rival and themselves? How quickly do they alter their own prices in response to a price change by a rival?

26 OVERSEAS ENVIRONMENT

> **Pass marks**. This is a fairly wide-ranging question, with a broad coverage of environmental issues. Interestingly, the *mode of entry* to this new market has already been chosen for you, although the firm has yet to decide on the *site* of its manufacturing plant. A low-wage economy suggests a lesser-developed country. In poorer countries there are inevitable problems relating to education and infrastructure. In part (b) you are specifically asked about cultural and human resources issues, not the marketing implications.
>
> **Examiner's comments.** A popular, well-answered question. Although a number of models - PEST, Porter's five forces, Porter's competitive advantage of nations - could be used, they needed to be applied to the question. In part (b) candidates should assess the impact of cultural influences on the effectiveness of the work force.

(a) **PEST factors**

Political and legal factors

(i) **Political conditions** in the individual overseas markets (eg overall stability) or sources of supply (eg risk of nationalisation).

(ii) **Relationships between country governments.** If the firm intends to use the plant as a basis for exports to other countries, the country's membership of international trade bodies is important, and political relationships with other states matter.

(iii) In some low wage countries, the **legal framework** is not secure (McDonalds was evicted from a prime leasehold site in Beijing when it was decided to redevelop the property irrespective of the legal agreement).

(iv) **Political connections.** Where the low wage economy has involved state planning, political connections may be more important than legality, and help might be needed to get round a complex bureaucracy.

(v) **Local labour law** may be different (redundancies are legally hard to achieve in some countries, eg India).

Economic factors

(i) The overall level of **economic activity** and growth.

(ii) The relative levels of **inflation** in the domestic and overseas market.

(iii) **Exchange rate,** its level and volatility. This is relevant if the new plant will source some of its raw materials from overseas.

(iv) **Exchange controls**. Will the firm be allowed to remit profits to London?

(v) The relative **prosperity** of individual overseas markets.

(vi) The state of the **labour market**. Cheap labour is often unproductive, because it is untrained and perhaps inefficient. While labour costs may be lower, the apparent saving may be reduced by lower productivity.

Social and cultural factors

(i) The cultures and practices of **customers** and **consumers** in individual markets.

(ii) The **media and distribution** systems in overseas markets.

(iii) The differences in **ways of doing business.**

(iv) The degree to which **national** cultural differences matter for the product concerned. For clothing, the firm might have to consider different sizes, materials and national stylistic preferences.

Technological factors

(i) The degree to which a firm can **imitate** the technology of its competitors.

(ii) A firm's access to domestic and overseas **patents**.

(iii) **Intellectual property protection** varies in different countries.

(iv) **Technology transfer** requirements (some countries regard investments from overseas companies as learning opportunities and require the investing company to share some of its technology).

(v) The **relative cost** of technology compared to labour.

(vi) An **appropriate infrastructure** to enable the technology to be used effectively. More basically, the firm has to rely on public supplies of electricity and water.

(vii) In some countries **telecommunications** are inefficient and expensive.

Currently, the firm is hoping to exploit low labour costs. How far is this realistic in the long term? If the market is to enjoy overall economic growth, rising prosperity will mean rising wages. If the firm is to make a substantial investment in the local factory, it will have to plan for productivity improvements.

The overall competitive environment

(i) This relates to the **five forces** analysis propounded by **Michael Porter**.

(1) **Barriers to entry**. Existing firms might have powerful political connections which they can exploit against the competitor from overseas. Customers may prefer the national products and brands. Also the distribution network may be effectively tied up.

(2) **Substitute products**. We are not told what type of clothing is to be made, and who the customers are. In some countries, traditional clothing, made at home, may substitute for factory produced products.

(3) **Bargaining power of customers**. No detail is given of distribution, and how the firm intends to sell its products, but distributors might have high power.

(4) **Bargaining power of suppliers**. Again, we are not told how the factory will be supplied. Local suppliers might welcome the new business.

(5) **Competitive rivalry**. In some countries, local businesses have strong political connections. Whilst overseas investment might be welcome, as official policy, it can be hindered at local level. Furthermore, existing producers are owned by the state, and there may be restrictions on competition.

(ii) We can also use Porter's diamond model of **national competitive advantage** to assess the venture.

(1) The **rivalry** between different firms has been discussed above.

(2) **Demand conditions.** The new market might help the firm compete elsewhere, by the demand conditions it possesses, but this seems unlikely.

(3) **Factor conditions.** What is the new market's supply of basic and advanced factors, apart from labour? To what extent is the firm evading other problems by concentrating on low-cost, and low-skill labour, as opposed to improving productivity at home?

(4) **Related and supporting industries.** A country in which there is a cluster of textile and clothing related industries? History often shows that industrialising countries often start off with textiles.

(b) **Cultural issues and the workforce**

The firm will have to deal with the national culture in a number of areas.

(i) **Local education and training**

If low labour costs are a reason for the move, this implies that the processes are fairly labour intensive. The influence of local **education** will make itself felt in a number of areas.

(1) **Basic literacy and numeracy**. Many relatively poor countries, such as Sri Lanka, have high literacy rates in the local language. Sadly, in other poor countries, this is not the case. If this is needed for the factory, the actual supply of labour might be smaller than appears.

(2) **Knowledge of English**. In order to ensure that the factory is properly run, at least some of the local managers and staff need a good working knowledge of business English. In some countries English speakers might be in short supply.

(3) **Technology**. Education and training implications are discussed in (ii) below.

(4) **Attitudes to work**. The firm will have to train its employees, in part to acclimatise them to the corporate culture of the firm. Professor Hofstede contrasted attitudes to work in different countries.

- In some countries, **disagreeing with the boss** is not acceptable behaviour, whereas a boss from the UK may be touting for new ideas.
- **Continuous improvement programmes** require people to show more initiative than a culture based on deference to authority might accept.

(ii) **Technology**

(1) The firm will have to **train** its workers how to use and maintain the machines so that their useful life is not shortened.

(2) If the plant is to develop further, personnel with an appropriate **technical knowledge** will need to be recruited. There may be a pool of qualified engineers available for recruitment. It is unlikely, according to Porter, that firms can compete on low labour costs alone, and the firm will invest to enhance the **productivity** of the labour force.

(3) As is mentioned above, **cultural attitudes** to technology and the work processes are important. Some labour disciplines regarding machinery need to be enforced, particularly with regard to **health and safety**.

(iii) **Working hours**

Even within Europe, different national cultures suggest different attitudes to **time, timekeeping and punctuality**. Clearly, the factory has to be operated efficiently, and this might require a greater degree of **labour discipline** than the people might have expected.

However the firm will perhaps be able to offer better wages than local firms, and will be able to choose employees for which this is not a problem.

Even poor countries have labour **regulations,** and a large factory would be more subject to regulation in this respect than local family businesses. Indeed, there might be legal restrictions on shifts and working hours which have to be respected.

(iv) **Domestic amenities**

Housing. In some countries in the past, firms were expected to take a paternalistic approach to employees, such as provision of dormitory accommodation. Few people in wealthier countries would tolerate such an arrangement, but it might be acceptable in poorer countries, especially if transport is expensive.

Other amenities. Such amenities can include subsiding the **education** of workers' children, a good **canteen,** and **health services** in the factory. The firm can prove itself a **good corporate citizen.**

27 THREAT OF NEW ENTRANTS

Pass marks. This is quite a specialised question dealing with only *one* of the five competitive forces in Porter's model: the threat of new entrants. Although not a scenario-based question you are expected to apply your knowledge of the threat of new entrants to a low-technology industry.

Other points. In our answer we have interpreted 'low technology industries' literally, ie such that entry barriers in terms of requiring, for example, the latest computerised production systems, are not present. This may not always be the case - a low technology industry may not necessarily have low barriers to entry and you may have put this into your answer. As always, if your argument is sensible, relevant and supported by evidence it will earn marks.

Examiner's comments. This question was popular and on the whole well answered, with appropriate examples. Some candidates mixed up parts (b) and (c). Answers to part (b) should have mentioned internal factors, as the competitive threat can be met by 'the efficiency and effectiveness of "our" organisation'.

(a) **Porter's Five Forces model** contends that the long-term profitability of an industry is determined by the interrelationship between five competitive forces: the threat of new entrants; substitute products; customer bargaining power; supplier bargaining power; and the intensity of competition.

A company is concerned with maintaining **competitive advantage** and all of these forces impact on that, especially in the sense that a profitable industry will attract new entrants (purely because it is profitable, if for no other reason). If these newcomers do enter the market, they will increase competition.

The **threat of new entrants** is that risk associated with other firms entering the industry. They will bring in new capacity and compete for the same customers. This may have the effect of driving down prices and profitability. It may also have the effect of driving existing firms out of business. The precise level of the threat posed by new entrants is determined by **barriers to entry** and the likely **response of firms currently in the industry**.

If the barriers to entry are significant and firms currently in the industry are prepared, for example, to cut their prices to protect their market share, new entrants may be deterred. Any new entrant is likely to have to make a significant investment to break into the market and will want to be able to obtain enough market share to provide an **adequate return** on that investment.

Low-technology industries are, however, likely to be characterised by a number of firms, as it is relatively easy to set up in business without significant outlay and with a relatively low cost of failure. There may not be so many barriers to entry (certainly in the technological sense) and so it is likely that competition will reduce industry profitability.

(b) An **assessment of the threat** of new entrants will depend on the following.

(i) The likelihood that new entrants will be **interested** in the industry and its markets, and will be **successful**.

(ii) Their effect on the **future of the industry** as a whole.

(iii) The ability of a firm already in the industry to **repel the threat**. This depends on its **internal capabilities** and the way it adds value for its customers.

By shrewd review of the environment, a firm might have some idea as to potential new entrants. Porter suggests that in carrying out a **competitor analysis** a firm can analyse the following.

(i) The competitor's future **goals**

(ii) The competitor's **assumptions**

(iii) The competitor's current **strategy** - (will it try the same approach to any new industry it enters?)

(iv) The competitor's **capabilities and competences**, which might be relevant to the industry. These include know-how in the area, financial resources, marketing resources and so forth.

All firms currently in the market must therefore use **external information** to assess the environment, as well as looking to their own operations.

The industry ought to be **monitored** for its continuing appeal to new entrants, by assessing what would happen, for example, if prices were decreased or products were altered. This may involve the company 'under threat' in some form of market research to see both how customers, competitors and new entrants would respond.

Customers will always welcome price reductions, which may decrease profitability and thereby deter new entrants. This will depend on the strategy of the new entrant, who may be prepared for initial losses and is taking a **longer term view**. Changing product specifications may be unpopular with customers and therefore an inappropriate strategy to adopt when dissuading new entrants.

This latter point may tie in with an assessment of where in the **product life cycle** the industry's various products lie. If many of them are in the growth stage then the market is attractive to new entrants, with customers increasing in number and companies better able to differentiate their product. An industry with products in a mature phase characterised by little market growth will, as a rule, be less attractive.

A new entrant may be attracted to even a mature market if the anticipated volumes are large enough and the new entrant has **cost advantages**. It is therefore important to ascertain where possible the **cost structure and capabilities** of new entrants. A new entrant may have such access to funds (such as large cash balances, bank loans or debenture stock) that it has plenty of available cash and is looking for places to spend it.

All this information can be collected and analysed in a firm's process of **strategic planning**. As an example, when conducting a corporate appraisal, SWOT analysis can include the likelihood of the threat of new entrants in the market, as identified by some of the above processes.

The firm needs to examine the **future** of its industry as well as the current picture. A number of scenarios can be devised and they can be used for decision-making. Analysing the scenario involves determining the future structure of the industry, developing the implications of the scenario for the attractiveness of the industry and identifying implications for future competitive strategies.

For example, a relatively low-tech industry such as footwear must take into account the likely entry by firms from countries with very low labour costs, such as Brazil and China and react accordingly, by product differentiation or moves to low cost production.

Internal information sources

Porter suggests that competitive advantage rests in **adding value** in a unique way. A model of the process is the value chain, describing the various activities of the firm. Each element of the value chain can be identified to see if there some activities which are weak and/or costly, or which a competitor will exploit.

Reducing weaknesses and **enhancing strengths** should make it that much more difficult for new entrants to compete profitably. The advantage of already being set up in the industry is significant and should be capitalised upon, but lapse of time and perhaps a previous lack of competition may serve to make incumbent firms complacent. Long established players will always be under potential threat from slimmer, younger companies.

(c) Various options are open to a company to counter the threat of new entrants to a low technology industry. The key is to make sure that potential new entrants are aware of them.

As we are trying to deter the threat of new entrants rather than existing competitors, the initial approach is to **discourage them from entry in the first place**, or to drive them off once they have decided to enter.

Raise barriers to entry. Here are some examples.

(i) Fill in any gaps in the product range which a competitor might exploit. Launching a number of **different brands** gives the impression of a market that does not need new entrants. New products from new entrants may be resisted.

(ii) Block access to **distribution** channels (eg by exclusive agreements, volume discounts).

(iii) Even in a low technology industry, effective use of **patents** can raise entry barriers.

(iv) Build or reinforce **customer loyalty** (eg match the entrant's guarantees). Building customer loyalty is not achieved overnight, however, and is expensive.

Raise the new entrant's perception of risk, by making the market appear less attractive and more risky, so that the new entrant goes somewhere else.

(i) The firm should indicate its intention to fight by publicising that it is investing in **new capacity**, brands etc.

(ii) Propose an aggressive **price-cutting strategy** which will make it harder for the new entrant to build market share. Cost savings could be investigated to mitigate the effect of this.

(iii) Challenge the **competitor's assumption** about the future of the industry (eg by reducing stated profit targets).

Counter attack

(i) Disrupt the new entrant's **test markets** (eg by amending the offer).

(ii) Introduce **new products**, processes or variants.

(iii) **Litigation**, if necessary. This could be costly, but it may be considered worthwhile in a cost/benefit analysis. It may buy valuable time while new entrants 'regroup'.

(iv) **Attack the entrant in its home market**, to divert attention and resources from the new entry strategy.

Not all of these tactics can be adopted easily. Much depends on the resources available within the industry. Firms which are weakly profitable will be vulnerable to new entrants, and may not have the resources to spend dealing with the threat or counterattacking.

Long term considerations

(i) **Diversify**. If the new entrant threat results from a long term and permanent change in the structure and profitability of the industry, then the firm might have to reconsider its place in the industry and perhaps diversify.

(ii) **Acquisitions**. The firm might have to accept the new entrant. Rather than attack the new entrant, the firm might seek to take over one of the existing competitors - or at least its market share - to build up size and strength. The new entrant may have the effect of consolidating the industry.

As a last resort, a firm might decide the threat is so big, or the returns so small, that it is best to give in to the threat and **abandon the market**. For example, if a small pharmacy hears that Boots or Superdrug has got planning permission to open next door, it might decide to withdraw.

Entry barriers might be falling for many reasons, so withdrawal might in any case be **economically sensible** if the structure of the industry is changing.

28 STRATEGIC PLAN FOR CHANGED ENVIRONMENT

> **Examiner's comments**. The examiner's general comment was that candidates should be realistic in their treatment of this scenario. Reading the financial press since the end of the Cold War would have alerted you to some of the long-term issues for companies involved in defence contracting.

(a) BG is in an unhappy position.

(i) It is being exposed to new and growing **competition in a declining market**.

(ii) Until now, the market has consisted of one customer, the government. BG is unlikely to have well developed **marketing skills** or commercial **contacts**.

(iii) The costing system used does not encourage operational **efficiency**.

The strategic plan needs to take the following **environmental factors** into account.

The **competitive environment** is hostile.

(i) There is a **declining market.**
(ii) There are **new competitors** (eg former eastern Europe).
(iii) **Barriers to entry** to BG's market segment are being reduced.
(iv) **New markets** may not be easy to find.

The political environment

(i) There will be no long term increase in defence spending in the home country. The defence business is peculiarly dependent on government thinking.

(ii) Other governments may continue to support national champions in arms industries as a means of ensuring domestic security, so while barriers to entry to the home market are being reduced, there is no evidence that this is happening abroad. However, see the points made under 'economic environment' below.

The economic environment is also likely to be unfavourable in the long term.

(i) Talk of a **peace dividend** in Europe will lead for pressures for reduced spending over the continent.

(ii) Governments of countries with sophisticated arms manufacturing industries are likely to be more **vigilant** over arms exports to regimes of dubious political legitimacy.

(iii) Many **poorer countries** can no longer afford to import defence equipment.

(iv) In particular the **re-established democracies** of Latin America are likely to reduce defence spending as the role of the armed services in society is reduced.

The **technological environment**. High technology weaponry is likely to be popular with governments to minimise bloodshed. These are very expensive to produce.

BG's reliance on one customer, in a very cosy relationship, has not prepared it for the rigours of the new competitive situation. As the company never really had a marketing objective, it would not have enough experience to reorientate itself. At the same time, its contacts with the government might enable it to benefit from government sponsored export drives.

Product range

(i) It is possible that BG's products were made according to detailed **government specifications**. These specifications might have laid down for the government's particular defence needs. There is no reason to suppose that other governments will have the same requirements.

(ii) Moreover, some defence products, especially of a high-tech nature, require that those who operate them have a high degree of **technical training**. This might not often be available, so the products might be too complex and over specified for some markets.

Accounting systems

(i) The **cost-plus system** may not be the cause of BG's difficulties, but it will certainly provide no remedies. If BG is losing contracts on grounds of price, this indicates that there is something wrong with the way BG has operated. It may be simply a reflection of size: competing firms might be much larger and so benefit from economies of scale. Or it may be that BG is **inefficient**, and lacks proper project management skills.

(ii) It may be that BG's **overhead recovery system** gives incorrect costing information, thus leading to **poor pricing decisions.**

Interested parties

BG has shareholders to satisfy, in the short and long term. They will expect performance to improve.

(b) **Strategic options available to BG**

(i) **Find new markets.** There is strong competition, and, as mentioned in part (a), BG's products may be too advanced or too specialised for many. Also, if it is losing government contracts at home, then there is no reason to suppose that it will be any more successful abroad, unless it can match competitors on price. Moreover, BG has little experience in marketing.

(ii) **Develop new products.** Most of BG's work has been on government defence contracts. Product development in this field is expensive, and it is not certain that BG has the necessary marketing skills to identify what would sell. Development of a new product and its failure to sell would probably mean the end of the company.

(iii) **More aggressive pricing.** The company still has strengths in that it is well attuned to the personnel and internal politics of the defence ministry of the home government. In the short term therefore, it can bid competitively for home government contracts at lower margins.

(iv) **Changing accounting systems** for better cost information. This will support the objective in (iii) above. It is unlikely that overhead absorption by direct labour hours is appropriate in a high-tech company.

(v) **Rationalisation.** BG will have to make itself more efficient in order to survive, and build up margins.

(vi) **Exploit civilian applications** of its military technology. If its technical expertise involves computer program writing it could set itself up as a specialist software supplier. A UK example has been the development by a defence company of software to provide computerised road maps.

(vii) BG could **share its resources** with other companies to cope with declining markets and increasing costs. This would also be a means of gaining **expertise**, and building up commercial **relationships.**

(viii) **Sell to a larger firm.** If BG fails to come up with a viable plan, or the plans it develops require large amounts of capital it should, in its shareholders' interests, consider selling itself to a larger company prepared to invest in its future. This would preserve jobs and skills, and enable shareholders to invest elsewhere.

(c) **The management accounting response**

(i) **Costing and pricing.** In BG's case, it is clear that the cost accounting system needs examining. After all, BG might be quite efficient in terms of quality and delivery, and the manufacturing process might also be adequate: from the information provided, inefficiency cannot be assumed.

(ii) **Overheads.** It appears that there is a problem with the system of overhead absorption.

(1) If all overheads are absorbed, this may include the overheads of inefficient departments.

(2) It may be the case that different projects use overheads at different rates. Perhaps an **activity based costing** (ABC) system should be introduced which will identify how overheads are actually generated, and so provide a more accurate allocation.

(3) The company has a history of over or under absorbing fixed overheads, a shift to a marginal-cost based pricing system might be appropriate.

29 COMPETING UNIVERSITY

> **Examiner's comments.** The examiner noted that many answers to this question assumed that PG has practically unlimited funds for student welfare. This is unlikely to be the case, at least in the UK. Candidates also assumed that advertising is the only way of competing.

(a) **Ways in which PG can compete with other institutions**

PG has a limited control over its own **cost structure**, as university lecturers' salaries are in part determined centrally, and university facilities involve a high degree of relatively fixed costs (eg buildings, laboratories and so forth).

PG might also have limited control over one of its major sources of **revenue**: the level of tuition fees per student is determined in the UK by central government. Central government, through the University Grants Committee, also determines how other government funds to universities are distributed.

Firstly, we must identify what the universities are competing for. In fact, the university is competing in a number of different **markets and market segments**. We can use the **fours Ps**: product, price, place promotion.

UK undergraduate students

Product. Generally, the university will be offering an honours degree at the end of a three year course. To compete, the university should identify popular subjects, or perhaps (more profitably) offer degree courses in subjects for which there might be a suppressed demand. Alternatively, if the university has recognised strengths in particular fields then these can be used as a basis for marketing.

Place. Capital expenditure might be limited and restricted. It can seek the cooperation of a local tourist board, which might be trying to enhance the image of the town generally.

Price. There is little that can be done here. Tuition fees are paid by the state. High rents for accommodation might deter students.

Promotion. There are a variety of promotional measures. Some universities are well known. Other universities, which might have equal academic strengths, need to alert prospective students to their virtues. Examples include:

(i) **prospectuses** sent to 6th form colleges and schools;

(ii) inviting teachers to inspect **key departments** in the hope that they will recommend the university to pupils;

(iii) having **open days** at convenient times for prospective students;

(iv) persuading **current undergraduates** to take students round the campus;

(v) well-publicised **ties with local businesses** to attract students from the immediate vicinity;

(vi) **'star' academics** who give publicity to their departments by appearing on television programmes;

(vii) the services of a **PR consultancy**.

Overseas students

Their fees are paid by their governments or families. As the UK university system has a good reputation, there is a demand from overseas. However, demand can still depend on the overall relationship between the countries involved. PG is competing with universities overseas.

Product. It might be harder to discover the sort of studies which overseas students are particularly keen on. If they are sent by the governments of poor or developing countries, they are likely to be interested in subjects such as engineering or medicine.

Place. In this case, price, another important element in the marketing mix, will be important, although PG has to convince overseas students that the place is right, too.

Price. Overseas students are often charged high fees. Offering courses at a lower price might attract more students.

Promotion. The co-operation of institutions like the British Council might be helpful. Also, maintaining contact with government agencies for public funds might gain some business.

Research students

A **research department** is a source of prestige to a university and it encourages the brightest individuals to study at the university. It also commands respect from the fund-granting authorities.

Mature students

Students who have worked before choosing to do a degree have their own special interests and needs. The **product** element must therefore include **flexible** course design, for those who continue to work. **Price** is likely to be a significant element in the marketing mix, as many mature students are **self-financing**: some might already have financial or domestic commitments. **Place** can therefore be important: perhaps mature students are likely to chose a local university.

Business sponsorship

Governments are trying to enhance the interconnection between universities and industry. It is held that the UK has been less successful at **exploiting research** in developing new products. Forcing universities to seek out **commercial sponsorship** is a way of building up those ties.

For the university, sponsorship by industry is a way of securing funds which are no longer available from the government.

Using the marketing mix, we can identify that the **product** will partly depend on the amount of money the business is prepared to invest and will partly depend on **people**: the university is effectively selling its research scientists.

The **price** depends on what the business requires or what the university can persuade the business to fund. **Promotion** is matter of publicising the university's facilities to the business community.

(b) **Establishing user satisfaction**

The university's product typically takes three years to consume, and so the final judgement can only be made once a student has left.

The university can ask its students what they think of particular elements of the learning environment offered by the university.

(i) **Basic facilities.** It is easy to assess students' views about basic services simply by handing out questionnaires, and monitoring complaints.

(ii) **Academic facilities.** Similarly, for services such as the use of libraries, market research would be easy and cheap to conduct. This might lead to changes in opening hours and other operational adjustments.

(iii) **Quality of teaching**. This is likely to be a contentious area. Brilliant researchers may be poor public speakers. The best communicators may have few original ideas. Or perhaps some academics see teaching as a necessary but resented distraction from their principal activity.

For those who have taken time off work, borrowed money, or are paying privately (eg mature students, overseas students), poor tuition is likely to be resented.

(iv) **Quality of research**. This can be assessed by the reputation the university builds up.

(v) **Social utility**. The university's main customer is the state, and through the state, the taxpayer. Education is one of the most important long term investments a society can make.

(c) **Measuring effectiveness**

A university's resources consist of:

(i) **tangible fixed assets** such as lecture theatres, halls of residence, laboratories and so forth;

(ii) **intangible assets** such as reputation, goodwill;

(iii) **liquid assets,** normally the funds provided by the government;

(iv) **spare time** (during university vacations some of the university's assets will not be used by students);

(v) **personnel** (lecturers, administrative staff).

The university is a **not-for-profit** organisation.

(i) The ultimate measure of **effectiveness** of use of resources is something that, perhaps, cannot be measured: have students been well educated for both their personal development and for society's needs?

(ii) However it possible to measure the **efficiency** with which resources are used to pursue particular objectives.

Both **quantitative** and **qualitative** measures of performance can be used.

Measures of students' satisfaction as noted in part (b) are an indication of how well the university is performing its basic task.

The university operates under **resource constraints,** which are basically **financial.** The university has to tie in the success of its primary objective, while minimising the cost of achieving it.

Some measures, therefore, will reflect the university's **use of resources** in the light of its operations.

(i) Student/lecturer ratio
(ii) Total cost per department
(iii) Total cost per student
(iv) Student cost per department
(v) Course fees received/ student cost per course
(vi) Administration costs / total costs
(vii) Cost drivers for administrative costs

(viii) Cost of research for business/ sponsorship fees.

The university will wish to spend as little as possible on administration in order to maximise resources available for its main objectives. If it does work for businesses, establishing the costs of this work will help to indicate whether this uses up more resources than it provides.

30 ENVIRONMENTAL MANAGEMENT ACCOUNTING

> **Examiner's comments.** This unpopular question was not well answered, and many answers, whilst expressing concern at environmental damage, did not address the role of the Chartered Management Accountant despite the clear hints given in the wording of the question. Candidates could have discussed how existing management techniques can be adapted. Few mentioned the potential marketing benefits of paying attention to environmental issues.

Concern with the physical environment and the use of natural resources has grown in the past decade. There is concern about pollution and degradation of the environment, as well as concern about the long term impact of global warming.

Pressure on businesses is exerted by **consumers**, by **pressure groups**, by **government legislation**, and international **treaties**. These influence firms' practices on diverse issues such as food production and waste disposal.

It is within this context that many firms, in order to respond to their various stakeholders, have introduced more **systematic** policies regarding **environmental reporting**. The CMA is a key information provider within the organisation and is thus an important link in these developments. The CMA provides information for planning, decision-making and control and is already used to translating **operational data** into **management information.**

Many of the CMA's existing techniques can be adapted to serve the organisation's environmental agenda.

(a) **Cost/benefit analysis.** CMAs working in the public sector may already use cost/benefit analysis in assessing various projects requiring public expenditure. Already, cost benefit analysis techniques are used to identify and quantify social benefits. The environmental impact can be built in to such assessments.

(b) **Eco-balance**. In reviewing the process of production, the firm identifies its raw materials and its outputs in terms of waste, noise and so forth. Raw materials have a ready available market price, but outputs of waste and so forth can also be given a 'cost'. The difficulty is giving these items an economic value to factor into decision-making.

(c) **JIT** and **TQM** are both concerned to eliminate **waste** from the production process. TQM techniques have the effect of reducing physical waste and are thus friendly to the environment. They can be adapted to concentrate on toxic material waste.

(d) **Liabilities**. Firms sometimes face large 'clean-up' bills and are made liable for de-contaminating sites they used to occupy. Already in the UK there is a **landfill tax** and the aim of government policy might be to ensure through the tax system that the 'polluter pays'.

(e) **Product life assessments**. The CMA can measure the total environmental impact of a product throughout its 'life ', from its raw materials, through usage to decay. Valuable or scarce raw materials can be replaced with alternatives; the product can be designed to use less energy in operation. Its components can be recycled when it is obsolete. Some car manufacturers – with some prompting from governments - have introduced recycling schemes.

(f) Normal methods of **cost control and variance analysis** can be used for environmental issues. Moreover, some innovations (such as Combined Heat and Power plants) can save money as well as be friendly to the environment.

Concepts of **sustainability** and **inter-generational equity** (that we should not leave the world worse off than when found it) are harder for the CMA get involved in directly.

(a) The CMA works for organisations, and provides information regarding economic **costs and benefits**. Sustainability is more controversial. Arguably it is a matter for **governments** to deal with, in order to develop frameworks of incentives and 'punishments' so that firms and non profit orientated organisations are stimulated to behave in a sustainable way.

(b) Some economists believe that the **price mechanism** will encourage more efficient use (in environmental as well as economic terms) of scarce resources. Already car engines are far more fuel-efficient than a few years ago, although much of the efficiency gain is eaten up by increased vehicle weight.

(c) Some firms do have policies on **sustainability**. Furniture makers might decide not to use hardwoods from tropical rain forests.

(d) A final problem is **global warming**. Arguably there is no shortage of oil available for burning, which would release vast quantities of carbon dioxide into the atmosphere. Yet many firms are developing alternatives to petrol. The **Economist** recently suggested that cars powered by hydrogen – which release only water vapour into the atmosphere - have a great future.

Organisations and the CMAs they employ work in a framework of costs and potential revenues which are partly out of their control. They can adopt good environmental practice, and in many cases there are good **profit orientated** and **environmental** reasons for doing so. In other cases, government must give the lead, so that all companies operating in a particular jurisdiction face the same 'carrots and sticks'. Ecological standards will, however, vary across the world.

The CMA, as a major provider of information within the company and for this reason alone will be involved in a positive way in good environmental practice. This role is not diminished by the fact that for any organisation, forces outside it lay down the rules.

31 GENERIC STRATEGIES AND THE EXPERIENCE CURVE

Pass marks. This should be a familiar topic. The question needed a bit of thinking before jumping in. Do not be tempted to merely describe the model rather than criticise it. The examiner made a distinction between these two approaches, and those candidates who went for the former in their answer did not achieve a pass mark, while those who provided some criticism in their answer were rewarded.

Other points. You may have included diagrams of the models in your answer, and this is fine as long as you were not then drawn into excessive description of the model rather than criticism of it. The suggested solution provided by CIMA also has diagrams. We have not included them here as they are not strictly necessary for providing a good answer. While the examiner points out (see below) that many candidates confused the generic strategies model with the five competitive forces, we believe it is relevant to refer to the latter briefly, in that the strategies identified by Porter can protect a company against the five competitive forces. As the examiner notes, models do not exist in isolation.

Examiner's comments. Overall, the answers to this question were disappointing. Some confused this model with Porter's Five Forces model, and had difficulty linking it to the Experience Curve. This served to demonstrate lack of awareness of what the question actually required. A number of candidates fell into the trap of describing the model in some detail, rather than critically appraising it as required by the question. There is a danger of candidates treating models and theories as operating in isolation. One model or theory can inform another.

(a) **Competitive advantage** is anything which gives one company a head start against its rivals, mainly in relation to the **products or services** which it provides. The environment within which many companies compete is characterised by the need to both **obtain** this competitive advantage, and **protect** it.

This need arises because, although any of the competitive advantage that a company might hope to achieve is determined to some extent almost automatically by the **nature, quality, price** or **image** of its products, this will be eroded as competitors rush to share in the market.

The strategies for competitive advantage devised by Porter are **generic** in nature, because the best strategy for a company is always going to be unique to its specific circumstances.

Porter states that a company may pursue either **low cost** competitive advantage (providing comparable value to the customer more efficiently than competitors) or **differentiation** competitive advantage, whereby the company has comparable costs to its competitors but provides a product which has better features or satisfies customer needs in a unique way.

Companies can apply either of these strategies to a **broad** or a **narrow** market. Porter identified the three generic strategies for competitive advantage as **cost leadership** in the market as a whole, **differentiation** in the market as a whole, and **focus.** The latter strategy applies only to a narrow market, where cost leadership or differentiation is pursued within a focussed market segment.

Overall **cost leadership** seeks the position of lowest cost producer in the market, and hence highest profits as unit sales increase. It depends upon having **economies of scale,** and it is a necessary feature of the strategy that the company pursuing it should aim for other significant advantages such as productivity improvements or distribution advantages. This is because in industries where economies of scale are achievable, actual cost leadership is going to be a realistic goal for more than one company.

Cost leadership has the advantage that economies of scale raise **entry barriers,** and the firm is less vulnerable to price competition than its less cost effective competitor. However, cost leadership tends to ignore **product design** or **marketing** issues.

A **differentiation** strategy assumes that competitive advantage can be achieved through **product characteristics**. Assuming that customers are not too **price sensitive,** then they may be prepared to pay extra for a better designed or marketed product. There is always the likelihood and risk that they will become price sensitive sooner or later, and not pay this premium. It is therefore advisable to differentiate along several lines wherever possible, for example by having a highly visible branch network and effective customer service as well as high quality products.

Differentiation and innovation can be achieved at a low cost, but it is more likely that a differentiating firm will have a large **research and development** budget, or a high **advertising** spend. Differentiating firms have to pay to stay ahead of the game, as **imitation** erodes perceived differences between products.

Therefore, while Porter's model is useful in identifying areas for company attention, it is always possible to find companies that go for a **mix** of strategies. It is likely that product differentiation will be sought, which will impact on the customer's decision to buy, but this may cost more than an aspiring cost leader would wish.

It is not realistic to assert that only the lowest costs or differentiation **in isolation** build competitive advantage (**pricing policy**, for example, is also a major influence), but both cost leadership and differentiation can be said to protect a company against the **five competitive forces** (also outlined by Porter) and for this reason are to be aimed for in some proportion. The model does not, however, tell companies how to get there.

(b) One feature of strategic management is cost reduction, so as to obtain an advantage over competitors. As a process is **repeated,** it is likely that costs will reduce due to **efficiency, discounts,** and **reduced waste**.

Economies of scale may arise through the employment of **technology,** with larger outputs yielding lower unit costs of production. Japanese companies have been quoted as examples of the drive for volume leading to substantial lowering of cost.

The **Boston Consulting Group** has identified substantial evidence to support the theory that all costs of output (not just labour costs on a learning curve) are related to the **experience curve**. The curve has the following implications for strategy.

A policy of **reducing prices** as process costs fall can help a company to win a **dominant market share**. As costs fall, the company may find itself in a **cost leadership** position.

Greater experience can also be used to **differentiate** a product, either via greater experience of the market and customer expectations, or the ability to utilise existing technology in a unique way. With experience, products can be **redesigned** to improve production efficiency.

New products often hold their price in the early stages of their life cycle, while costs are going down, creating increasing profit margins. Expectation of these increasing margins can inform strategic decisions in other areas of the business.

32 TUTORIAL QUESTION: CORPORATE STRATEGY DEVELOPMENT

(a) A **position audit** is a detailed review of an organisation's current position, and is a useful starting point for developing strategies for the future. Position audit is defined in the CIMA's **Official Terminology** as:

'Part of the planning process which examines the current state of the entity in respect of:

(i) resources of tangible and intangible assets and finance;
(ii) products, brands and markets;
(iii) operating systems such as production and distribution;
(iv) internal organisation;
(v) current results;
(vi) returns to stockholders.'

The position audit will include a marketing audit and a resources audit.

(i) The **marketing audit** will establish information about **market share** for the company's products, the size of its **customer base**, the size and frequency of **orders**, the split of sales between **exports and domestic** markets, sales and contribution **growth** over the past few years, current sales **revenue** and **profitability** for each product, product group and in total etc.

(ii) A **resource audit** will provide information about the resources that the organisation uses, such as the number of **materials** suppliers, prices for materials, **supplier** reliability and quality, the size and skills of the labour force, **wages** costs, labour efficiency, labour **turnover**, industrial relations, the cost, age and efficiency of **machines** and other fixed assets, fixed asset utilisation, management experience and skills, **working capital** requirements, periods of credit given and taken, **stock levels** and turnover, **financial resources**, and intangible items such as **brands**, patents and goodwill.

(b) A **corporate appraisal** (**SWOT analysis**) follows on from a position audit and environmental analysis. Corporate appraisal is defined in the CIMA's **Official Terminology** as:

'A critical assessment of the strengths and weaknesses, opportunities and threats (SWOT analysis) in relation to the internal and environmental factors affecting an entity in order to establish its condition prior to the preparation of the long term plan.'

Strengths and weaknesses analysis involves looking at the particular strengths and weaknesses of the organisation itself and its product/service range.

(i) The strengths and weaknesses analysis is **internal** to the company but is intended to shape its approach to the **external** world. For instance, the identification of shortcomings in skills or resources could lead to a planned acquisition programme or to more staff recruitment and training.

(ii) In essence, an internal appraisal seeks to identify:

(1) shortcomings in the company's present skills and resources; and
(2) strengths which the company should seek to exploit.

The **external appraisal** of **opportunities** and **threats** follows on from the environmental analysis and position audit.

(i) The analysis of opportunities would involve:

(1) identifying business opportunities and their inherent potential (eg for making profits);

(2) assessing whether the organisation has sufficient strengths to exploit these opportunities, and whether competitors are better placed to exploit them.

(ii) The analysis of threats involves identifying potential threats to the organisation, from economic change, government regulations, competitors, technological change, social/demographic changes and so on.

SWOT analysis should help the planners to develop strategies that will exploit attractive opportunities, take defensive measures against threats, exploit strengths and reduce weaknesses.

33 TUTORIAL QUESTION: GAP ANALYSIS AND VALUE CHAIN

(a) **Gap analysis** is 'a technique which attempts to analyse the 'gap' between an entity's **ultimate objective** and the **expected performance** from projects planned and under way, identifying means by which any identified difference, or gap, might be filled' (CIMA).

The two broad stages in gap analysis are as follows.

(i) To assess the **size of the gap** between the organisation's targets for achievement compared with a projection of what the organisation will actually achieve.

(ii) Considering strategies to **close the gap**.

Gap analysis will cover the planning period, year by year, and the size of the gap will vary over time.

A **variety of gaps** can be analysed. These include a profit gap, a performance-risk gap, a sales revenue gap, a manpower gap, an EPS gap, and so on.

If gap analysis is applied to a product/market situation, the organisation will be considering its targets for the type of products it wants to be making and the markets or market segments it wants to be selling them in.

The **product/market targets** might be quantified as follows.

(i) The organisation should have targets for the numbers of **products** it would like to be selling, classified perhaps into:

(1) those in the introductory stage of their **life**, those in the growth stage, those at maturity and those in decline;

(2) alternatively, using the **BCG classifications**, cash cows, rising stars, dogs and question marks;

(3) another way of targeting products would be to determine what **sort of products** the company wants to sell - eg does it want a more diversified range of products?

(ii) There should also be targets for the **markets or market segments** that the organisation would like to be in, and targets for:

(1) market **share** or market segment share, both in existing markets and markets it would like to break into; and

(2) market **positioning**. Positioning is concerned with such matters as product quality, image and reliability, price, distribution outlets, type of customers.

A projection of the organisation's products, and the market shares and market positioning for each of its products, would be made on the assumption that:

(i) no new products are developed;
(ii) the marketing mix for existing products remains the same.

The 'gap' could be analysed in terms of:

(i) what products the organisation will be missing from its product range (eg how many cash cows will it fall short of target, how many rising stars will it lack, how many newly-developed products will it lack etc);

(ii) what markets or market segments it is failing to sell into, or failing to win an adequate share of;

(iii) how far 'out of position' in the market the product will be.

Strategies to close the gap would include:

(i) new product **development strategies** or new market development strategies;
(ii) a strategy of product and market **diversification** through a takeover policy;
(iii) a marketing **mix strategy**, to gain the required position in target markets.

(b) The **value chain** is a model of how the organisation's **activities** and the **links** between them add value. It is 'the sequence of business activities by which, in the perspective of the end user, value is added to the products or services produced by an organisation' (CIMA). It describes activities where costs are incurred and where value is added to inputs.

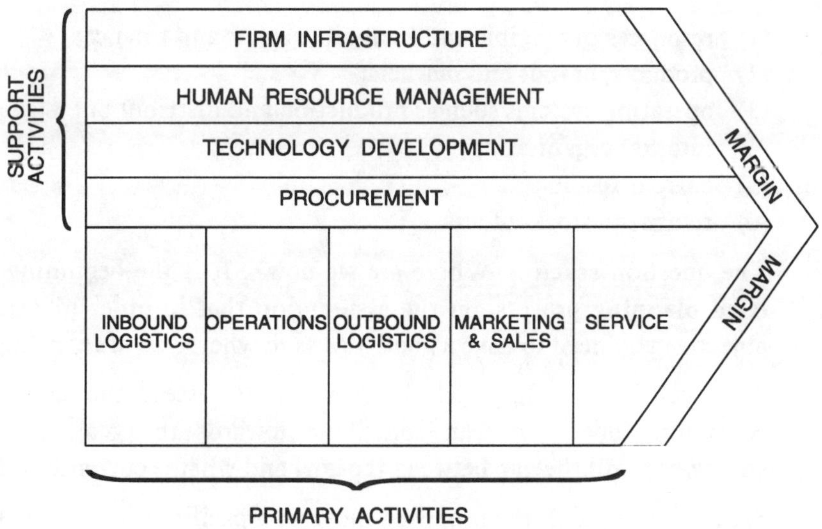

Primary activities are those activities which **directly add value.**

(i) **Inbound logistics** relates to the receipt and storage of raw materials, stock control, and distribution within the factory and so forth.

(ii) **Operations** relates to manufacture, assembly and packaging goods for distribution.

(iii) **Outbound logistics** refers to warehousing and distribution and order processing.

(iv) **Marketing and sales** are those activities involved in generating demand for products and services, and include advertising and sales promotion and so forth.

(v) **Services** involve maintenance and repair, training and so forth.

Secondary, or support, activities are those which provide the **framework** for the primary activities to occur. For example, a firm's productive capacity can be severely impeded by a poor technology policy.

(i) Firm **infrastructure** relates to finance, management, quality control and accounting.

(ii) **Human resource management** refers to personnel recruitment and training.

(iii) **Technology development** refers to research and development relating:

(1) to new products;

(2) to new production technology and work organisation;

(3) to information technology to enhance other activities (such as the development of marketing databases).

(iv) **Procurement** refers to the purchasing of materials, temporary staff, and other inputs.

34 IMPERIAL TRADERS

Pass marks. Remember, it is only Head Office which is being transferred, not the entire company. In part (c) don't generalise into discussions about tax and exchange rates: it is cultural issues which interest us.

(a) (i) A **position audit** is defined in the CIMA's Official Terminology as follows.

'Part of the planning process which examines the current state of the entity in respect of:

(1) resources of tangible and intangible assets and finance;
(2) products, brands and markets;
(3) operating systems such as production and distribution;
(4) internal organisation;
(5) current results;
(6) returns to stockholders.'

The question asked is 'Where are we now?'. It is the beginning of the **long term planning** process, on the assumption that in order to reach a desired objective you need to have a good idea as to where you are starting.

This will enable Imperial Traders plc to assess the extent to which continuing operations can contribute towards the goal, and to develop strategies to fill the **gap** between the goal and what is currently achievable.

When dealing with the proposed move to a pacific rim location, the position audit will deal with all the factors noted in the CIMA's definition:

(1) for the company as a whole;

(2) for the Head Office entity in particular, in more detail in the context of the firm's **internal operation**, and in its relations with the **wider commercial environment** and with investors and bankers.

Obviously a crucial part of the position audit will be the gathering of **comparative cost information** for London and various regional sites. The current role of Head Office in its location must be assessed.

Only after such a position audit is carried out, can management decide:

(1) **whether to move** at all;
(2) if a move is desirable, **where to go to**;
(3) **how** the move will be implemented successfully.

(ii) A formal position audit in respect of this decision will enable a balanced assessment of the role of Head Office to be made.

(1) We do not know the **degree of control** Head Office exercises over the local businesses. It might, like Hanson or BTR, simply set **financial targets** for the businesses to meet, avoiding interference with tactical or day to day decisions. The role of Head Office is to **communicate** with the investment community, to be a central location for **financial**

reporting, and to act as a **domicile** for the company so that it can take advantage of a favourable tax regime.

If it is felt that Head Office has a minimal **operational** function, it might be better to keep it in the UK for the benefit of the company's investors. Moreover, the City of London is a centre of world finance.

(2) On the other hand, the Head Office role has a **hands-on approach** to the running of the company. It may be the case that all its activities are heavily interrelated, and Head Office **co-ordination** is essential for the company's successful functioning.

(3) A position audit of the company as a whole would identify those **regions** which are most **critical** to its long term success. If that region is Japan, for example, this might be a good reason for relocating to that country.

More broadly, the position audit should identify all the major costs and benefits of such a move, in a formal way, and so should result in a better decision.

(b) **Effects of relocating to a Pacific Rim country**

The term Pacific Rim is normally held to encompass the west coast of the USA, Indonesia, the Philippines, and the rapidly growing region of southern China as well as the area of Imperial Traders plc's current operations which comprises Japan, Korea, Malaysia, and Australia.

The final choice as to which of the latter countries will be the site of the new Head Office will be as significant as the decision to move away at all.

(i) **Tangible assets**

(1) Imperial Traders will need to sell its London accommodation. The price it receives may be a major factor in the **economic benefits** of the relocation decision.

(2) Office space in the country of choice will have to be purchased. Two considerations matter here.

- The **relative price of office space** in each country will differ significantly. Japan, despite the current slump in land prices, is extremely expensive. Perhaps an Australian location would be cheaper.
- There may be **legal restrictions** in some countries on the purchase of land by foreign companies.

(ii) Imperial Traders will be moving away from London, which has one of the world's most developed **capital markets**. Will its needs be as well satisfied in one of the Pacific Rim countries? A country with a relatively open financial system, such as Australia, might be better than, say, Korea. Tokyo is also one of the world's leading financial centres, and so might be attractive on that count. The company already deals with providers of trade finance, so this should not be any great problem.

(iii) We do not know which products are Imperial Traders plc's particular speciality. It might specialise in trading commodity products (such as wool from Australia to textile factories elsewhere), it might specialise in trading manufactured goods or it might not specialise at all.

If Imperial Traders plc is basically a **transport and distribution** company, then the domicile of its Head Office is unlikely to matter in terms of its trade, or in attracting business. It might, however, bring the head office closer to its main markets, so **market knowledge** by head office staff might be enhanced, and **decision making** speeded up.

If Head Office plays a co-ordinating role, it might be able to develop a better **strategic vision** as to where it wants to be if this function is located in its main market.

(iv) **Operating systems**. Savings will be made on those systems which merely connect the region to the London head office. The firm will have to arrange appropriate **telecommunications** links.

(v) The **internal organisation**. This is where the difference will be greatest. The company may wish to avoid the expense of relocation, and prefer to **recruit** staff locally. There are likely to be redundancy costs in the UK, and the cost of hiring and training staff in the area.

(vi) **Current results**. There will be a number of costs entailed in the move. Careful planning should minimise this risk.

It is possible that the firm might receive relocation subsidies from some countries, or it may be able to negotiate a tax holiday if the country wishes it to locate there.

(vii) **Returns to stockholders**. Initially, there might be an adverse effect, owing to the costs of the move. The firm might have used sterling more often as there was a London Head Office. As currency flows are likely to remain within the Pacific Rim region, the currency risk will be different. This might significantly affect the reported returns to stockholders, who would seem to be based in the UK. If the company can find capital at cheaper rates than in the UK this will reduce its interest charge, and might make certain activities appear more attractive.

(c) **Cultural differences**

Imperial Traders plc's activities are divided between two Commonwealth countries (Australia and Malaysia) and Japan and Korea.

(i) **Language**. If any Head Office staff relocate to Australia, there will be no problem with language. In Korea or Japan, however, staff will need a good working knowledge of the local knowledge.

(ii) **Business culture.** Different cultures have different ways of doing business.

(iii) **Different legal systems.** Australia probably has the legal system most like the UK's.

(iv) **Women**. Female executives may find it harder to be accepted by Japanese counterparts.

(v) **Personal problems.** Newly expatriate staff will need to adjust to different climate, diet, and working hours. Those with families will have to find education provision for their children, and perhaps employment for spouses.

35 ORIENTATION AND CUSTOMER PROFITABILITY

Pass marks. Although a fairly straightforward knowledge-based question, this requires you to combine your knowledge of **two** aspects of the syllabus, marketing orientation and customer profitability, to see how they relate to each other. You were given a helping hand, as the wording of the question identified the main elements of the marketing and sales orientation.

Examiner's comments. In part (a) candidates were required to **discuss** the issues - in other words, a list was not enough. A discussion should mean an explanation of the opposing arguments. Despite the contrast between the two orientations outlined in the question, many candidates confused them in part (b). The whole point about a marketing orientation is that it is centred around the customer.

(a) **Benefits from carrying out customer profitability analysis**

Customer profitability analysis (CPA) is, according to CIMA's Official Terminology, the 'analysis of revenue streams and service costs associated with specific customers or customer groups'.

Historically, many firms monitored costs in relation to products rather than customers. However, as Ward notes, 'an immediate impact of introducing any level of strategic management accounting...is to destroy totally any illusion that the same level of profit is derived from all of customers.' In other words, **profit does not always increase with sales revenue,** and this can be influenced, not only by increased production costs, for example, but also by the ways in which different customers are treated.

Causes of different levels of customer profitability

(i) Volume discounts, frequency of orders, complexity of orders, size of orders, frequency of deliveries, distance, transportation costs, sales mix, customisation costs, working capital costs (of slow) payers, are obviously costs that can be traced to individual customers.

(ii) Other costs can be specifically related to **particular market segments,** such as tailored advertising, the cost of complying with different regulations in different markets and so forth.

Advantages of identifying customer profitability

(i) A company can **focus its efforts** on customers who offer the highest profit.

(ii) If the behaviour/aspects of different customers cause different level of costs then the firm can **rationalise its approach** to different groups of customers. Low cost customers can be rewarded with lower prices; high cost customers can be made to pay more for the service or, alternatively, the firm can review its operations with a view to reducing the cost of the customer-generated activities. For example, electronic data interchange can reduce order processing costs.

(iii) CPA can be used as part of a comparative analysis of **competitors' costs,** especially in relation to a focus strategy. A firm which services a customer more cheaply than a competitor can use this cost advantage to offer benefits to the customer or segment which the competitor cannot afford.

(iv) CPA can be used in **negotiations.** A firm which knows what level of profit can be earned from a customer will not negotiate over-generous terms.

(v) Cross-subsidy has often been the practice of utilities - high charges to business customers has enabled them to subsidise domestic users. with **competition and regulation,** utilities pricing has to be more transparent.

Although these benefits are real, they do not always apply and a true estimate of customer profitability, especially for market segments, is not always easy to find.

(i) Firms need to identify precisely which costs would be **avoided** by ceasing to serve a particular customer or group. Giving up some customers will mean that current unavoidable costs are spread over the smaller number of customers who remain.

(ii) The **practicality and cost** of collecting information might be prohibitive for the benefit gained. For example, the Post Office does not track each letter through the system even if each costs a different amount to sort and deliver.

(iii) It may not be possible to **trace the effect** of an advertising campaign to a particular customer or segment's purchasing decision.

(iv) Even if CPA information **is** collected, a firm may be unable to use it to pass on costs to customers. A customer with **high bargaining power** may be in a position to refuse to pay or may defect to a competitor.

(v) Some of the costs of reaching customers or segments may be **borne by distributors** anyway, who have their own objectives.

(b) **CPA and sales or marketing orientation**

A **sales orientation** is an approach to the market which focuses on the needs of the seller rather than the needs of the customer. A sales orientated firm believes that customers are by nature sales-resistant and have to be persuaded to buy more.

Typical management accounting information in a sales orientated firm would therefore include the following.

(i) Total **volume sales**, with a target to be achieved over a period or in relation to another period.

(ii) Total **sales revenue**, with a similar target to be achieved over a period

(iii) (i) and (ii) above will be broken down into **sales areas** or even by sales person. Every sales person will have to achieve a particular target in order to win a bonus or a certain level of commission. (i) and (ii) can therefore be turned into **performance indicators.**

(iv) Non-financial performance indicators might be included, such as number of **customer leads** generated, number of customer contacts, the ratio of sales to customer leads.

Of course sales figures are not the only story, and a sales orientated firm will also require data on production and other costs.

(i) **Cost** per product

(ii) **Capacity** utilisation

(iii) **Functional costs** for the sales department, the warehouse, the fleet, the marketing department (eg advertising, marketing research), and relevant performance indicators

(iv) Total **profit** for the period

Overall the firm might also monitor **market share** in relation to competitors, especially consumer products industries.

The management accounting system may contain data which can be configured to identify customer profitability, but such an analysis by customer will not be made.

The **marketing orientation** focuses on the needs of customers: marketers understand that a customer is buying a package of benefits to satisfy needs.

CPA is an analysis of costs - in part (a) of the question we suggested that, for reasons of practicality, cost and commercial value, it may not always be relevant. A firm could have a genuine marketing orientation without undergoing the rigours of CPA.

However, many marketing-orientated firms will benefit from CPA, and, in order to satisfy the **'profit' aspect of the marketing orientation**, they may need to identify customer profitability.

A marketing orientated company will require all the sales volume and product cost information outlined for the sales orientation, but might **structure** it in a different way, or might set up a **database** so that the costs can be appropriately classified. An example, adapted from Ward, is offered below.

		£'000
Sales revenue		X
Less direct product cost		(X)
		X
Customer-specific variable costs:		
- distribution	X	
- rebates and discounts	X	
- promotion etc	X	
		(X)
		X
Other costs		
- sales force	X	
- customer service	X	
- management cost	X	
		(X)
		X
Financing cost		
- credit period	X	
- customer-specific inventory	X	
		(X)
		X

There is no point in identifying unavoidable costs in the statement. For example, the sales director's salary is unavoidable in the short term. However, for **cost control** purposes, an **activity-based costing** approach can identify where costs can be reduced.

A problem with applying CPA to **market segments** is identifying which segmentation variable is most important. For example, information might be collected by area because that is how the sales force is organised. However, the natural segmentation basis might be customer size.

36 BCG MATRIX I

Pass marks. Part (a) was surprising as you would expect the application of the BCG matrix in the strategic management of the firm, rather than the mechanics of its construction, to be the main subject of the question, even though this was partly addressed in section (b). Also the BCG model does not only apply to SBUs. It applies to a portfolio of products.

Examiner's comments. A very popular question but poorly answered. Candidates did not read the question and explicitly ignored instructions to disregard the contents of each quadrant of the matrix. Instead candidates were supposed to concentrate on the two axes, market growth and market share. Part (b) asked for a critical appraisal.

(a) A diagram of the **BCG matrix** is given below. A product or an SBU can be positioned on the matrix and compared with other products or SBUs.

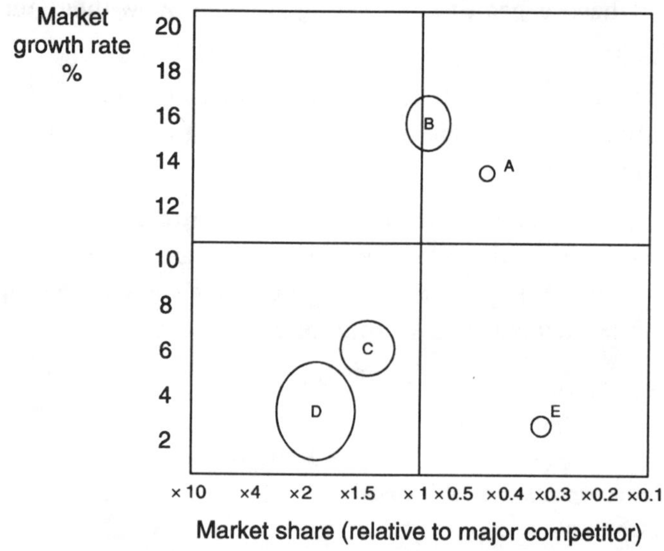

(i) The vertical axis represents the **growth rate of the market** for a product, in annual percentage terms. The matrix typically shows growth rates of up to 20% pa, with growth rates over 10% being considered high. Of course in fashion goods industries, markets for some products grow much faster than this, if only to peak and fall at a later date.

(ii) The horizontal axis represents the **market share** of a product or an SBU. It refers specifically to market share relative to the **largest competitor**. For example, a relative market share of 0.1 means that sales of the product are only 10% of the leader's volume. A score of 4, suggests that the SBU or product is the leader and has four times the market share of the next biggest competitor. A score of 1 on this axis suggests joint leadership.

(b) The matrix divides into **four quadrants**, with different combinations of growth and share. The assumption is that products/SBUs in each quadrant have different profit and cash characteristics.

For example products with high market share in a low-growth market (**cash cows**), need little investment other than expenditure to maintain the position and can be milked for cash to be invested in products with a low share of a high growth market (**question marks**), which can be turned into **stars**, with high shares of high growth markets.

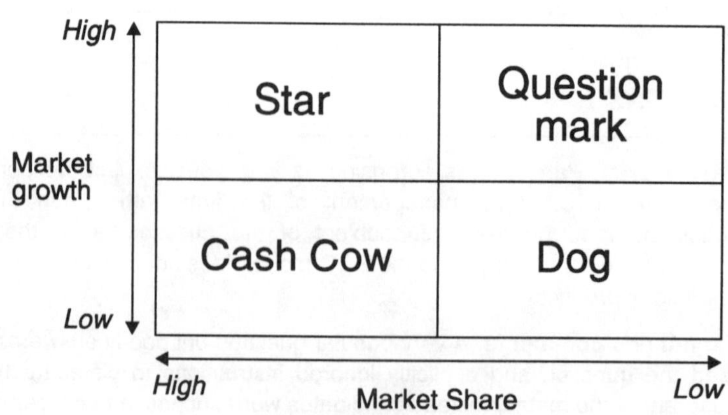

The BCG matrix is one of several **'portfolio' approaches** to managing a business. Such approaches see a business as a collection of cash-generating or cash-using investment projects, which have to be balanced for the business to be successful. In principle, as suggested above, a firm needs cash cows to generate cash to invest in new stars or question mark products. **Dogs** (low shares of low growth markets) should be killed off as the cash can be more profitably used elsewhere.

There are a number of **criticisms** of the approach.

(i) By concentrating on external matters only, it **ignores the internal configuration** of the business. After all, a high growth market will be attractive for that reason. Used on its own, it could generate **unfocused diversification**. For example, some Japanese steelmakers diversified into IT without conspicuous success.

(ii) According to Kotler, they may lead managers to place '**too much emphasis on market-share growth businesses** to the neglect of managing the current businesses, thereby leaving themselves vulnerable to competitors who can configure the value chain in different ways.

(iii) The results of the matrices can be **manipulated**. A lot of businesses, according to Kotler, can be positioned in the middle of the matrix, even though their underlying characteristics are very different.

(iv) They **fail to identify synergies** between different businesses and over simplify the cost structure. Deleting dogs from a portfolio might save money, but only if all the costs of the dogs are avoided.

(v) They provide no advice on markets which are in **decline**. It is possible to make profits in declining markets with the right strategy (eg by consolidating the industry).

(vi) **Identifying the market and market share**. Markets can be segmented, and so measures of 'relative market share' must be taken with caution. Firms can build entry barriers round their favoured segments.

37 BCG MATRIX II

Pass marks. The first part of this question is a chance for some easy marks, as long as you are familiar with the model. Brief discussion of the product life cycle helps to put the BCG matrix into context. Remember that models do not exist in isolation. Do not lose sight of the fact that the question refers to SBUs, not products.

The question does not look for specific application to public sector organisations until part (b), which requires a bit more original thought. Public sector organisations are, as the data in the question indicates, subject to increased competition and the BCG matrix may well be a useful tool for them when devising strategy. We have taken the UK Post Office as an example.

Examiner's comments. This was the most popular question in Section B. It was clear that most candidates were comfortable with the BCG matrix. Regrettably, some confused it with Ansoff's growth vector matrix. Part (a) was generally well answered, although some failed to relate their answers to cash flows as requested. Part (b) was not well answered in the main, with most candidates having great difficulty relating the matrix to the public sector. Some good answers looked at the application of the matrix within such areas as health, higher education, postal services and local authority sports centres.

(a) The Boston consulting Group (BCG) Growth Share Matrix can be a useful tool in **portfolio planning**. The **aims** of portfolio planning are both to identify the current strengths or weaknesses of an organisation's **products** or SBUs in its **markets**, and the state of **growth or decline** in each of these markets, and to identify what **strategy** is needed to maintain a strong position or improve a weak one.

The BCG matrix incorporates the concepts of the **product life cycle** into a matrix assessing products' strategic position. Many firms provide a number of different products with different characteristics. The combination of products will influence the performance of the firm. Products' profitability and sales are likely to change over time, and the product life cycle attempts to track this history, from introduction of the product, through growth and maturity and into decline.

Different product forms will have different life cycles, and while it is true that the product life cycle concept has its limitations (some products such as Kellogg's Corn Flakes never seem to decline, for example) it is a tool which is useful for firms attempting to look to the **longer term** and estimate how much each product or business unit is likely to contribute towards sales revenue and profitability.

Many large firms are organised into strategic business units (SBUs). A **SBU** is a section, within a larger organisation, which is responsible for planning, developing, producing and marketing its **own products** or services. This may be one product or several. Managers control their own resources. SBUs have an external market **distinct** from those of other SBUs.

The BCG matrix can analyse SBUs by **relative market share, growth rate** and **sales value.** It may compare SBUs with each other, or compare products within an individual SBU.

The relative market share is measured in comparison with the largest competitor and so can demonstrate a business unit's strength in its relevant market. The matrix is expressed diagrammatically below.

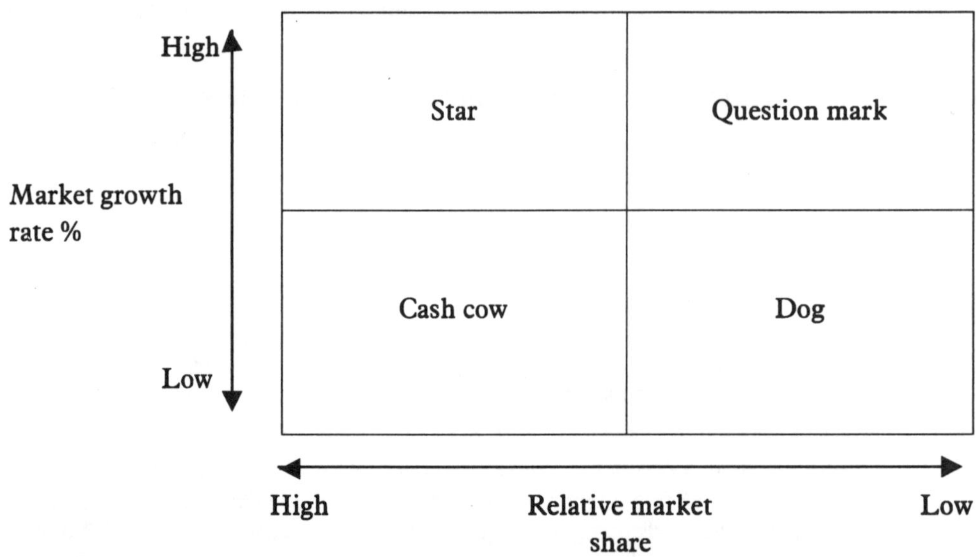

Stars are business units with a high share of a high growth market. They generate cash, but possibly less in the short term than the capital expenditure required to initiate them. They promise high returns in the future. An example may be a business unit manufacturing high specification computer components.

Stars become, as the cycle goes on, **cash cows,** with a high share of a low growth market. The market beds down for a period of stability and the cash cows in it can generate high levels of cash income. This cash can be invested in more stars so as to improve market share where growth opportunities are strongest. An example of a cash cow may be the Mars bar in the UK chocolate market. The SBU in the Mars organisation responsible for chocolate bars may well be financing (directly or indirectly) new product development.

A **question mark** is a product in a high growth market with low market share. A decision will need to be taken about whether the product or unit justifies considerable expenditure, in the hope of increasing its market share. An example is provided by Philips consumer products division, which has relatively poor recognition in the UK when compared with rivals such a Sony. Question marks will usually be poor cash generators and show a negative cash flow, and need **considerable investment** to convert them to star status.

Dogs are products with a low share of a low growth market. Although they will show only modest cash flows (in or out) they tie up funds and provide a poor return on investment when the money would be better spent elsewhere.

Stars and questions marks corresponds to a market in a growth phase, while cash cows and dogs represent a mature market. In the introduction phase of a product or division there may be **infants** (in the early stages of development), while in market decline there are **war horses** (products that were cash cows in the past and are still making acceptable sales and profits even now) and **dodos** (negative growth and cash flows).

The components of the BCG matrix provide a useful approach to the analysis of the product/market mix, assuming that the company is able to decide where on the matrix its various divisions sit. Providing that this initial position analysis is accurate, the company can decide where to focus its attention within its overall **strategy** and plan its deployment of cash resources.

(b) The term **public sector** represents a wide field of operations. It includes government, local government, the health service and the nationalised industries. It is quite difficult to try and define a **primary objective** for a public sector organisation. Government funding in most cases means that '**survival**' as an objective is inapplicable. The organisations often exist to provide a service, so **profitability** as a sole objective is not appropriate either - a bus service seeking higher profits might stop providing buses on an unprofitable route, but this would damage the service provision.

One approach is to aim for the most **effective deployment** of **resources** in a responsible manner, so as to maximise the service provision and **minimise the cost**. However, it is important to bear in mind that the circumstances of different organisations vary so widely that a strategy which is appropriate for one organisation will not be appropriate for another.

The BCG Growth Share Matrix was described in part (a) and may be applicable when considering the strategic development of a public sector service facing competition. The development of a strategy broadly involves identifying the customer, determining their needs, preparing a mission statement, preparing a list of goals, translating those goals into specific measurable objectives and planning a strategy to achieve those objectives.

Taking the example of the Post Office in the UK, we can examine the usefulness of the BCG matrix.

The Post Office is one of the notable non-nationalised industries in the UK, but is facing increased competition for its services from fax, e-mail, parcel delivery organisations and privatised European counterparts, for example in Germany and the Netherlands. A recent package of reforms has still left it with less commercial freedom than other European postal services, at a time when it needs to move quickly to keep its position in the global market. The Post Office needs funds to finance acquisitions and joint ventures. The level and type of investment is to stay under government control.

The Post Office therefore faces a challenge in maintaining a hold in the market. Applying the matrix, we can classify some examples of Post Office products as follows.

Stars. Parcel delivery is a growth market but the Post Office share is threatened by private delivery companies. The Post Office could benefit from strategic alliances in this area to enhance its network, which would promise high returns in the future. As mentioned above, however, it is subject to financial and investment controls by the government, which guarantees its debts.

Cash cows. Letter delivery, one of the Post Office's 'basics', is threatened by fax and e-mail. The Post Office has strong cash flow from this area, with the bulk of its turnover coming from the commercial sector. These high levels of cash could be used to invest in lucrative new markets. It should be noted that the basic Post Office services also include an element of cross-subsidisation of socially useful areas. These include a network of small branches, and the delivery of letters to remote places for the same price as that paid by customers in areas which are easier to reach. This service provision is unprofitable, and in a profit seeking company would in all probability be discontinued.

Question marks. Services such as mailshots could be provided for commercial clients, but the Post Office share of this lucrative market is low and would require considerable expenditure. As stated already, however, government funding means government control of investment projects.

The example of the Post Office shows that while the matrix is a useful tool for classification and indication of growth opportunities, it cannot enable a public sector service to escape from any of the constraints that are imposed upon it. It may provide a starting point for development of a strategy that would support the service in its negotiations with the government over funding and control, and possible privatisation in the longer term.

38 VALUE CHAIN ANALYSIS

Pass marks. A straightforward question about a useful business model –it asked for more than just a description. If you bring in examples, make sure that they are relevant. Apply your knowledge carefully.

Other points. We have discussed the value chain beyond the boundaries of the organisation. For example, it operates throughout the entire supply chain. The examiner noted that this point was overlooked by the vast majority of candidates. Well done if you have extended your discussion to cover this aspect.

Examiner's comments. This was one of the most popular questions on the paper. A mere description of Porter's model was not sufficient, as the thrust of the question was in applying the model to strategic decisions such as resource allocation.

The **value chain model** shows how the activities of the firm should be **configured** to ensure that a firm provides a product/service which its clients will value. The value chain describes **all the activities** of the firm (not necessarily the departments in which those activities are managed).

Value chain

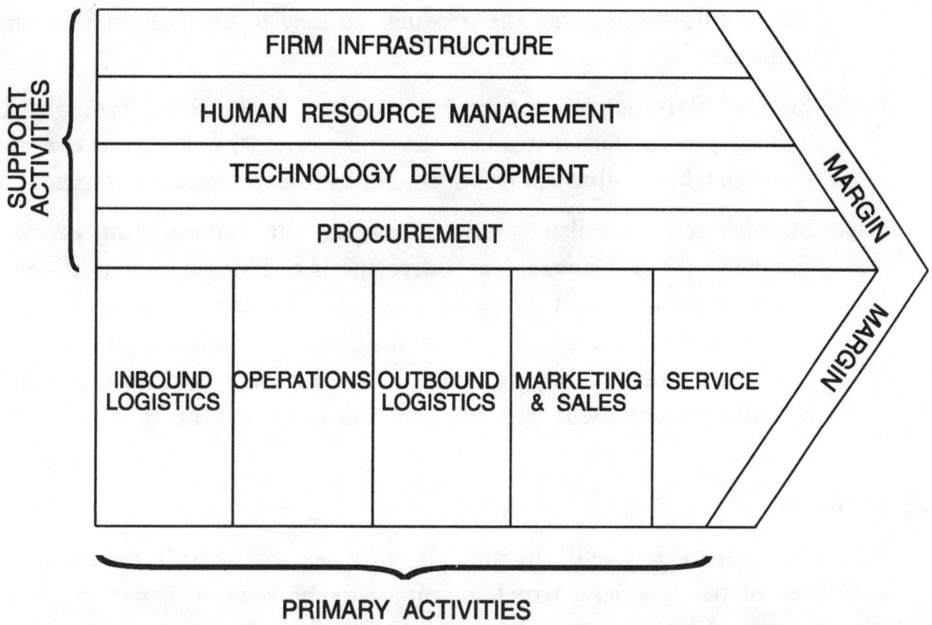

Primary activities relate to the production of goods and services. They cover inbound logistics, such as warehouse operations, the production process itself, delivery, selling and after sales service. Supporting these activities are human resources, R & D and so on.

The value chain suggests that all these activities are part of the process of transforming **inputs,** perhaps from other suppliers' outputs, in order to earn a **margin or profit** for the business. In fact, a firm's value chain is one of several linking suppliers and customers in a **value system.**

Value chain analysis provides a model of the firm. Effort should be devoted to those activities which **add value.** Those activities which do not add value in the long and short terms are wasteful. In this, value chain analysis echoes the **quality** movement.

Value chain analysis can be used in the following way.

(a) **Assess each activity in the chain** to see how it adds value or whether there are better ways of adding value.

   (i) **Inbound logistics** - warehousing is a cost incurred to support production operations. Perhaps just in time purchasing would reduce the waste involved - although JIT may not be right in all cases.

   (ii) **Operations are extensive**. But do they add value most effectively? Some operations, such as sub-component manufacture, can be outsourced. For example, most manufacturers of computers outsource their supply of memory chips to firms such as Intel and Motorola.

   (iii) **Outbound logistics involves physical distribution** - getting the goods to the customer. Again, the best way is to maximise customer benefits for the minimum of cost. IKEA dealt with this problem by, effectively, outsourcing assembly and distribution of furniture to its customers. Customers carry the pieces away in their cars, and assemble them at home. Other furniture suppliers manufacture the items themselves and deliver by lorry.

   (iv) **Marketing and sales communicate the product to the customer.** They add value because marketing techniques can be used to identify customer needs, thereby avoiding wasted effort by the firm on products which will not sell.

   (v) **After sales service is very important in some contexts.** A good example is computer and network upgrades or helplines for new software. Of course, the aim should be to make the products so easy to use that they do not need a helpline.

(vi) Support activities are not directly involved in the short term with the value adding process but instead in the long term with **creating the conditions** through which value can be added, hence research and development.

(vii) Support activities also involve **managing the value-adding process,** hence the need for a management infrastructure. Human resource development refers to training and developing people . **Procurement** refers to obtaining inputs to the process - by some definitions this includes both recruitment of personnel and also buying components. In some businesses, such as retail, effective procurement is part of operations, so central is it to the success of the firm.

(b) **Linkages**

The value chain is useful because it provides an **overall perspective of the activities** of the business, which might easily be seen in isolation in functional departments. For example does the marketing department provide relevant information to the production function or to research and development? Does the firm infrastructure promote or impede such communication?

The role of the value chain in strategic resource allocation

Porter identified three aspects of **competitive strategy.**

(a) **Cost leadership,** in the industry as a whole.

(b) **Differentiation,** again on an industry wide basis.

(c) **Focus** on a segment (but pursue cost leadership or differentiation within that segment).

Focus is based on a review of customers and their needs, and thus does not initially involve looking at the firm's internal operations.

(a) In a **cost leadership strategy**, the value chain can be used to identify all the cost-incurring activities.

(i) Management attention can focus on investing in those activities which offer the greatest scope for **efficiencies** and **cost reduction**

(ii) As cost leadership concerns efficient use of **capacity** it can also consider investing resources in selling and marketing to build up **market share**

(iii) Some activities might be **outsourced,** if money can be saved.

(b) In a **differentiation** strategy, the value chain can be used in a more creative way in developing ways of satisfying customers. Each activity in the value chain can be configured in a different way to offer a differentiated product/service.

This can be best illustrated with an example.

(i) **Amazon Books** is the world's largest internet bookshop. The firm is sited near book wholesalers; it takes orders from all over the world via the internet and delivers by post.

(ii) **Books Etc** and other firms create a physical environment conducive to browsing and book purchase.

These are two very contrasting examples as to how books can be sold to the customer. In practice, because barriers to entry in the internet bookshop business are so low, many more established companies are offering the service. Bookshops also differentiate themselves by the **product range** they offer.

This suggests that the value chain **should support the differentiation strategy**. Amazon Books is more likely to concentrate on IT systems and logistical issues, whereas Books Etc will concentrate on customer service and creating the right retail environment, including, for example, staff who are well informed.

39 CUSTOMER ACCOUNT PROFITABILITY

Pass marks. Make sure you are clear about what CAP analysis is for. It is founded on the belief that it is more expensive to go out and find new customers than it is to retain existing ones. Given that, companies are well advised to find out which of their existing customers are the most profitable. The examiner commented that few candidates expressed this. Make sure in your answer to part (b) that you relate your points to EPS and shareholder value.

Examiner's comments. Good answers to this question were rare. Few candidates pointed out that it is more expensive to develop new customers than retain existing ones. Many candidates did not relate their appraisal of CAP to increasing EPS or enhancing shareholder value. The issue of short versus long termism is also relevant to this question, in that CAP may enhance the overall profitability of companies in the long term (thereby at odds with shareholders seeking short term returns from increased dividends). This issue was not explored by most candidates.

(a) Customer account profitability (CAP) analysis examines the revenue streams and service costs (and hence the profitability) associated with **specific customers or customer groups**, rather than products.

Customers do not all generate the same levels of profit. The **costs associated with customers can vary** depending on how customers are serviced. Some customers will get volume discounts, and others may be charged different rates (for example, the distinction made by power companies between domestic and business users). Some customers may be more difficult to get to, and therefore have higher associated distribution costs.

CAP analysis suggests that the profit from two different customers does not increase by the same amount (if at all), given the same increase in sales revenue. This will affect **marketing policy**. With CAP a company can focus its efforts on customers who promise the highest profit, and rationalise its approach to those who do not. A company may decide to focus on its existing customers rather than overspend on attracting new ones. It is well recognised that it is **cheaper to retain existing customers than to recruit** others.

(b) Increasing **EPS** and **returns to shareholders** is likely to be a key organisational objective. Shareholders seek short-term dividend income, but also longer term capital growth via the market value of their shares. These objectives may conflict. CAP can help to increase the market value of a company by identifying those customers which it is most profitable to retain. Companies often find that they spend too much time and effort on customers who desert them for cheaper competitors at the first opportunity.

Customers worth investing in are those who remain loyal, who spend money on repeat visits and encourage others to do the same. Repeat sales are important to the continued success of a company, generating higher revenue and therefore more opportunity for profit. Focusing attention on the needs of the most profitable customers is likely to lead to improved levels of customer service which will in turn please customers and encourage repeat business.

Different customer costs can arise from differing order sizes, the sales mix, order processing and complexity, transport costs, management time, cash flow problems caused by slow payers, stockholding costs and the customer's own negotiating strength. A strong customer may have used duress to negotiate terms which the supplier would not ordinarily have agreed to. CAP should lead to a review of such unprofitable relationships, and renegotiation of terms on a more favourable footing.

How do you identify which customers, or customer groups generate the most profit? This is a consideration that must be brought into the design of **management information** and administration systems. The firm's existing customer groupings, as reported in management accounts, may reflect administrative measures rather than their **strategic value**.

To analyse customer profitability successfully it may be necessary to structure accounting **information systems** to take account of the many factors by which customers can be analysed. The information systems will probably benefit from the attention that they receive.

Reports thus generated can highlight the differences between the cost of servicing different customers, which can then be applied to **maximising shareholder returns** as follows.

(a) **Directing effort to cutting customer specific costs**. Installing an electric data interchange system (EDI) can save the costs of paperwork and data input.

(b) **Identifying those customers who are expensive to service**, thereby suggesting action to increase profitability.

(c) **Using CAP as part of a comparison with competitors' costs**. A firm which services a customer more cheaply than a competitor can use this cost advantage to offer extra benefits to the customer.

(d) Indicating cases where **profitability might be endangered**, for example by servicing customers for whom the firm's core competence is not especially relevant.

CAP might provide answers to the following questions. All of them are relevant to improving EPS and maximising shareholder value (both through dividends and capital growth).

- What **profit/contribution** is the organisation making on sales to the customer, after discounts and selling and delivery costs? Does it need to revise the selling price?
- What would be the **financial consequences** of losing the customer?
- Is the customer buying in order sizes that are **unprofitable** to supply?
- What is the **return on investment** on plant used?
- What is the level of **inventory** required specifically to supply these customers?
- Are there any other **specific costs** involved in supplying this customer, eg technical and test facilities, R & D facilities, special design staff?
- What is the ratio of **net contribution per customer to total investment**?

CAP analysis can be expensive to undertake in the short term, especially if information systems have to be reviewed. This will have a short term impact on profitability, which will disappoint shareholders seeking dividend growth, and it may divert resources, but it should in the long term improve company performance and increase the market value of shares.

40 TUTORIAL QUESTION: GENERIC STRATEGIES

> **Pass marks**. It is not sufficient to simply describe the three strategies. The question specifically asks you to indicate how each strategy will result in competitive advantage so you must make sure that you do this in your answer.

The three strategies identified in the question are **generic strategies** which provide a guideline to the strategic competitive positions which are open to a firm.

(a) **Overall cost leadership**

A cost leadership strategy seeks to achieve the position of **lowest-cost producer** in the industry.

The competitive advantage that results from producing at the lowest cost is that the manufacturer can **compete on price** with every other producer in the industry and can earn the highest unit profits.

(b) **Differentiation**

A differentiation strategy attempts to make the product unique in terms of attributes which are desirable to the customer.

The assumption is that competitive advantage can be gained through the particular **characteristics of a firm's products**. With a successful differentiation strategy, loyalty to the firm's products will build up and customers are not so **price-sensitive.** The firm can then sell its products at prices that are higher than the least-cost producer in the market.

(c) **Focus**

A focus strategy is based on **segmenting the market** and targeting particular segments.

The competitive advantage which results is that '...the firm is thus able to serve its **narrow strategic target** more effectively or efficiently than competitors who are competing more broadly. As a result the firm achieves either differentiation from better meeting the needs of the particular target, or lower costs in serving this target, or both.' (Porter)

41 TUTORIAL QUESTION: TO BUYOUT OR NOT TO BUYOUT?

> **Pass marks**. Past examination questions have asked candidates to evaluate takeover strategies or management buyouts. Have a go at preparing your own list in answer to this question. It will make you think about the sort of factors to consider in a proposed buyout. You may have thought of other equally valid points. When you have finished, make a checklist of the factors and try to memorise them so that you have the basis for the answer to a question on buyouts.

(a) Would they be interested in being part of a buyout? What other **career options** do they have?

(b) What are the **reasons** for the parent company's decision to sell?

(c) What is the **state of the market** for the company's products? - How big is it? Is it static? Is it declining, or expanding? Is it new?

(d) How **well-developed** are the company's products?

(e) What will be the **assets** of the company?

(f) Who will work for the company? Will there be **redundancies**?

(g) Will the company achieve **profitability**? If so, when?

(h) How much **finance** will the company need, and how much can the managers put up themselves?

(i) Which **venture capital organisations** might back the buyout?

(j) Why should the parent company prefer a **buyout** to a **straight sale**?

42 STRATEGIC MODELS

> **Pass marks.** The examiner commented favourably on the answers to part (a). In response to a BPP enquiry, he has stated that many students suggested that mission or objectives were the logical starting point to the planning process, and that this approach is valid. As for answers to part (b) the examiner's report states that 'Most candidates were able to describe the two models. However, many did not appreciate that the models do not in themselves generate strategies'. Part (c) was answered badly.

(a) The **strategic planning process** is adopted in different ways in different organisations. Whilst internal and external **appraisals** are an important part of the strategic planning process, the starting point can be located further back.

(i) **Mission**

An organisation's mission, according to Mintzberg, describes its **basic function in society**. Mission is often held to have two purposes.

(1) **Embodying the values** of the organisation.

(2) Setting its overall strategic direction by asking the questions: '**What is our business and what should it be?**'.

A **mission statement** should be relatively enduring. It is the logical starting point of the planning process.

Many firms follow sophisticated planning procedures every year.

(ii) The mission is translated into **goals and objectives**. Often these terms are used interchangeably, but some goals may be quantified and others not. For any business, satisfying shareholders is an important **goal**, and this might be translated into **quantified** objectives for profitability and shareholder value.

(iii) The **internal appraisal** is necessary in order to assess the organisation's existing competences. It is sometimes called a **position audit**, which CIMA defines as 'part of the planning process which examines the entity in respect of resources of intangible and tangible assets and finance, products brands and markets, operating systems such as production and distribution, internal organisation, current results and returns to stockholders'.

This identifies any **limitations in the resources** available to the organisation which put constraints over what can be achieved.

(iv) The **external appraisal** identifies development in the environment which can affect the organisation. These can be general political, economic, social and technological developments (**PEST**). They can be more specific to the industry or to the firm (eg a new competitor).

(v) These appraisals might be combined into a **SWOT analysis**. Together with a **gap analysis**, which identifies the achievement necessary for the firm to fulfil its objectives when compared to its current performance, these suggest the necessary issues the strategy must deal with.

(b) (i)

		Competitive advantage	
		Low cost	*Differentiation*
Competitive scope	*Broad target*	Cost leadership	Differentiation
	Narrow target	FOCUS (a) Cost focus	(b) Differentiation focus

Competitive scope refers to whether the organisation chooses to target the entire market, or whether it chooses to concentrate on a more narrowly defined segment. **Competitive advantage** refers to the route taken to serve the market or segment.

(1) A firm pursuing a **cost leadership strategy** aims to be the **lowest cost producer in the market** as a whole or, in the case of a cost-focus strategy, in a segment. Cost leaders cannot be undercut on price, and can enjoy higher profitability.

(2) Not every firm can be a cost leader and many choose to use **differentiation,** which is the exploitation of unique aspect or features of the product in the market as a whole or in a segment of it.

Porter argues that firms must choose **between** these strategies and a firm that stays **stuck in the middle** is doomed.

(1) The choice of generic strategy is likely to be a **long term one**.

(2) Also, most firms employ some form of market segmentation, and the model cannot identify which segments the firm should pursue if it follows a focus strategy.

(3) The model can highlight confusions in the firm's existing strategy, if it is applied to the current competitive situation of the firm.

(ii)

Market \ Product	Existing	New
Present	(1) Market penetration	(3) Product/service development
New	(2) Market development	(4) Diversification

The **Ansoff matrix** identifies four different kinds of **product-market strategy** that the organisation can pursue, depending on whether the firm concentrates and existing products and/or markets or embarks upon new ventures.

Market penetration involves trying to milk more from existing products and existing markets. If the market as a whole is growing, this might appear a fairly **low-risk strategy** to adopt. Where the market is stagnant, market penetration might involve increasing market share at the expense of other producers.

Market development uses existing products in new markets. Exporting is perhaps an example of this strategy. This might be attractive if the firm has to achieve high sales volumes to **utilise capacity** efficiently.

Product development involves offering new products to existing markets. Firms with an expensive **distribution network** may choose this to make most efficient use of it by marketing more products through.

Diversification involves moving into new market with new products. However, this need not always be as risky as it sounds, especially if the products and or markets have some **similarities** to existing ones.

The Ansoff model is a **framework** for discussing alternative directions. It cannot take the decision.

(1) As suggested, market penetration may not be profitable if the markets are mature; only examination of the specifics will identify which is the best approach.

(2) Obviously, it is too **general** on its own to suggest which markets should be targeted.

(c) **Limitations of models**

All models are **abstractions and simplifications** of real life situations.

(i) **Porter's generic strategy model**

Porter's statement that no firm can pursue a stuck in the middle strategy is not entirely borne out by the facts. Instead, a variety of approaches can be adopted to price and the differentiating product features. Firms do strive for cost leadership and differentiation at the same time.

Cost leadership

(1) **Cost refers to internal measures,** rather than the market demand. It can be used to gain market share: but it is the **market share** which is important, not cost leadership as such.

(2) If cost leadership applies cross the whole industry, only one firm will pursue this strategy successfully.

(3) Having low costs does not mean you have to charge lower prices or compete on price. A cost leader can choose to 'invest higher margins in R & D or marketing'. Being a cost leader arguably gives producers more **freedom to choose other competitive strategies.**

- Low costs give you **more opportunity to differentiate** the product.
- Low costs also enable you to **serve many segments,** in other words to pursue a focus strategy.

Differentiation. Porter assumes that a differentiated product will always be sold at a higher price; however, a differentiated product may be sold at the same price as competing products in order to increase market share. Differentiation can be achieved by keeping costs down; the savings can be reinvested in unique product features. Two other points can be mentioned.

(1) **The object of differentiation.** The firm must discern who are its competitors, whether they serve other market segments and if they compete on the same basis.

(2) **The source of differentiation.** This can include all aspects of the marketing mix. Restaurants aim to create an atmosphere, as well as serving food of good quality.

Focus probably has fewer conceptual difficulties, as it ties in very neatly with ideas of market segmentation.

(ii) **Ansoff's product-market matrix**

(1) **No criterion for choice.** As indicated in (b) the matrix is only a framework for **identifying** product-market opportunities. There is nothing to stop a firm carrying out all four strategies simultaneously. A firm can pursue a penetration strategy in its existing markets as well as diversifying into new ones.

(2) **Limited scope.** Another problem is that there are various strategic developments not covered in the matrix. New technology and manufacturing techniques can also alter the dynamics of the market.

(3) It does not address the degree of **change** in each product-market area: it suggests they are static.

(4) The Ansoff matrix does not identify the role of **profit**.

(5) **Withdrawing** from a market or product is not offered as an option.

43 DIVERSIFICATION AND THE PLANNING GAP

Pass marks. The three parts of this question might appear to merge into each other. In part (a) we have considered diversification compared to other approaches to product market strategy, using Ansoff's approach but mentioning the BCG matrix on the way. Part (b) refers specifically to the strategic management of markets, so product market and competitive issues are important here, although there might be other reasons for diversifying. We have included some industry examples.

Examiner's comments. Answers to part (a) should have defined the planning gap and diversification. Part (b) was generally well answered. In part (c), however, many candidates failed to distinguish between 'the potential risk of related compared with unrelated diversification'.

(a) **Why diversification may be adopted**

(i) **Filling the planning gap via product market strategies**

The planning gap identifies the difference between the results needed to satisfy the firm's growth objectives, and the results which will be obtained as a result of continuing with current policies and projects. If the latter is less than the former, then the firm will have to consider new ways to increase sales and profits. Ansoff identified the options which firms can pursue for identifying products and markets.

(1) **Market penetration** is where the firm concentrates on existing markets with an existing product range.

(2) **Product development** is the sale of new products to existing customers. This assumes that the firm has a distinctive competence which can be carried over to the new product range.

(3) **Market development** is the entry of a firm's existing products into new markets.

(4) **Diversification** is the marketing of new products to new markets. A firm might diversify when none of the other options (i), (ii) or (iii) above offers a chance of filling the planning gap. Related diversification can take the form of forwards or backwards integration, whereby a firm becomes its own supplier or distributor and is able to hold on to more of the **added value** in the **supply chain**.

(ii) **Diversification and the product portfolio**

The firm's **portfolio** of products may be **unbalanced,** with a surfeit of **dogs** and few **stars** to offer future profits. The BCG matrix notes that at different stages products have different cash characteristics. Rebalancing the portfolio may enable a firm:

(1) to enter markets where **stars** are available;

(2) to acquire a **cash cow,** to generate financial resources for investment elsewhere.

(b) Diversification involves moving to new markets, with new or different product offerings.

The **advantages of diversification** appear when the firm's existing product market areas are unattractive for whatever reason.

(i) **Related diversification** is where the new products and markets bear some similarity with existing product offerings. A possible example might be Sony's decision to enter the market for computer games, competing with Nintendo and Sega.

The example of Sony and computer games might be called **horizontal diversification.**

(1) **Competitive advantage.** CD technology is becoming the format for many new multimedia products, and developing **expertise** in this area may be essential for Sony to retain its competitive advantage.

(2) **Competitive leadership.** Moving into computer games may be an essential strategy. When markets and technology change, diversification may be essential in order to harness these developments for the company's benefits.

Allied Lyons acquired Pedro Domecq (a drinks firm) in the early 1990s partly in order to benefit from Domecq's distribution network in markets where Allied Lyons wished to expand. This arrangement:

(1) enables products of both firms to find new markets;

(2) enables the wider exploitation of Allied's competences (eg in building brands).

(ii) **Unrelated or conglomerate diversification** is the entry of completely dissimilar product market areas, either organically, or more commonly, by acquisition. An example of unsuccessful diversification is provided again by Sony, which purchased a Hollywood film studio. The rationale was that Sony produced hardware (eg video recorders) and there would be marketing advantages in producing 'software' (films) as well. These advantages have failed to materialise. Running a film production business requires a wholly different set of management skills to running a manufacturing business.

(iii) **Reasons for diversification which do not directly affect the strategic management of markets.**

(1) **Vertical integration.** A firm might expand by buying a supplier or a distributor, to garner more of the wealth in the supply chain, or to secure supplies. In many cases, it is not true diversification, if the final consumer stays the same. A problem is that the acquired business cannot benefit from **economies of scale** in the industry as a whole, and that different management expertise may be required.

(2) **Spreading risk** across several businesses, and possible synergies in which different businesses can contribute to each other. These are discussed in (c) below.

(3) **Competitive strategy** in each market depends on the circumstances of the diversification. If resources can be spread across different business, diversification might support a **cost-leadership** strategy. However, the firm is exposing itself to competition in many different markets, and the generic strategy to each depends on the precise competitive position.

(c) **Risk and diversification**

> **Pass marks**. Approach this part of the question by taking time to brainstorm the word 'risk'. You might have considered business risk, financial risk, operating risk, foreign exchange risk, interest rate risk or political risk. A consideration of all of these points, as applied to proposed diversification into new business areas, would ensure a comprehensive answer.

(i) **Defining risk.** In statistical terms, some **risks** can be measured by relating it to **probability**. If a firm applies probability analysis in its planning process, it might calculate a number of values for profit, each of which has a different probability of occurring.

(ii) Sometimes it is not always possible to measure risk quantitatively, and the riskiness of an action will be assessed by **managerial 'hunch'**.

Different people have **different perceptions of risk**. This is especially pertinent for diversification decisions.

(i) **Managers** of firms have a powerful motive to pursue growth diversify. In any business decision, managers face a career risk.

(ii) **Shareholders** can spread their risk by buying a **portfolio of shares** with the required risk/return characteristics.

Selling the shares to a bidder may be a convenient way of changing the management of a firm. The acquirer might be better able to release the added value in a firm. Some conglomerates, such as ICI, have de-merged so that their constituent parts are quoted separately on the stock market.

(iii) **The business**

For the business as a whole, diversification would appear to be a higher risk strategy than the others.

(1) **Uncertainty.** The diversifier is maximising the degree of uncertainty which it faces.

(2) **Learning.** The diversifier will need to climb a learning curve, in both production and marketing terms. (Devising and marketing computer games to teenagers requires different marketing and product development skills to those needed to sell hi-fis or televisions.)

(3) **Turbulence.** Diversifying increases the degrees of environmental turbulence to which the businesses are subject. An example is offered by British Aerospace. For some time it had a property subsidiary, Arlington Securities, which was supposed to generate profits and cash but which lost a lot of money, forcing the exit of the chairman and severe cutbacks elsewhere.

(4) **Competitor behaviour.** The diversifier may be a new entrant, and competitors may respond by building higher barriers to entry or other spoiling tactics. Competitor behaviour is often hard to predict.

(5) **Management problems.** Many diversified businesses are run at arms length from each other, but there may be problems in corporate culture. This was reported when UK clearing banks purchased stock-broking firms where management styles and systems were very different. Diversification perhaps increases the risk of management failure.

(6) Related diversification may appear safer, but vertically integrated businesses still depend on the same end market, and will be investing more resources in servicing it. (Moreover, many firms **outsource** non-core functions, if a third party can manage them more efficiently.) The acquirer will not benefit from economies of scale if the former supplier and another similar firm were to merge. The acquired supplier will need to be given resources and suitable management to develop.

Although diversification is unfashionable at the moment, there are arguments in its favour.

(1) In practice, it may be **less risky** than the other options. Just because something is familiar does not mean that it is secure. Doing nothing is often not the safest option. Carrying on as at present may be the riskier strategy. A competitor might enter the market, completely overturning its dynamics.

(2) Diversification may be a **competitive tactic**, if potential competitors are attacked on their own turf, and dissuaded from attacking the diversifier's core market.

(3) The risk inherent in diversification might be reduced if there is **synergy**. **Synergy** is the advantage to a firm gained by having **existing** resources which are compatible with new products or markets that the company is developing. It can be described as the 2 + 2 = 5 effect. The combined performance is greater than the sum of its parts.

    There are different ways in which synergy can be obtained.

    - **Sales synergy:** the use of common **marketing** facilities such as distribution channels, sales staff and administration, and warehousing.
    - **Operating synergy:** the common use of operational facilities and personnel, bulk purchasing, a greater spread of fixed costs and the advantages of common learning curves.
    - **Investment synergy:** the wider use of a common investment in fixed assets, working capital or research.
    - **Management synergy:** the advantage gained when management skills concerning current operations are easily transferred to new operations because of the similarity of problems in the two industries.

44 TUTORIAL QUESTION: ACQUISITION VS INTERNAL GROWTH

(a) An **acquisition strategy** has risks and disadvantages, as well as advantages, and it is difficult to evaluate the advantages without also recognising the disadvantages.

(i) **Market entry.** The purchase of an established brand name will enable the purchasing company to enter a market more quickly than if it tried to develop its own product internally.

(ii) **Established brand.** The purchasing company will be obtaining ownership of an existing brand name, which will have an established customer loyalty and distribution channels. If a company tried to develop a product internally, customer support and distribution channels would have to be established from scratch.

(iii) **No learning curve.** The purchase of an established brand name avoids the costs of internal developments, such as R&D costs and the 'learning costs' of operating staff, management and marketing staff.

(iv) **Cheap.** The existing supplier of the product is under-capitalised, and this might possibly have the advantages that:

(1) the supplier is willing to accept a lower price for selling the brand name, because of its urgent need for cash from the sale;

(2) further investment by the purchasing company would overcome the problem of under-capitalisation, and might help to boost the sales and profits from the established branded products.

(v) The external purchase of an established brand name might **release R&D resources** for the development of other products (instead of having to devote available R&D resources to the development of an in-house product as a rival to the existing brand).

(b) **Operational strategy** decisions can be re-assessed after an acquisition, but many aspects of strategy take time to be implemented and altered. A company that makes an acquisition might therefore be obliged to continue with many policies of previous management, at least in the short term, even if it would like to introduce new policies in the longer term.

(i) The existing range of **products** that carry the **brand name** cannot be increased at short notice, since it will take time to amend existing products or develop new products for the range. Some existing products could be scrapped fairly quickly, but the acquiring company might not wish to reduce the number of branded products, and so it will be obliged in the short term to accept the product range that previous managements have established.

(ii) The **pricing policy** for the branded products will be difficult to alter at short notice, because price is a key element in brand image.

(iii) **Distribution** might be restricted by existing distribution/supply agreements: for example, a retailing organisation might have exclusive local distributorship rights for the branded products.

(iv) **Promotion.** Some brands might be under-utilised, and the acquirer might purchase the brands in order to expand their sales. Promotion expenditure might be increased, perhaps to reposition the product.

(v) Previous management might have taken various investment decisions that could be impossible to reverse or alter; for example, the investment in new machinery and current output capacity might not be changeable in the short term.

It could therefore be argued that of the '**four Ps**' in the marketing mix only promotion (advertising, sales promotion, publicity etc) can be changed fairly easily in the short term.

45 UNBUNDLING

> **Pass marks**. The examiner reported some conceptual confusion in answers to this question. Students did not mention shareholder wealth; they talked about synergy when asked to describe conglomerate diversification; they confused demerger with decentralisation.

(a) **Growth as a strategic objective**

All businesses want to survive. In order to do so many feel they have to grow. After all, if the economy as a whole is growing, most shareholders and managers would wish the businesses they own and/or control to share in the general prosperity.

Measuring growth can be done in a number of ways. The various measures of growth outlined are often contradictory, and in certain circumstances there are cases when 'small' can mean 'beautiful'.

(i) Increase in sales volumes
(ii) Increase in market share in comparison with competitors
(iii) Establishment of new products
(iv) Entry to new markets
(v) Growth in profits
(vi) Growth of shareholder value
(vii) Growth in management prestige

Survival. In competitive markets, growth is sometimes necessary to survive. If competitors expand, they might eventually take away your business if you become a small player in the market, thus losing economies of scale.

Timescale. Growth must also be measured over a particular time horizon. Japanese companies are reputed to take a longer term view about certain measures of growth, such as profits, provided that others, such as market share are successful.

Market share. Long term gains in market share are purchased at the expense of current profits or short term financial performance. Growth in market share in one market may mean that other opportunities are lost. Some companies do better by restricting themselves to high profits in niche markets. A growth in sales volume may not be what is required, if it is at the expense of sales value.

Growth in shareholder value is the yardstick by which UK companies measure their success. In the UK and US this is the objective by which all growth is judged. As shareholders own companies, to maximise shareholder value is to maximise the returns available to shareholders. This takes precedence over other growth objectives such as size, market share and so forth.

Growth can be managed in two ways.

(i) **Organic growth** derives from the successful and profitable expansion of current businesses.

(ii) **Acquisition** is the purchase of already existing businesses from their current owners.

Growth can lead to unwieldy organisations and in inefficient distribution of resources within the growing enterprise. Good businesses can be brought down by bad.

(b) **Conglomerate diversification**

Conglomerate diversification is one of the means by which an organisation can grow. A conglomerate organisation is a group of companies which do not really have anything in common. Some conglomerates own companies in diverse fields as batteries and ladies' stockings.

Conglomerate diversification has a number of objectives.

(i) **Risk to managers.** From the point of view of management, owning a number of businesses reduces the risk that they will be out of a job if one of the businesses fails.

(ii) **Risk to shareholders.** In some companies, conglomerate diversification is supposedly undertaken to reduce the risk to shareholders (but there is nothing to stop them diversifying their own risks directly - they may not need a conglomerate's management to do it for them).

(iii) **Business mission.** The main business activities of some companies are buying and selling other businesses, after these have been 'turned round'. The successful sale of acquired businesses can reduce the cost of acquisition. The purchase of the US firm SCM by Hanson Trust, and the later sale of many of SCM's assets, is an example of this.

(iv) **Resources.** The management of a company feel that they have resources which could be put to better use. The current businesses do not therefore give potential for growth (but again, shareholders can buy direct stakes in insurance companies - why not just increase dividends and so them the money to do so directly?)

(v) It gives a stake in **new markets.**

(vi) Management of acquiring businesses feel that they can run the businesses they purchase better than existing management. Their shareholders must agree. This might be because they can bring in investment, or because they appear tougher.

(c) **Demerger**

Demerger is the opposite process to conglomerate diversification, although, paradoxically, it follows a similar objective.

(i) Unbundlers believe that conglomerates do not maximise shareholder value and that in fact a **centralised** head office management subtracts from shareholder value rather than adds to it.

(ii) Unbundlers believe that if the constituent business streams were separate companies many would be worth more to shareholders. Shareholders could identify the profitable opportunities so that successful businesses would not be propping up unsuccessful ones, as there would be transparency and no cross-subsidy.

(iii) Some companies divest themselves of certain businesses to concentrate on **core activities.**

Unbundling may also defend management against **hostile takeovers,** and release funds for investment in core businesses.

46 DF EXPORTERS

> **Pass marks**. The wording of the question provides three convenient sub-headings that you can use to structure your answer. This is a fairly straightforward question but make sure that you relate the points you make to DF's situation and that you can develop them properly. Remember that DF is only considering whether or not to go abroad – your answer should help them in that decision, and not assume that the decision has already been made!
>
> **Examiner's comments**. This was the most popular question in Section B and was generally well answered, although most candidates did not develop their points. Some candidates were able to demonstrate their knowledge of strategic financial management issues.

After experiencing declining sales and profitability, DF has decided to set up a manufacturing and distribution base overseas, after many years' experience as an exporter from its home base. Firms which intend a heavy involvement in an overseas market need to have experience of that market, so DF is well placed from that standpoint. However, servicing the market through exports has suffered after the company increased prices because of rising shipping costs, and the perception by overseas customers that DF is too remote. The risk of losing touch with customers is currently a real one.

Direct foreign investment will involve DF in a number of strategic issues, with different **opportunities and threats,** and increased **risk**. DF is not alone. Firms that are fully committed to international marketing are often drawn into overseas manufacture. It gives rise to consideration of organisational management, financing and government regulatory issues.

Organisational management issues

Location abroad can offer, eventually, a better understanding of the problems and needs of **customers** in the overseas market. As DF has been exporting to this market for many years, its knowledge of the market is likely to be very good. The issues with running an overseas plant will however be very different to those encountered in a purely export market.

There may be difficulties in training and retaining competent **labour,** especially if other international companies set up plants in the same market after DF has laid the groundwork. The **distribution infrastructure** may not be what DF is used to in its home country and supplies for the plant may not be supplied on time.

Production overseas by a wholly owned subsidiary gives a firm absolute **control,** but DF may find it difficult at first to know how much **centralised control** it must exercise. Suitable managers, whether recruited in the overseas market or posted abroad from home, may be difficult to obtain. **Culture and language** may create difficulties, as ways of doing business may differ. Local managers may resent excessive head office interference.

Financing issues

If we accept that DF has sufficient resources to set up and run a production facility overseas, it is still true that establishing and running a production facility in an overseas market demonstrates the fullest commitment to that market. This obviously exposes DF to greater **financial risk**. Setting up an overseas production facility would be inappropriate if sales are expected to be low in volume or if the product is only going to be on sale for a limited period.

The most likely risks are those arising from **exchange rate** fluctuations. **Remittance of profits** from the overseas subsidiary may be restricted by local **government policies.**

Steps (such as hedging strategies) can be taken to minimise foreign exchange risk, but the danger to the profitability of the foreign investment must be recognised.

Other issues related to the financing and costs of the overseas investment for DF to consider are these. Not all of them are negative.

(a) Overseas production can overcome the effects of tariff and non-tariff **barriers to imports.**

(b) Some markets are so large that **economies of scale** can still be gained from overseas production.

(c) **Production costs** are lower in some countries than at home.

(d) For firms producing weighty or bulky products (eg brewers), overseas production can reduce **storage and transportation costs.**

Government regulatory issues

If the overseas government is one of DF's customers, manufacturing in the overseas market may be a factor in winning orders. However, **regulatory requirements** imposed by some foreign governments can often be difficult to overcome. Local **business culture** can mean that it is very important who DF knows if tasks are to be achieved, or approval given. The time taken for decisions to be approved, or the appropriate strings pulled, can sap resources.

The **political stability** of the country is also important. Government policy affects the whole economy, and governments are responsible for enforcing and creating a stable framework in which business can be done. Political change can complicate the planning activities of DF, because it may invalidate the strategy and severely damage the firm.

Some overseas governments discourage, and sometimes prohibit, 100% ownership of an enterprise by a foreign company. Taxation policy may create problems. Political risk, and the risk of expropriation of overseas assets by foreign governments, may discourage DF.

DF must consider these issues when deciding whether or not to set up an overseas operation. It may decide that the shipping costs it will save are not enough of an incentive for the significant extra risk and management resources it will be committing itself to. Taking over a firm in the overseas market can be a more effective way of establishing a production facility overseas than building one from scratch. Alternatively DF may enter into co-operative agreements with firms in the overseas market, as a way of spreading the risk.

On the other hand, the benefits of having an enhanced and fully controllable local presence may generate many years of business which will justify the additional costs and risk.

47 DIVISIONAL PERFORMANCE MEASUREMENT

Pass marks. Subjects do overlap at stage 4 and it was appropriate to bring in material from other areas on performance appraisal. In part (a) we have applied the general theory behind strategic and operational targets to the example of a tyre-fitting division in a garage. Distinguish 'strategic' from 'operational', but only in the sense of how *measurement of performance* is affected. Do not fall into the trap of limiting your answer to explaining the differences between the types of target.

Examiner's comments. Overall, the question was quite well answered and most candidates seemed comfortable with the topic area. In part (b) candidates often failed to relate their answer to the circumstances and culture of the hospital.

(a) A **strategic target** is prepared by following the broad lines of the **mission statement**, which defines the aims of an organisation. The level of detail in the mission statement varies from company to company, but the identification of **specific objectives**, and specific **criteria** which are capable of **measurement**, will follow from it. Different courses of action for achieving company goals can then be evaluated.

Specific **operational targets** are the means by which strategic targets can be monitored on a day-to-day basis. To take an example, a strategic objective for a company operating a network of garages might be to 'enhance customer satisfaction'. An example of a **measurable** operational target when monitoring achievement of this objective could be: 'decrease the number of customer complaints in the tyre-fitting division by 40% between May and June'. This target becomes a **step** that must be taken if the **longer term objective** is to be achieved.

New systems of performance measurement may need to be established to achieve this. As indicated above, strategic objectives may be non-financial. The tyre-fitting division should be assessed regularly on the number of complaints received, possibly in comparison with **competitors** if this information is available. This will indicate progress towards the ultimate aim of enhanced customer satisfaction for the company as a whole, leading (ideally) to the long term profitability of the company.

Other operational targets may be more **short term** in nature, and might be closely aligned to the budget cycle and the allocation of **resources**. Such targets could include **financial measures** such as levels of spending, or efficiency of the labour in the tyre fitting division. Such targets would contribute to short term objectives, such as immediate returns to shareholders.

Strategic plans are always broken down into their **operational components** to **allocate the work** of achieving the plan throughout the organisation. In our example, one division alone could not bear the entire responsibility for enhancing customer satisfaction because a range of divisions might have an impact.

(b) Division performance should be assessed on the basis of **measurable** targets. When establishing a new system, it is also very important to consider the effect upon the **motivation** of staff and management.

The scenario in the question reflects recent moves to impose private sector practice on non-profit making organisations. There is increased emphasis on **performance** with the main purpose of the **internal market** being the **efficient allocation of resources**. This requires a re-think of the measures that will be used to assess performance.

The **motivation** of divisional senior managers and their staff is more likely to be enhanced if they have **participated** in establishing both the financial and non-financial goals, and regard them as both **controllable** and **attainable**. They need to be reflective of J's overall aims.

This may need some sensitive handling as the new divisional manager are senior medical officers who may not be used to thinking about patient care in purely financial terms. This has been a problem experienced by some NHS trusts. A divisional manager might take decisions that will improve his own centre's performance at the expense of the whole hospital. There needs to be **goal congruence**.

A divisional manager needs to be clear that his divisional goals (for example supplying more services to hospitals outside the immediate area) is both **controllable, achievable** and **measurable** and related directly to J's goal of becoming more competitive in the health services market. Part of that objective might be obtained by cutting costs and becoming a **cost leader** in his divisional area of responsibility (children's medicine, for example).

As has been stated above, in a non-profit organisation **efficient** use of resources is the key because 'outputs' often cannot be easily measured. In the case of J, **provision of services** as outputs to other hospitals is a key performance measure but the organisation also needs to be sure that all resources (nurses' time, machine availability) used in providing that service are properly allocated. Resource allocation and usage can be monitored according to the principles of **economy, efficiency** and **effectiveness.** These may include comparing a division with similar divisions in other hospitals, that is, via **benchmarking**. Each operation may be given an expected cost, which the divisional manager must strive for.

Some management theory writers consider it essential that managers are judged on **outputs** rather than **inputs.** A divisional manager ought to be judged by what he actually **achieves,** rather than the hoops he jumps through to get there. If a divisional manager in J, for example, manages to increase the number of contracts for supply of services to the purchasing organisations (in line with the Board's stated objectives) but spends over his budget on nursing staff because of historical labour turnover problems, he should not be judged harshly.

A very good manager may achieve considerably less than an average manager, purely because of ingrained problems which he is nevertheless managing to address over the **medium to long term.**

The performance appraisal system of J ought really to be based upon both financial (number of operation contracts supplied) and non-financial (such as patient satisfaction or positions on government sponsored 'league tables').

These changes are likely to require a **cultural change** in the management of the organisation. The organisation structure itself is no longer based on **functional** responsibility but could be said to be based upon **product.** The change will need to be implemented carefully so as not to alienate staff. Some conflicts may arise as staff and managers settle in to their new responsibilities.

48 PERFORMANCE INDICATORS AND QUALITY

Pass marks. This question is slightly unusual, especially part (a), in that quality of service is often measured by non-financial performance indicators. The question as a whole seeks to explore the effect of accounting and performance indicators on managerial behaviour, at an operational level. It is possible that there was a misprint in the question paper, which should have read 'the impact on quality of service(s) which is not subject to a performance indicator'.

Examiner's comments. This question was unpopular. Candidates failed to grasp the point of part (a) 'which required an assessment of how much attention is paid to indicators that do not measure the performance of operational managers. Too many candidates saw part (b) as an opportunity to rattle off everything they knew about TQM'.

(a) **Performance indicators and service quality**

The effect of any one performance indicator on managerial behaviour might depend on the following factors.

(i) **The other performance indicators** which are used to assess performance. Managers might have to make a **trade off** between a number of indicators. For example, some supermarkets have promised extra staff, if queues get beyond a certain length, even though this costs more money.

(ii) **Controllability of underlying factors.** Some performance indicators are genuinely attributable to the manager, but others result from factors outside the manager's control. Managers will respond to performance indicators which they can influence, and seek other ways of dealing with those they cannot.

(iii) **Performance indicators and the performance appraisal and reward system**

(1) If indicators are crudely used to punish or reward, then they can be detrimental to service quality or indeed to business profitability. Bank managers who are rewarded solely for increasing the volume of lending will increase this by lending **riskily**.

(2) On the other hand, if the performance information is used scientifically, in order to improve performance rather than punish individuals, service quality should not suffer.

(iv) **Mission and professional ethics.** In occupations such as medicine, where there is a genuine sense of vocation, or indeed in any jobs where people take pride in their work, quality of service should not suffer, because people care: this requires care for the job not just performance indicators.

(v) **Culture.** The culture of the organisation may discourage or encourage slavish adherence to simple indicators of performance.

(vi) **Measurability.** Some aspects of service quality can be measured (eg customer surveys or satisfaction, queuing times, levels of complaints), and be used as performance indicators.

(vii) **Power and politics.** The relative importance of different performance indicators can be influenced by the internal or external political environment of the organisation.

(viii) **Manipulation.** It might be easier to manipulate the performance indicator than it is to improve performance. For example, firms can change the bases on which performance is measured. Managers who are expert in creating budgetary slack will probably be able to influence performance indicators.

(ix) **Participation.** If managers participate in developing the indicator they might adhere to it more readily than if not, imply because their credibility is at stake.

(x) **Priorities.** Management priorities may be uncertain. Management desire for profit can lead to employees ignoring other safety matters.

In short, the influence of performance indicators on managerial behaviour depends on the use to which they are put, any **trade offs** between them, the **personal/professional outlook** of the manager, their role in the reward structure, and the culture of the organisation.

(b) **Performance indicators** in an organisation might cover all of the following areas.

(i) **Competitive performance,** focusing on factors such as sales growth and market share.

(ii) **Financial performance,** concentrating on profitability, liquidity, capital structure and market ratios.

(iii) **Quality of service** looks at matters like reliability, courtesy, competence and availability.

(iv) **Flexibility** is an apt heading for assessing the organisation's ability to deliver at the right speed, to respond to precise customer specifications, and to cope with fluctuations in demand.

(v) **Resource utilisation**, not unsurprisingly, considers how efficiently resources are being utilised. This can be problematic because of the complexity of the inputs to a service and the outputs from it and because some of the inputs are supplied by the customer .

(vi) **Innovation** is assessed in terms of both the innovation process and the success of individual innovations. Individual innovations can be measured in terms of whether they have improved the organisation's ability to meet the other five performance criteria - have they improved competitiveness, for example? The innovation process can be measured in terms of how much it costs to develop a new service, how effective the process is (that is, how innovative is the organisation, if at all?), and how fast it can develop new services.

Total quality management is a business philosophy based around performance measurement, providing the right things are being measured. **TQM** as a management philosophy is relevant to items (iii), (iv), (v) and (vi) in the list above.

TQM has been widely employed in both manufacturing and service contexts. Its aim is to **reduce waste** and **improve the quality** of the product/service delivered to the customer. According to CIMA, TQM is 'the continuous improvement in quality, productivity and effectiveness obtained by establishing management responsibility for processes as well as outputs. In this, every process has an identified process owner, and every person in an entity operates within a process and contributes to its improvement'.

The principles of TQM can be summed up as follows.

(i) **Zero defects** and 'right first time'.

(ii) **Reduce variation** in outputs. This is measured by statistical process control.

(iii) **Continuous improvement**. This can be measured by identifying costs saved, employee suggestion schemes etc.

As a lot of the work of TQM involves measurement and changing behaviour, it is clear that TQM and performance measurement are intimately related.

(i) **Conflicts.** TQM, like J-I-T, requires concentration on certain aspects of performance, but there may be conflicts between old performance industries and new. For example, if a manager is rewarded on the volume of output, this can be detrimental to quality.

(ii) **Measurement.** All the costs of quality need to be taken into account. The old system of performance indicators may fail to measure or take into account the new quality requirement.

(iii) **Application.** There is a danger of dysfunction if TQM indicators are merely tagged on to the other indicators, or are restricted to one part of the organisation. Although some TQM techniques are used in isolation, successful implementation of the philosophy requires co-ordination amongst all departments, who should see themselves as internal customers.

(iv) TQM requires that attention be paid to **non-financial indicators** of performance, which therefore have to be included in how managers are judged.

TQM includes non-financial performance indicators, and changes the validity of older measures of performance.

The extent to which managerial behaviour changes at operational level also depends on **senior management priorities,** and so quality indicators will only affect operational managers' behaviour if the senior managers take them seriously.

(c) Quality inevitably encounters a variety of organisational problems. In practice all the techniques and approaches to TQM involve a significant shake up.

(i) TQM is associated with giving employees a say in the process (eg in the **quality survey**) and in getting them to suggest improvements.

(ii) TQM implies a **greater discipline** to the process of production and the establishment of better linkages between the business functions.

(iii) TQM involves **new relationships** with suppliers, which requires them to improve their output quality so that less effort is spent rectifying poor input. Long-term relationships with a small number of suppliers might be preferable to choosing material and sub-components on price.

(iv) TQM requires both work **standardisation** and **employee commitment**.

Participation is important in TQM, especially in the process of continuous improvement, where workforce views are valued. The management task is to encourage everybody to contribute. **Barriers to participation** include:

(i) an **autocratic chief executive**, who believes he or she is the sole key to the process;

(ii) **individualism,** in which people 'possess' ideas in order to take credit for them rather than share them for mutual benefit;

(iii) ideas of managers as **leaders and directors** rather than facilitators and supporters;

(iv) **middle managers** who feel their authority is threatened.

In addition there are other '**cultural barriers**' to the acceptance of TQM. The British emphasis on individual development can be very destructive of team working. Often the hardest aspects for managers to accept are as follows.

(i) **Social and status barriers** are removed with the removal of office partitions.
(ii) Administrative functions must now be seen as **supporting** the shop floor.
(iii) The **shop floor** is the most important area.
(iv) Managers are judged by their contribution to **team spirit.**
(v) Meetings are used to gather **information,** not to take decisions.
(vi) **New personal skills** are needed (eg the ability to listen and communicate).
(vii) A manager's role is in supporting and training, not **disciplining** and **restricting.**

Holmes believes that managers most suited for a TQM culture will 'understand how people **motivate** themselves and direct this motivation towards good team results. They are concerned with achieving the **goals of the team,** supporting the individual members of the team, and keeping the team together'. They will 'ensure time is spent setting objectives, planning, briefing, controlling, evaluating. These activities will be conducted in a participatory or controllable way'.

49 TRANSFER PRICING ISSUES

Pass marks. Transfer pricing appears elsewhere in the CIMA syllabus, particularly in Management Accounting Applications at Stage 3, and elsewhere in Stage 4 (Management Accounting Control Systems). This question discusses the problems in applying the theory of transfer pricing in practical situations and applying it to multinationals.

Examiner's comments. 'This question was extremely unpopular...[and]...those few candidates who did attempt the question did not provide good answers. In part (a), candidates should have related their answers to short-run profit maximisation. Part (b) dealing with the problems faced by multinationals was answered better, although candidates should have made more comparisons with companies operating only in the domestic market.'

(a) **Validity of traditional theory**

According to Tomkins and McAulay, 'transfer pricing situations apply where organisations decide to structure themselves into divisions which make decisions independently. A transfer price is then needed when divisions trade with each other. The **transfer price is a cost to the buying division and revenue to the selling division**, so whatever transfer price is set will influence the profitability of each division. In addition the transfer price will also significantly influence the buying and selling divisions' input and output decisions and thus the total company profits.'

The traditional theory

The traditional theory of transfer prices is based on economics, and is underpinned by the assumption that organisations are profit-maximising entities. In an ideal world, the transfer price will reflect the **opportunity cost of sale** to the supplying division and the opportunity cost to the buying decision (ie the purchase price available externally, and/or the contribution obtainable from the extra output that can be made with the transferred items).

If unit variable costs and unit selling prices are constant, the following rules apply.

(i) In many cases, if there is a perfect external market for the item to be transferred, this **external market price** should be the transfer price, to enable the firm to use its resources efficiently.

(ii) With **no external market**, the transfer price can best be set in the range where the marginal cost to the selling division of producing the item is equal to the net marginal revenue (selling price less variable costs) in the receiving division. Ideally, this should be based on the **opportunity cost**.

If unit variable costs and unit selling prices are not constant other problems arise.

(i) There is an optimum level of output for the firm as a whole: this is because there is a certain level of /output over which net revenue declines. The ideal transfer price should motivate managers to produce at this level of output.

(ii) Effectively this means that some divisions might have to produce at less than full capacity, and that a transfer price might have to be imposed centrally.

Problems with the theory

There is nothing wrong with the traditional theory **as a theory** at all. Problems arise when, even in the domestic market, we try to apply the theory to practical situations faced by real companies.

(i) **Problems in identifying/classifying costs**

(1) New manufacturing techniques make it **harder to identify fixed/variable costs,** which may be needed to draw up schedules identifying what the marginal costs of the transferring division truly are.

(2) There are differences between accountants' variable costs and economists' marginal cost in practice.

(3) Some variable overheads my not be avoided by buying on the external market (eg salaries of order processing staff).

(4) Opportunity costs are often very hard to identify.

(ii) **Problems of identifying the short run.** UK and US managers are often accused of short-termism. In practice, transfer prices will be set with the long-term relationship in mind, and short-term profit maximisation sometimes has to take second place. This trade-off can be more easily made when the costs, benefits and risks are properly identified.

(iii) **Risk.** The motivational impact of the transfer pricing model does not take into account the risk for the buying or selling division. For example, a division may for some time have bought a key component from outside suppliers, which is then manufactured by another division of the buyer's group. The new internal supplier sets the transfer price according to the external market price - but there may be problems of quality and delivery. On the other hand, the producing division may be taking a higher risk, if the buying division can easily get supplies elsewhere, but if the producing division cannot so easily change what it manufactures.

(iv) **Politics.** Recently, Volkswagen has dealt with excess capacity by deciding to manufacture more components in-house, to keep its workforce employed. Managers may not be free to reduce 'resources', especially human resources, in line with make-or-buy decisions elsewhere in the firm.

(b) **Domestic and international transfer pricing**

A transfer pricing system in theory has to meet two objectives, according to Tomkins and McAulay.

(i) 'A fair distribution of profits arising from inter divisional trading'.

(ii) 'A reliable basis for divisional managers to make sound decisions and thus encourage goal congruence between the divisions and the whole corporate group. This will happen when the actions which divisional managers take to improve the reported profits of their own division also improve the profit of the corporate group.'

Part (a) described some of the difficulties in applying this - no mention was made of the additional problems caused by **trading in different countries,** with different laws, currencies and tax requirements. The transfer pricing system has to deal with many other issues, which are perhaps tangential certainly to objective (i) above. Objective (ii) is probably more relevant - but with the proviso that the objective will be to maximise profits for the group as a whole - minimising the tax paid, for example, might mean that a transfer price is set which benefits neither division individually.

Some of the main differences between domestic and multinational transfer pricing are outlined below.

(i) **Exchange rate fluctuation**

When a subsidiary company or profit centre in one country transfers goods to a subsidiary or profit centre in another country, there will be a transfer price but the value of the revenue/cost to each profit centre could depend on fluctuations in the currency exchange rate.

(ii) **Taxation in different countries**

The rate of taxation on profits is likely to be different from country to country. For example, suppose that a company has two subsidiaries, one in Country A and one in Country B. If taxation on profits is 20% of profits in Country A and 50% on profits in Country B, the company will presumably try to 'manipulate' profits so that profits are maximised in the subsidiary in Country A, by reducing profits in Country B.

Profits between a subsidiary in one country and a subsidiary in another country can be manipulated by means of raising or lowering transfer prices or by invoicing the subsidiary in the high-tax country for 'services' provided by the subsidiary in the low-tax country.

In this way, the subsidiary's profits in the low-tax country can be increased, by reducing profits of the subsidiary in the high-tax country

Artificial attempts at reducing tax liabilities could, however, upset a country's tax officials if they discover it and may lead to some form of penalty. Many tax authorities have the power to modify transfer prices in computing tariffs or taxes on profit, although a genuine arms-length market price should pass muster. The Internal Revenue Service in the USA and the Inland Revenue in the UK are alert to manipulation possibilities.

(iii) **Import tariffs**

There might be import tariffs on goods transferred from one country to another. If the tariff is set as a percentage of the value of goods imported, a multinational company might benefit from manipulating the transfer price.

For example, suppose that Country A imposes an import tariff of 20% on the value of goods imported. A multi-national company has a subsidiary in Country A which imports goods from a subsidiary in Country B. In such a situation, the company would minimise costs by keeping the transfer price to a minimum value.

(iv) **Exchange controls**

In contrast, if a country imposes restrictions on the transfer of profits from domestic subsidiaries to foreign multinationals, the restrictions on the transfer can be overcome as follows.

(1) Head office should provide some goods or services to the subsidiary.

(2) The subsidiary should be charged exorbitantly high prices for these goods or services. In this way, the 'profits' can be disguised as sales revenue, and transferred from one country to the other.

The ethics of such an approach should, of course, be questioned.

(v) **Anti-dumping legislation**

Governments may take action to protect home industries by preventing companies from transferring goods cheaply into their countries. They may do this, for example, by insisting on the use of a fair market value for the transfer price.

(vi) **Competitive pressures**

Transfer pricing can be used to enable profit centres to match or undercut local competitors.

50 CENTRALLY DETERMINED TRANSFER PRICES

Pass marks. Transfer pricing appears regularly in the new syllabus. This question considers transfer pricing from a behavioural point of view – by mentioning that divisional managers are not consulted – but also from an ethical point of view. Other questions covering ethics have covered matters such as pollution and redundancy.

There are number of frameworks you can use, the stakeholder view or the profit-maximisation view – whatever view you take, your argument should be consistent and logical, setting out the advantages and disadvantages. On the issue of tax avoidance/evasion, some countries have catch-all provisions outlawing schemes whose sole purpose is to avoid paying tax. The UK does not (yet) have such a provision. Do not ignore the international aspect of the question.

Other points. We have mentioned Sternberg's model in our answer to (b). You may not have done so, and yet could still achieve a pass. Indeed the examiner himself pointed out that there is no single correct answer to this question. Remember however that social responsibility and professional ethics are important aspects of the syllabus that will be examined regularly.

Examiner's comments. There was little critical appraisal of the company's policy, as was required by part (a). Too many candidates in part (b) were not clear about the ethical issues. These included the legality of the policy, tax considerations and the advisability of a policy where subordinates' evaluated performance was affected by actions of superiors over which they had no control.

(a) Although P plc is a multi-national, it is incorporated in the UK, and investors using stock markets in the UK are the ultimate destination of its dividend stream. **P plc's performance is measured** by profits and earnings per share figures which are reported **in sterling**. As P plc is a business it is **profit-maximising** and its directors have an obligation to **minimise costs**.

Transfer pricing regimes can be very complex. P plc not only faces the business problems of operating in different countries, but also **currency risk** and **varying rates of taxation.**

P plc's transfer prices have to be designed on the understanding that **unit variable costs** and **sales prices** from the point of view of P as a whole are not constant, if only because of the currency risk.

(i) **Output optimisation**. The firm will seek to gain a profit-maximising level of output. Transfer pricing decisions will be made from the point of view of the organisation as a whole.

(ii) **Tax avoidance**

(1) Calculating a profit-maximising level of output will involve for the firm as a whole consideration of **tax liabilities**. Doubtless, P plc has **tax accountants** who are able to deal with the complexities of international tax law. This needs to be **centralised** to take into account how the tax regimes of different countries interact with each other.

(2) **Excise duties** can be minimised with low prices.

(iii) It is very hard in practice to identify a level of output which will enable each part of a multi-national business to maximise its own profits. Currency risk make it very hard to determine such a price on a mechanical basis.

(iv) Most countries in the industrialised world enable free **cash flow** between countries, but some developing economies place limits on currency transactions. Transfer prices can minimise this problem.

(v) It is often hard to determine where in the value chain 'value' is added. The only use for **part processed products** is further processing. P plc can probably justify its transfer prices to the authorities if there is no external market as a reference point.

Problems with the system

(i) **Governments and multinational bodies are increasingly vigilant** about the use of transfer prices to minimise tax/excise payments or to hinder competition.

(ii) **Divisional performance assessment is made a lot harder**. If transfer prices are distorted, it becomes difficult to get a genuine picture of how efficiently a manufacturing plant is working. Some plants might have an unrealistically high reported 'profit'.

(b) According to **Elaine Sternberg**, the actions of an entity can be analysed according to their **guiding purpose**. The fundamental purpose of a profit-orientated business is to maximise wealth for the owners over the long-term. This fundamental purpose is subjected to two constraints.

(i) **Distributive justice:** people should be rewarded according to the value they add to the business

(ii) **Ordinary decency:** theft, dishonesty and coercion are never 'ethical'.

Violations of these principles are **unethical.**

Designing appropriate transfer prices to maximise the profits of the business is in **accordance with its fundamental purpose**, which is to maximise owner-wealth in the **long term**. While P is not breaking the law, governments might put restrictions on its activities.

Furthermore, letting tax considerations dominate commercial decisions puts emphasis in the wrong place. Tax rates change easily, and so good tax planning one year can be rendered invalid the next. The same is true of transfer pricing. If tax considerations dominate decision-making, adverse consequences might include a harsher tax regime.

P has invested in certain countries due to a favourable tax climate. It could be argued that manipulation of transfer prices goes against **distributive justice** for the reason that the firm benefits from public expenditure on infrastructure, education, law enforcement and so forth, and so avoiding the tax means that other people are paying unduly. Arguably this could be construed as violation of distributive justice. P's ethical consultants could argue that P brings employment and prosperity, which are **social benefits.**

P's subsidiaries prepare tax returns and if these are **honestly** prepared, the transfer pricing system is clear and open to government officials. P plc is deceiving no-one, nor is it guilty of any coercion and distortion. Tax evasion is **unethical and illegal,** but there is no evidence that P is doing this.

51 EXPERIENCE CURVE AND LIFE CYCLES

> **Pass marks**. This question is a challenging one because it links two models together and explores their connection. You should present arguments for and against the view expressed. Might experience curve theory actually shorten product life cycles? You need to have a full and detailed understanding of both models to be able to do this. Mere description of the models, with no attempt to link them, would have gained few marks. As the examiner noted, most candidates did not rise to the challenge posed by the question.
>
> **Examiner's comments**. This question linked two theories together and explored how they might affect each other. It was very unpopular. Many candidates confused the experience curve with the learning curve.
>
> The greatest impact of the experience curve will be felt in the later stages of a product's life, but as techniques improve then demand patterns change and new products are demanded thereby decreasing the life of the original product. This presents an interesting conflict.

The **experience curve** can be used in strategic control of costs and hence in contribution to profitability. Its basic principle is that as output increases, the cost per unit of output falls. It is usually expressed diagrammatically as follows.

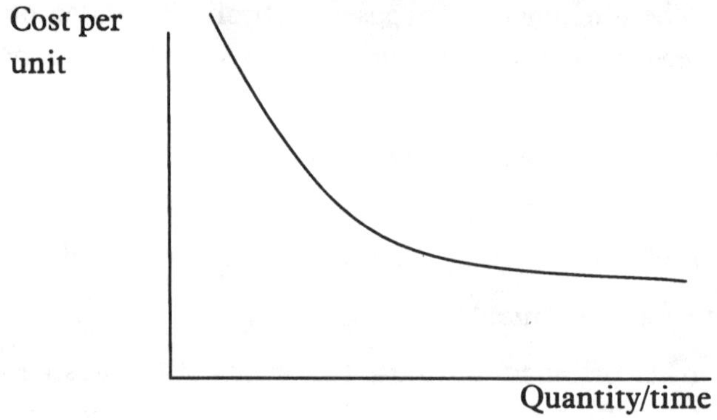

This curve results from a variety of factors.

Economies of scale will be at work. In other words, an increased volume of production leads to lower unit costs. In addition, as the workforce becomes familiar with the job and learns to carry out the task more efficiently, there will be a genuine **'learning effect**.' As a process is repeated, it is likely that costs will reduce due to **efficiency, discounts** and **reduced waste.**

The experience curve applies not just to labour costs, but also to **innovation** and **technological improvements**, marketing and **management expertise**. Economies of scale apply equally to production and marketing processes.

New products often hold their price in the early stages of their **life cycle,** while costs are going down, creating increased profit margins. A policy of reducing prices as costs fall can help a company to win a dominant share of the market. Organisations which have a high market share are generally among the most competitive and profitable.

An alternative to this method of pricing is to set a 'target' price according to **target costing,** an approach used in Japan. When a product is first manufactured, the target cost (ie the eventual cost that is 'aimed' for) will usually be well below the current cost, which will be determined by, amongst other factors, experience curve effects.

Management then sets **benchmarks** for improvement towards the target costs by improving technologies and processes and thereby benefiting from the experience curve as more **production experience** is gained. Target costing is thus in effect a process of establishing what the cost of a product should be over the entire **product life cycle**. In the short run, because of development costs and the learning time needed, costs are likely to exceed price. In the longer term, costs should come down to their target level.

There are other aspects to the **strategic importance** of experience curves, which managers must be aware of when making decisions. For example, businesses **can predict their likely future costs,** and plan more effectively in the project appraisal process.

As noted above, the **product life cycle** is relevant. We can add another dimension: can the benefit of **prolonged experience of its production** necessarily **prolong the life** of a company's product? The profitability and sales of a product can indeed be expected to change over time, but the general pattern of introduction, growth, maturity and decline may vary from product to product, and so it is difficult to forecast the stages that particular products will follow or indeed how long those stages will last. Some products have no maturity phase, and go straight from growth to decline.

A company might be prepared to make losses in the short term, in order to build up sales volumes, so that the product is profitable over its entire life cycle and enjoys a prolonged maturity phase. Knowledge of the stages of the PLC for each product will mean that appropriate marketing mix strategies can be planned, in order to prolong the maturity phase and keep sales at a strong level. In practice, however, the different stages of the product life cycle can be difficult to recognise.

In reviewing strategy, planners should where possible assess the **stage** of its life cycle that any product has reached, its **remaining life** and the urgency of the **need to innovate**. The greatest impact of the experience curve will be felt in the later stages of a product's life as more and more experience is gained (the growth and maturity stages), but it could be said that in some cases as techniques improve, demand patterns will change and new products are required, which will **decrease the life** of the original product.

On the other hand, if there is a very steep experience curve (ie the benefits are obtained quickly), the first into the market may reap all the advantages and build up a commanding position by obtaining an early leadership in market share. This can lead to increased profitability.

Greater experience can also be used to **differentiate** a product, either via greater experience of the market or the ability to utilise technology in a unique way. Products may be **redesigned**, or the distribution channel may be amended. New **promotional techniques** may keep the product in the mind of customers for longer than before.

An experience curve which models production costs can be related to **customer demand** schedules. If the experience curve suggests increased quantities of production, then it is possible that the increased volume will have to be sold at a lower price, in order to prolong the life of the product. Therefore, the management accountant might usefully relate experience curves to demand schedules, in particular **price elasticity,** to establish likely profitability of the product.

Furthermore, the strategy as a whole needs to take the entry of **competitors** into account. It is essential that the offering to the customer is better than or at least matches that of your competitors, and prolonged experience of competitor reactions and the environment in which the company operates should make managers better able to respond.

52 QUALITY AND ADDED VALUE

Pass marks. Think about the strategic focus of a management accountant and its external nature. We have interpreted the key words in the question (aside from *quality*) to be *competitive advantage* (what constitutes this?) and *added value* (what does this mean?). How can investment in improved product quality help in these areas? We have tended in our answer towards the angle of the opportunity cost of a *lack* of improvement in product quality. You may have taken a different approach. The management accountant should be able to find examples to show how product quality adds value to a business by demonstrating that failure to invest in it drains resources.

Examiner's comments. Many candidates thought this question was about quality and nothing more. Too many candidates failed to appreciate the differences between 'quality' and 'cost reduction' – the latter does not necessarily lead to the former! Too few candidates made the point that increased costs, whilst being a short term disadvantage, could lead in the longer term to better quality and added value. Hence, answers often did not address the central theme of the question (how the management accountant can assist an organisation to obtain added value from improved product quality). A number of good answers were produced (the use of value chain analysis was an appropriate approach) but there would have been more good marks if more candidates had looked carefully at the requirements of the question.

The worldwide nature of **competition** has pushed **quality management** to the fore. Japanese companies have managed to show that high quality does not necessarily mean high cost and high prices for the customer, and Western firms are finding that **sustainable competitive advantage**, and indeed any presence in the market worth having, is dependent upon a basic level of quality. Further, most organisations believe that product or service quality **improvement** will mean that your position is enhanced relative to competitors.

Many of the performance criteria associated with quality monitoring may be **non-financial**, but a management accountant's role in measuring the impact of quality improvement on business competitiveness and performance begins from the premise that **quality costs money**. This will be felt, in the case of poor quality, in rectification costs, poor customer perception and lost goodwill. **Resources** are wasted if there are errors or bad workmanship.

Investing in quality **improvement**, on the other hand, costs money but is likely to **add value**. Although added value can be measured in different ways, the main concept is that added value equals **sales minus the costs of materials and bought-in services**. One of the costs may be the costs associated with quality improvements, which could help to differentiate an organisation's products from its competitors.

The implication for a management accountant in an environment where quality is pervasive is that he must support quality performance measures with management accounting **information**. This may include cost information that will enable management to take decisions where any **trade offs**, for example between product choices, are to be made.

The management accountant is aiming in this context to develop performance measures which will support a firm's strategy of securing competitive advantage over other organisations. This demonstrates the external focus of the strategic management accountant and has two implications.

(a) **Competitive advantage is relative**. To have competitive advantage, you must have competitors. Understanding competitors is therefore of prime importance. Rivalry among existing firms is one of the competitive forces in Porter's model. New entrants may come in to the market with a better quality product.

(b) **Customers** determine if a firm has competitive advantage. It is something a firm gains from interaction in the market place. The bargaining power of customers is another of Porter's competitive forces. Any quality targets must take into account **customer's perception** of quality, which may not agree with that of management, and a set of criteria may need to be developed.

From the quality perspective, an organisation should therefore be made fully aware of the levels of quality achieved (and achievable) by competitors and potential new entrants, and the levels of quality expected by customers.

If an organisation subscribes to the concept of **total quality management** it will, amongst other things, seek **continuous improvement**. Quality management is concerned that products and services meet planned quality specifications. Management needs to set clear standards, plan how those standards will be met, track achievements by monitoring the costs of the strategy, and take action where necessary. The management accountant can assist in presenting the following types of information.

(a) **Sales and contribution information**. Sales and margin figures for products before and after quality improvement initiatives are implemented should be provided, showing product contribution and return on the overall investment. This can be compared to project targets and the organisation's required rate of return. Such analysis will show whether the quality improvement initiative has added value, although some investments may take a long time to show benefits.

(b) **Forecast benefits of selected quality improvement proposals**. These could be assessed by DCF analysis or the application of decision theory where appropriate. The expected benefit from a range of outcomes can be given, comparing those benefits to the initial planned investment. This involves an element of uncertainty.

(c) **Likely competitor reaction**. Efforts are likely to be made by competitors to counter any product quality improvements by the organisation. Increased promotion is a very likely reaction, and the management accountant may be able to provide analysis of likely competitor response, by liaison for example with the marketing department to find out about previous experiences. An expected response which is likely to be damaging to the organisation may lead management to conclude that the quality improvement will not add value.

(d) **Analysis of quality performance**. This may involve a survey of customers, the competition and suppliers as well as internal study of the firm itself. Strategic management accounting, as has already been said, has an external focus. Customer satisfaction surveys may show improved results after quality improvements. The organisation may receive quality awards.

(e) **Opportunity cost** of any lack of quality improvements may be significant. Poor quality products, or simply those of a standard, non-differentiated quality, may make losses due to having to bear a lower selling price than competing, higher quality products. Poor quality may lead to lost orders. Information on the financial effect of this could be provided by liaising with sales teams.

(f) **Staff costs**. Analysis of employees' time will provide a view of whether one department's efforts are being spent on correcting errors made by another department. As many employees as possible should be working on core activities, rather than on tasks related to quality deficiencies. Releasing them to focus on more value adding activities will benefit the organisation.

(g) **Analysis of quality costs**. These can be divided into **prevention** costs, **appraisal** costs, **internal failure** costs and **external failure** costs, and the management accountant can present these as a way of showing how investment in quality is saving money.

The term 'prevention costs' broadly covers the cost of any **action taken** to investigate and prevent or reduce defects and failures. 'Appraisal costs' are associated with the costs of **assessing quality,** such as performance testing. 'Internal failure' costs are those that result from failure to achieve the quality specified, and may include reinspection costs and costs of revising product specifications. 'External failure' costs arise after transfer to the customer, and may include administration costs in the customer services division, costs of repairing returned products and, in extreme cases, product liability costs.

The cost examples listed above may not be available from the accounting system as it is currently set up. Quality related costs may be hidden because of inadequate coding, so new accounting **procedures** may have to be implemented. The management accountant could be involved in redesigning the system and accounting procedures, to make sure that such costs can be identified and a thorough analysis presented.

53 RUS PLC: SERVICE QUALITY

> **Pass marks**. The examiner reported that candidates were able to describe TQM but were less able to indicate its relevance to RUS plc. Also, candidates did not show with sufficient precision the management accountant's distinctive contribution to the new strategy: instead they discussed management accounting in general terms.

(a) **Relevance of TQM**

TQM is relevant to both the previous and the new strategy.

(i) TQM deals with two issues.

(1) **Design quality:** the services should be designed to meet customer needs in the most appropriate way.

(2) **Conformance quality:** the service actually delivered should conform to the service promised.

(ii) **Scope of TQM**. Developed in manufacturing industry, TQM is an approach to dealing with production, which involves getting things right first time, zero defects, reducing variation etc. It tries to involve the customer's needs in the very process of production.

(iii) **Relevance to service industries.** Bad service cannot be inspected and scrapped after it is delivered: services are generally consumed as they are produced. As much of the success in a service industry depends on repeat business, getting things right first time (as that is, indeed, the only time) must be a priority.

(iv) **Measurement.** TQM also involves a detailed analysis of the process of production. An aspect of TQM is the reduction in variation. Restaurant service should be predictable; food quality must be consistently good, not outstanding one day and mediocre the next, otherwise the hotel will get a reputation for being unreliable.

(v) **Culture of TQM**. Employees must be encouraged to come forward with suggestions, and they must be engaged in the process of improving service. An almost obsessional interest in service quality should be encouraged.

These considerations apply to the family and medium-priced business accommodation as well as to the hotel's new strategy. However, as the new guests will be paying more, their expectations will be so much more exacting than before.

The design quality of the service (what these new customers actually want) is paramount, and conformance quality (what is actually given) must be faultless.

(b) **Financial and organisational implications**

RUS is chasing a new market, targeting high spending customers whose requirements will be different.

(i) Investment in buildings and fixtures includes the following.

(1) Decoration
(2) Changes to room sizes (eg conversion of pairs of single rooms into suites)
(3) More luxurious furnishings
(4) Perhaps expanded restaurant and kitchen facilities
(5) Swimming pool, gymnasium etc
(6) More opulent spaces
(7) Enhancing the hotel's grounds and gardens
(8) Carparking facilities

(ii) Other expenditure will arise from the following.

(1) More staff, to provide the service required

(2) More training

(3) The greater variety of food offered to guests (hence kitchen costs will rise)

(4) Advertising to reach the target segment

There will be fewer customers but they will be paying more.

(iii) **Organisationally,** the increased numbers in staff must be given more training, and existing staff will have to learn to cater differently for the new customers. Furthermore, there is unlikely to be the same deployment of staff as before, catering for family and business customers at different times. More effort will need to be spent on management and marketing. Quality circles should be introduced.

(c) The **management accountant's contribution** to the new strategy is as follows.

(i) To provide cost and revenue information in the initial research and planning phase, and to forecast future income and expenditure.

(ii) To cost any improvements to buildings and furnishings.

(iii) To suggest an appropriate pricing policy.

(iv) To raise external finance (eg from the bank) if substantial capital investment is needed and borrowing is necessary.

(v) To draw up tactical plans and budgets for the changeover.

(vii) To set up and operate new management accounting systems to monitor and control the hotel's performance.

(viii) To suggest appropriate non-financial performance measures, in particular with relation to quality of service.

(ix) To consider if the hotel's new clients will need services such as travellers cheques encashment etc, if they are from overseas.

(x) To provide regular and suitable management information.

54 SALES TEAM BENCHMARKING

> **Examiner's comments.** this was a popular question and reasonably well answered. Part (b) required an application of the principles to the scenario: a thorough understanding of existing operations is thus necessary.

(a) **Objectives and uses of benchmarking**

According to CIMA, **benchmarking** is 'the establishment, through data gathering, of targets and comparators, through whose use areas of performance (and particularly areas of underperformance) can be identified. By the adoption of identified best practices it is hoped that performance will be improved'. CIMA then goes on to identify the following types of benchmarking.

(i) **Internal benchmarking** compares one operating unit or function with another in the **same industry**. A firm will normally choose another with superior performance, which can be matched. In evaluating operational performance, this enables managers to see where they fall down in comparison with industry best practice.

(ii) **Functional/operational/generic** benchmarking involves the comparison of a business's internal functions with those of the best external practitioners of those functions, regardless of the industry they are in. For example a bank setting up a telephone banking service might benchmark a telephone sales operation, for matters such as speed of answering, courtesy and so forth. This is because answering the telephone is a generic skill, not restricted to banking.

(iii) **Competitor benchmarking**. The firm uses competitors as a benchmark for performance. **Strategic benchmarking** is a type of competitor benchmarking aimed at strategic action and organisational change.

The **objectives and value of benchmarking** are as follows.

(i) To keep up with industry best practice - perhaps to negate a competitor's operational competitive advantage.

(ii) To enhance the efficiency and effectiveness of the function involved in the benchmarking exercise.

(iii) To reduce the need to 'reinvent the wheel' - a firm can climb the learning curve to achieve best practice much quicker if it uses another firm's experience: of course a competitor or even a firm in the same industry is unlikely to be too helpful.

(iv) As performance indicators to motivate managers: the **benchmark standards are achievable,** as other firms **have** achieved them.

In all these respects, benchmarking can be used for planning and control. As **planning measures,** they can be used to design systems and to assess the resources required to achieve a certain standard of performance. In evaluating operational performance, benchmarks can be used as the 'plan or standard' of a **control system,** and feedback can be used to see whether the plan has been met. Such non-financial performance indicators can be introduced ready-made into the strategic control system.

Problems with benchmarking in evaluating operational performance are as follows.

(i) The benchmark standards do not always take the use of resources into account.

(ii) Managers will be satisfied when they have reached the benchmark standard and will be less motivated to exceed it.

(iii) There may be better ways of enhancing performance (eg by exploiting different linkages in the value chain, outsourcing some value activities etc).

(iv) It is based on copying industry leaders, rather than doing things in a different, more innovative way.

(b) (i) **The sales team as a whole**

Subject matter of benchmarking exercise. Many organisations have field sales forces organised on an area basis, and so the company is not unique. It can therefore learn from other companies as to the best way of managing and controlling its sales personnel. Benchmarking techniques can be used, for two types of information.

(1) The best way to **design and run** a field sales force (eg the optimum balance of salary and commission, the most appropriate way of designing and setting targets).

(2) The **performance** of the sales team, as it is currently managed in the light of other field sales forces (in other words the content of the targets).

Choice of company to benchmark. Competitor benchmarking is probably out of the question, given that any useful and coherent information will be hard to obtain, unless the firm poaches disaffected sales personnel. There is no indication that the firm is considering any major change in strategy, so the approaches which **can** be used are **internal benchmarking** and **functional benchmarking.** Obviously, the consent of the benchmarked company needs to be obtained, and the firm will pay a fee for this.

(1) The firm could choose a firm of similar size, hopefully with similar markets, to ease comparisons.

(2) On the other hand, the use of firms **outside the industry** offers a wider pool of expertise and new ideas.

Identifying areas to be benchmarked. The company needs to identify and describe its **current practices** and performance.

(1) **Systems issues** include remuneration systems, territory design and size, and the basis on which targets are set by territory.

(2) **Performance issues** include typical mileage and expenses, the number of sales leads generated and the number of sales leads converted into real orders.

Timescale. The benchmarking exercise needs to carried out over a meaningful timescale, both from the firm's point of view and in terms of the operational realities of the benchmarked firm. **Seasonal factors** need to be taken into account as do any other special circumstances. Whilst the demand for industrial oils is unlikely to be too seasonal, this may not apply for the benchmarked company.

Review. Once the information has been gathered, it can be analysed and converted into a meaningful form by the benchmarking company. The information must be comparable and so a number of adjustments will have to be made. Once this is done, the benchmarking firm can then identify areas of performance or systems where deficiencies are found.

Action. The firm can then take steps to improve its performance and make any necessary changes to the achieve the benchmark.

(ii) **Individuals**

Individual direct benchmarks are not appropriate. Applying benchmarks to the individuals is a logical extension of the process of benchmarking the team. Whilst the sales team can be reviewed as a whole, and its performance measured on an average basis, individual sales personnel will differ in their performance. Furthermore, it is unlikely that any single individual sales person in the benchmarked company (covering the same region, say) could be used for benchmarking purposes. The benchmarked company may have a different sales territory structure.

Group average. Applying benchmarking to individual sales people will therefore happen at one remove. From the comparison between each company, an overall average measure of performance will be derived, on whatever measures are deemed necessary. For example, the benchmarked company may show a much better record of converting sales leads into orders, on average. These techniques can be adapted.

Suggest and announce changes. This may involve making current targets harder to reach, or introducing new measures, or changing more fundamentally the structure and operations of the sales function. In the company described, changes could include the following.

(1) **Redesign of the sales territories.**

(2) The use of **different targets** per individual - in other words setting different targets per territory, depending on the nature of the territory, the ease with which it can be traversed and so forth.

(3) **Amend the payment system** to increase the element of bonus/commission and reducing the level of basic salary.

Introduce changes. Clearly, these matters will be better resolved if a **participatory approach** is adopted. Sales staff may offer suggestions to improve performance. The new systems should be fiddle-proof, in other words not easy to manipulate. An appropriate time might be needed for people to get used to the new system, and so learning curve effects must be allowed for. Indeed, performance might dip in the short term as people become accustomed to the new system.

New comparisons. Once the new measures are in place, the performance of the sales staff can be compared. To ensure fair comparisons, matters such as the overall level of prosperity and industrial structure of the sales territories can be taken into account to enable more appropriate targets to be set.

55 TUTORIAL QUESTION: SEGMENTATION

(a) The simile of **segmentation** being like the precise use of a rifle, rather than the indiscriminate use of a machine gun, has often been quoted.

Market segmentation is the division of a market into **fairly homogeneous subsets** where each subset can be chosen, reached and served by its own tailored marketing mix. Each such homogeneous subset is made up of people with approximately similar needs and aspirations which distinguish them from other subsets.

Segmentation applies to the personal customer market and the business market.

(b) **What are the criteria for effective segmentation?**

According to Kotler the criteria for effective segmentation are measurability, accessibility (of the segment to the organisation's selling efforts), actionability and substantiality (ie a segment must be sufficiently large and profitable to justify its own campaign).

(c) **What are the benefits of segmentation?**

There are benefits to both the organisation and to its customers.

(i) The firm can choose segments with **greater profit potential.** No firm has unlimited resources and must concentrate their use to promising segments.

Segmentation allows **tailoring** of all the elements and sub-elements of the marketing mix.

(1) Products and services themselves may be find-tuned to the segment. The costs involved in product testing/development can be reduced by concentrating on specified segments only.

(2) The firm can consider differential pricing. Lower unit costs can be achieved.

(3) The four promotional sub-elements (advertising, sales promotions, publicity and personal selling) can likewise be better directed towards the target segment.

(4) Facilities can be located and furnished in accordance with the exigencies of the segment. For example, in a banking context, the more affluent personal customers will expect fairly plush offices, whereas corporate treasurers expect to be visited on their own premises. (If they visit the bank at all, it may be to the dining suite, not the offices themselves.)

(5) Managerial and staff training can be more specific, rapid and effective.

(6) The firm also benefits because it forces itself to look at not only the present situation but also the future. The firm therefore puts itself in a better position to be able to meet upcoming changes in the composition of the market, and likely competitive moves.

(ii) **Customers benefit** from segmentation by being offered those products and services which they are seeking at prices pitched at their level, and the products and services can be packaged in the combinations of interest to the segment. As the firm is specialising, it should be more efficient, and the staff should be more conversant with the products in question, and get to know their customers better, thus being able to give customers better and faster advice and service.

56 BUYER BEHAVIOUR

Pass marks. An unusual question in that whilst a model was referred to in part (b), it was not in part (a). A number of models of the consumer buying process exists. Below we have chosen a simple model of problem recognition, information search, evaluation of alternatives, purchase decision and post purchase evaluation. You might just as well used AIDA or Howard-Sheth. You could have used this to structure your answer, to describe how cultural, social, personal and psychological factors influence each stage. Part (a) offers sixteen marks, so using a structured approach will help you avoid leaving things out.

Examiner's comments. Not a popular question, although not a difficult one. Answers to part (a) were required to show exactly how each factor influences buyer behaviour. Part (b) referred to the buying decision. 'Irrespective of whether the candidate identified the categories (users, influences, deciders, approvers, gatekeepers), marks were awarded for functions if appropriately discussed.'

(a) **Consumer buyer behaviour**

Cultural factors include the values, belief systems and behavioural patterns which consumers share with others. Examples of cultural influences include religion and the belief that sexual roles should be highly differentiated.

Social factors and cultural factors are closely but not entirely, related. Social factors include a person's socio-economic status and the status to which that person might aspire.

Personal factors include the individual's age, occupation, sex, life style choices and personality.

Psychological factors relate to person's motivation, perception, learning styles and attitudes.

These categories are not hard and fast. Cultural factors reflect socio-economic status (eg in some poor countries, the elite is educated in the west). Cultural factors can also influence an individual's life style choices and indeed the individual's motivation (psychological factors). The distinction should not be taken too rigidly. These factors influence the process of buying in the following ways.

Problem recognition. The buyer must recognise a need and be sufficiently motivated to satisfy it. Let us take the example of the purchase of **critical illness insurance**.

(i) **Psychological.** A person with a pessimistic or nervous psychology is more prone to buying insurance than someone who is happy living with risk.

(ii) **Personal.** Personal factors are also relevant: some occupations are riskier than others, hence consumers in some industries will be more willing to buy critical illness insurance to tide them over if their firm is not generous to those who are sick.

(iii) **Social factors** include whether the purchase of critical illness insurance is something which other people in the person's social network do or talk about.

(iv) **Cultural.** It is hard to think of specific cultural factors - although in such cultures, insurance is regarded as slightly blasphemous (as it is 'second-guessing' divine providence).

Information search. This is the process of hunting round for information about how the need can be satisfied. Let us take the example of **choosing a holiday**.

(i) **Psychological.** Some people rely on verbal rather than textual information. Those who are risk averse will be concerned with the reliability of the source of information and will go to what they consider a reputable travel agent - it might even influence the choice of holiday ('we like to visit the same place every year' rather than 'we like to see different countries').

(ii) **Personal factors.** Age might be a factor in information search. Younger people may be happier with electronic means of communication, such as the Internet. Those more elderly people not familiar with this method may prefer a brochure or even a trip to a travel agent for 'advice'.

(iii) **Social factors.** A person might ask people in his/her role set for advice. Word of mouth recommendations can be important. (For example 'so-and-so is a good firm to go on holiday with'). Other social factors include spurning some destinations as being 'down market'.

(iv) **Cultural factors.** Newspapers and magazines are cultural products, as are TV holiday programmes. Choice of newspaper influences buyer behaviour if people rely on the newspaper as an accurate source of information - which advertisers can then exploit.

Evaluation of alternatives. If there are a number of solutions to the buyer's needs, then each will be considered. Let us take the example of **buying a car**.

(i) **Psychological.** Some people find the process of comparing alternatives too irritating and go for the first offer that looks even half decent. Risk-averse people will go for reliability (perhaps consulting **Which**? magazine in the information search phase); others might feel a particular make of car is exciting. Much advertising is devoted towards psychology.

(ii) **Personal.** Occupation is an important factor in choice of car, if only for the reason that many cars (in the UK) are 'company-cars' paid for by the employer, which limits choice. Other choices include whether the purchaser drives to work or commutes by public transport.

(iii) **Social.** Cars function as status symbols for some people - hence, perhaps, the rush in the UK to own a new car when the registration year reference letter changes. Some brands (eg Skodas at one time) are the target of jokes - but other consumers may not take cars seriously as social identifiers. Social class and status are obviously identified with some cars (each Rolls Royces).

(iv) **Cultural.** A concern with ecological greenery may lead some people to choose cars which do least damage to the environment, or at least they will respond favourably to advertising which emphasises these issues.

Purchase decision. The product/service is now to be bought. The marketers most difficult task is to convert interest to action. A variety of techniques are used. Let us take the example of **selling cable television and telephone services.**

(i) **Psychological.** Cable TV is sold in a variety of ways - by advertising, by direct mail and by door-to door selling. Some consumers may respond better to some advertising media than others. Some may resent door to door or telephone selling if they feel pressurised into buying.

(ii) **Personal.** Socio-economic status may have an impact, in that not everybody can afford to own cable TV. Consumers' existing use of satellite TV may make cable less attractive. An interest in sport or other special interest channels may make cable more attractive. There is the economic constraint: can the purchase be afforded?

(iii) **Social.** The decision to purchase may be taken at a time when other people are doing it. A person who has been interested for a while in cable TV may change over when someone he or she knows has done so.

(iv) **Cultural.** The decision whether or not to purchase cable TV services is almost certainly a cultural factor - if only for the reason that television by definition is a cultural product, and the mix of programmes may not appeal to some people. Some religious groups eschew television completely.

Post-purchase evaluation is when, having acquired a product or service, a person reviews his or her decision and is either pleased or disappointed with it. This may lead the person to buy again.

(i) **Psychological.** Anxious people need to be reassured that they have made the right decision and some sales literature emphasises the benefit of the product even after the sale. Guarantees and promises of after-sales service can help make this stage less stressful.

(ii) **Personal**. A person may have particular expectations based on his or her previous experience or lifestyle. For example, service quality may be unfavourably compared to service enjoyed elsewhere. People who are hard up might be especially concerned with value-for-money issues.

(iii) **Social**. People might show their purchase to friends and seek their approval ('do I look nice in this?').

(iv) **Cultural**. In the former Soviet Union, people were accustomed to shoddy goods. Cultural expectations of service quality can rise.

(b) **Organisational buyer behaviour**

Organisational buying behaviour is, in theory, more rational than individual buyer behaviour. They do have certain feature in common. Many domestic purchases result from co-operative activity. for example, a child might have a need, which the parents have to satisfy - at least two different people, the child and parent(s) form the decision-making unit. In companies, the decision making unit or buying centre is much more significant.

The organisational buying behaviour process has some similarities with consumer buyer behaviour, but is supposedly more rational. Crucial questions are these.

(i) **How are needs recognised in a company**? How are customer needs connected with product specification? The role of the decision making unit is crucial here.

(ii) What is the type of buying situation?

(iii) How is a supplier selected? Some firms seek to build long term relationships with suppliers, other employ sophisticated rating systems.

(iv) How will performance be reviewed after purchase?

The **decision-making unit (DMU)** is a term used to describe the person or people who actually take the decision to buy a good or service. The marketing manager needs to know who in each organisation makes the effective buying decisions - this might be one person, or a group of people - and **how decisions are made**: the DMU might act with formal authority, or as an informal group reaching a joint decision. Many large organisations employ specialist purchasing departments or 'buyers' - but the independence of the buyers will vary from situation to situation. The DMU might include the following.

(i) The **gatekeeper** controls the flow of information about the purchase. This role can be senior or junior but is important because it influences the communication flow within the organisation.

(ii) **Influencers** do not take the purchase decision but their opinions count. In this environment, the salesperson can be a respected technical link with the buyer able to influence the purchasing process.

(iii) **Users**, employees or managers in sales and production etc might make recommendations about what type of supplies should be purchased.

(iv) A **junior buying manager** might decide what to buy, but might have to submit his or her recommendation to a superior for approval.

(v) In large organisations, there will be **several buying managers**, who might work independently, but might also work closely together, either formally or informally.

(vi) Technical specifications for component purchases might be provided by **engineers or other technical staff**.

(vii) **Accountants** might be able to set a limit on the price the organisation will pay.

(viii) Large items of purchase might require approval from the **board of directors.**

In the case of **large contracts**, a firm might use several salespeople, each with the responsibility for promoting their product to particular members of the decision-making unit. For example, technical experts might be called on to speak to the buyer's technical staff; directors of the selling company might discuss the contract with the directors of the buying company; another salesperson might deal with the buyer's purchasing staff etc.

57 BRAND STRATEGY APPROACHES

Pass marks. As with all scenario based questions, remember to relate your knowledge to the question set. You need to be able to differentiate between the different strategy types. Do not confuse line extension with brand extension. This was a common error in the examination. Line extension means extending a brand into existing products, whereas brand extension means extending it into new ones.

Other points. We have brought in real-life examples of branding in organisations which are relevant to H plc. This would earn marks and show the examiner that your knowledge is not limited to the textbook. We are surrounded by brands every day and it is not too difficult to think of examples. You may have thought of others.

You may have come to a different conclusion as to the recommended strategy for H plc, but this is fine. The CIMA suggested answer comes up with no firm recommendation and tends towards giving the circumstances under which each strategy would be appropriate. This does not seem to satisfy the requirements of the question. Be confident enough to make a choice and support it with argument.

Examiner's comments. On the whole the question was reasonably well answered, although it seems that many candidates were lying in wait for a question on branding and tended to write about brands in a general sense rather than addressing the scenario. Most candidates did not give adequate support for their recommended strategy and tended to list out advantages and disadvantages of each, with little further application.

H plc has built up a successful umbrella **corporate brand name** which stands for good quality. To this extent, the work of giving **identification** to its goods has been successful, but the company is finding that competitors are encroaching on its territory.

Branding and firms' **reputations** are heavily linked, so it is appropriate for the directors to consider a new approach to branding which will build upon the excellent reputation that the company currently enjoys.

There are various approaches to **branding strategy.** Taking each of the options under consideration by H plc's directors we can say the following.

Line extension

This involves pushing the existing brand further into existing product lines, by introducing new flavours, varieties or package sizes. The H plc brand is synonymous with quality, but the danger of the approach is that competitors may be perceived as offering more **variety** of **product types.**

Customers may prefer a choice of types of tinned vegetable rather than merely a choice between 50g or 100g tins of the same types, however excellent the quality. Customers, once lost to competitors, may stay away. It is far more effective to retain loyal customers than try to win them back.

Brand extension.

H plc is in the canned food business, although the scenario presented does not say whether this is limited to certain types of food. Brand extension would involve extending the brand both to **other types of product** (such as pet food) in cans, but also other types of food, such as fresh food or frozen ready meals, as well as completely new products, like household cleaning supplies. The question of how far H plc wants to go to will depend upon how much of its market is being threatened by rival brands.

Brand extension assumes **high customer loyalty** to the existing brand if it is to be successful. For example, a customer well accustomed to H plc's brand of canned tomatoes will be less resistant to buying a new H plc furniture polish. Supermarkets are likely to want to stock new products from H plc as they are likely to be strong sellers.

Extending the brand to other types of product should only be done if H plc is happy that sales of **existing products** will not be harmed. If the products are completely different, there is no reason why this should happen, although there is a danger of **brand dilution** which may weaken **customer loyalty**.

Extending a brand is cheaper than starting a new one, with all the attendant **promotional activity** that would require.

As H plc supplies a **worldwide** market, it may be that extending the brand to other products provides an opportunity to enter **new markets**. A country which has previously resisted H plc's canned fruit because of a strong domestic supplier could welcome H plc's frozen range. Assessing the likelihood of such an outcome would involve H plc in **marketing research**.

Multi-branding

With this approach, H plc would develop **different brand names for similar goods** serving similar customer tastes. An example of this in the UK is the soap market, where Procter and Gamble and Unilever each produce a large number of different brands of soap products.

This strategy makes it very difficult for new entrants because, although the market seems very fragmented, it is in fact **dominated** by a small number of players.

H plc would only consider this approach if it wanted to maximise the perceived differences between the various products of the company. Setting up various new brands would be **expensive** and it would take some time for customers to be aware of the different brands.

New brands

This would involve H plc in establishing **new products** with new brands. As with multi-branding, it is not territory they are used to. The culture of H plc is probably very tied up with its brand and corporate identity, much like Heinz or St Michael (Marks and Spencer). The use of new brands should be the least favoured of the strategies, because it is both expensive and **risky** for the already strong name that H plc has.

The above discussion of advantages and disadvantage would tend to support **brand extension** as the recommended strategy for reasons of cost and related benefit, the adequacy of response to competitors, adequacy of offer to the customer and suitability for a worldwide market.

It is appropriate to continue with the 'umbrella' branding strategy of quality, which is of key importance in the food industry. Marks and Spencer have stretched their brand name from food to plants to clothing with its reputation for value and quality seeming to be easily transferable.

Finally, the company should make sure that the brand strategy it adopts is in line with its overall **corporate strategy.** If its stated aim is to 'Promote the H plc brand all over the world and see sales revenue increase by X%', then a policy of brand extension will support that, by encouraging sales of new products in a potentially wider market.

58 NOT FOR PROFIT MARKETING

Pass marks. This straightforward question asks for a textbook description more or less of the marketing concept, followed by its application to a club or charity. Did you remember to use report format in part (b)? There is some ambiguity as to whether it should also be adopted for part (c). We have chosen to do so, because the question states that your recommended strategies should be drafted to respect the culture of the society: this implies an attention to style and format. How practical were your suggestions in (c)? You should have tailored your ideas to the specific circumstances outlined.

Examiner's comments. Despite the detailed description, many candidates assumed the society was aiming for a profit. Many also confused the marketing concept with the marketing mix, and their ideas suggested the application of the product rather than the marketing concept.

(a) The **marketing concept** is 'a management orientation or outlook, that accepts that the key task of the organisation is to determine the needs, wants and values of a target market and to adapt the organisation to delivering the desired satisfaction more effectively and efficiently than its competitors.'

The marketing orientation concentrates on the needs of the customer, whereas other orientations concentrate on the needs of the seller or producer. A production orientated firm acts on the basis that all it needs to do is make a good quality product, and that people will buy it. A sales orientation suggests that customers are naturally resistant to buying and this resistance must be broken.

(b) REPORT

To: Smalltown Horticultural Society Date: 21/X/19XX
From: A.N. Accountant
Re: The Society's Annual Show

Background

There is considerable public interest in horticulture and gardening generally, as witnessed by the variety of television programmes on the subject, and the success of flower shows generally. The Society should be able to flourish in such a setting, as there appears to be no dearth of public interest.

Although the Society should be flourishing, it has not succeeded in tapping the wealth of public interest. This is shown in the slow decline of people attending the annual flower show.

This decline has prevented the Society from pursuing some of its traditional activities in the local community, such as providing seeds for the elderly. The club is not paying its way.

Possible causes

There have been significant social changes since the Society was founded. One significant change, identified by the Chairman's plea to the ladies of the town, is the changing role of women. Perhaps women are just not available to carry out the Society's functions any more. Reasons for this might include the increase in female employment.

Another significant change is the overall increase in car ownership. This has meant it is a easier than before for people to travel the distance to the next town with its competing flower show. This means that the catchment area of any show has grown larger, and people's activities may not be restricted to the strictly local environment.

The marketing concept

Although the Society is not a business seeking to make a profit, the marketing concept is still relevant to the past and future of the society. There has been no decline in public interest in horticulture, but it is clear that the Society is failing to tap the interest that does exist in the subject.

It is clear that the marketing concept has not applied to any significant degrees.

(i) The Chairman believes the Society is of benefit to the local townsfolk, but the declining interests and attendances would indicate that this is definitely not the case. Fewer people are attending the shows, and this implies that people are being put off.

(ii) The Chairman is simply trying to carry on with the existing practices. This is at best a sales or a production orientation.

(c) **Suggested strategies**

In order to address the slow decline in public interest, first of all an analysis should be carried out as to why there is a decline in interest.

(i) Existing members of the society should be asked for their views, as those who are not on the committee of the society may have their own views.

(ii) The society should conduct a survey to identify the following.

(1) The population profile of Smalltown, to see how this relates to the Association's traditional membership.

(2) The general interest in horticulture amongst residents.

(3) How well known the Society is.

(4) How many people knew about the show last year.

(5) For those that attended the show, what they liked and disliked about it: reasons for non-attendance etc.

(6) What they would expect to see at a show.

(7) What they liked about the show 60 miles away.

(8) The best date for a show (eg in school holidays etc).

(9) Any other activities they would like to see the Society perform.

(10) Their image of the society, whether they think it is relevant and friendly.

The research is quite important. It may suggest that the society is simply not publicising itself or the show properly; perhaps it needs to arrange advance coverage in the local news media or local BBC or commercial radio station.

On the other hand, the society may have a poor but unjustified image; perhaps people perceive it as being run by a clique, who are out of touch with current demand. Certainly the Chairman's plea to the ladies of the town to perform their traditional duties suggests he is out of touch.

The study might reveal other activities that the society could carry out.

(i) It does some **charitable work** and this could be publicised.

(ii) It could run **evening classes** for those residents who might be interested, but who work during the day. This might enable the society to attract a new audience.

(iii) Society members could run a column in the local paper giving useful advice.

(iv) The society might **get involved** with local schools, promote competitions etc.

The cost of the survey would not prohibitive, and the Society's reserves of £12,000 would suggest that it could be afforded.

The Society should also consider how to promote the annual flower show more effectively, as this is its main source of funds.

(i) Ensure that the show does not clash with larger ones held elsewhere.

(ii) Give proper notice in local papers, or indeed by leafleting local people, or buy advertising at local garden centres, DIY stores.

(iii) Try and obtain sponsorship from local businesses. Such funds might be used for advertising.

(iv) Most importantly, address the identified deficiencies in the show, so that people are not disappointed.

59 RR CONTRACTORS

Pass marks. Read the scenario carefully and you should be able to deduce what is going on, so part (a) should present few difficulties. In part (b) make sure your strategy is a sensible one and addresses the key point that RR is in desperate trouble and needs to take action quickly.

Examiner's comments. On the whole, candidates were able to provide an answer to part (a) by drawing from the scenario. The main point to recognise was that the product was unsatisfactory, and the company had a poor reputation.

In part (b), few candidates suggested the possibility that the company was a lost cause, although this could certainly have been argued. They key factor was the speed that was needed to turn the situation around – long term and ornate marketing strategies were unlikely to be of much benefit. Improved quality, and quick communication of the improved service, were needed, but the local market place may have given up on the company.

Strategy suggestions from candidates ranged from the unethical ('repaint the van and change the company name') to the desperate ('pray for a hurricane').

(a) RR Contractors has experienced a decline in the number of its customers because it has neglected its **product** in the **marketing mix**, and concentrated instead on being able to charge low **prices**.

The scenario suggests that this policy has led to quality defects, with the exercising of guarantees by customers indicating sub-standard workmanship and the use of cheap and poor quality materials.

As most of the customers are local, word will spread quickly about RR's shortcomings and new business will be hard to generate in the local area. Roof repairs are, for most customers, a one-off investment and so the company has to rely on new business rather than repeat custom. Adverse word-of-mouth **publicity** in the local area will have been seriously damaging.

Competitors will have been able to take advantage of RR's poor reputation and will have been able to emphasise their own product quality, reinforcing customer perceptions.

(b) RR needs to conduct an investigation and implement a new marketing strategy if it is to take control of the situation and remedy the serious loss of confidence in its products. It is possible that given the 'one-off' nature of the product, and the adverse local publicity, RR may never recover. RR is faced with the task of immediate damage limitation to restore market confidence, and then of ensuring long term survival. This will involve a review of the company's marketing mix. Taking each of the elements of the marketing mix in turn:

Product

Management of RR must recognise quickly that product is the most important aspect of its marketing strategy. High quality roof repairs are fundamental if RR is to rescue its reputation. In the frequently wet English climate, customers need to be sure that the repairs will stand up to adverse weather conditions and last for a long time. Customers will pay a premium for a quality service when the quality of what they are buying is fundamental to the purchase deccision.

To ensure quality repairs, RR must use quality materials and employ competent labour. It has no choice in this. It will cost more, but there is likely to be scope for RR to increase its prices.

RR would benefit from the introduction of a **quality control programme**, set up to inspect each job and monitor customer satisfaction. The policy of providing guarantees for its work should continue, as this increases customer confidence.

Price

It is likely that customers would sooner pay a higher price for a quality product, than have a roof that continues to leak and needs further costly repairs. RR needs to revise the emphasis of its strategy, which currently focuses on price when the market for roof repairs may not be price sensitive. It is likely that there is scope to increase prices, and invest that extra revenue in better quality.

Most customers for building repairs will collect several quotes, so price is indeed a consideration, but reputation and recommendations are also likely to be key factors in the purchase decision. If a service is too cheap, it is unlikely to be trusted, because customers usually have an idea of what is a 'fair' price to pay.

Place

RR operates largely in its local area and the damage to its reputation here has been severe. It may not be able to recover unless it undertakes some better work in other areas (not too far away, for reasons of cost), after which its improved reputation may filter back to its own area.

As a small firm, a policy of expansion into outlying areas cannot be pursued too far, but an increased catchment area of potential customers will be to RR's advantage.

Promotion

As already mentioned, word of mouth in the local area has probably had a devastating effect, so RR needs to move quickly and limit the damage by emphasising to potential customers that the quality of its service has been improved. Local press is likely to be one of the best media. Satisfied customers from other areas could be used in this campaign to illustrate the better product.

This is likely to take time to implement and may do little to encourage local custom. Competitor activity is likely to be capitalising on RR's difficulties, although a promotional campaign will at least keep RR in the public's mind for the short term while immediate difficulties are addressed.

60 MARKET ATTACK STRATEGIES

> **Pass marks.** Marketing strategies sits in part (d) of the syllabus, Strategy in the Market Place, but analysis of specific attack strategies is marginal and fairly specialised, and the question therefore seems to carry a disproportionately high number of marks. From that standpoint it may be regarded as a prizewinner's question. In the actual exam it is likely that, for the majority of candidates, it was attempted only as a last resort.
>
> **Examiner's comments**. This question exposed a gap in knowledge! Very few candidates attempted the question – those that did either knew and understood the strategies very well, or did not know them at all. For those who did know them it was a chance to earn high marks.

The **market share** and **profitability** of A Ltd ('A') is under threat from B plc ('B'), and consequently A needs to **reposition** itself and recover market share. It may not be able to regain the leadership it once enjoyed, because B appears to have the **resources** to defend itself from attack as well as pursue **innovation** and **promotion** of its product. B may also enjoy a strong reputation and is likely to have **economies of scale** not available to A.

The **marketing mix** of product, price, promotion and place could be used by A as a basis for attack. B may be failing in one of these areas and A could exploit this. Research, comprising **competitor analysis** and **marketing research,** could be appropriate.

The suitability of each attack strategy depends on the resources available to A what its **strategic objectives** are. The directors must be clear what they want to achieve, the resources available to them and the length of time within which they wish to see improvements in market share.

(a) **Frontal**

This is based upon a **direct attack** upon B's strengths rather than its weaknesses. The outcome depends upon the **defensive capability** of B, which is likely to be strong in a conglomerate with six times A's turnover. A would have to match or improve upon aspects of B's marketing mix in all its markets.

The fact that the component is specialised could mean that A is able to match or even exceed B in terms of product specification, or it may be able to bear a lower price because it may have lower operating or administration overheads than a larger company. A may start off by offering lower prices to attract customers and then match B on other fronts such as product quality, distribution network and promotional activity.

This amounts to an assault in two stages, accepting a lower level of profit initially to recoup market share that can be sustained in the longer term by cost cutting. However, B is likely to cut its prices too, and may be better able to survive a price war than its smaller rival.

(b) **Flanking**

This strategy should be more attractive to A as it involves attacking B's market share at the points where it is weakest. This means that A's comparative lack of resources is less significant. B may be weak in particular **geographical areas** or in particular **market segments,** so A can try to target these new areas and segments where B pays less attention. There may be market needs that B is not meeting with its version of the component, so A may be able to adapt its own product. This will enable it to increase market share at relatively low cost.

(c) **Encirclement**

This is only possible where the aggressor has more resources. This is not the case for A. Attacking B on all sides by developing the marketing mix in all areas (improved product, better distribution networks, enhanced promotion and lower price) is likely to be beyond A's capabilities. It is unlikely that it would be able to overwhelm B on several fronts.

(d) **By-pass**

This strategy would involve A bypassing B altogether and concentrating on entirely **new products and markets** as a way of coping with B's dominance in one particular segment. This would be done with the aim of increasing A's resources and maybe enabling it to undertake more direct attack strategies in the future. A may choose unrelated products, new geographical markets or, most likely, **new technologies** where B is not active.

The latter will involve A in **research and development**, instead of hanging on where B has overtaken it. This strategy will take time to bring returns, although the advantages gained could be considerable. Research into new technology could bring unexpected spin-offs, and A may command significant market attention on the strength of its new developments and products.

(e) **Guerilla**

This is another strategy suitable for smaller aggressors. **Small attacks** could be waged by A on various fronts in the marketing mix to undermine B's position. **Intense promotional activity** could be an option, seeking to undermine B's share of the market for the component in a relatively small area of activity which may be weakly defended by B, and where it is less willing to retaliate. As a general observation, substantial promotional spending is only a good idea if A can exhibit demonstrable superiority over B's product. If customers can see no appreciable difference, then B's position as market leader is unlikely to be threatened.

The aim of guerilla attacks is to gain a **foothold** as a prelude to a more sustained and aggressive challenge. Conducting a guerilla campaign of any duration can be expensive, and A would have to decide when and if it should step up its activity into a stronger attack.

On the basis of the above review, it would seem that A's best option if it is to regain market share is to launch either a frontal or flank attack, depending on the exact **nature of the market** for the specialised component (for example, are there possible substitutes?) and the **characteristics of the product** itself, which are not clear in the question.

Encirclement can be ruled out as A has a resource disadvantage, and a bypass strategy will take longer to come to fruition than is likely to be in the contemplation of A's directors. Guerilla tactics need considerable planning and intense activity, which again may be beyond A's capabilities both in terms of resources and time available. B as a conglomerate is unlikely to cave in over the odd pricing attack here and there.

61 TUTORIAL QUESTION: MARKETING MIX

(a) A **manufacturer of domestic washing machines** is a supplier of **consumer durables** to the consumer market. Here, the marketing mix has to be consumer-orientated, so that the main principles behind the marketing mix and the smaller sales mix must be such that the arrangement and the allocation of the resources maximise returns per unit of outlay. The ideal mix for such a product would differ, then, from (b) below. The washing machines are bought for use, and also for **personal satisfaction,** and they are purchased in single units by individual buyers.

Product. With a consumer capital good like a washing machine, the **product** itself will be important. The customer will want quality, a wider variety of features, a well known name with good reliable service back up and guarantees. Packaging may be important, but technological specification will certainly be.

Under **place**, ready availability, good service cover and prompt delivery will be important.

Promotion. This applies to goods which an individual will buy infrequently (eg a motor car). The customer will look at all promotional literature, want demonstrations and possibly consult a consumer advisor.

Price.

It is an expensive product. Price discount, any trade-in allowances, any bonuses will all be important. Credit terms and payment periods will also be important.

(b) A manufacturer of **heavy commercial vehicles**, however, produces for the industrial market. Here the purchase is made by a professional buyer who buys for **use** and not personal satisfaction.

Under the '4 Ps' obviously quality, features, options, and style and sizes will be important characteristics for the **product**. Packaging will be irrelevant.

The **place** may be important for service back up while promotion will depend on trade advertising, technical publicity and reports, service back up and the personal selling.

Price will again be important, although more in the context of value for money. Mercedes do not claim to be the cheapest, but they emphasise quality, reliability and long life. Credit terms may be important, although this may well be dealt with separately. Discounts and allowances will be important.

62 TUTORIAL QUESTION: PRODUCT DEVELOPMENT AND PRICING

(a) **Product development** involves an organisation seeking to create new products to replace existing ones. The new products could represent either completely new products or revised versions of existing ones.

The framework of an overall **corporate strategy**, determines the **marketing strategy.**

Within a marketing strategy, the structure of a company's competitive advantage is determined by its overall product-market mix, and **product development strategy** is part of this.

Portfolio. Many firms attempt to have a combination of current and new products in current and new markets so that it is able to grow and survive. Other product-market growth strategies that will be co-ordinated with the product development strategy are strategies for market penetration, market development and diversification. A company will attempt to have a mixture of these strategies which is consistent with its overall marketing strategy.

The product development strategy must ensure that the products which are developed are appropriate for the target market and for the product's intended position in that market. Product development is a high cost activity therefore it is essential that a co-ordinated approach is adopted to develop products with the correct features such as appropriate quality, availability and price.

Product development activity performs a number of specific roles as part of an overall marketing strategy, including the following.

(i) The **replacement** of products which are in the mature phase of their product life cycle so that the company can retain market share and maintain growth.

(ii) The **reduction of risk** through the production of a range of products.

(iii) **Brand extension.** The ability to gain through **cross-selling opportunities** from established brands.

(iv) **Response.** The ability to respond to developments by competitors or the emergence of substitute products.

(v) The ability to enter **new markets,** or to exploit existing ones better.

(b) A direct relationship between the costs of production and a selling price is the basis of a **cost plus pricing** policy. It may be inappropriate as a pricing strategy for the following reasons.

(i) **The link between price and demand**

Cost plus pricing fails to recognise that since sales demand may be determined by the sales price, there is likely to be a profit-maximising price which is not directly related to the cost of the product.

(ii) **Determining the costs of production**

The determination of production cost is a subjective exercise because of the need to apportion and absorb overhead costs and joint production costs. Arbitrary apportionment decisions can dramatically affect the apparent production cost and this would have a knock-on effect on the selling price. Use of such arbitrary cost information does not provide a consistent foundation for a firm's pricing policy.

(iii) **Lack of flexibility**

A cost plus policy can lead to a lack of flexibility in a firm's pricing decisions. For example a firm may have spare capacity and could be anxious to attract marginal business. The use of a cost plus policy could lead to high prices which would lose potential customers.

(iv) **Perceived benefits**

A firm will not necessarily incur high costs in providing valued benefits and they may lose the chance to command a price premium if they use cost as the basis for determining selling prices.

For example the use of gold foil to package loose tea may substantially increase the customer's perception of the product's value and would therefore enhance the product's ability to command a premium price. However the foil may be relatively cheap to provide and a price based on product cost would be unnecessarily low.

(v) **Volume of production**

Unit costs tend to reduce as output increases because of the **spreading of fixed costs**. In the early stages of a product's life cycle in particular it may incur high unit costs, before economies of scale and learning curve benefits are achieved. Firms which base their prices on these high costs may not attract sufficient demand to be able to achieve the desired market share.

The Japanese in particular work on the premise that cost should not be a determinant of selling price for this reason. They establish a **target price** which must be charged in order to achieve a desired market share and then set about reducing costs to below the target price.

In addition, the use of cost plus pricing can lead to an upward spiral of price increases if it is applied rigidly. If prices are high then sales volume is likely to fall. This will increase unit costs which would then dictate higher prices. Sales volumes would then fall still further, and so on.

(c) A marketing specialist should take account of the **perceived value of the benefits** to the potential buyer and of the **level of differentiation** offered by those benefits.

(i) **Perceived benefits that are of value**

The marketer should ensure that the benefits are actually perceived by the customer and that the customer values those benefits.

For example a new model of a video cassette recorder may have a fast rewind facility. Many potential customers may not be aware of the facility, and those that are aware may not include the facility as an important factor in their purchasing decision.

If this is the case then the marketer would not be able to charge a price premium for the benefit of a fast rewind facility.

(ii) **Unique/differentiated benefits**

Even if the potential buyer does perceive the product's benefits to be beneficial they may not be sufficiently differentiated from competing products. A lack of differentiation will erode the ability to charge a premium price.

(iii) **The target customer group**

In order to determine whether the product has unique benefits which are perceived to be of value, a marketing specialist will need to carry out research among the target group of customers.

(iv) **Product positioning**

The price of a product may affect its position in the market. For example an ostentatious good such as a Rolls Royce car has a high price. The customer's perception of the benefits provided by the product could change if the price is reduced dramatically.

63 PRODUCTS AND BRANDS

> **Pass marks**. The examiner was pleased with answers, although some candidates found it hard to distinguish between products and brands: denim jeans are a product, but Levis is a brand. In part (a) you were asked to discuss the validity of the statement in the question, and you could have argued the case either way. The statement asks you to contrast products and brands, but it is also worth asking how relevant the life cycle model is to products anyway.

(a) **Products and brands**

Definitions

A **product** can be defined as something which is offered to a market in order to satisfy customer needs in some way: it is a package of benefits. A **brand** on the other hand is rather different: it is a name, term or symbol or design or combination of them which is intended to signify the goods or services of one seller of group of sellers and to differentiate them from those of competitors.

For example (as in the Pass marks above), denim jeans, the product, **underpin a number of brands**, such as Levis jeans, Wrangler, Lee or Pepe. These brand names do not only apply to jeans, and these brand names can be found on shirts. (Doc

Martens, the shoe manufacturer, has recently diversified into clothing; Mars has diversified into ice cream.)

Product life cycles

The life cycle model suggests that a product goes through distinct phases, with different financial and marketing characteristics. The phases are development, launch, growth, maturity and decline.

(i) This model applies to some products but not to all. For example, the same **customer need** for recorded music has been satisfied by a number of different formats which have undergone life cycles of their own. The 78 record is no longer made, and vinyl generally has been replaced by the CD. In industrial economies, black and white TVs have by and large given way to colour.

(ii) On the other hand, some products do not have a life cycle. Denim jeans show no signs of fading way, nor does toothpaste, although some stages of the life cycle model still apply; the toothpaste market might be fairly mature in western economies, which is why manufacturers might look for **growth** in developing countries.

Brand life cycles

With brands, the situation is equally ambivalent.

(i) Some brands appear immortal, despite the changes in the products they support. This is because they are adequately supported. The Kelloggs **family brand** is independent of any one of its breakfast cereals, and would still remain if one of the products the Kelloggs brand supported were to be taken off the market.

(ii) On the other hand, some brands do die, if they are not properly supported by advertising and promotion.

The statement is thus a false dichotomy. **The life cycle model is a tool for marketing** managers, not a scientific prediction. What drives both products and brands is **customer needs.**

(b) **Brands and entry barriers**

A **barrier to entry** makes it difficult for a new entrant to gain a foothold in a market. Barriers to entry include economies of scale, product differentiation, capital requirements, switching costs, access to distribution, and other cost advantages (eg patents). Brands function as entry barriers in the following ways.

(i) **Product differentiation**. Porter discusses two features of a product: use criteria (what the product actually does) and signalling criteria (how the product appears). Brand image is built up through advertising and other special features and reflects both use and signalling criteria.

(ii) Existing firms in an industry may have built up a good brand image and strong customer loyalty **over a long period** of time, through advertising, product quality etc.

(iii) A firm might develop a variety of brands to 'crowd out' the competition. Some firms own many brands (eg detergent companies) to make it harder for competitors to get noticed by consumers, as there are so many 'alternatives'. This creates a barrier to entry, because new entrants would have to spend heavily to overcome the existing brand loyalties and to build up a brand image of their own. These high 'start-up' losses might deter would-be competitors because they would be unwilling to suffer short-term losses, given that the chances of eventual success in the new market might be fairly slim anyway. (Breaking into new industries is often a high-risk strategy.)

(iv) With some brands thereare also quite **high switching costs,** which is why many people are unwilling to change bank accounts because of the inconvenience of so doing. The same applies to industrial goods, which are less subject to brand considerations.

(v) **Economies of scale are also relevant.** A certain amount of volume may be necessary to justify the promotion of the brand. Existing producers may already have built up a **distribution network** which functions best at this level.

(c) **Financial criteria for assessing different stages of the product life cycle**

Ward suggests that, because each stage of the life cycle involves different risks and has different financial characteristics, no one measure is suitable throughout. The table below offers a summary.

	Launch	**Growth**	**Maturity**	**Decline**
Characteristics	High business risk. Negative net cash flow. DCF evaluation for overall investment	High business risk. Neutral net cash flow	Medium business risk. Positive cash flow.	Low risk. Neutral-positive cash flow.
Critical success factors	Increasing time to launch	Market share growth. Sustaining competitive advantage	Contribution per unit of limiting factor. Customer retention.	Timely exit.
Information needs	Market research into size and demand	Market growth, share. Diminishing returns. Competitor marketing strategies	Comparative competitor costs. Limiting factors	Rate of decline; best time to leave; reliable values of assets.
Financial controls	Strategic 'milestones'. Physical evaluation. Mainly non-financial measures owing to volatility (eg rate of take up by consumers)	DCF. Market share. Marketing objectives.	ROI. Profit margin. Maintaining market share.	Free cash flow (for investment elsewhere).

(d) **Capitalising brands on the balance sheet**

The subject of brand valuation has been a matter of considerable dispute in recent years, and has formed part of wider concern as to the value of statutory financial reporting.

The **effect of capitalising brands** on the balance sheet is to increase the value of the firm's fixed assets; brands are thus considered to be intangible assets, like patents or capitalised development costs. After all, brands can be sold, and it is felt that they generate income. This affects a number of accounting ratios.

(i) Although ROCE will fall (as capital employed increases), **gearing ratios** will also fall, and shareholders' funds are effectively increased. High borrowings look less serious if there are high levels of assets to support them.

(ii) Furthermore, some firms believe that existing financial reporting undervalues these **intangible assets**, making them more attractive to a takeover. However, capitalisation of internally generated brands has effectively been outlawed, because brands are considered a type of **goodwill**. Goodwill is an intangible asset, and is easy to manipulate.

The arguments against capitalisation are related by and large to **prudence**, whereas those in favour aim to show that capitalisation better reflects the **realities** of the business: brands can be seen as **'investments' which generate income.**

Valuation

(i) A brand can **fall in value very quickly**.

(ii) Brand valuation is often very **subjective**, although consultancy firms such as Interbrand have developed valuation methodologies.

(iii) The value of a brand is **affected by competitor behaviour**, whereas this is less true, say, of freehold properly.

Use of values

A wider issue relates to the use of accounting information.

(i) For **management accounting purposes**, if brand values aid decision making then they should be capitalised.

(ii) The main debate is about **financial reporting to shareholders**, and this is part of wider concern as to what published financial statements are actually for.

64 SPORTS CENTRE: MARKETING MIX AND LIFE CYCLE

> **Pass marks**. The PLC can be applied at any stage of strategic planning process, both to identify the firm's overall product portfolio and in devising marketing strategies for each product or service.
>
> **Examiner's comments**. Part (a) was satisfactorily answered, and 'good marks were usually earned by those who applied an appropriate model, such as the marketing mix': some candidates, however, took too restrictive a view and concentrated on promotional activities. Also, in answering part (a) you could have used the PLC for the sports centre as a whole as the starting point for your answer. Part (b), on resource allocation, required each service to be discussed separately: the word 'resources' should be interpreted widely to include human resources etc, not just capital investment and cash, important though these are. Very few candidates 'acknowledged the public service nature of the sports centre' such as the use of the swimming pool by schools. Answers to part (c) should have been justified by (a) and (b) and should have taken into account the competitive reference point. And finally - the question specifically said that you were **not** required to **draw** the product life cycle, but many candidates did so.

(a) **How the local authority can market its sports centre services**

The sports centre as a whole might be positioned at the maturity stage of the product life cycle. It is well established, but other service providers have entered the market. Of course, there does not have to be a decline stage at all, and many marketing strategies can be deployed to maintain and enhance the centre's attractiveness.

Investigate customer needs. A marketing orientation is built around satisfying the needs of the customers; these have to be discovered first of all. The sports centre has many users, including leisure/sports enthusiasts, schools and so forth. Unlike a business, it is partially funded by public money and so part of its remit might be to promote social objectives (eg keep fit classes for the elderly). It should be possible to discover groups of potential consumers with common characteristics: these are **market segments.**

The sports centre is offering a service. We can thus apply, in a coherent and integrated way, the 7 Ps of the **service marketing mix.**

(i) **Product/service.** The sports centre basically provides facilities for recreational use. It can vary its product offering by offering new facilities (as with martial arts), improving current facilities (eg fitness training) and by amending the circumstances when the service is delivered. The badminton court could be adapted at times for dancing classes, for example. Some additional revenue might be earned by providing a restaurant or bar.

(ii) **Price.** The users of the centre only pay for part of its costs, as user fees. Other funding is provided by the local council. However, prices will have to rise to cope with the cutback in central funding. The council has the discretion to vary prices. It can raise prices for some users, but still keep to its social remit (eg free entry for pensioners) or it can offer a leisure pass (eg £25 pa) which will allow people to get reductions for frequent use. The centre can also price its services by time of day, day of week (eg more at weekends).

(iii) **Promotion** covers all aspects of communications with the consumer. Some promotional techniques (eg personal selling) are of little relevance. Advertising is probably most important, for example, in local newspapers, on local radio, perhaps a leaflet with other local council communications (eg council tax demands). Perhaps the supermarket could be persuaded to assist in this. Promotions need to show the benefits of the centre (eg that it is cheap) as well as basic facts about it (eg opening times). Public relations (eg articles rather than advertising copy) in the local newspaper can also help.

(iv) **Place** is the channel of distribution for the services - this is given, and the service is delivered directly on site.

(v) **People**: the quality of a service depends crucially on the people giving the service. Some staff are involved in administration - basic issues of courtesy and friendliness are important here. Other staff are involved in running the centre and providing training and other services (eg in the gym).

(vi) **Process** denotes the way in which the service is delivered, such as access to the pool, ticketing, booking systems for the squash courts etc. These should be designed for ease of use.

(vii) **Physical evidence** denotes the environment in which the service is delivered. As well essentials such as basic cleanliness and security in the locker room, an attractive environment will encourage people to return.

The elements of the mix have to be **integrated** with each other, in the light of the marketing objectives (to increase usage) and available resources. As the centre is not a business, one marketing objective might be to encourage use by people who would not normally visit the centre, or those groups in the community with special needs.

(b) **Strategic resource allocation implications for each life cycle stage**

The sports centre as a whole is well past the introduction stage. Most of its capital costs were incurred by the supermarket development, and so the basic facilities have been quite cheaply provided. Any further development, however, will not be funded by the supermarket. The resources needed by any of its individual services are these.

(i) **Cash** to spend on capital equipment (eg gym machines)

(ii) **People,** properly trained

(iii) A **time** slot
(iv) Special **materials**

Introduction

Martial arts is a service in the introduction phase, with little take-up yet, presumably because too few people know about it and interest has yet to grow.

For physical products, the introduction stage requires cash outflows both on production and on marketing. There is always a certain amount of risk that the product will fail or that demand will be less than hoped.

The main introductory costs for martial arts will be **certain special equipment** (eg judo mats).

(i) The capital equipment is unlikely to be costly.

(ii) Instructors have to be hired or trained: instructors' time is effectively an issue of capacity, which will be built up ahead of demand.

(iii) Promotion will be the principal drain on resources, so that people know that martial arts are available

(iv) Finally, there are the opportunity cost of not offering the space to other activities.

Growth

Squash courts are in the growth phase. Growth requires investment in new capacity to cope with demand which according to the scenario is growing rapidly.

(i) **Capital investment**. Unlike martial arts, squash does require quite heavy capital investment, in the construction of the squash courts. People generally bring their own equipment, but the centre might choose to hire out rackets and squash-balls.

(ii) **Capacity rationing**. Some flexibility in pricing is useful here. Higher prices, in the short term, could ration demand, and prices could be lowered later (skimming pricing). However, this would go against the centre's public service remit - but there is nothing to stop charging higher prices at peak periods and lower prices at relatively slack periods (during the day, for example) to use the capacity as much as possible.

(iii) **Revenue costs**. Squash courts require continual maintenance, particularly with regard to cleanliness and the quality of the floor.

The rapidly increasing demand suggests that the local demand for squash is not being met: if there is such a demand, the commercial sports centres might be encouraged to provide their own facilities.

Maturity

At maturity stage are the **gymnasium** and the **swimming pool**.

The **gym** is obviously a **cash cow**, which generates resources rather than consumes them. This surplus can be applied to the sports centre's other activities. The gymnasium can perhaps be used to generate for income (eg aerobics classes).

Swimming pools are fairly expensive to maintain, particularly with regard to purification, and to run (the need for life guards in permanent attendance). In theory the swimming pool should be generating cash - but the best way to do so is to persuade as many as possible to use it.

(i) The pool is perhaps at the heart of the **public service** ethos. Few sports clubs are big or wealthy enough to provide a pool, and a pool is of value to school sporting provision and family use particularly at weekends.

(ii) **The pool at least should cover its costs,** although in the mature phase of the life cycle in theory it should, like the gym, provide surplus cash for reinvestment elsewhere.

(iii) **Demand in the pool might be developed further**. For example, at weekends, families might enjoy the use of a wave making machine; perhaps a separate area of the pool can be cordoned off for children; some local authorities have women-only swimming sessions; others offer swimming classes to adult non-swimmers. Thus, many service innovations and extensions which can be built around this supposedly mature product - all will involve expenditure.

Decline

The decline stage features lower sales, and falling profits. Although **badminton** is in the decline stage of the life cycle, there are three contrasting approaches to dealing with it.

(i) **Reverse the decline**. Conduct market research to find out why the badminton facilities are becoming less popular. Research will discern whether the decline can be reversed and, if so, how (eg extra promotion, upgrading the facilities and so forth). Reversing the decline might require a commitment of extra resources.

(ii) **Ignore the decline for the time being.** The badminton facilities can be run down slowly - although, as the sports centre is a public service, it has to cater for a variety of tastes. After all, even if it is in decline, it might still have more current attendees than martial arts. Few extra resources need be committed. The only problem is whether, in the long term, badminton represents the best use of available space - there might be an opportunity cost consideration here.

(iii) **Dual use of badminton facilities.** The badminton facilities may be shared with other sports (eg soft-ball),. This would require some new equipment.

(c) **Future services and competition**

The sports centre is not a profit-orientated organisation, but is instead a public service, funded by the local council, to serve the community as a whole and groups within it who might not otherwise have access to sports facilities at reasonable cost. Whilst it is competing to some extent with the private centres, this is not its purpose; it is seeking to cover its operating costs at least, but will still require a subsidy.

The competitive threat

The competitive threat is that users will abandon the sports centre for commercial firms. The consequence for the council will be that the facilities are increasingly expensive to maintain, but they will not disappear. All the council needs to do is to increase usage, and it might target customer groups who cannot afford commercial sports organisations or who want specialist services.

The sports centre might best exploit activities which commercial sports centres do not provide. Although martial arts is in the growth phase, no projections are given for its future development - it may be the case that martial arts tuition is widely available elsewhere, so is there any need for the council to replicate it?

The swimming pool can be further promoted - indeed, this can be used as an introduction to some other services - for example, combined pool and gym tickets might encourage swimmers to use the gym and vice versa; or combined pool-and-squash tickets might enable the pool to be used by squash players.

The services are likely to be a lot cheaper than those offered by private sector providers - however, demand might be higher.

As suggested in (b), badminton facilities might be available for dual use, and so other sports could be offered. Whilst there is still a demand for badminton it should not be run down, but it might be easy to switch facilities.

The centre might provide a cafe or even a bar, as a major leisure facility in a supermarket development.

To encourage use by shoppers, it might offer a crèche (for a fee of course) - this will enable day-time users to combine shopping with trips by their children to the sports centre - under qualified supervision of course. Again this would be in line with the public service remit.

65 MARKETING RESEARCH PROGRAMME

Pass marks. This question focuses on how the management accountant can contribute to the programme, so do not be tempted to write about marketing research as a general catch-all topic. The mini-scenario lays down the context of the question: strict financial control and a budget which must not be exceeded. The MA is acting in a control role as well as in an advisory role –but note that the sales director has no experience of this area either.

Examiner's comments. This was not a popular question, possibly because it did not ask about the four Ps. A disappointing number confused 'marketing' research with 'market' research. Most recognised that the management accountant had a role to play, but were uncertain what this should be. Part (b) was better answered, probably because it concerned the more familiar territory of budgets.

D is probably not a marketing orientated company. If it were, it would have a marketing director and not just a specialist sales director.

(a) The research programme can be analysed into five stages.

Define the problem

Both the Q and M know that the problem is the rapid decline in sales of the product. The market research needs to discover why. Sales might be falling because of:

(i) a genuine fall in customer **interest**;
(ii) problems in **distribution**;
(iii) **competition**, for example at a lower price;
(iv) **substitute** products on the market;
(v) a genuine **contraction in the market** as a whole.

The research might even be formulated in terms of the **product life cycle** – is the product reaching the end of its life?

Define the objectives of the programme

The research programme's outcome will be a report, explaining the reasons for the fall in sales and some ideas as to how this situation can be turned round, produced within a particular timescale.

The research may be used for example to **develop a demand schedule** for the product and to estimate how elastic demand is.

Collect internal data

M's information provision role might lead to investigation of the firm's internal information systems to detect any patterns in the sales data.

(i) There might be problems of quality, customer returns and so forth.

(ii) Sales data might reveal that the decline is confined to particular regions.

(iii) The sales director can also carry out an informal survey of his own sales personnel, by enquiring what difficulties they are having.

Very little of this internal data costs money.

Collect external data

(i) **Published research**, for example by government or trade associations, can indicate overall trends in the market although the information may be out of date. The **internet** might provide some useful information at a low cost. Thus research might indicate broader reasons why sales are falling. The fall of D's sales has been rapid.

(ii) **Published survey data**. A variety of surveys can be purchased. They may be carried out by a trade or consumer association. Q is probably already aware of some.

(iii) **Commissioned, specialist research**. If D sells consumer products, a specialist agency to devise appropriate surveys will be needed. If D has a limited number of customers (eg if it sells to specialist segments in the business-to-business market), then they can be addressed directly.

Analyse data

Data collected has to be input and analysed, using appropriate modelling techniques. The statistical basis of the research should be understood so that accurate conclusions can be drawn.

Present findings

Both Q and M are likely to have some **experience in report writing**. M will be able to interpret the financial consequences of the conclusions drawn. If price is a problem, M can present a demand schedule showing how volumes can be improved.

(b) **Sales** of the product range are in free fall.

(i) If they shrink to half their previous level, this is equivalent to a fall in turnover of 20%.

(ii) The effect on **profit** is harder to gauge. Fixed costs will be spread across a smaller sales volume and D will face problems of **over-capacity.**

(iii) **Other marketing problems will ensue** – if sales are falling, distributors might refuse to stock the product or demand better terms.

The Board is beginning to panic about profits but in the short term they should also be concerned about **cash flow**. It would be disastrous if D did not rein back its manufacturing volumes and instead built up large stocks, eating up **working capital**.

Providing cash flow and working capital are under control, the issue is whether the research exercise can be justified.

(i) D has **no experience of marketing research** and, consequently, has not even considered putting a value to the information it needs. The budget figures have probably been picked out of thin air.

(ii) The key issue is to assess the **value of the information** the market research programme can supply.

(1) By applying the results of the survey, D's product range can **regain market share,** or at least slow down the fall in sales. The survey's cost is likely to be relatively inexpensive compared with the likely benefit.

(2) On the other hand, the survey might reveal that sales of the product range are falling inescapably. This information would enable D to plan for **exiting** this market – the savings would be that money would not be spent unnecessarily on marketing programmes which do not work.

M is best advised to take the **opportunity cost** approach to the problem. The Board should be advised of the financial consequences of not having the information, with the marketing research project being used as a profit-saving device.

If the Board are unconvinced, M will have to show that a cheaper survey would be less accurate and less reliable. Doing without a survey might be even more risky, in that data gleaned from desk research may be less relevant and less focused.

66 PHARMIA PLC: NEW PRODUCTS

Pass marks. The examiner reported that parts (a) and (b) were answered well. Most candidates failed top understand part (c). Part (d) required a more general discussion than that provided. Sonprex appeared from the analysis to be the best option, but this conflicted with the marketing strategy of the business. The merits of all options should be discussed.

(a) **Product portfolio and product life cycle**

A product portfolio is the range of products that a firm supplies to its markets. Some writers mention a **product-market portfolio**, a slightly more sophisticated concept, in that it identifies the markets and/or market segments to which these products are supplied. **Portfolio planning** is a term used to describe methods of analysing the product(-market) portfolio in order:

(i) to identify the current **strengths and weaknesses** of an organisation's products, and the state of growth or decline in each of those markets;

(ii) to identify the **strategies** needed to maintain a strong position or improve a weak one.

Examples of portfolio planning models include the **Boston matrix** and the **product life cycle.** Both of these suggest that a firm should have mix of products with different commercial characteristics, so as to minimise the risk to the company of a product failure. Some products earn healthy profits in mature markets. Others will generate high profits in future but require heavy investment now. The cash flow from one can support the other.

The **product life cycle** suggests that products have a life of four stages: **introduction,** in which sales are low and money has to be spent on promotion; **growth,** in which the market as a whole expands or the product's share expands; **maturity,** where profits are stable, but demand is not likely to expand; **decline,** where the product's sales fall, as it has been superseded by other products, new brands and so forth.

Portfolio planning in Pharmia

Pharmia plc has a portfolio of 34 products, not all of which have yet been brought to market. It thus has a portfolio of existing and potential products.

Clearly, Pharmia plc uses the **life cycle** model to maintain a mix of new and mature products. Moreover, scientific and marketing uncertainties lead it to explore many product options in the hope of finding a winner. Its high expenditure on research and development indicates that it chooses to be an innovator rather than a follower: technological innovation is thus a key strategic and marketing issue.

(b) **Expected values**

A decision tree is provided on page 249. The outcomes are multiplied by the probabilities which are then aggregated. Before the initial investment of £5m is taken into account, the expected value (EV) of each option is as follows.

EV of Tyrix = 0.03 × £150m = £4.5m
EV of Medvac = (£48m × 1/6) + (£27m × 1/3) + (-£10m × 1/2) = £12m
EV of Sonprex = £14m

The net payoff, after the investment cost, is as follows.

Tyrix £4.5m – £5m = £(0.5m) (ie a loss of £500,000)
Medvac £12m – £5m = £7m profit
Sonprex £14m – £5m = £9m profit

(c) **The appropriateness of expected values and subjective probabilities**

Any strategic decision is taken in a state of partial ignorance as to the future: this is why strategies are necessary. You cannot be sure that a quantitative exercise necessarily gives the right result without questioning the **assumptions** on which it is based and the **context** in which it is made. The probabilities in this example are merely **subjective** quantifications of uncertainty. In the cases of the options suggested we can note the following.

(i) **Possible overconfidence about Sonprex.** Can we really be 100% certain about Sonprex's success? The answer has to be **no**, as this would imply that the company's forecasters had an absolute knowledge of the future. However, this does indicate that the project is low risk, but that is all it indicates.

(ii) **Sensitivity to the 'risky' Tyrix.** The decision is sensitive to the low (3%) probability of Tyrix's success. Tyrix offers a huge reward. Were the success of Tyrix to have a 5% probability, the EV before investment would be £150m × 5% = £7.5m. A 10% probability of success, still very low, would give it an EV before investment costs of £15m, which would make it, on the basis of EVs alone, an attractive option even though a high risk. The decision is thus sensitive to changes in probability estimates. As these are subjective anyway, they need to be taken with a pinch of salt.

(iii) **Bizarre profit/market share figures for Medvac.** How realistic are the market share projections for Medvac?

(1) It is hard to see how an **increase in market share,** even if only 10%, could lead to a loss of £10m, especially after £5m had been invested in advertising, and the loss did not take this advertising into account.

(2) The difference in payoff between a 10% market share and a 15% market share is extraordinary (£37m). This needs to be looked into. It is unlikely that there would be a sudden jump in market share. When would the outcome be positive? at 11%? or 12%?

To summarise, the decision cannot be taken in isolation from the firm's commercial strategy of innovation, its need to maintain a balanced portfolio of projects in the present, and its need to invest in future successful projects. Furthermore, especially in the case of Medvac, more information is needed.

(d) The relative merits of each drug

This decision should not be taken without considering other products in the portfolio, about which we know little. Nor can we ignore the circumstances of the decision: the £5m is 'unexpected', additional to the existing allocation of resources. The company's policy is to take a scattergun approach, investing large sums in R & D in many projects in the hope of producing a sure fire winner.

(i) *Tyrix* is an innovative investment. It might be favoured for a number of reasons.

(1) **Cheap.** The actual investment (£5m) is small in comparison to the potential reward (£150m) even though the probability of achieving the reward is very low.

(2) **Safe.** The investment of £5m is hardly critical to the firm's success: otherwise it would not have been conjured out of a hat and made unexpectedly available. The risk is perhaps less important than it would be normally.

(3) **Strategic conformity.** The firm's overall approach to the market is product **innovation.** Tyrix conforms to this strategy. Sonprex does not.

(ii) **Medvac** can also be favoured.

(1) It has already been successfully introduced. The chances of the advertising campaign being successful is about 50%.

(2) Despite the competition, and the rather bizarre negative payoff resulting from an increase in market share, there are substantial benefits to be had from supporting it. Again, this will depend on the firm's attitude to risk. Risk is spread through a number of different products in the portfolio, and so Medvac may be worth it in the light of the rest of the portfolio.

(iii) Sonprex gives the **highest payoff** compared to the other two, but that is the only thing in its favour.

(1) Investing in Sonprex will be an investment in a product which would shortly be superseded: a **harvesting strategy**.

(2) If this means that the firm's portfolio is too heavily weighted towards mature products, the firm's **long term future** is in danger.

Remaining uncertainties

We do not know much about the timing of the cash flows, however.

(i) If Sonprex brings in £14m in the year after the investment, this might be used to subsidise investment in the other two. Nor do we know if Medvac's condition will get much worse if the money is not invested.

(ii) If the price of investing in Sonprex is the failure, say, of Medvac, then this must be taken into account when devising expected values. Tyrix is an opportunity: it does not need the investment, whereas Medvac's competitive position may be undermined if it is not supported.

The EVs provide some useful information to make a decision, but because we do not know:

(i) the state of the entire **product portfolio**; and
(ii) the firm's attitude to **risk,**

a comparison of EVs cannot be used as the determining factor in this case.

Expected value of different products

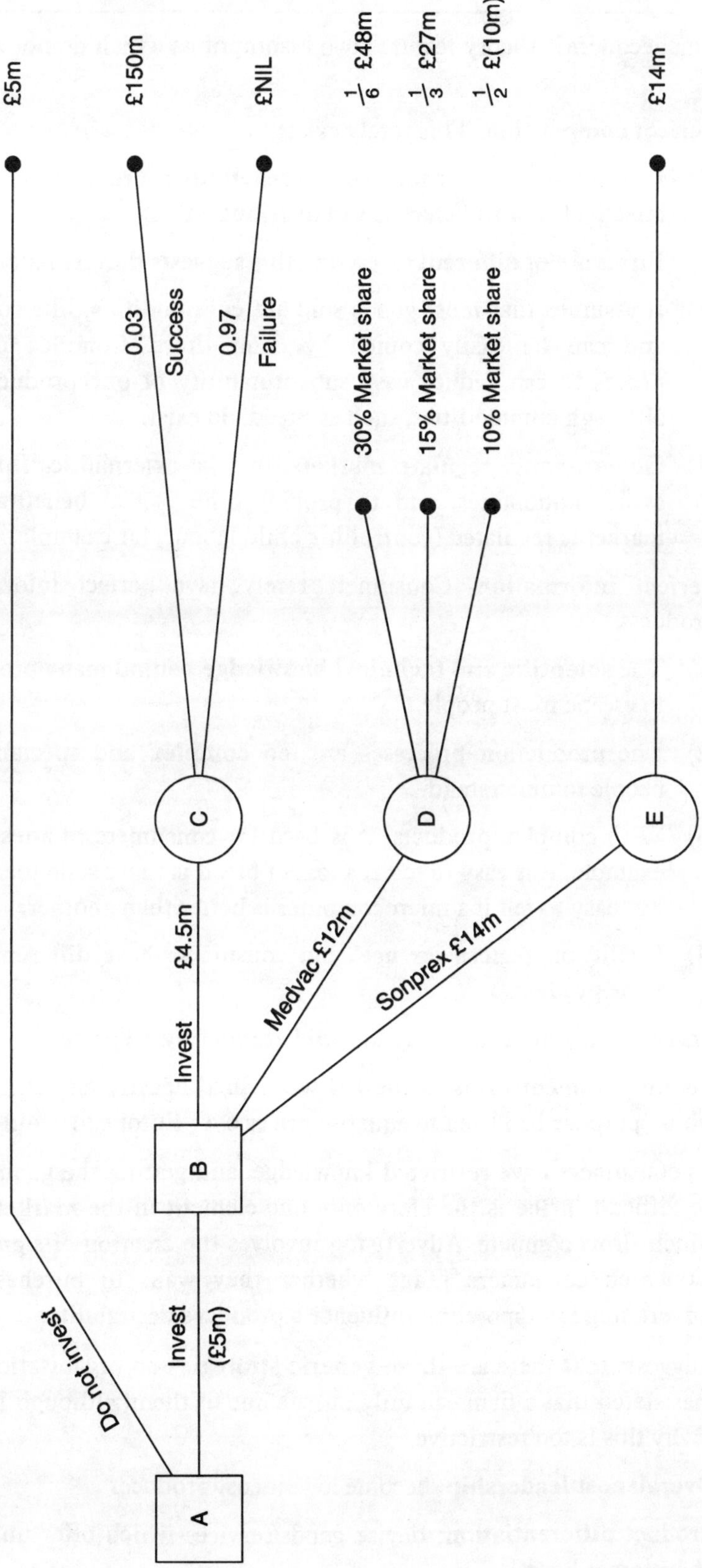

67 PRICE COMPETITION

> **Pass marks**. This question is about the role of price in securing competitive advantage. You could have taken a number of angles; price as part of the marketing mix; price as a weapon in competitive strategy and so forth.

(a) Traditional economic theory features two assumptions which do not always hold in practice.

(i) **Perfect competition**. This rarely exists.

(1) It is not always easy for firms to **reach the market place**, if competitors effectively control channels of distribution.

(2) Firms are of **different sizes**, and this suggests different strategies.

(3) It assumes that most goods sold are **commodities**, like coffee or wheat, and can be easily copied by competitors. Complex manufacturing processes can reduce easy substitutability of one product by another, although commodities, such as bread, do exist.

(4) **Governments regulate markets**, to take externalities into account, to avoid monopolies, and to provide other social benefits. The labour market is regulated (controlling child labour, for example).

(ii) **Perfect information**. Consumers rarely have perfect information about products.

(1) The **scientific and technical knowledge** behind many products is likely to escape most people.

(2) The production processes are too **complex** and specialised for most people to understand.

(3) With complex products, it is hard for consumers to attest **quality**. For example, it is easy to tell if a loaf of bread is more stale than another, but less easy to tell if a microcomputer is better than another.

(4) Quality is '**fitness for use**', but consumers have different uses for the same product.

Many firms will go out of their way to **avoid competing on price**.

(i) Recently, cement firms in the EU were fined heavily for setting up a cartel, whose purpose had been to equalise prices over Europe to avoid imports.

(ii) As consumers have restricted knowledge, and getting the goods to them can be difficult, **price** is therefore only one element in the **marketing mix** with which firms compete. Advertising involves the creation of signalling criteria by which consumers judge whether they want to purchase a product. Advertising is supposed to influence a product's desirability.

(b) Porter suggests that there are **three generic strategies** an organisation can pursue. Porter has stated that a firm can only pursue one of them, although there are good reasons why this is too restrictive.

(i) **Overall cost leadership**: become lowest cost producer

(ii) **Product differentiation**: devise goods/services which offer unique packages of customer benefits

(iii) **Focus**: concentrate on a restricted number of market segments.

A firm's strategy will in part be dictated by the structure of the industry; small firms will challenge competitors in different ways.

Price competition can be relevant in the following circumstances.

(i) **Cost leadership.** A firm pursuing overall cost leadership can, if it chooses, compete on price; it will always win a price war. However, such firms may choose instead to earn the highest profits in the industry (which can be handed back to shareholders or recycled into other strategic investments), rather than charge the lowest prices. The relevance of price competition in the competitive strategy of a cost leader will depend on a host of other factors in addition to whether a firm can possibly win such a battle.

Price competition in an industry is a powerful barrier to entry.

(ii) **Differentiation.** Price competition can feature in a product differentiation strategy, as price is one of the features of a distinct marketing mix. Price can be used as a source of differentiation. A firm might sell a low-price, low 'quality' product, as its differentiated product, if there are advantages in so doing. Examples are provided by the pricing strategies of discount stores when compared with supermarkets in the UK. The discounters offer a restricted range of goods at very low prices; supermarkets offer a much larger choice, but prices have generally been higher. The discounters' retail-package to consumers involves selling a differentiated products in which low prices are part of the marketing mix. (This does not mean they pursue cost leadership strategies, however; profit in retailing can be obtained through increased volume as when as increased margins.)

(iii) **Focus strategy**. Price competition can be used in a focus strategy. In its early days, Mercury Communications targeted the business market for telecommunications with trunk and international calls lower than that offered by BT. This was price competition directed at a particular segment. However, focus strategies can be analysed into cost-focus and differentiation-focus; Mercury was pursuing a cost-focus strategy. Both telecommunications operators are now facing competition from even cheaper suppliers such as Energis.

(c) **Other roles of a pricing strategy**

Some of the roles of a pricing strategy have already been suggested in (b) above, in that price competition can be used to support a number of **different generic strategies.**

Price strategy does have a number of other roles in a firm's activities.

(i) **Product differentiation**. Price is part of a package of customer benefits. There has been documented evidence that consumers have taken price to be an indicator of product quality (if it is so expensive it must be good). As suggested in part (a), consumers often have little expertise about the quality of the products they are buying.

(ii) **Promotion role.** Price can suggest an image of exclusivity, and so a high price can be used to support the value of a brand. Price is part of the marketing mix of product, place, price, promotion. To succeed, these should be internally consistent.

(iii) **Achieving the objectives of a firm** (for example its desire for profit, and the return required for investors). Many firms are unwilling to trade profit for market share. Pricing strategy is the essential means by which revenue is brought into a company.

(iv) **Influence a firm's costs**. Japanese firms have been known to use target pricing. A market price for a product over its life cycle is established, and this is used as a target for the firm's manufacturing operations to cut their costs.

(v) **Manage a product's progress through its life cycle**. In the growth phase, skimming prices will be charged; in the decline phase, harvesting prices might be charged.

(vi) **Demand management**. Price strategy can be used to manage demand. For example, a firm may not have enough production capacity to supply all customers. Price strategies restrict demand, until new capacity is built up.

(vii) **Aid distributors**. For example, many publishers offer discounts to booksellers to stock their products. Pricing strategies can be used to manipulate the distribution chain.

68 OPERATIONALISING SOCIAL RESPONSIBILITY

(a) (i) **Social responsibility and shareholder wealth maximisation**

Many businesses pursue a policy of enhancing shareholder value, or **'long-term owner wealth'**. This is a different concept to profit in one year. Instead it is taken to refer to the total market value of a company's shares. According to some models of share valuation, such market value is determined by expectations of future performance (as reflected in dividends), rather than past performance.

Theorists such as **Elaine Sternberg** have suggested that a business's guiding purpose is to pursue long term owner wealth, but they also offer some arguments that there are reasons why businesses should be socially responsible.

(1) No business exists in isolation, and economic activity is only possible within the context of **social institutions**. For example, all businesses are expected to honour contracts, freely made. Of course, this process is backed up by **legal sanction**, but it is evident that there are occasions where shareholder value of an individual firm has to take second place to supporting the system so that businesses could flourish at all. Where people cannot rely on agreements made, the whole system is brought into disrepute.

Furthermore, the relationship of business to society is not only an economic one. Businesses provide benefits and also cause social costs (**externalities**) which they do not pay for. Pollution is such an **externality**, and it is increasingly the case that businesses will expect to deal with them. Sternberg suggests that **distributive justice** and **ordinary decency** are the ethical considerations in business ethics.

(2) When it comes to the examples mentioned in the question, the situation is more complex, for a number of reasons. It is not, after all, the purpose of business to determine **wider social policy**, which should be a democratic choice by society as a whole. All of the options suggested in the question involve costs and impact on profits, and if these are too low then shareholders may have depressed expectations about the company's future performance, and the share price, and hence their wealth, will fall.

However, issues of social responsibility can be presented as:

- a tradeoff between the **long and the short terms** and
- a matter of **enlightened self interest**

If the political trend is towards **increased pollution regulation,** businesses can preempt this by setting standards for best practice, or even selling their expertise. The initial cost of the extra improvements may not be so great. Many modern business practices identify the elimination of waste in the production process (**JIT and TQM**). Finally, businesses which pollute needlessly might be forced to pay for the clean-up afterwards.

Paying wages above national minimum levels may be necessary, to **retain the commitment and loyalty of the workforce** if these are valued. Skilled employees are unlikely to leave to another employer. Another problem is **bad publicity**. Although of uncertain impact, Burger King suffered bad publicity because of employment practices which resulted in one employee receiving only £1 for a day's work. Bad publicity can mean loss of custom, especially when this is orchestrated by a successful pressure group.

Declining to trade with objectionable governments is a harder nut to crack. Business can be a force for good, if it uses its influence wisely. If the government is shunned by the international community (eg with sanctions) then trade conditions are unlikely to be very favourable. Again, perhaps the principal impact will be on **customers' attitudes** to the firm. It has been reported that Barclays lost potential student customers because of bad publicity surrounding its investments in South Africa when apartheid was practised. **If the firm violates distributive justice and ordinary decency then its actions cease to be ethical.**

Social responsibility therefore does not necessarily conflict with shareholder wealth maximisation, but this is not to say that conflicts never happen. What is important to realise is that a firm owes a moral obligation to its owners.

(ii) **Acceptability of conflicts in objectives**

According to some models of the firm, businesses are profit-maximising entities. In other words the overriding objective is that of profit. Another model of the firm, however, suggests that as social institutions, businesses are inevitably more complex; they contain a variety of systems and personnel with different objectives and desires. In this case, arguing about the acceptability of conflicts in objectives is missing the point: conflict of objectives is inevitable, and it is management's job to direct and control it, in the owners' interest.

Examples are offered below.

(1) **Time horizons.** There are conflicts between the **long term** and the **short term**. Profits are needed now to satisfy shareholders, and they cannot all be reinvested in the business. At the same time, investments need to be made so the long term future of the business, and hence shareholders' wealth, is maintained and enhanced. This applies to any new project, not just capital equipment. Colloquially, firms talk about advertising and marketing expenditure as an investment in brands, necessary to bring in the customers. As argued in (a) above, pursuit of social responsibility can sometimes be viewed in this light.

(2) **Stakeholders.** There are possible conflicts of objectives between different stakeholders in the business.

- **Managers** benefit from the growth of the organisation in terms of job interest and prestige; conglomerate diversification might be the result, whereas shareholders do not need to invest in a conglomerate to spread risk.
- Other conflicts might include disputes between **workers** and **shareholders** over the distribution of the value added by the firm (as wages or in dividends).

(3) **Conflicts between different departments or divisions of the organisation.** Systems theory suggests that sub-optimality occurs when subsystems pursue their own objectives to the detriment of the organisation. Setting correct **transfer prices** can avoid this problem.

(b) **Operationalising social responsibility**

Assuming a firm wishes to act ethically, it can embed **social responsibility** in its decision processes in the following ways.

(i) Include it in the **corporate culture**, or, at the very least, in codes of practice.

(ii) Managers can set by example by ensuring that incentive systems are designed to support **ethical behaviour** (eg safety).

(iii) Identify social responsibility in the **mission statement**. As a public declaration of what the organisation is for, this can have a moral force over corporate decision making, assuming of course that the mission statement is taken seriously and has not just been designed as an exercise in public relations.

(iv) Introduce **ethical considerations into the strategy evaluation** process.

(1) Employing ethics consultants, as some US firms do, can help sort out tricky dilemmas. Some environmental pressure groups would be very happy to offer advice.

(2) Undergo **an ethics audit**, particularly in relation to environmental projects.

(3) Conduct **ethical benchmarking,** to compare the firm's procedures with best practice in other firms.

(4) Apply for **environmental standard BS 7750.**

(5) Enforcing ethical standards elsewhere in the system. This might mean refusing to do business with suppliers from poorer counties who employ child labour, or actively promoting higher standards, and offering educational opportunities.

(6) Having regard to **sustainability.** This involves developing strategies so that the company only uses resources at a rate which allows them to be replenished in order to ensure that they will continue to be available, while at the same time **emissions of waste** are confined to levels which do not exceed the capacity of the environment to absorb them.

This is relevant, as in the long-term, **wasteful use of resources** will make it harder for business to flourish in future.

(v) For **performance measurement**, targets can be set for decreased waste, lower emissions, less noise, and so forth.

(c) **Feasibility of including stakeholder requirements in wider social responsibilities**

A **stakeholder** is any person, group or organisation with an interest in the activities of the entity. Stakeholders include shareholders, managers, employees, suppliers, customers, bankers, local government, national government, pressure/interest groups and the general public.

(i) **Shareholders and investors** expect a **high return**. Given that many investors are **pension funds** investing people's savings, the pursuit of profit is responsible in part. Shareholders as members of the public will also benefit from a company's exercise of social responsibility as society as a whole will benefit.

(ii) **Employees** might expect to be beneficiaries of social responsibility. Good practice towards employees can be of wider public benefit, if it means that people are kept in work and off the dole queues, or that abject poverty, with all its attendant **social costs** in poorer health and educational disadvantage.

(iii) Other stakeholders have a direct relationship with the business, such as **suppliers and customers**. A firm's pursuit of social responsibility can affect them directly and indirectly. A firm wishing to minimise pollution might require components that use less energy. The firm might acquire **waste management** equipment, and so new suppliers will be created. Similarly, customers will also be affected, possibly in terms of higher prices or different products.

(iv) **Bankers and financiers** are stakeholders who would be less affected by social responsibility. One possible problem is that security for their loans might be adversely affected if the property used as security was badly polluted; in a receivership, the firm might face severe **cleanup bills** in order to sell polluted land and to realise the bank's security.

69 FORWARD LOOKING DISCLOSURES

Pass marks. The slant of the question, asking about the provision of this type of information to stakeholders, may be slightly different from what you are accustomed to when talking about collecting and providing information. Ask yourself what the stakeholders and the company want from the information that is published.

Other points. We have briefly discussed other types of stakeholder in our answer. You may not have done in yours. Do not forget that 'stakeholders' does not just mean shareholders, although it is appropriate in this question to focus mainly on them. If you have done so to the exclusion of all other types, that is acceptable. Just be aware that more detail on other stakeholders may be relevant in other questions.

Examiner's comments. This was the most popular question in section B of the paper and was in the main well answered. The interest of stakeholders of all kinds in receiving forward looking information was generally clearly recognised, especially when related to the concept of maximising long term owner value. Breach of confidentiality is a potentially damaging consequence which was concentrated on by the majority of candidates in part (b), although some were unrealistic in maintaining that a company should expect to be able to keep its strategy completely secret. There is a wealth of information in the financial pages every day that gives clear indication of individual corporate strategies, without necessarily going into damaging detail.

(a) **Stakeholders** are defined as those in society who are associated with a company, either **externally, internally** or **connected** in some other way. Depending upon the exact nature of their relationship with the company, they will be interested in forward looking information to a greater or lesser extent.

Employees are examples of internal stakeholders and they will be interested in the future of the company as it affects their own careers. More information may make them better motivated workers. The **government** or certain **pressure groups** may be interested to know about plans to apply for planning permission to build a new facility. Plans to create new jobs by opening a new factory will please local development agencies.

Other groups who may be interested in forward looking information are **customers** (happy to place long-term orders), **creditors** (happy that they will be paid) and **lenders**. The more information that lenders such as banks receive from a company, the more comfortable they will be in continuing to provide finance. Companies with strategic plans to invest will need access to **sources of finance**. Any relevant information they can provide on such plans (forecast returns, capital expenditure forecasts), will help lenders assess the risks and maybe make them able to negotiate a better deal on finance costs.

Shareholders are the most significant stakeholders to consider in the context of this question and they are concerned with growth in the **value of their investment** via both capital growth and dividends.

Company management want to show them that the company is successful and, by implication, well-run. Strategic aims and objectives frequently feature in the (mainly historical) **published accounts** of a company as a glimpse of the future, but it could be said that, as owners, shareholders need and deserve more detail than is commonly provided. **Existing shareholders** may want to increase their shareholding, or **potential new shareholders** may want information on the future of the company to be able to decide that an investment is worth making, particularly from the point of view of expected future dividend streams and share price.

Any future strategy as provided by management will generally be intended to present a rosy picture, and the temptation may be to put a gloss on otherwise uncertain activities.

(b) The danger in making forward looking information freely available to stakeholders is that it will not be possible to keep it **confidential** when communicating with external or connected shakeholders.

It may be possible to keep information internal, or asks banks and other advisers such as solicitors to keep plans confidential, but **publishing** information for the community at large will inevitably mean that information falls into the hands of **competitors.**

Management (the management accountant would be included here) would therefore face the challenge of providing enough information to satisfy the stakeholder needs outlined in part (a), but not so much detail that strategic plans are anticipated, and the impact of them possibly diluted by **competitor activity**. A compromise position needs to be reached.

The published accounts of a company are required by the regulatory framework to contain certain **minimum** disclosures. Other information, such as plans to open a certain number of new branches over the coming year, are likely to feature in the Chairman's statement and, while interesting, may not necessarily contain much other detail (for example exact location, expected costs, expected shutdowns of other branches, planned redundancies).

Before deciding to disclose this information, it would be necessary to gauge the impact both for stakeholders and competitors. Information may be disseminated in stages. Employees affected by a string of branch closures would be told first. Plans to open a new branch may only be disclosed when the relevant planning permission has been achieved.

Where possible, a form of **cost/benefit** analysis may be undertaken by the management accountant which sets out the overall recommendation as to how much information to disclose, if any. The decision will always depend upon the company's own circumstances. If it is a dominant market player with significant cost leadership and other advantages, the impact of competitor activity may not be enough of a downside to discourage the full disclosure of plans to stakeholders, with the attendant advantages as outlined in part (a).

70 ACQUISITION: ETHICS AND STAKEHOLDERS

> **Examiner's comment.** This was a wide ranging question, covering an acquisition and its effect on stakeholders, followed by the issue of pollution. Part (a) was generally well answered. Candidates confused parts (b)(I) and (b)(ii). Part (b)(ii) was focused specifically on pollution.

(a) **Strategic factors to be considered before the acquisition**

The disappointing performance of the share price, compared to dividend growth, suggest that investors are not confident that dividends can be maintained in future.

(i) **Competitive environment**. Stern competition is driving down profits. This might be caused by excess capacity in the industry. If there is excess capacity and C buys K, C can benefit in two ways.

(1) C can close down K, reducing the over capacity - but every other firm in the industry will be better off because of this, but at C's expense.

(2) C can use K's capacity, either by reaping economies of scale or by investing in K to improve its record and to make it a more fierce competitor. This is a more expensive option.

It appears that the industry needs to be consolidated - the problem is to ensure that C reaps as much benefit as possible from this.

(ii) **Competitive strategy**. We are not told of C's or K's competitive strategy, but cost leadership would appear to be an option. Alternatively, the capacity could be used in a competitive strategy of product differentiation.

(iii) **Business risk**. The possibility of prosecution for effluent discharge makes K far less attractive as a target, at least until a settlement is agreed. C should wait until the case is settled. C would not wish to be lumbered with any liability. Moreover, a large fine might make K cheaper to buy. Either way, the timing is not right.

(iv) **Product-market strategy.** The industry is consolidating, and the purchase of K implies that C intends to pursue a **penetration strategy**, in existing markets. Although supply will be consolidated the firm will have to consider whether existing product-market mix can generate the profits that shareholders want.

(v) **Wait until K goes bankrupt** - then the capacity can be acquired even more cheaply, and K would not be a going concern.

(vi) Acquisition in this case is a way of increasing **market share**. As the competitor is in the same industry, the board of C do not have to climb a learning curve as they grapple with a completely unfamiliar business.

(vii) There are often **management problems** in acquisitions.

(viii) C plc has to set itself **strategic objectives** for the acquisition. For shareholders to support it, it must offer an increase in shareholders' wealth.

(ix) **Cost.** No details are given as to how the acquisition would be financed and how much it would cost. These are obviously related to shareholders' wealth. C will also have to **invest** in K.

(x) **Other prospective purchasers** may drive up the price.

(xi) The underlying **capital structure** might change. C will find it more costly to raise capital, and may have to follow to fund the acquisition.

(xii) **Contingency plans.** If the bid is unwelcome, then C will have to consider a better means of growth.

(b) (i) **Social and ethical implications**

Employees. Significant redundancies are forecast whichever strategy is adopted. These redundancies would happen anyway if there is over capacity in the industry. If K is failing then redundancies, liquidation or receivership would ensure in the medium term. This is a fact of life. It may be the case that C offers the best hope that at least some of K's employees will have a future.

(1) According to **Elaine Sternberg,** firms have an ethical obligation to act according to the dictates of **distributive justice and ordinary decency,** in pursuit of their overall purpose, the growth of long term owner wealth. No ethical implications are involved in the acquisition or even the redundancies as such.

(2) The **manner in which the redundancies are dealt with** is a matter for ethical concern, in that the guiding principles mentioned above should be understood. Distributive justice suggests that people should be rewarded according to the value of their contribution. This can be taken into account in the redundancy settlement. Ordinary decency can be satisfied by honest dealings, a refusal to raise expectations deceitfully, and adherence to contracts.

(3) In practical terms, the effects of the changes on employees involve other issues for the company including **morale and insecurity**. These can be bad for business - large scale sackings are known to increase the stress levels suffered by those who remain.

(4) For employees and managers of C, the acquisition may create **career opportunities**. C will certainly want to inject management to 'turn round' K.

Shareholders, not managers' interests. Most shareholders are financial institutions. In the UK at least, financial institutions include pension funds, insurance companies and so forth, who look after people's savings. They have a responsibility to their own investors to **maximise the return** available. The ethical implications are that both K and C must pursue their goals with the benefits of maximising long term owner wealth in mind. The ethical considerations include the benefit to shareholders, rather than managers. For example, K's shareholders may prefer to sell the business, and so K's managers should seek to get the best deal for its shareholders even though K's managers might want to carry on.

(ii) **Environmental issues faced by C**

Although it was suggested in (a) that C wait until the outcome of the litigation, there may be good reasons to proceed before this is dealt with. The following issues should be dealt with.

(1) **Discover the cause of the pollution** at K and deal with the problem.

(2) **Estimate the likely financial penalty**. Offer to settle early, perhaps, to avoid the expense and bad publicity of a court case. Devote management's attention to dealing with the problem.

(3) For C and the newly acquired K, put steps in place to improve its **environmental record** (eg BS 7750, the environmental standard). This will promote best practice, and help the company avoid liability in future.

(4) **Waste reduction** can be pursued in tandem with a quality management programme.

(5) The firm will pre-empt legislation or legal action by bringing its environmental practices **up to date**.

(6) In the short term, **crisis management techniques** will be needed to deal with the public relations problems at K.

(7) C may incur **some short term costs** up front.

Stage 4 **MOCK EXAM**

Paper 14 November 1999

Strategic Management Accountancy & Marketing

SMM

INSTRUCTIONS TO CANDIDATES

You are allowed three hours to answer this question paper.
Answer the ONE question in section A. *Answer TWO questions only from section B.*

DO NOT OPEN THIS PAPER UNTIL YOU ARE READY TO START UNDER EXAMINATION CONDITIONS

SECTION A - 60 MARKS

ANSWER THIS QUESTION

All parts of this question relate to the scenario

The P Group

Background

The corporate history of the P Group (P) stretches back 30 years. During that time, P has developed internationally and how trades in many diverse areas. Fifteen years ago, the company launched P Airlines, which has proved to be one of its most successful business ventures. Five years ago, the company established P Rail and obtained franchises for running rail services in its home country. However, P Rail has not achieved the success that P had intended and is frequently publicly criticised for providing services which do not run on time.

The brand

The group has a distinctive brand name which was established when P's charismatic founder and chairman launched the first business venture. The majority of the citizens in its home country have heard of the brand which has over time been applied to many diverse areas of business. The chairman believes the reputation of the brand name places a heavy burden of responsibility on P not to disappoint its customers. The chairman himself has impressed his own personality on P by pursuing personal publicity in business ventures and becoming involved in high-profile and sometimes dangerous 'leisure' activities.

P has achieved a reputation for entering markets which are dominated by major companies, and has been successful in taking business from some major competitors by exposing their consistently poor service and complacency.

The principal business approach which has been adopted is that of 'brand stretching' across different products and services. Each company within the group runs its own affairs but they are all encouraged to help each other resolve their particular problems in a kind of family spirit.

Key strategic factors

The chairman has stated that P is in business 'to be different' and that the P brand name should be clearly associated with this.

It is considered essential by the directors that any products or services incorporated within the brand must help to build its good reputation, provide an opportunity to add value, and yield an appropriate trade-off between risk and rewards.

The chairman considers that there are a number of key factors which have contributed to the success of P. The brand name is associated with being the consumer's champion, and has been very successful in delivering what the chairman refers to as a 'sense of excitement' in most ventures to which it has been applied. In addition, the business contacts which have been established are important and he recognises that his own personality attracts customers and venture partners. P also encourages talented staff within the group to interact with each other in order to solve problems. The management style of P is therefore seen as a major contributory factor in its corporate success. Much weight is placed on its corporate image. The chairman explains that the quality of a customer's experience when coming into contact with P is the most important item in determining its success.

Management style

The directors agree that the first priority in being able to achieve success is for P to ensure that the group employs personnel of the best quality and calibre. Their simple philosophy is that motivated staff lead to satisfied customers which results in repeat and new business and provides benefit to the shareholders.

P has a flat management structure with few authority levels within the hierarchy. The chairman himself is committed to providing good communication channels within and outside the group. He believes very firmly that managers within the organisation must be prepared to listen both to the customers and also the staff.

Financial performance

The business approach which has been developed is that the brand name is provided by P with a cash injection from a joint venture partner. This has generally proved to be a very successful formula although this has not been the case with the latest venture into the domestic railway market. The directors consider that the performance of P Rail will improve following a programme to upgrade the infrastructure inherited from the previous nationalised rail network.

Comparative financial information relating to P Airlines and P Rail for the last two years at 31 December is as follows.

	1997	1998
	$m	$m
Turnover		
Airlines	570	678
Rail	410	423
Pre-tax profit		
Airlines	60	80
Rail	30	32
Capital employed		
Airlines	750	790
Rail	530	640

Other performance indicators

The following information is provided relating to P's airline and rail businesses.

Airline	*1997*	*1998*
Number of passengers carried	1.2 million	1.4 million
Passengers miles travelled	3,000 million	3,300 million
Ratio of cabin staff to passengers (excluding aircrew, ie pilots and navigators):		
Economy class	1 to 10	1 to 12
Business and first class	1 to 4	1 to 5
Number of airline routes flown	40	44

- P Airlines sells economy, business and first-class seats to passengers. The prices reflect the level of comfort and service. For example, first class seats cost double the price of business class seats and ten times the price of economy seats.
- Airline passenger numbers are expected to increase by 3% in the next two years in the long-distance economy-class market from which P attracts most of its customers.
- There is an increasing level of partnerships emerging among airlines whereby each carries the other's passengers as well as its own on designated routes. P is engaged in such partnerships for two of its routes.
- A general survey of satisfaction among airline passengers carried out by independent representatives from the travel industry in P's home country ranks P as being within the top three for most services.

Rail	*1997*	*1998*
Number of passengers carried	4.5 million	4.3 million
Passenger miles travelled	160 million	150 million
Ratio of customer attendants to passengers		
Standard class	1 to 100	1 to 120
First class	1 to 20	1 to 25
Number of routes travelled	25	25

- P Rail sells standard and first-class seats to its passengers. The first-class seat is priced at about double that of a standard priced seat.
- An increase of 5% in total rail passengers is expected over the next four years.
- P operates the railway services under a franchise agreement, which is due for renewal in five years' time.
- The government has established a Railway Regulatory Authority to monitor the quality of the services provided by the P Group and other railway franchisees, and is constantly increasing pressure on the franchisees to improve their services.
- A general survey of passenger satisfaction carried out by the Railway Regulatory Authority was highly critical of P's services with regard to its record relating to punctuality and service on its trains.

Future development

P has enjoyed considerable success in its ventures within its domestic market. However, the directors believe there is much opportunity to develop the brand name within the emerging highly-populated retail markets elsewhere in the world where currently it is relatively unknown.

1. REQUIREMENTS:

(a) Discuss the importance of the external forces which P faces in its worldwide business development. **10 Marks**

(b) With reference to the comparative financial and other performance indicators, evaluate the performance of the P Airlines and P Rail companies. Recommend ways in which they may increase their individual contribution to the future development of the group. **20 Marks**

(c) Advise the directors of P how their brand extension strategy may be successfully implemented in countries where the brand is relatively unknown at present. **15 Marks**

(d) Explain the main factors which have contributed to P's commercial success so far. Comment on the chairman's personal responsibilities to the group's shareholders, employees, joint venture partners and customers. **15 Marks**

Total Marks = 60

SECTION B - 40 MARKS

ANSWER TWO QUESTIONS ONLY - 20 MARKS EACH

2 SE plc is a manufacturer of commercial security equipment. It has applied a successful strategy of acquisitions over a number of years to counter the threat of increased competition. Five years ago the company acquired an overseas competitor in order to expand outside its domestic market. This was very successful and the overseas subsidiary (ML) became market leader in its own country following a programme of downsizing and the introduction of improved efficiency measures. A competitor, of approximately the same size in terms of turnover and profitability, has now entered the market overseas and is threatening ML's market dominance.

The directors of SE plc have become acquainted with the following market defence strategies: position defence; flanking defence; pre-emptive defence; counter-offensive defence; mobile defence and contraction defence. They are concerned to protect the market share which has been achieved by ML and have turned to you for advice.

REQUIREMENT:

Discuss the benefits and disadvantages of these defence strategies. Advise the directors of SE plc which should be applied to defend its overseas market share.

20 Marks

3. A plc is a company which supplies industrial cleaning services. After it was founded, fifteen years ago, AL Ltd (as it then was) achieved rapid growth and high levels of turnover. The board of directors at the time believed that its traditional scientific management style, based on Taylorian principles, was the main reason for the company's success. As the company grew, the directors found that the company had insufficient capital resources to meet the increasing levels of demand for its services. As a result, AL Ltd was floated on its domestic stock exchange and increased capital resources flowed into the business, allowing it to maintain its rate of expansion. This seemed to be further evidence of the success of the traditional management style employed.

In each of the last three years, however, AL plc has found that its turnover and profit have fallen below the industry average and that its market share has reduced. There is increasing concern among the shareholders about the long-term decline in turnover and profitability. The finance director of AL plc (to whom you report as management accountant) has quoted the performance of CC Ltd, a similar sized company in the contract catering industry. While CC Ltd is not a competitor, it is often viewed as a benchmark against which AL plc can measure its own performance even though it employs a different management style which requires the consent and commitment of employees. CC Ltd has managed to increase its market share, turnover and profitability consistently over the last five years and the finance director has turned to you to analyse why AL plc seems to be producing continuously unsatisfactory results.

REQUIREMENT:

(a) Explain to the directors of AL plc how value can be added by carrying out a programme of benchmarking. **7 Marks**

(b) Explain how you would implement a benchmarking exercise comparing the performance of AL plc with CC Ltd. Discuss the possible implications for the style of management which should be employed by the company after carrying out such an exercise. **13 Marks**

Total Marks = 20

4. GC is a conglomerate which comprises five strategic business units (SBUs), all operating as subsidiary companies. Information relating to each SBU (and the market leader or nearest competitor) is given in the following table.

	Current Market Share			**Market growth expected by GC**
	GC	*Market leader*	*Nearest competitor*	
	%	%	%	
Building brick manufacturer *(Declining profitability)*	3	25		Small
Parcel carriage service *(Long established, faces strong competition. Turnover and profitability over last three years have been stable but are expected to decline as competition strengthens.)*	1	6		Nil
Food manufacturer producing exclusively for household consumption *(Long established with little new investment. High levels of turnover and profitability which are being sustained.)*	25		5	Slowly declining
Painting and decorating contracting company *(Established three years ago. Continuous capital injections from group over that period. Currently not making any profit.)*	0.025	0.5		Historically high but now forecast to slow down
Software development and supply company *(Acquired two years ago. Market share expected to increase over next two years. Sustained investment from group but profitability so far is low.)*	10		8	Rapid

REQUIREMENTS:

(a) Comment on GC's overall competitive position by applying the Boston Consulting Group Growth/Share Matrix analysis to its portfolio of SBUs. **8 Marks**

(b) Discuss how GC should pursue the strategic development of its SBUs in order to add value to the overall conglomerate group. **12 Marks**

Total Marks = 20

---

5. (a) Explain why an organisation may outsource some of its primary or support activities. **7 Marks**

(b) The Directors of AB plc are facing increasing pressure from shareholders to increase earnings per share. The overhead costs of the company have increased as a proportion of total cost over the last three years and the directors are considering outsourcing the financial accounting, payroll, creditor payments and debtors functions in order to reduce the levels of operational gearing. However, the directors are concerned that AB plc will not receive the same level of service from these functions after they have been outsourced.

REQUIREMENT:

Summarise how AB plc should proceed to outsource the financial accounting, payroll, creditor payments and debtors functions. Discuss how the directors may be assured of the quality of the service which is subsequently received for these activities. **13 Marks**

Total Marks = 20

SUGGESTED ANSWERS

DO NOT TURN THIS PAGE UNTIL YOU HAVE COMPLETED THE MOCK EXAM

The Examiner for SMM offers to future candidates and to lecturers the following background and guidance on the questions included in this examination paper

General

The examination paper comprehensively covers the SMM syllabus. In addition to testing theory, the paper requires candidates to apply knowledge in respect of the case study and scenarios presented. The first question particularly crosses boundaries within the syllabus and candidates are invited to apply knowledge which has been acquired through study for earlier Stages and for other Stage 4 subjects. The syllabus topics mainly addressed are environmental and performance appraisal, branding, benchmarking, identification and closure of the planning gap, marketing strategies and corporate responsibilities.

Section A - compulsory

Question 1 concerns a conglomerate group which has achieved considerable success by promoting its brand name. The group has a charismatic chairman who applies the basic management principle of valuing the services provided by the group's staff. The group's brand name has been stretched across numerous different products and services into areas where it is believed the industry is capable of providing better value for money to customers. The question addresses the issue of external forces which the group faces and requires its performance to be evaluated. In addition, brand extension into countries where the group is relatively unknown is explored as well as analysis of its critical success factors and responsibilities to stakeholders. The question addresses all sections of the syllabus and the first, second and third syllabus Aims.

Section B - two questions from four

Question 2 relates to the implementation of appropriate defence strategies to protect the market share of an overseas subsidiary. This question's subject matter is firmly contained within section (d) of the syllabus and relates principally to the fourth Aim of the syllabus, but also includes some consideration of the third Aim.

Question 3 provides a scenario of a company which has applied a traditional scientific management style but after flotation has found that its trading results in the recent past have been unsatisfactory. The question seeks to explore the application of benchmarking and couples this with appreciation of the need to implement an appropriate management style in order to satisfy organisational objectives. This question relates to sections (b) and (c) of the syllabus, and addresses the first and second Aims.

Question 4 presents the market share and market growth position relating to the five strategic business units which make up a conglomerate group. In addition, further information is provided on each SBU's level of profitability and candidates are required to analyse the performance of each of the SBU's by applying the BCG Growth/Share matrix and to discuss how strategic development may be pursued. This question relates to sections (a) and (c) of the syllabus. It addresses the first and fourth Aims.

Question 5 concerns outsourcing and presents a small scenario which reveals that a company's directors are facing increasing pressure to increase earnings per share. The question relates to sections (c), (d) and (e) of the syllabus. It addresses the second and third Aims of the syllabus specifically, but also includes an element of the fourth Aim.

1

> **Pass marks.** You may have realised that this case study is based upon the experiences of the Virgin group. Part (a) is a reasonable question on the competitive forces faced by the P Group that should have caused few problems, while part (b) required some fairly basic numerical analysis. Do not overlook the important fact that the airline and rail companies are service businesses, so non-financial performance indicators such as customer satisfaction are fundamental to long term success.
>
> The question on brand extension strategy in part (c) brings in the marketing section of the syllabus. You should have noted the key point that brand extension into unknown markets is risky, even for a successful group such as this. Brand extension implies a high level of customer recognition of a brand, and if this is missing then it is necessary to go back to some basics of international marketing strategy, covered in Chapter 18 of the Study Text. P Group can alleviate some of the risk by using its familiar formula of a local joint venture partner.
>
> The question finishes up with a consideration of the factors behind the commercial success of the group, and stakeholders and their relationship with the Chairman. So, as we have come to expect from the case study, there is quite wide syllabus coverage!

(a) Despite trading in many areas, the P Group has managed to establish itself as a successful company with diverse interests. These will nevertheless be subject to various external **competitive pressures.**

Porter's Five Forces model provides a framework for analysing those pressures which the P Group must respond to in order to maintain its **competitive advantage** and ensure that customers continue to enjoy and respect the strong brand. These forces influence the level of competition faced by the P Group businesses.

(i) **The threat of new entrants**

A new entrant into an industry will being extra capacity and more competition. This can be countered by **barriers to entry** and the response of existing competitors. The P Group prides itself on being different and exciting. This may have the effect of shutting some competitors out of the market (especially if they are seen as complacent by the public). The strong **brand loyalty** and charismatic leadership enjoyed by P Group also has the effect of excluding competitors.

In its airline business, barriers to entry may be created because of the high levels of **capital investment** required, although P Airlines is always at risk from existing airlines who may want to expand their networks and fly new routes (possibly by forging alliances, subject to government regulation). A new entrant into rail services may threaten to take over the P Group's operating licence if the service improvements expected by the Regulator do not happen.

(ii) **Substitute products or services**

A substitute product is a good or service that is produced by another industry and which satisfies the same **customer needs.** As P Group companies operate in diverse fields, these customer needs (and attitudes and lifestyles) are going to be many and various, so the P Group must make sure that its **marketing strategy** addresses these differences.

For example, its rail services will compete with domestic airlines and cars, so advertising needs to convey the advantages that rail travel enjoys (ease of journey, lack of traffic congestion and so on).

(iii) **The bargaining power of customers**

At the moment, the P Group is well perceived by customers as the **consumer's champion** and the scourge of corporate complacency. This perception has worked in the P Group's favour, but it must make sure that it does not become complacent itself. Customers will continue to want better quality products and services, at lower prices, and this might force down profitability.

Where P Group's products or services are specialised, however, this may reduce consumer power. It may also be the case that the brand carries a premium that renders some consumers **price insensitive** because of their perceptions about quality. Managers need to have knowledge about different customers in different markets, including market conditions such as cultural environments.

(iv) **The bargaining power of suppliers**

P Group needs to make sure that there are enough suppliers available who can support its successful business and guarantee **availability** and **quality** of materials and services. If there are one or two dominant suppliers then they may be able to charge monopoly or oligopoly prices. It is likely that the P Group is an important customer for many suppliers.

(v) **Rivalry amongst current competitors**

P Group is trying to enter new markets and will find itself facing established **local competition**, which may have distribution, cultural and other advantages (these can be significant in emerging markets such as China and India which have previously been closed to Western companies). Competitive actions might take the form of price competition or advertising battles, the introduction of new products or improving after-sales service to attract market share.

Rivalry is intensified when success in a market is a prime **strategic objective**. Success in the highly populated emerging retail markets, for example, (where there are potentially billions of new customers) will be hard won as many Western companies are beginning to target these markets for turnover and profit growth.

The external forces described above are all important considerations in pursuit of worldwide business development and competitive success. The prime consideration for the management of P Group is that the focus on the company's **objectives** is maintained.

The strong impact of the Chairman and the brand is a distinct advantage in the home market, but competitive forces overseas could combine to dilute this influence. The P Group needs to be sure that sufficient **resources** are devoted to new ventures to ensure their success.

(b) The comparative financial information given on the two companies can be analysed as follows.

		1997	1998	Increase/ (decrease) %
AIRLINES	**Turnover**	$570m	$678m	18.9
	Revenue per passenger	$475	$484	1.9
	Revenue per mile travelled	$0.19	$0.21	10.5
	Profit before tax	$60m	$80m	33.3
	Profit margin %	10.5	11.8	
	ROCE %	8.0	10.1	
	Asset turnover	76%	85.8%	
RAIL	**Turnover**	$410m	$423m	3.2
	Revenue per passenger	$91	$98	7.7
	Revenue per mile travelled	$2.56	$2.82	10.2
	Profit before tax	$30m	$32m	6.7
	Profit margin %	7.3	7.6	
	ROCE %	5.7	5.0	
	Asset turnover	77.4%	66.1%	

Note. Revenue per passenger has been calculated by dividing turnover by the number of passengers carried to give an approximate indication of an average fare. A similar calculation was made for revenue per mile travelled.

Airline

The airline company generates **higher profits** than the rail company and is also a more successful **investment**, with a higher return on average capital employed in 1998. **Asset turnover** has improved between 1997 and 1998, with each $ of investment generating more sales.

Turnover and profits have increased between 1997 and 1998 and testify to the overall success of the airline venture and **public satisfaction** with it, with more passengers being carried and more air miles being travelled. Four **new routes** (and therefore new markets) were opened in 1998 and this will have contributed to the turnover increase. Passenger numbers are expected to increase in the future. **Revenue per passenger** has only increased slightly in 1998. **Revenue per mile** is small in absolute terms because of the great distances covered by air travel, especially as most of P's customers are from the long-distance economy market. This market is forecast to grow.

Rail

Railways require significant investment in rolling stock and other capital assets, so its **capital employed** figure is high. **Asset turnover** has deteriorated between 1997 and 1998 and may still worsen. The capital employed figure is likely to rise over the next few years with the proposed upgrade of the **infrastructure** that was inherited when the business became part of the P Group. Returns could be low for several years to come.

Profit margins are lower than the airline, and **turnover growth** has been small, although revenues per passenger and per mile travelled have increased quite significantly. Part of the reason for slow growth in turnover will be the public dissatisfaction with the service which has deterred passengers. Both the number of passengers carried and the number of miles travelled has declined, which will have offset some of the benefit of any **fare increases.**

The Group is unlikely to invest in any **new routes** until the problems with the existing service have been corrected, and will rely for turnover growth instead on gaining more **market share** from the expected 5% increase in rail passengers over the next four years.

Other performance indicators

Airline

In customer perceptions of the airline industry, a key **differentiating factor** between competitors is the in-flight **service**. Airlines go to great lengths to advertise to potential customers about such features as the amount of leg room and the standard of food and entertainment, often saying very little about prices.

P Airlines has cut the ratio of cabin crew to passengers in 1998, which will have cut costs. This will have affected service levels, although the cuts are not drastic and are likely to have gone unnoticed by the majority of passengers. This is borne out by the results of **customer satisfaction** surveys.

Rail

As has happened in the airline business, the ratio of customer attendants to passengers has decreased, but this ratio is traditionally quite low for rail services, even in first class, so the changes again may have gone largely unnoticed and costs will have been saved.

Service improvements must be made if the company is to retain its **operating licence**. Passenger irritation with delays and cancellations, and possibly long standing concern about safety on the railways generally, is reflected in the low customer satisfaction ratings that P Group's services achieve.

Government pressure on the company will increase until the service is improved. This will distract the directors from other ventures, but it is very important, both for the success of P Rail and the overall **perception of the brand** in all its activities, that the service regains public confidence.

Recommendations for increasing individual contribution

Air

As has been noted above, the average fare has increased by only a very small amount between 1997 and 1998, so there may be an opportunity to **increase fares** on some routes or in some **segments** of the market.

Economy passengers make up the bulk of P's market and it may be time for the company to consider increasing the number of **business** and **first class** passengers that it carries. These passengers provide **higher margins,** with first class passengers being charged ten times more than economy passengers even though they do not cost ten times more to service.

British Airways has recently announced that the focus of its **future strategy** is the attraction of these higher paying passengers, so much so that it is actually cutting the number of economy seats in its aircraft. This strategy will increase **average revenue per passenger** and the average revenue **per mile** travelled. Business class travel is also a lucrative market although there is evidence to suggest that concern with cost control is limiting the amount that companies are prepared to spend on employee flights.

Engaging in more **partnerships** with other airlines will open up new routes and markets. These should be carefully chosen to make sure that P Airlines has an attractive and lucrative **global network** of routes. If such **incentives** are not already in place, passengers should be encouraged to participate in air miles schemes and qualify for loyalty rewards for flying on some or all of these routes.

Rail

The long term success of this company depends on being able to deliver service improvements in the future, not only because of the importance of public opinion but because it stands to lose its operating licence in five years' time.

Such improvements will require **expensive investment** and a long time to show a return. It is unlikely that **fare increases** will be countenanced by either the regulatory authority or the travelling public until the service is improved. There is scope for attracting more first class passengers, because first class train travel by businesses is popular and widely advertised as a good **alternative to travelling by car** on congested city roads ("Business brains take Virgin trains" is a slogan seen in the UK, for example).

P Rail must attempt to halt the decline in the number of passengers carried and attract a share of the growing market for rail travel. Advertising in the business press and on television should attract more customers as the services begin to improve.

(c) Firms with a well established brand have an advantage when introducing new products, because the new product enjoys **instant recognition** which can save heavy advertising costs. In addition, it has been claimed that **globalisation** of the world market is leading to increased **homogeneity** in consumer tastes thanks to modern communications and travel.

A **brand extension strategy** involves stretching a brand over new products and implies a **high consumer loyalty** to the existing brand. Other products can be introduced into the brand range by 'piggy-backing' on the articles already known to the customer. In this way, for example, major supermarkets like Sainsbury in the UK have introduced financial services (including savings schemes, loans and credit cards) which have been taken up by customers who trust the strong supermarket brand and do not worry that banking is not a supermarket's core competence.

Such a strategy poses few problems to the directors of P in its home country, where citizens are familiar with the brand and the high profile chairman, but it is more difficult in countries where the brand is not so well known. Some of P's products are likely to be genuinely **global** ones and the group's prestige will be enhanced, so it is a worthwhile strategy to pursue, but the company must acknowledge the **risks** involved (which may include a greater likelihood of political instability or government intervention). There will also be a greater investment of financial resources (more debt), working capital and human resources.

This is made more complex by the avowed aim of the business 'to be different'. Finding suitable products and services in new countries which fulfil this aim, and do not disappoint customers both in the new countries and more established markets, is a challenging task. The brand name must be appropriate for the chosen product.

Having made the **strategic** decision to stretch the brand into new overseas markets, the company must consider **tactical** issues, and ask and answer the following questions.

(i) How can the company get to understand customers' **needs and preferences** in foreign markets? Buying habits will also be different. P's brand may not be as appealing as locally chosen ones.

(ii) Does the company know how to **conduct business abroad,** and deal effectively with foreign nationals? It would seem that the P Group does have this knowledge.

(iii) Are there foreign **regulations** and associated hidden **costs**? There may be product regulations and price controls.

(iv) Does the company have the necessary **management skills**? The management skills of the company have been attested to, but they might not transfer so well to emerging markets.

The **emerging** highly populated retail markets (India and China are key examples) provide the company with the potential for billions of new customers who can be segmented in terms of wealth and lifestyles, rather than strictly national or ethnic terms.

However, some understanding of the **culture** of these new international markets will be required and the key to this (and understanding which products will be successful) will involve P in using **local expertise**. P's brand name may not be appropriate in some overseas cultures because of difficulties in pronunciation, or because it is amusing, meaningless or offensive. Some companies have to market the same product under many different names in different countries, which would not be acceptable for the P Group's very distinctive brand philosophy.

McDonalds cannot sell burgers containing beef in India because cattle are sacred animals, and P may also find that some of its products and services do not travel well to these markets. Local expertise or commissioned **research** will be needed to find this out. Mistakes made at an early stage could have a disastrous effect upon public trust and have the effect of barring P Group companies from such markets.

A programme of **advertising** of the brand will have to be embarked upon, assuming that there is an adequate **communications infrastructure**. The chairman is not averse to publicity and his charismatic appearance at promotional events could give the brand a kick-start.

As has already been noted, the initial strategy is likely to involve using resources and expertises that are already present in the target market. **Alliances** or **joint ventures** are a familiar way of doing business for the P Group and such arrangements with well known domestic companies in the emerging markets, such as Tata in India (whose interests range from computer services to motor vehicles) might provide the benefits of shared expertise to both sides. **Franchising** is also a common method of expanding a business, with the franchisee supplying capital, personal involvement and local market knowledge.

Once the brand is better established and P Group has become accustomed to business in the new market it will be able to operate without such support and will be better able to withstand competition. As the brand extension strategy develops, however, P Group must be careful that it is not **overextended** and loses its special position in the consumers' minds.

(d) The commercial success of the group so far can be attributed to the following factors. These factors are likely to combine to enable the Group to survive the poor start to its rail venture, and when P Rail is improved the brand could emerge stronger than ever.

(i) **Strength of the brand**. The group is intensely brand driven. It enjoys strong recognition and a good reputation, and the directors and staff pay careful attention to the products that are to be associated with the brand (rather than the other way round). The key emphasis is on adding value, balancing risks and reward and maintaining a strong corporate image. It does not always get it right, as demonstrated by the rail company, but even here the directors have faith in the brand and it would seem that the rail problems are not yet dragging the overall brand name down, which is a considerable feat.

(ii) **Age of the company**. The company is fairly young (established 30 years ago) and has been able to make a name for itself as being energetic and dynamic. It has enjoyed considerable success in taking market share from more inflexible and complacent competition in the markets it has targeted with its brand.

(iii) **Emphasis on the customer**. It is becoming a fundamental of marketing and business success that any organisation that does not pay attention to its customers is destined not to enjoy long term prosperity. The P Group is very strongly customer focused and is recognised as the consumer's champion, taking on less agile companies whose customer service policies and attitudes become outdated. Motivated staff contribute to this success, and the company enjoys high customer satisfaction ratings.

(iv) **Management style and staff policy**. The management structure is flat and communication and participation is encouraged within and between group companies. A highly participative, 'family' culture is equated with motivated staff, which should ensure a quality of customer service which is a key element of competitive advantage.

(v) **Dynamic and forward looking**. The company is not complacent about its success and is determined 'to be different', looking out for new markets to sustain its future. With this in mind, the emerging highly populated retail markets are now being considered.

(vi) **International ambitions**. Being internationally diverse and willing and able to stretch the brand could have been a disastrous strategy and there may still be the danger that the brand could be stretched one product too far. Conglomerates are unfashionable organisations but the P Group has overcome this with its business approach of providing the brand for joint venture partners who in turn provide a cash injection. This helps to spread the risk. The airline has been particularly successful in promoting the P Group's international credentials.

(vii) **High profile**. This is largely thanks to the activities of, and publicity provided by, the charismatic Chairman, who attracts customers, media attention and joint venture partners alike.

The chairman and the stakeholders

The chairman has set himself up in a high profile and publicity hungry role, and by doing so has identified himself, probably more strongly than most chairmen, with the fortunes of the group and its stakeholders. This has meant that a greater degree of responsibility falls to him.

Responsibility to stakeholders such as customers and shareholders falls to all chairmen, but because the group's fortunes are so closely tied to him as a personality, the pressures are greater. Failures reflect on him personally, and successes serve to endorse his position. His high risk leisure pursuits could conceivably put his life in danger, and his loss would prove disastrous for the group's fortunes. It may be seen as dangerous to tie the Group's fortunes so conspicuously to one man, and the grooming of a successor may eventually be seen as desirable by larger shareholders.

Shareholders. The objective of shareholders (increase in shareholder value) is taken as the prime objective which company management must fulfil. The chairman has a responsibility, as long as he is prepared to shoulder it, to these shareholders to continue with his strong and dynamic leadership of the group because he is a very important factor in its success and growth.

Employees. The participative management style of the company and open communications policy is not unique, but it is distinctive and makes the P Group a pleasant and exciting place to work, and is probably a reflection of the Chairman's own personality. As long as the group is successful and continues to attract and employ high calibre staff, employees will be encouraged to remain and share in the success of the company.

Joint venture partners. These are often attracted to the P Group by the chairman's reputation and past successes, and it is his responsibility to make sure that their trust (and investment) is not misplaced. They may find that they have less involvement with him than they expected, but as he is the chairman of the group and the driving force behind the brand they are investing in, they are entitled to his support.

Customers. They will continue to expect ever higher standards of product and service from management, and are likely to hold him personally responsible for any shortcomings. He must ensure that the highest standards are met and that he can explain failings, being able to deal with the bad (as well as the good) publicity. If customers are lost, the shareholders could see turnover and profits fall.

2

> **Pass marks.** Another question from a marginal area, testing specifics not detailed in the syllabus. After the question in November 1998 on attack strategies, here is one on the defence strategies described by Kotler. The examiner noted that the November 1998 question exposed 'a gap in knowledge', and this question may have proved equally unpopular. Our answer relates the defence strategies to ML's particular circumstances. Although the question wording does not specifically require it, we have set out our answer in the form of a report. Our conclusion differs from that of CIMA's model answer, but as long as you can support a conclusion you will gain credit.

REPORT

To: Board of Directors, SE plc
From: Management Accountant
Date: November 1999
Subject: Defence strategies and ML

As the directors of SE plc are aware, there are six military-style **defence strategies** that a dominant firm such as ML can use when faced with **intensified competition**. These can be described as follows.

Position defence

This involves ML in merely **defending the position it already has,** by 'digging in' with **competitive pricing** and building a barrier between itself and the competition to protect its own current territory and product. It is a straightforward defence, but it will eventually become stagnant and backfire, because although ML is indeed protecting its market share it will be doing nothing to **develop** that territory (through, for example, product enhancements, new ventures or promotional activities) or to prevent **competitors** from entering elsewhere and developing their own competitive position without challenge.

Such reliance on an existing position will hinder future **growth and profitability** especially if there is a **price war.** It has become a fact that ML is sharing the market with a competitor (with similar **resources**) which can afford to develop its own attack, and that ML must do more than sit still. For this reason, such a strategy is not recommended.

Flanking defence

This would involve ML in setting up activities that build upon its dominance and provide a base for the development of future ventures, always related to its **core business** of manufacturing commercial security equipment. It may, for example, strengthen **market awareness** of its products by entering into alliances with retailers of security equipment, or expand its **product line** to include residential security equipment, such as burglar alarms. The recent downsizing and efficiency measures will have paved the way because management can now at least consider new activities for the leaner business. A flanking defence does require significant commitment of time and resources, however, that management may feel they cannot yet afford.

Pre-emptive defence

A pre-emptive defence strategy requires ML to **get in early** and spoil the party for the new competitor before it starts its concerted attack against ML. It may already be too late for this, but assuming that it is not, ML must retain the upper hand and keep the new competitor guessing. This could take the form of a price cut, promotional activity or distribution of its security equipment to a larger number of sellers in an attempt to 'crowd out' the competitor's product from the potential market. Such aggressive tactics are expensive.

We know that the new competitor is at least as strong as ML, and ML would have to be very confident of its product to do nothing about the threat.

Counter-offensive defence

This strategy reflects a belief that **attack is the best form of defence.** Most market leaders will respond to a counterattack when they are attacked by a competitor, but it is the **timing** of that counterattack which can be crucial. The exact nature of the competitor's threat to ML (for example, lower prices or better products?) has not been described, but ML is currently dominant and is enjoying the benefits of improved efficiency. It can probably afford to wait a bit, identify 'chinks in the armour' and attack the competitor where it will hurt the most. ML may be able to attack the competitor's markets in areas where it is weak. For example, it may have a poor distribution network and availability problems that ML can capitalise on.

Mobile defence

To use this defence, ML must stretch its territory and innovate to cover totally new areas, via **market broadening** (getting involved in other areas related to the core business of manufacturing security equipment, such as the servicing and installation of all types of security equipment, or provision of outsourced security services) and **market diversification** into completely unrelated industries. The attacking company will find it has a bigger challenge.

This must not be carried too far or ML's key business and competitive strengths will become diluted, and it does not seem an appropriate defence to adopt. It would involve SE plc in significant commitment to totally new activities in a relatively new geographical market that it may not have the expertise or resources for, and may leave it exposed in other areas.

Contraction defence

This applies to large companies who find that they have spread their resources far and wide and **cannot defend everything** that they have. They decide to withdraw from some, probably weaker, areas to concentrate on others where the position is stronger and the market is of central importance.

This strategy does not seem to apply to ML's circumstances because it is in a fairly specialised field in a local market, and they should be able to retain their share.

Conclusion

Having considered the above defences, it is recommended that SE plc should defend its overseas market share using a **pre-emptive defence**. It is a fairly aggressive approach, requiring control and careful management at group and local level. However, the resources and experience are available to SE plc to **set up immediately** and subsequently **maintain** the initiative. Management should not forget however, that the competitor has strong resources and can attack back.

A counter-offensive defence is an alternative option, but local management may feel that it involves more **risk** as the competitor may be as yet an unknown quantity. Sitting back and waiting for a weakness to appear will give the competitor too much time to establish itself, whereas a head-on counter-attack may waste resources and be deflected by a resourceful opponent.

3

Pass marks. Benchmarking is a technique for evaluating performance and identifying improvements, and the question addresses two aspects of its use – the adding of value, and the way in which a programme can be implemented. Do not ignore the 'management style' implications in part (b). You should not have been put off by this element – it is clearly pointed out in the scenario and provides a practical twist to the question, with the application of benchmarking leading to the likely updating of business practices. It is apparent that the company has held on for too long to possibly outdated management methods.

Other points. You may not be familiar with Taylorian scientific management theory, but you should have been able to deduce from the scenario wording that it is very different from the management style off CC Ltd that encourages employee involvement and participation. Unlike us, you may have set out your answer in the form of a report. This is appropriate, given the question wording.

(a) **Benchmarking** can be described as a technique whereby a company tries to emulate or exceed the **standards** achieved or **processes** adopted by another company, generally a very successful one. The company carrying out the benchmarking does not necessarily have to be in the same industry as the 'model' organisation Benchmarking exercises usually reveal improvements and benefits for both sides.

Activities in Porter's **value chain,** such as the support activity of human resource management, incur costs and combine to provide a product or service which earns revenue. In the case of AL plc, that service is industrial cleaning. By studying **business processes** to identify the weakest elements, and then comparing them with other companies, solutions to problems can often be found and these solutions will often lead to new or better ways of doing things, often at a lower cost.

For example, the Taylorian **management practices** highlighted at AL plc (possibly involving tightly timed, highly regulated and profoundly unsatisfying work schedules, with close supervision and little opportunity for employee involvement) may have resulted in high staff turnover. If AL, after carrying out a benchmarking exercise, decides to try and emulate the more participative management style of CC Ltd, staff turnover and absences may be reduced, and so recruitment and training costs will be lower. The quality of the service may improve because staffing is consistent and better motivated, and increased **customer satisfaction** means a greater likelihood of repeat business.

Benchmarking therefore focuses on improvement in key areas and sets targets which may be challenging for AL, but are certainly achievable. It can be a spur to **innovation**, with new ideas and processes suggesting new products and services for the company's market, but it requires the commitment of all staff.

(b) CC Ltd must be willing to participate fully in the exercise if AL is going to learn anything from it. CC must be confident that they too can learn from the programme. The benchmarking exercise can be divided into stages.

(i) **Set objectives** and determine the areas to benchmark. This will include understanding why CC is performing consistently well in its sector and trying to relate that directly to why AL is underperforming. The respective management styles of the two companies are a key point of difference which clearly merit attention.

(ii) Establish **key performance measures**. Studying management styles may include related measures such as absenteeism, staff turnover and recruitment and training policies. Detailed discussion of the costs of these may not be willingly shared, but the two companies can probably learn from each other's experiences and may even find that they have common problems with common solutions.

(iii) **Measure** own and others' performance. CC Ltd should in theory be prepared to open its doors and let AL, a non-competitor, see how it operates. This does not have to involve detailed discussion of confidential figures relating to turnover, costs and profitability, which are likely to be irrelevant to the exercise because the companies are in different industries. A related programme of customer and employee satisfaction surveys will be a good source of information

(iv) **Compare** performances. This should clearly indicate where CC is stronger than AL, and why. It may be done using a points scoring system, for example rating customer satisfaction on scales from 1 to 10.

(v) Design and implement an **improvement programme**. Having studied CC and identified where it does things well , AL will be in a position to apply what it has learnt to its own business and design a package of improvements. This will require the full involvement of the senior management of AL and will also have to be 'sold' to the staff. The expected benefits from the programme must be clearly identified and quantified where appropriate, for measuring against actual results.

(vi) **Monitor** improvements. The benefits from the improvement programme (reduced staff turnover, less absenteeism, fewer customer defections) must be measured against expectations and systematically reported upon. This final stage is crucial because the programme must have the full commitment of management if it is to be sustained and deliver the required benefits, because improvements will not happen overnight.

The management style adopted by AL plc after carrying out the benchmarking exercise is likely to be far more **participative**, and this will require significant **cultural** adjustment for both the employees and senior management, long used to Taylorian principles of scientific management and authoritarian control of work practices. Some managers in the company may find it very difficult to believe that workers lower in the hierarchy have valid suggestions for improving the way that the company's service is delivered to customers. It is vital however that the new management style has the commitment of senior executives.

It is likely that the historical relationship between workers and management has been confrontational and may have led to disputes, strikes and maybe even lost contracts. Attitudes on both sides may have become entrenched. Some employees may not want additional responsibility and may be suspicious of what they see as having to do more work without additional pay. The process will have to be very carefully managed.

The improvements may initially be expensive to set up, with for example additional training costs (in addition to the cost of the benchmarking exercise already undertaken). However, it is being recognised by many industries that motivated employees translate directly to satisfied customers and repeat business.

4

Pass marks. Practical application of the BCG matrix is the theme with this interesting question, rather than simple description or discussion of its features. Indeed, you are forced to apply it by the very way the question is presented, having to slot the different SBUs into the familiar (or at least they should be familiar!) categories, and then go on to discuss overall competitive position and suggestions for strategic development. Candidates who were unfamiliar with the model would have found this progression very difficult.

Other points. We have used a diagram to present our analysis of the SBUs in a concise format, with expanded commentary below.

(a) Applying the Boston Consulting Group Growth / Share Matrix to GC's portfolio of SBUs reveals the following position.

		Market share	
		High	***Low***
Market growth	***High***	**Stars** Software company	**Question marks** Painting /decorating
	Low	**Cash cows** Food manufacturer	**Dogs** Building bricks Parcel carriage

As can be seen from the matrix, the overall competitive position of GC is not strong. Only one business unit operates in a sector where strong market growth is expected. Three out of the five SBUs operate in sectors where market growth will be low, and two of these are categorised as **dogs** which are using up cash resources that would be better utilised in areas of the business which have greater potential. The painting and decorating business can be regarded as a **question mark,** historically absorbing cash in the hope of turning it into a high market share star, but the slow down in market growth may have defeated those ambitions.

Parcel carriage has become a **dog** with the expected decline in turnover and profitability as competition intensifies. The **cash cow,** food manufacture, may become the only SBU capable of delivering the cash required to finance future **stars.** Its market growth, however, is slowly declining and could eventually be nil.

Currently, only the software development and supply company can be categorised as a star. While capital expenditure in this SBU has been high, its share of a growing market is expected to increase, along with its cash generation potential.

The future prosperity of the conglomerate is possibly dependent on two out of five business units, the cash from one supporting the development of the other. If cash from the food manufacturing business becomes inadequate to finance the software company as its market slows down, the position will be even more unstable.

(b) GC's **strategic development** of its SBUs will have to address the points noted in (a) above. The group is widely **diversified** across very different industry sectors, and the conglomerate itself is now a less usual form of business than it was, for example, in the 1980s, when companies such as Hanson had widely differing business interests. It may be possible to find **synergies** between the businesses and their **value chains** to enable further development.

GC may have to consider **divestment** of poorer performing businesses in order to concentrate resources on those areas of the business where potential for adding value is greatest. This may include further **acquisitions** in carefully chosen ventures in the future, but the immediate priority must be to address the existing SBUs.

The building brick manufacturer is facing declining profitability, and expected small growth in a market where GC's share is low. If such expectations are borne out then this division will become a drain on resources, although recent reports in the British press about the South East needing over one million new houses over the next few years will give a boost to the construction industry, and demand for building bricks will obviously increase.

Unless GC can reasonably expect to be involved in such developments as new housebuilding activity, it should consider disposing of the building bricks division. The current market leader, with a 25% share, may be interested in acquiring its small rival.

The painting and decorating contracting company has not been part of the group for long and has received continuous cash injections. Even if it was profitable in the past (this is not known), it is currently not making any profit and market growth is forecast to slow down, which may make it difficult to gain a large enough share to ensure **sustained profitability** in the future.

The present situation in painting and decorating mirrors that of the building brick manufacturer, and the fortunes of the two are tied together on expectations of a housing boom. It may be more difficult to sell this business as the market is characterised by numerous companies with no dominant player, so GC will have to decide whether to hold on to this business and try to restore it to profitability. It may consider investing in a different area of the market (for example, branching into commercial contracts if it has previously concentrated on residential) to try and expand its market share and **differentiate** itself from competitors.

The parcel carriage service faces strong competition and GC could consider ways of facing that competition before turnover and profitability decline, possibly through **improved services** or offering different ones. Although market growth is expected to be nil, the business has been long established in the market and should be able to use this **reputation** to develop other services. This could include use of the **Internet** to take customer orders and monitor delivery schedules. Services and resources for this may be developed by the software development and supply company, so GC already has the expertise that competitors may lack. Alternatively, the decision may be taken that this SBU does not warrant additional investment.

The food manufacturer is facing a slowly declining market, but GC is by far the dominant business in the market and enjoys high levels of **turnover and profitability**. To ensure that this continues in the future and that **cash flows** are maintained, GC should consider producing for larger scale catering concerns (restaurants, hotels, schools and hospitals, for example) to reduce its dependence on the declining household market. Its reputation and dominance should mean that it has the resources to make this expansion successful.

The development of food manufacture is very important for GC as it is the most viable source of the steady cash flows needed to finance its one 'star', the software development and supply company. This sector is highly volatile due to the speed of technological innovation, and GC needs stable resources to be able to invest in research and development and staff with the necessary expertise. This is the only way to make sure that market share grows and that it offers **innovative** products to an increasingly computer literate public. It has a close competitor (8% of market share compared with GC's 10%) and GC may be in a position in a few years' time to acquire this competitor and reinforce its position.

5

> **Pass marks.** There was an article on outsourcing (written by the senior examiner) in the *CIMA Student* section of the October 1999 issue of *Management Accounting.* For those candidates who took the hint and read the article, it must have been gratifying to see this question on the paper. The article is reproduced on pages (xxiv) to (xxvi) of this Kit, and covers the issues raised by the question, which combines a straightforward description of the reasons for outsourcing in part (a) and its application to a particular business situation in part (b).

(a) An organisation will outsource some of its activities to improve **efficiency,** and for **cost control**. The outsourced services are usually those that are supplementary to the core business activities, such as IT, facilities management, administration and human resources.

By outsourcing functions such as payroll and creditor payments a company gets the **benefit** of such services (its employees and creditors get paid) without itself having to provide (and therefore **finance**) the resources needed. A **specialist** organisation has the necessary resources and **economies of scale** and should be able to provide the service more efficiently, but it does have to cover its own costs and make a profit.

Some of the main reasons for outsourcing can be summarised as follows.

(i) Better use is made of what **resources** the company has, focusing on the **core business** rather than trying to carry out functions that it does not have the resources to manage, including supervision time;

(ii) There is a reduction in **costs** and cash may be realised from selling assets to the outsourcing organisation;

(iii) **Capital** resources are freed up;

(iv) **Risks** are shared with the outsourcing provider, such as keeping up with changes in **legislation** affecting payment of employees. The recent imposition of the minimum wage would be a good example.

(b) The directors of AB plc are clear about the **objectives** of their outsourcing strategy. They are under pressure from shareholders to increase EPS, and they have identified **overhead cost control** as one way of achieving this, rather than relying on increased revenue. Overhead costs have been increasing and the expectation is that outsourcing the chosen activities will reverse this.

An important point to make is that the directors have to be careful that they are not over-emphasising **short term shareholder concerns** at the expense of the overall quality of the company and the **sustainability** of its success in the **long term**. The correct balance of in-house and outsourced service provision must be achieved in order to achieve **competitive advantage**.

The directors do need to be sure that the costs of the in-house functions that have been earmarked for outsourcing are the source of the cost control problems. **Cost accounting principles**, such as consideration of the allocation of **fixed overheads,** need to be applied to be sure that the savings that are expected do indeed materialise. For example, certain fixed costs associated with the financial accounting function may not necessarily disappear when that function is outsourced.

Certain phases have been identified in the process of outsourcing and they provide an indication of the procedure that AB must follow. These are described below.

Sourcing strategy is the identification of those activities which are to be outsourced. The directors of AB have already done this and have decided that financial accounting, payroll, creditor payments and debtors are non-core activities for the resources of the company.

Sourcing preparation establishes the levels of improvement needed in the soon to be outsourced services. This will involve collecting detailed information on how these functions currently operate, including the costs associated with them.

Supply selection involves identifying the appropriate supplier for each service, with quotes being obtained as the first step. The services may all be provided by one organisation. Some of the large accountancy practices and management consultancies provide comprehensive outsourcing services. Using a large and reputable organisation will help to assure the directors of AB that they will be receiving a quality (and possibly world class) service.

A **transition period** will be needed for the handover of the functions to the supplier(s). This may include a period of parallel running.

The contract will then need to be **managed** and **monitored** to ensure satisfactory performance by the outsourcing organisation and compliance with the **supply contract**. This is probably one of the most complex areas as it will depend upon the negotiated terms and also upon accurate presentation of the **expected benefits** from the outsourcing programme.

Investment should be made in a staff team set up to manage the contract, which will cover roles such as managing the **financial control** of the contract, its **legal** aspects and the **technical** strategy.

For example, AB may want to see an improvement in **debtors collection** periods, and the outsourcing company will be expected to provide regular details such as aged debt reports. **Deadlines** for production of reports from the financial accounting function may be tighter than were imposed on the in-house service.

If the supplier performs well then the **reselection process** at the end of the contract will be smoother. AB may eventually decide to bring some of the functions back in-house if new resources (more space in a new building, for example) become available.

The directors have quality concerns and it is certainly true that with outsourcing there is a **loss of control** of potentially sensitive areas. External suppliers need to be reliable in terms of product quality and reliability of delivery times, and one way of vetting them is to check that they have certification of the standard of the service they deliver, such as the British certification BS EN ISO 9000.

There may also be loss of **internal skills** that may be needed in the future if employees are made redundant as a result of the outsourcing programme. Employees who remain in the company may feel threatened and this could have implications for the performance of those functions which are retained in house. There may be increased absenteeism, staff turnover and hence high recruitment and training costs.

See overleaf for information on other
BPP products and how to order

CIMA Order

To BPP Publishing Ltd, Aldine Place, London W12 8AA

Tel: 020 8740 2211. Fax: 020 8740 1184

Mr/Mrs/Ms (Full name)

Daytime delivery address

Postcode

Daytime Tel   Date of exam (month/year)

	7/99 Texts	1/2000 Kits	1/2000 Psscrds	1999 Tapes	1999 Videos	1999 CDs
STAGE 1						
1 Financial Accounting Fundamentals	£18.95 ☐	£9.95 ☐	£5.95 ☐	£12.95 ☐	£25.00 ☐	£34.95 ☐
2 Cost Accounting and Quantitative Methods	£18.95 ☐	£9.95 ☐	£5.95 ☐	£12.95 ☐	£25.00 ☐	£34.95 ☐
3 Economic Environment	£18.95 ☐	£9.95 ☐	£5.95 ☐	£12.95 ☐	£25.00 ☐	£34.95 ☐
4 Business Environment & Information Technology	£18.95 ☐	£9.95 ☐	£5.95 ☐	£12.95 ☐	£25.00 ☐	£34.95 ☐
STAGE 2						
5 Financial Accounting	£18.95 ☐	£9.95 ☐	£5.95 ☐	£12.95 ☐	£25.00 ☐	£34.95 ☐
6 Operational Cost Accounting	£18.95 ☐	£9.95 ☐	£5.95 ☐	£12.95 ☐	£25.00 ☐	£34.95 ☐
7 Management Science Applications	£18.95 ☐	£9.95 ☐	£5.95 ☐	£12.95 ☐	£25.00 ☐	£34.95 ☐
8 Business and Company Law	£18.95 ☐	£9.95 ☐	£5.95 ☐	£12.95 ☐	£25.00 ☐	£34.95 ☐
STAGE 3						
9 Financial Reporting	£19.95 ☐	£10.95 ☐	£5.95 ☐	£12.95 ☐	£25.00 ☐	£34.95 ☐
10 Management Accounting Applications	£19.95 ☐	£10.95 ☐	£5.95 ☐	£12.95 ☐	£25.00 ☐	
11 Organisational Management & Development	£19.95 ☐	£10.95 ☐	£5.95 ☐	£12.95 ☐	£25.00 ☐	
12 Business Taxation (FA 99)	£19.95 ☐	£10.95 ☐	£5.95 ☐	£12.95 ☐	£25.00 ☐	
STAGE 4						
13 Strategic Financial Management	£20.95 ☐	£10.95 ☐	£5.95 ☐	£12.95 ☐	£25.00 ☐	
14 Strategic Management Accountancy & Mktg	£20.95 ☐	£10.95 ☐	£5.95 ☐	£12.95 ☐	£25.00 ☐	
15 Information Management	£20.95 ☐	£10.95 ☐	£5.95 ☐	£12.95 ☐	£25.00 ☐	
16 Management Accounting Control Systems	£20.95 ☐	£10.95 ☐	£5.95 ☐	£12.95 ☐	£25.00 ☐	
					£	

POSTAGE & PACKING

Study Texts

	First	Each extra	
UK	£3.00	£2.00	£
Europe*	£5.00	£4.00	£
Rest of world	£20.00	£10.00	£

Kits/Passcards/Success Tapes

	First	Each extra	
UK	£2.00	£1.00	£
Europe*	£2.50	£1.00	£
Rest of world	£15.00	£8.00	£

Master CDs/Breakthrough Videos

	First	Each extra	
UK	£2.00	£2.00	£
Europe*	£2.00	£2.00	£
Rest of world	£20.00	£10.00	£

Grand Total (Cheques to *BPP Publishing*) I enclose a cheque for (incl. Postage) **£**

Or charge to Access/Visa/Switch

Card Number

Expiry date   Start Date

Issue Number (Switch Only)

Signature

We aim to deliver to all UK addresses inside 5 working days. Orders to all EU addresses should be delivered within 6 working days. All other orders to overseas addresses should be delivered within 8 working days.

* Europe includes the Republic of Ireland and the Channel Islands.

REVIEW FORM & FREE PRIZE DRAW

All original review forms from the entire BPP range, completed with genuine comments, will be entered into one of two draws on 31 July 2000 and 31 January 2001. The names on the first four forms picked out on each occasion will be sent a cheque for £50.

Name: ______________________ **Address:** ______________________

____

____

How have you used this Kit?
(Tick one box only)

☐ Home study (book only)
☐ On a course: college ______________
☐ With 'correspondence' package
☐ Other ______________

Why did you decide to purchase this Kit?
(Tick one box only)

☐ Have used complementary Study Text
☐ Have used BPP Kits in the past
☐ Recommendation by friend/colleague
☐ Recommendation by a lecturer at college
☐ Saw advertising
☐ Other ______________

During the past six months do you recall seeing/receiving any of the following?
(Tick as many boxes as are relevant)

☐ Our advertisement in *CIMA Student*
☐ Our advertisement in *Management Accounting*
☐ Our advertisement in *Pass*
☐ Our brochure with a letter through the post

Which (if any) aspects of our advertising do you find useful?
(Tick as many boxes as are relevant)

☐ Prices and publication dates of new editions
☐ Information on Kit content
☐ Facility to order books off-the-page
☐ None of the above

Have you used the companion Study Text for this subject? ☐ Yes ☐ No

Your ratings, comments and suggestions would be appreciated on the following areas

	Very useful	*Useful*	*Not useful*
Introductory section (Advice on revision, question practice and exam technique, question and answer checklist, etc)	☐	☐	☐
'Do you know?/Did you know?' checklists	☐	☐	☐
Tutorial questions	☐	☐	☐
Examination-standard questions	☐	☐	☐
Pass marks	☐	☐	☐
Content of answers	☐	☐	☐
Mock exam	☐	☐	☐
Structure and presentation	☐	☐	☐

	Excellent	*Good*	*Adequate*	*Poor*
Overall opinion of this Kit	☐	☐	☐	☐

Do you intend to continue using BPP Study Texts/Kits? ☐ Yes ☐ No

Please note any further comments and suggestions/errors on the reverse of this page or write by email to alisonmchugh@bpp.co.uk

Please return to: Alison McHugh, BPP Publishing Ltd, FREEPOST, London, W12 8BR

REVIEW FORM & FREE PRIZE DRAW (continued)

Please note any further comments and suggestions/errors below

FREE PRIZE DRAW RULES

1 Closing date for 31 July 2000 draw is 30 June 2000. Closing date for 31 January 2001 draw is 31 December 2000.

2 Restricted to entries with UK and Eire addresses only. BPP employees, their families and business associates are excluded.

3 No purchase necessary. Entry forms are available upon request from BPP Publishing. No more than one entry per title, per person. Draw restricted to persons aged 16 and over.

4 Winners will be notified by post and receive their cheques not later than 6 weeks after the relevant draw date. Lists of winners will be published in BPP's *focus* newsletter following the relevant draw.

5 The decision of the promoter in all matters is final and binding. No correspondence will be entered into.